R. Gupta's®

POPULAR MASTER GUIDE

SSB

Sashastra Seema Bal

Assistant Sub-Inspector
(Steno)

Head Constable
(Ministerial)

Recruitment Exam

2020
EDITION

RAMESH PUBLISHING HOUSE, New Delhi

Published by

O.P. Gupta *for* Ramesh Publishing House

Admin. Office

12-H, New Daryaganj Road, Opp. Officers' Mess,
New Delhi-110002 ☏ 23261567, 23275224, 23275124

E-mail: info@rameshpublishinghouse.com
Website: www.rameshpublishinghouse.com

Showroom

● Balaji Market, Nai Sarak, Delhi-6 ☏ 23253720, 23282525
● 4457, Nai Sarak, Delhi-6, ☏ 23918938

Book Code: R-1262

ISBN: 978-93-87918-71-9

HSN Code: 49011010

SELECTION PROCEDURE

The selection process shall consist of following stages:

- (*i*) Physical Efficiency Test (PET)
- (*ii*) Physical Standard Test (PST)
- (*iii*) Documentation,
- (*iv*) Written Examination
- (*v*) Detailed Medical Examination (DME)
- (*vi*) Appeal Against Findings of detailed Medical Examination
- (*vii*) Final Selection

PHYSICAL EFFICIENCY TEST

- ✦ All candidates will have to undergo Physical Efficiency Test, which will be qualifying in nature and the candidates must qualify the event as under: **For Male:** 3.2 kms. race in 14 minutes. **For Female:** 1.6 kms. race in 08.30 minutes.

WRITTEN TEST /SKILL TEST NORMS ON COMPUTER

Candidates who qualify documentation will appear in written examination i.e. Paper-I and Paper-II and skill test as per details given below:

- ✦ **Paper-I (duration: 2 hours):** Paper-I will be of 100 multiple objective type question focusing on General Knowledge, Numerical ability, Quantitative aptitude, General English/General Hindi and General Reasoning carrying 100 marks.

- ✦ **Paper-II (Descriptive nature of 2 hours duration):** Paper-II will be a descriptive examination consisting 01 essay writing (25 marks), 01 precis writing (25 marks), 01 letter writing (25 marks) & 01 comprehension (25 marks) and will be conducted to test the writing capability of candidates.

  NOTE: Candidates will have choice to answer Essay writing & Letter writing either in English or in Hindi. But the answer of precis and comprehension will have to be given in English language only.

- ✦ **Skill test norms on computer:** Candidates who qualify **Paper-I** & **Paper-II** (Descriptive nature) will be called for Skill test. Skill test will be qualifying in nature.

  Final merit list will be prepared on the basis of marks obtained in the **Paper-I** (Common Entrance Test) & **Paper-II** (Descriptive nature).

CONTENTS

MODEL PAPER (SOLVED)

▼

GENERAL ENGLISH

▼

NUMERICAL ABILITY/QUANTITATIVE APTITUDE

▼

GENERAL REASONING

▼

ESSAY & LETTER WRITING

▼

PRECIS WRITING & COMPREHENSION

▼

GENERAL KNOWLEDGE

Model Paper (Solved)

SASHASTRA SEEMA BAL (SSB)
ASI (STENO)/HEAD CONSTABLE (MINISTERIAL)

PAPER-I
General Knowledge

1. In which country was the FIFA World Cup–2018 held?
   (*a*) Sau Polo (*b*) Brazil
   (*c*) Argentina (*d*) Russia

2. Buenos Aires is the Capital of which country?
   (*a*) Argentina (*b*) Brazil
   (*c*) Costa Rica (*d*) Jamaica

3. How many non-permanent members are there in the Security Council?
   (*a*) 10 (*b*) 12
   (*c*) 15 (*d*) 8

4. The minimum age to qualify for election to the Lok Sabha is:
   (*a*) 18 years (*b*) 21 years
   (*c*) 35 years (*d*) 25 years

5. The National Integration Council (NIC) is chaired by the:
   (*a*) Prime Minister
   (*b*) President
   (*c*) Finance Minister
   (*d*) Home Minister

6. October 2, the birthday of Mahatma Gandhi is internationally observed as:
   (*a*) Non-violence Day
   (*b*) Vegetarians Day
   (*c*) Martyrs' Day
   (*d*) Communal Harmony Day

7. Bhagat Singh and B.K. Dutt threw bombs in the Legislative Assembly as a protest against:
   (*a*) Passage of Public Safety bill
   (*b*) Death of Lala Lajpat Rai
   (*c*) Jallianwalla Bagh massacre
   (*d*) Visit of Simon Commission

8. Sonepur, the venue of one of the largest cattle fairs is located in which of the following States?
   (*a*) Gujarat (*b*) Rajasthan
   (*c*) Bihar (*d*) Uttarakhand

9. Cancer is a disease where we find uncontrolled:
   (*a*) Cell division
   (*b*) Cell swelling
   (*c*) Cell inflammation
   (*d*) Cell deformity

10. If the lens in eye becomes opaque, the disease is called:
    (*a*) Myopia
    (*b*) Astigmatism
    (*c*) Glaucoma
    (*d*) Cataract

11. In which city is the Indian Institute of Petroleum (IIP) located?

    (a) Digboi (Assam)
    (b) Mumbai (Maharashtra)
    (c) Ankaleshwar (Gujarat)
    (d) Dehradun (Uttarakhand)

12. The Governor of a State can be removed by:
    (a) Chief Minister
    (b) Union Home Minister
    (c) Prime Minister
    (d) President -

13. Telangana became the 29th State of Union India on:
    (a) 1 June, 2014
    (b) 2 June, 2014
    (c) 3 June, 2014
    (d) 4 June, 2014

14. National Song 'Vande Mataram' has been taken from:
    (a) Gitanjali
    (b) Constitution
    (c) Anand Math
    (d) Train to Pakistan

15. Where is 'Statue of Liberty' located?
    (a) London   (b) New York
    (c) Ahmedabad (d) Bonn

16. The theory of economic drain of India during British imperialism was propounded by:
    (a) M.K. Gandhi
    (b) Jawaharlal Nehru
    (c) Dadabhai Naoroji
    (d) R.C. Dutt

17. Alamatti Dam is situated on which river?
    (a) Godavari   (b) Kavery
    (c) Krishna   (d) Mahanadi

18. Gandhi Sagar Dam is a part of which one of the following?
    (a) Chambal Project
    (b) Kosi Project
    (c) Damodar Valley Project
    (d) Bhakra Nangal Project

19. Which Bank has the largest number of branches in India?
    (a) P.N.B.   (b) Central Bank
    (c) SBI   (d) HDFC

20. McMahon line is the line that divides:
    (a) India and Myanmar
    (b) India and Nepal
    (c) India and China
    (d) India and Bangladesh

21. Lord Mahavira died at:
    (a) Pava Puri   (b) Sanchi
    (c) Vaishali   (d) Varanasi

22. Who is called the "Father of Indian Cinema"?
    (a) A.K. Hangal
    (b) Amitab Bachhan
    (c) Alok Nath
    (d) Dada Saheb Phalke

23. What is instrument for measuring blood pressure called?
    (a) Electrocardiogram
    (b) Anemometer
    (c) Stethoscope
    (d) Sphygmanometer

24. Name the continent where 'Tundra' type of climate is found:
    (a) Europe   (b) Asia
    (c) Africa   (d) Australia

25. Which is NOT a Greenhouse Gas?
    (a) Nitrous oxide
    (b) Ozone
    (c) Sulphur dioxide
    (d) Carbon dioxide

Numerical Ability/Quantitative Aptitude

26. What will principal amount be ₹ 496 in 6 years at the rate of simple interest of 4% per annum?
    (*a*) ₹ 456   (*b*) ₹ 500
    (*c*) ₹ 400   (*d*) ₹ 460

27. A car covers a distance of 420 km at a certain speed. If its speed 4 km/hr more, it will take one hour less to cover the same distance. What was its speed?
    (*a*) 60 km/hr   (*b*) 50 km/hr
    (*c*) 40 km/hr   (*d*) 55 km/hr

28. A train 110 m long is running at 60 km/hr. A platform is 240 m long, what time will it take to cross the platform?
    (*a*) 21 secs   (*b*) $5\dfrac{5}{6}$ secs
    (*c*) $14\dfrac{2}{5}$ secs   (*d*) 4 secs

29. On the river, a man covers a distance of 3 km against the flow of stream or 15 km in the direction of stream flow in 3 hours, what is the speed of the stream flow?
    (*a*) 9 km/hr   (*b*) 2 km/hr
    (*c*) 4 km/hr   (*d*) 6 km/hr

30. In a race of 200 metres A and B can complete the race in 22 secs and 25 secs respectively. When A complete the race then B will be at how much distance from the finishing line?
    (*a*) 54 m   (*b*) 30 m
    (*c*) 48 m   (*d*) 24 m

31. If the difference between the circumference and the radius of a circle is 37 m, what is its radius?
    (*a*) 14 m   (*b*) 5 m
    (*c*) 7 m   (*d*) 12 m

32. A room is 12 m long, 9 m broad and 8 m high, what will be the length of its diagonal?
    (*a*) 17 m   (*b*) $6\sqrt{3}$ m
    (*c*) $4\sqrt{6}$ m   (*d*) 12 m

33. Two electronic music system were purchased for ₹ 8000. The first was sold at a profit of 40% and the other at a loss of 40%, if the selling prices of the both were same, then what were the cost prices of both the music systems?
    (*a*) ₹ 2400, ₹ 5600
    (*b*) ₹ 3000, ₹ 5000
    (*c*) ₹ 4000, ₹ 4000
    (*d*) ₹ 3500, ₹ 4500

34. If the marked price is 30% more than C.P. and there is a discount of 10% at the marked price, what is the profit?
    (*a*) $18\dfrac{1}{2}\%$ (*b*) 20%
    (*c*) $15\dfrac{1}{2}\%$ (*d*) 17%

35. A man had ₹ 2000, some part of this he lends at 5% per annum and rest of this at 4% per annum on simple interest. The whole annual interest was ₹ 96. How much did he lend at 4% per annum?

(*a*) ₹ 1600 (*b*) ₹ 1200
(*c*) ₹ 600   (*d*) ₹ 400

36. The sum of the present ages of A, B and C is 90 years. Six years ago, their ages were in the ratio of 1 : 2 : 3. What is the present age of C?

(*a*) 45 years (*b*) 36 years
(*c*) 42 years (*d*) 40 years

37. The sum of salaries of 'A' and 'B' is ₹ 2100. 'A' spends 80% of his salary and 'B' spends 70%. If their savings are in the proportion of 4 : 3, then what is the salary of A?

(*a*) ₹ 700   (*b*) ₹ 1400
(*c*) ₹ 1200 (*d*) ₹ 900

38. ₹ 1290 is divided among A, B and C such that A's share is $1\frac{1}{2}$ times that of B and B's share is $1\frac{3}{4}$ times that of C. What is C's share?

(*a*) ₹ 350 (*b*) ₹ 240
(*c*) ₹ 420 (*d*) ₹ 630

39. Five litres of water is added to a certain quantity of pure milk, which costs ₹ 3 per litre. If the mixture is sold at same price of ₹ 3 per litre, a profit of 20% is made (ignore the cost of water). What is the amount of pure milk in the mixture?

(*a*) 30 litres (*b*) 20 litres
(*c*) 28 litres (*d*) 25 litres

40. Fifteen men working 8 hours a day, take 21 days to complete a work. How many days will be taken by 21 women to complete the same work, working 6 hours a day?

(3 women do as much work as 2 men)

(*a*) 28 days (*b*) 25 days
(*c*) 30 days (*d*) 33 days

41. 'A' can knit a pair of socks in 3 days. 'B' can knit the same pair in 9 days. If they are knitting together, in how many days will they knit two pairs of socks?

(*a*) 3 days (*b*) 4 days
(*c*) 5 days (*d*) $4\frac{1}{2}$ days

42. A reduction of ₹ 2 per kg in the price of sugar enables a man to now purchase 4 kg more sugar in ₹ 16. What was the original price of sugar?

(*a*) ₹ 2 per kg
(*b*) ₹ 16 per kg
(*c*) ₹ 8 per kg
(*d*) ₹ 4 per kg

43. 33% marks are required to pass an examination. A candidate who gets 210 marks fails by 21 marks. What are the total marks for the examination?
(*a*) 550   (*b*) 700
(*c*) 650   (*d*) 600

44. The ticket for admission to an exhibition was ₹ 5 and it was later reduced by 20%. As a result, the sale proceeds of tickets increased by 44%. What was the percentage increase in number of visitors?
(*a*) 80%   (*b*) 50%
(*c*) 25%   (*d*) 75%

45. The average weight of 8 men is increased by 2 kg when one man of 50 kg is replaced by a new man. What is the weight of the new man?
(*a*) 66 kg   (*b*) 58 kg
(*c*) 68 kg   (*d*) 60 kg

46. Cost of nine pencils is equal to the cost of four pens. Cost of thirteen pencils and six pens is ₹ 159. What is the cost of twenty one pencils and seventeen pens together?
(*a*) ₹ 345.50   (*b*) ₹ 354.50
(*c*) ₹ 342   (*d*) ₹ 355.50

47. Ramesh is five years older than Suresh. Respective ratio between Suresh's age and Madan's age is 3 : 8. Raju is 8 years younger than Madan. Raju's present age is 48 years. What is Ramesh's present age?
(*a*) 16 years
(*b*) 21 years
(*c*) 26 years
(*d*) Cannot be determined

48. In a test, minimum passing percentage for girls and boys are 45% and 60% respectively. A boy scored 767 marks and failed by 313 marks. What are the minimum passing marks for girls?
(*a*) 910   (*b*) 920
(*c*) 840   (*d*) 810

49. Train–A crossed a stationary train in 39 seconds. It also crossed a man standing on a platform in 19 seconds. The length of the train–A is 456 metre. What is the length of the stationary train?
(*a*) 460 metre
(*b*) 480 metre
(*c*) 490 metre
(*d*) Cannot be determined

50. In a metro train there are 600 passengers out of which 34 per cent are females. Fare of each male is ₹ 20 and each female's fare is 25 per cent less than each male. What is the total revenue generated by all the passengers together?
(*a*) ₹ 10,880   (*b*) ₹ 10,980
(*c*) ₹ 10,740   (*d*) ₹ 10,680

General Reasoning

51. If the letters in ACE are coded as 135 and in BAD are coded as 214, then how can BED be coded?
(a) 215   (b) 254
(c) 245   (d) 345

52. If in a code language AND is written as BOE and RENT is written as SFOU, then how is DEAF written in that code?
(a) EFBG   (b) FEBG
(c) EGBF   (d) PQRS

Directions (Qs. 53 and 54): *Find the missing numbers/letters from the given responses.*

53. 5, 9, 13, 17, ..., 25.
(a) 27   (b) 23
(c) 21   (d) 19

54. BMO, CNP, DOQ, ...
(a) FAT   (b) EPR
(c) EOR   (d) BNS

55. Which one of the given responses would be meaningful order of the following?
1. Adult   2. Child
3. Infant   4. Boy
(a) 2, 3, 1, 4   (b) 3, 2, 4, 1
(c) 1, 2, 3, 4   (d) 3, 4, 2, 1

56. Which one of the given responses would be meaningful order of the following words?
1. Wall   2. Clay
3. House   4. Room
5. Bricks
(a) 5, 2, 1, 4, 3   (b) 2, 5, 4, 1, 3
(c) 2, 5, 1, 4, 3   (d) 1, 2, 3, 4, 5

Directions (Qs. 57 and 58): *Find the odd word/letters/number from the given responses.*

57. (a) refuse – accept
(b) give – take
(c) cold – cool
(d) reward – punishment

58. (a) 20   (b) 64
(c) 27   (d) 125

Directions (Qs. 59 - 62): *Select the related letters/word/number from the given alternatives.*

59. ABC : 123 : : BCD : ?
(a) 456   (b) 234
(c) 345   (d) 243

60. Physician : Treatment : : Judge : ?
(a) Judgement
(b) Lawyer
(c) Court
(d) Management

61. 12 : 15 : : 24 : ?
(a) 36   (b) 34
(c) 30   (d) 18

62. Long : length : : broad : ?
(a) Breadth   (b) Bread
(c) Breed   (d) Spread

63. Find the missing number.
594, 198, 66, _____
(a) 33   (b) 22
(c) 44   (d) 11

64. F is the brother of A and A is the daughter of B. How is F related to B?
(a) Brother-in-law

(*b*) Son
(*c*) Uncle
(*d*) Son-in-law

65. Arun travels 10 km towards North. From there he travels 7 km towards South. Explain his final position from the starting point A.
(*a*) He is 3 km South of A
(*b*) He is 4 km North of A
(*c*) He is 3 km North of A
(*d*) He is 1 km South of A

66. A word given in capital letters is followed by four answer words. Out of these, only one cannot be formed by using the letters of the given word. Find out the word.
INTERNATIONAL
(*a*) NOTE   (*b*) ALONE
(*c*) LATER   (*d*) RADIO

67. Keep the odd one out. (Identify that one which does not belong to the group)
(*a*) Seek   (*b*) Sang
(*c*) Went   (*d*) Came

68. Keep the odd one out.
(*a*) Maharashtra (*b*) Chennai
(*c*) Kerala   (*d*) Punjab

Directions (Qs. 69 - 71): *Study the information given below and answer the given questions.*

In a certain code—
"facing problems with health" is coded as "mip hit ngi snk"
"health problem on rise" is coded as "hit sa rtv mip"
"rise with every challenge" is coded as "snk rtv lne riy"
"facing challenge each day" is coded as "ngi riy ncp hus"

69. What does the code "lne" stand for?
(*a*) Facing   (*b*) With
(*c*) Every   (*d*) Rise

70. What does the code "riy rtv snk" stand for?
(*a*) Rise above challenge
(*b*) Rise health challenge
(*c*) Day rise challenge
(*d*) With rise challenge

71. Which of the following is the code for "facing"?
(*a*) ncp   (*b*) rtv
(*c*) ngi   (*d*) snk

72. In a class, Sneha is 4th from the bottom. Harsha is 10th from the top. In between them there are 6 students with various ranks. How many students are there in the class?
(*a*) 25   (*b*) 20
(*c*) 30   (*d*) 28

73. Identify the one which does not belong to the group:
(*a*) Mend   (*b*) Rectify
(*c*) Trouble   (*d*) Repair

74. Identify the one which does not belong to the group:
(*a*) Syndicate Bank
(*b*) Corporation Bank
(*c*) South Indian Bank
(*d*) Canara Bank

75. Five students are sitting in a row. P is sitting between M and R. M is sitting next to B who is sitting on the extreme left and Q is sitting next to R. Who are sitting adjacent to M?
(a) B and P   (b) P and Q
(c) P and R   (d) R and Q

General English

76. Choose the phrase which best completes the sentence. Having a hobby is the best way—
(a) To be lazy
(b) To relax
(c) To have leisure
(d) None of these

77. Pick out the most appropriate synonym of the given key word.
Access—
(a) An addition
(b) Means of entering
(c) Large surplus
(d) None of these

78. Choose the word with the correct spelling—
(a) Restaurant (b) Restaurent
(c) Restorent (d) None of these

79. Choose the alternative which means the same as the given key word—
Druggist
(a) Dealer in intoxicants
(b) One who sells opium
(c) Person qualified to sell drugs
(d) None of these

80. Choose the correct alternative which substitutes the given bold word—
Ineligible
(a) That cannot be read
(b) Not qualified
(c) Not lawful
(d) None of these

81. Choose from the list below the permissing from the word in brackets in the following sentence—
You can't wear this dress to a party. It is old and ... (coloured)...
(a) un....   (b) dis...
(c) re...   (d) None of these

82. Choose the correct phrase to complete the sentence grammatically. They were talking very loudly. I couldn't help .... them.
(a) to overhear
(b) to overhearing
(c) over hearing
(d) None of these

83. Fill in the word that best fits the context in the given sentence—
She is fond of me but visits me.
(a) seldom   (b) often
(c) frequently (d) None of these

84. Choose the correct helping verb to complete the sentence grammatically—
The population of the world ___ risen very fast.
(a) have   (b) has
(c) were   (d) None of these

85. Choose the phrase which best completes the sentence—

He has had to ____ smoking since his illness.
(*a*) cut out   (*b*) cut down
(*c*) cut off   (*d*) None of these

86. Choose the correct alternative to complete the sentence—
The man _____ I was sitting next to on the plane talked all the time.
(*a*) whom   (*b*) that
(*c*) who   (*d*) whose

87. Fill in the blank with the correct connective. _____ all our careful plans, a lot of things went wrong.
(*a*) Although (*b*) In spite of
(*c*) Because of (*d*) None of these

88. Choose the correct preposition to complete the sentence—

She is not well. She often suffers ______ very bad headaches.
(*a*) in   (*b*) from
(*c*) on   (*d*) None of these

89. Choose the word that best completes the given sentence—

My companion was a very _____ fellow who bored me with his endless chatter.
(*a*) tiring   (*b*) tireless
(*c*) tiresome (*d*) None of these

90. Pick out the correct alternative to complete the sentence grammatically .... she is injured, she should win easily.
(*a*) As long as (*b*) Unless
(*c*) Supposing (*d*) None of these

Directions (Qs. 91 to 95): *In the following items, some parts of the sentence have been jumbled up. You are required to re-arrange these parts which are labelled P, Q, R and S to produce the correct sentence. Choose the proper sequence.*

91. Many (P) way to fuel growth (Q) economists argue that (R) and alleviate poverty (S) free trade is a magic bullet—the quickest
Which one of the following is the correct sequence?
(*a*) Q-P-S-R   (*b*) R-S-P-Q
(*c*) Q-S-P-R   (*d*) R-P-S-Q

92. As a (P) maestro appeared to be enjoying every bit of it (Q) and followed every composition the (R) thunderous applause from (S) an appreciative audience preceded
Which one of the following is the correct sequence?
(*a*) P-Q-S-R   (*b*) R-S-Q-P
(*c*) P-S-Q-R   (*d*) R-Q-S-P

93. Keeping (P) farmers to smoke their fields during (Q) in view the prevailing weather conditions (R) agricultural experts have advised (S) the night to protect vegetables from cold
Which one of the following is the correct sequence?
(*a*) S-R-P-Q   (*b*) Q-P-R-S
(*c*) S-P-R-Q   (*d*) Q-R-P-S

94. It is (P) stressful or joyful (Q) with the belief in the evanescence of life itself (R) necessary to rise above the situations, (S) and in the philosophical quest of the purpose of life
Which one of the following is the correct sequence?
(*a*) R-P-Q-S   (*b*) Q-S-R-P
(*c*) R-S-Q-P   (*d*) Q-P-R-S

95. The difference (P) and development on the other affects (Q) in the relationship between death and birth rates on the one hand (R) but the age structure of the population (S) not just the rate of population growth

Which one of the following is the correct sequence?

(*a*) S-R-Q-P (*b*) Q-P-S-R

(*c*) S-P-Q-R (*d*) Q-R-S-P

Directions (Q.N. 96-97): *Choose the most suitable 'one word' for each of the following expressions given below.*

96. The belief that good must prevail over evil in the end

(*a*) Optimism (*b*) Sophtism

(*c*) Truism (*d*) Radicalism

97. Hater of women

(*a*) Misochist

(*b*) Misogamist

(*c*) Misogynist

(*d*) Misanthropist

Directions (Q. N. 98-100): *Read the sentence carefully and choose suitable preposition for the purpose.*

98. She is proud .... her beauty.

(*a*) at (*b*) on

(*c*) of (*d*) about

99. Mohan belongs .... the upper strata of the society.

(*a*) from (*b*) for

(*c*) to (*d*) of

100. They have invited us ...... attend the function.

(*a*) for (*b*) to

(*c*) upto (*d*) at

ANSWERS

1	2	3	4	5	6	7	8	9	10
(*d*)	(*a*)	(*a*)	(*d*)	(*a*)	(*a*)	(*c*)	(*c*)	(*b*)	(*d*)
11	**12**	**13**	**14**	**15**	**16**	**17**	**18**	**19**	**20**
(*d*)	(*d*)	(*b*)	(*c*)	(*b*)	(*c*)	(*c*)	(*a*)	(*c*)	(*c*)
21	**22**	**23**	**24**	**25**	**26**	**27**	**28**	**29**	**30**
(*a*)	(*d*)	(*d*)	(*a*)	(*c*)	(*c*)	(*a*)	(*a*)	(*b*)	(*d*)
31	**32**	**33**	**34**	**35**	**36**	**37**	**38**	**39**	**40**
(*c*)	(*a*)	(*a*)	(*d*)	(*d*)	(*c*)	(*b*)	(*d*)	(*d*)	(*c*)
41	**42**	**43**	**44**	**45**	**46**	**47**	**48**	**49**	**50**
(*d*)	(*d*)	(*b*)	(*a*)	(*a*)	(*d*)	(*c*)	(*d*)	(*b*)	(*b*)
51	**52**	**53**	**54**	**55**	**56**	**57**	**58**	**59**	**60**
(*b*)	(*a*)	(*c*)	(*b*)	(*b*)	(*c*)	(*c*)	(*a*)	(*b*)	(*a*)
61	**62**	**63**	**64**	**65**	**66**	**67**	**68**	**69**	**70**
(*c*)	(*a*)	(*b*)	(*b*)	(*c*)	(*d*)	(*a*)	(*b*)	(*c*)	(*d*)
71	**72**	**73**	**74**	**75**	**76**	**77**	**78**	**79**	**80**
(*c*)	(*b*)	(*c*)	(*c*)	(*a*)	(*c*)	(*b*)	(*a*)	(*c*)	(*b*)
81	**82**	**83**	**84**	**85**	**86**	**87**	**88**	**89**	**90**
(*b*)	(*c*)	(*a*)	(*b*)	(*c*)	(*c*)	(*b*)	(*b*)	(*c*)	(*d*)
91	**92**	**93**	**94**	**95**	**96**	**97**	**98**	**99**	**100**
(*c*)	(*b*)	(*d*)	(*a*)	(*b*)	(*a*)	(*c*)	(*c*)	(*c*)	(*b*)

PAPER-II

(Descriptive Examination)

Essays & Letter Writing, Precies and Comprehension

1. Write an essay on any one of the following topics:

A.   Clean India Drive

B.   Corruption in India

C.   The Value of Sports

2. Write a letter to your grandfather who has been suffering from frequent ill health for the last six month.

3. Make a precis of the following passage and give a suitable heading.

Character is destiny. Character is that on which the destiny of a nation is built. One cannot have a great nation with men of small character. If we want to build a great nation, we must try to train a large number of young men and women of character. We must have young men and women who look upon others as the living images of themselves. But whether in public life or in student life, we cannot reach great heights if we are lacking in character. We cannot climb the mountain when the very ground at our feet is crumbling. When the very basis of our structure is shaky, how can we reach the heights which we have set before ourselves? We must all have humility. Here is a country which we are interested in building up. For whatever services we take up, we should not care for what we receive. We must know how much we can put into that service. That should be the principle which should animate our young men and women.

4. Read the passage carefully and answer the questions the follow each.

"Unless we think of new ways to work, the discoveries, or at least those that can be proved through clinical trials, are going to dry up," says one researcher. To truly appreciate aspirin, it helps to know a little of its history. This marvel didn't appear from nowhere. It's the product of thousands of years of ingenuity and endeavour. Its origin lies in prehistory, when humans first began experimenting with plant and mineral remedies to alleviate pain and discomfort. Aspirin's key ingredient is drawn from the salicylates, chemicals found in a range of plants, the most famous being the willow tree.

Questions

1. What does one researcher want in connection with aspirin?

2. Why is it necessary to know a little of the history of aspirin?

3. How did the marvel that aspirin is appear?

4. Where does the origin of aspirin lie?

5. From where is the key ingredient of aspirin drawn?

1. (B) Corruption in India

Corruption is one of the burning topics of today. It is also one of the most serious problems of society these days.

Corruption is there in all the government departments. It is there from the lowest to the highest level. If you want to get any work done in any department, you have to grease the palms of many officials there. The peons, the clerks and the officers, all are corrupt. It has, however, to be admitted that some exceptions are also there. Those who do not take bribes can be counted on fingers.

Corruption is there in many countries. But it is not so common in developed countries. India is one of the most corrupt countries in the world. In this respect, her place is with

Pakistan, Bangladesh, Nigeria, etc. The European countries are the least corrupt in the world.

In India, it is said, nobody can get a government job without paying bribe. This became clear when the biggest recruitment scam was unearthed a few years ago in Punjab. Only the UPSC and the like may be an exception. As far as the state public service commissions are concerned, nothing can be said with certainty unless their working is thoroughly scrutinised by some investigative agency.

India has become a land of scams. During the last few decades, we have seen a number of scams unearthed. Some of them are 2G Spectrum scam, Coalgate, Railways scam, Securities scam, Hawala scam, Fodder scam, Bofors scam, Housing scam, Sugar scam, Wheat scam, Urea scam, Recruitment scam, Petrol pump scam, Coffingate, etc. Indeed, the list is endless. So many frauds are committed in banks. The money meant for the pension to the aged, widows, orphans and the handicapped is swindled. Unfortunately, this virus of corruption has spread even in the judiciary, at least at the lower level. It is heartening to note that the Supreme Court and the High Court are trying to root it out from judiciary. Let us hope for the best.

2. Examination Hall,
XYZ
February ....

My dear Grandpa,

I received a letter from uncle yesterday stating about your health. I am very disappointed to know that you have been suffering from frequent ill health for the last six months. I pray for your early recovery.

Grandpa, uncle's letter shows that you are not paying attention to the doctor's advise.

So, it is my request to take proper rest and do as the doctor says. Take care because we all love you dearly and need you.

I am coming to visit you and Grandma early next month. So, be ready and out of bed to come back here with me. The weather here is pleasant and I am sure you will regain your lost health.

Get well soon. Convey my best regard to Grandma.
Yours affectionately
ABC
(Full name and address of the recipient)

3. Precis: Character is Destiny

It is character on which the destiny of a nation depends. If the people have strong character, the nation will certainly rise high. If, however, they have no character, the nation cannot reach the goal which it has set before itself. People should, therefore, work on the principle that they should work without any regard for personal gain.

4. Comprehension : Answers

1. One researcher wants in connection with aspirin that there should be devised new ways to work.
2. It is necessary to know a little of the history of aspirin in order to truly appreciate this marvellous drug.
3. This marvel is the result of thousands of years of ingenuity and endeavour.
4. The origin of aspirin lies in prehistory when humans started experiments with plants and minerals to get rid of pain and discomfort.
5. The key ingredient of aspirin is derived from the salicylates which are found in a range of some plants, the most notable among them being the willow.

TEST OF ENGLISH LANGUAGE

Test of English Language

What does this test measure

The test of English language measures your knowledge of English language through questions/items of functional grammar, reading comprehension, context based vocabulary, etc. There will be no question on English literature, or on poetic expressions.

The different types of questions which are used in this test can be classified as :

(A) Spotting the Error

(B) Sentence Completion or Fill in the blanks

(C) Reading Comprehension

(D) Sentence Structure

(E) Rearrangement of sentences.

Each of which measures one or more areas of language abilities.

(A) Spotting the Error

Candidate's familiarity with the conventions and grammatical rules of standard written English is tested in this type of question. Emphasis here will be on assessing knowledge of correct expression. A correct sentence should be grammatically and structurally correct.

Each question in this section, is divided into four parts and each part is numbered. You have to decide whether there is any error in the sentence and find out in which of the parts the error exists, if there is any. If the sentence is correct, your answer is 'E' *i.e.* "No error". Study the example given below :

(1) (A) Last week/(B) Arun and Kuldeep/(C) do the work/(D) which was pending./(E) No error.

Note that the sentence has been divided into four parts and each part is numbered. The sentence is about the completion of pending work two persons did the previous week. The error is in the verb used. The verb should denote an act that is already completed. The verb should read as "did" and the correct sentence should be "Last week/Arun and Kuldeep/did the work/which was pending". Since the error is in the third part, the correct answer is "C". Now try the example given below:

(2) (A) Before they left/(B) the office/(C) they switched off/(D) all the lights./(E) No error.

In the above sentence you will note that there is no grammatical error. It is also meaningful. Therefore, this question has no error and your answer should be "E" which is "No error".

(B) Sentence Completion or Fill-in-the Blanks

This type of questions measure your ability to recognise words and phrases that both logically and grammatically complete the meaning of the sentence. A sentence is given with a word missing in it. The missing word will be indicated by a blank. You have to find the most appropriate word/phrase from the given alternatives. In deciding which of the five words best fills the blank space, you must consider the context provided by the sentence.

Given below are two items for practice :

(3) We were so late, we .... had time to catch the train.

    (A) nearly   (B) almost   (C) simply

    (D) not   (E) hardly

"So late" sets the tone of the sentence. Because the people were late they just managed to get into the train and only "E", *i.e.*, "hardly" conveys this meaning. "Nearly" and "simply" could have been the right choices if the sentence were to read as "missed the train" after the blank. "Almost" and "not" are not correct grammatically.

(4) Ratesh's shirt has a pattern of boats all .... it.

    (A) on   (B) over   (C) down

    (D) round   (E) with

In the above example, the only word which grammatically fits is "over". So "B" is the answer.

You may also be given a passage like the one given below :

Instructions : In the following there are blanks, each of which has been numbered. These numbers are given below the passage and against each, five words are suggested, one of which fills the blank appropriately in the context of the whole passage. Find out the appropriate words.

My father waved me goodbye and the bus **(5)**, The person sitting **(6)** to me was a Government Engineer **(7)** to Hyderabad, **(8)** inspect the roads.

    (5) (A) going   (B) started   (C) arrived

          (D) stopped   (E) travelling

    (6) (A) next   (B) besides   (C) near

          (D) side   (E) neighbour

    (7) (A) coming   (B) arriving   (C) going

          (D) visiting   (E) flying

(8) (A) to   (B) for   (C) was

      (D) so   (E) then

In the above passage you have to fill up the blanks in such a way that the whole passage becomes meaningful in the context of the entire passage. It is not sufficient that the sentence alone is meaningful and grammatically correct.

In the first blank the word which would fit in the blank (5) is "started". Even though "arrived" or "stopped", "going" and "travelling" are not grammatically correct and also not meaningful.

In the next blank (6) only "next" fits properly. This is decided by the preposition "to" which comes after the blank. It is unidiomatic to use "near" or "besides" with the preposition "to". To use the words "side" and "neighbour" one has to change the sentence and therefore they are not correct answers.

The blank (7) has to be filled by keeping the entire passage in view. Since the passage is about a bus journey "flying" is a wrong answer. The description of the bus journey is of someone travelling to Hyderabad and therefore "coming" is a wrong alternative. "Arriving" and "visiting" are grammatically incorrect. Therefore, the correct answer is "going".

For the blank (8) "to" is the correct answer. To use "was" and "then" is ungrammatical. The other words "so" and "then" are meaningless.

(C) Structuring Sentences

The questions of this type assess the ability to comprehend, organise and structure sentences. The question consists of a set of five words. These five words have to be arranged to make a meaningful sentence. Note that all the five words should be used and each word should be used only once.

The alphabet in the bracket preceding the word is the code given to the word. Each choice given represents a certain way in which the words can be arranged. You have to find which of the arrangements forms a sentence which is meaningful and grammatically correct.

See the following illustration and try to solve it :

(9) (A) NOW   (B) REPLACE   (C) THE

      (D) PLEASE   (E) BOOK

      (A) DBAEC   (B) BDCEA   (C) DBCEA

      (D) DEACB   (E) DECAB

You should rearrange mentally the words so that a meaningful sentence is formed. You may take one word as a starting point and rearrange various other words to see whether they will form a sentence *e.g.* you may try starting with the word "book" as the first word and rearrange the other words. By referring to the alternatives given you may also be able to decide which of the words to use first as a reference point to arrive at the correct answer. Needless to say, you should be able to do this rearrangement in your mind itself. In the above illustration, the correct answer will be "Please replace the book now". The correct order of letters therefore would be "DBCEA". The correct answer therefore will be "C".

(D) Reading Comprehension

Questions on reading comprehension measure the ability to understand, analyse and apply information and concepts presented in the written form. All questions are to be answered on the basis of what is stated or implied in the given passage. Reading comprehension, therefore, evaluates your ability to :

- understand words and statements in the given passage.
- understand the logical relationships between points and concepts in the given passage.
- draw inference from facts and statements in the given passage.

Guidelines for Answering the Reading Comprehension Test

Given below are some guidelines which would be of use to you in answering satisfactorily the questions set on the passage.

(1)   Answer all questions on the basis of what is stated or implied in the passage itself. Even when you do not agree with what the author of the passage is saying, do not let your opinions or knowledge and information influence your judgement of what the author is saying.

(2)   Read the questions carefully, making sure that you understand what is being asked. If need be refer back to the passage for finding the answer.

(3)   Read all the alternatives carefully. Never assume that you have selected the best answer without first reading all the alternatives.

(4)   Remember that understanding is the critical factor in reading comprehension.

(Q. 10-14) Read the following passage carefully and answer the questions given below it. Certain words in the passage have been *italicised* to help you locate them while answering some of the questions:

Malaria is always associated with damp and marshy land. This is not because the land is damp but because still water is the breeding place of the mosquito, which begins its life as a larva living in water. Malaria does not frequently occur in dry desert countries. We should destroy mosquitoes to prevent their breeding in still water. This can be done by *draining* all ponds and pools, and by keeping them covered in breeding season with a film of kerosene oil, which kills the larve.

(10) Where is malaria not very common?
    (A) In cold countries.
    (B) In dry countries.
    (C) In countries having a lot of rain.
    (D) In hot countries.
    (E) Not mentioned in the passage.

In the above illustration alternative "B" is correct. It is stated in the passage that mosquitoes carry malaria and mosquitoes breed in swamps or in a damp condition. Dry countries are the place where damp and marshy conditions are absent. A country is called a "dry country" because the country is not only hot but also without rains. An alternative that comes closest to this is "In hot countries". However, this cannot be selected because it does not mean that it does not rain in hot countries and consequently there is no dampness. The chances of damp conditions prevailing in countries having lot of rains is very high, so alternative "C" also cannot be a right choice. Same thing is true about alternative "cold countries". The fifth alternative cannot be the right choice because in the passage the conditions under which mosquitoes breed and do not breed is mentioned. So the right answer is "B".

(11) What is the breeding place of the mosquito?
    (A) Flowing water   (B) Shallow water   (C) Dirty water
    (D) Deep water   (E) Still water

For the above question you should refer back to the passage. You will find the second sentence in the passage says "_______ because still water is the breeding place of the mosquito". Therefore, the correct answer to the above question is "still water", *i.e.*, "E" is the answer.

(12) What is the use of kerosene oil in preventing Malaria ?
    (A) It kills the fully grown mosquitoes.
    (B) It cleanses the pools and ponds.
    (C) It kills the developing mosquitoes.
    (D) It helps in burning the things around the ponds.
    (E) It purifies the air.

Referring to the passage you will find the correct answer given in the last sentence of the passage where it says "_______ by keeping them covered in breeding season with a film of kerosene oil which kills the larve". A larve as you know is a developing mosquito and therefore among the given alternatives "C" is correct.

You may have questions like this also.

(13) Which of the following words is most SIMILAR in meaning of the word *Draining* as used in the passage?

    (A) Depleting   (B) Discharging   (C) Emptying

    (D) Straining   (E) Clearing

"Draining" means letting water off. So "Emptying" is the right choice, as the one with similar meaning of "draining".

(14) Which of the following words is most OPPOSITE in meaning of the word *Still* as used in the passage ?

    (A) Noisy   (B) Flowing   (C) Living

    (D) Yet   (E) Steady

"Still" here means without movement or motion. So the choice "Flowing" is appropriate, as the one opposite in meaning of "still".

(E) Rearrangement of Sentences

Another set of questions, in which ability to understand what is read and to extract information is assessed is discussed below. These questions test your ability to organise your thoughts and ideas in a suitable sequence.

Questions of this type requires the candidates to rearrange the given sentences in the proper sequence so as to form a meaningful paragraph.

(Q. 15-19) Rearrange the following five sentences A, B, C, D and E in the proper sequence so as to form a meaningful paragraph; then answer the questions given below them:

A. When he reached home, he found his father hale and hearty.

B. He decided to rush home after finishing some urgent work.

C. Suresh received a telegram saying that his father was sick.

D. He realised that it was a trick played by someone.

E. In a few hours, he boarded the train for his home-town.

(15) Which sentence should come FIRST in the paragraph?

    (A) A   (B) B   (C) C   (D) D   (E) E

(16) Which sentence should come SECOND in the paragraph?

    (A) A   (B) B   (C) C   (D) D   (E) E

(17) Which sentence should come THIRD in the paragraph?

    (A) A   (B) B   (C) C   (D) D   (E) E

(18) Which sentence should come FOURTH in the paragraph?

    (A) A   (B) B   (C) C   (D) D   (E) E

(19) Which sentence should come LAST in the paragraph?

    (A) A   (B) B   (C) C   (D) D   (E) E

The correct form of meaningful paragraph will be as under:

A.   Suresh received a telegram saying that his father was sick.

B.   He decided to rush home after finishing some urgent work.

C.   In a few hours, he boarded the train for his home-town.

D.   When he reached home, he found his father hale and hearty.

E.   He realised that it was a trick played by someone.

Accordingly, the answer to Question Nos. 15-19 will be as under:

    15 (C)   16 (B)   17 (E)   18 (A)   19 (D)

SPOTTING THE ERRORS

All kinds of errors are possible in using English as a tool of communication. Errors may be due to grammatical mistakes or due to slips in idiomatic uses. A sentence may be defined as a group of words that make a complete sense. A sentence consists of a noun phrase and a verb phrase. When we look at a sentence we have to ensure first that the subject agrees with the verb in number, the correct tense is used, appropriate propositions are used and correct article is used.

Directions (1-100) : *Read each sentence to find out whether there is any error in it. The error, if any, will be in one part of the sentence. The number of that part is the answer. If there is no error, the answer is 'E'. (Ignore the errors of punctuations, if any.)*

1. (A) In spite of working/(B) very neat and careful/(C) he could not win/(D) even third prize./(E) No error.

2. (A) He has been working on/(B) the problem a long time/(C) but is not still/(D) able to solve it./(E) No error.

3. (A) Although the policemen/(B) ran after the thieves/(C) only one of them were/(D) caught by them./(E) No error.

4. (A) Between June to August/(B) the rain fall in/(C) this part of the/(D) country is always low./(E) No error.

5. (A) When I reached his office/(B) I found that/(C) he had almost ready/(D) to leave for home./(E) No error.

6. (A) The teacher said/(B) that Vishal was/(C) capable of doing/(D) more better work./(E) No error.

7. (A) The boy asked/(B) his father why/(C) he cutting/(D) down the tree./(E) No error.

8. (A) One of the issues/(B) which was discussed/(C) in the meeting/(D) was raised by me./(E) No error.

9. (A) The thirsty/(B) children drank/(C) up all/(D) the water./(E) No error.

10. (A) Rohan was fastest than/(B) Somesh, but was not/(C) fast enough to defeat/(D) Shiny in the race./(E) No error.

11. (A) It was decided not/(B) to be included him in/(C) the team for the/(D) world-cup competition./(E) No error.

12. (A) He has been trying to/(B) develop a medicine for/(C) this disease for/(D) the last ten years./(E) No error.

13. (A) No sooner did she/(B) receive the award, there/(C) was a loud applause/(D) from the audience./(E) No error.

14. (A) As sooner did the/(B) actress stepped out/(C) of her car, people/(D) gathered around her./(E) No error.

15. (A) Ten new members/(B) have got enrolled/(C) and seven have/(D) resigned./(E) No error.

16. (A) From thirty and/(B) forty percent of the/(C) people of this village/(D) suffer from malaria./(E) No error.

17. (A) Edison has not only invented/(B) the electric bulb but/(C) also the film projector/(D) used in cinema theatres./(E) No error.

18. (A) Hardly had the/(B) sad news reacher her/(C) ears when she/(D) broke into tears./(E) No error.

19. (A) He is smarter/(B) enough to get/(C) selected for this/(D) prestigious post./(E) No error.

20. (A) No sooner the plane landed/(B) at the airport than/(C) a group of armed/(D) commandos surrounded it./(E) No error.

21. (A) Manindar has not only opened/(B) a restaurant, but also/(C) a grocery shop in the/(D) village where we live./(E) No error.

22. (A) I was to about/(B) go out of my house/(C) when it suddenly/(D) started raining./(E) No error.

23. (A) We are trying/(B) to locate the/(C) historical city for/(D) the past two years./(E) No error.

24. (A) One of the party/(B) members were dismissed/(C) for speaking against/(D) the leader./(E) No error.

25. (A) After listening to/(B) his advice I/(C) decided to not/(D) go abroad for studies./(E) No error.

26. (A) The daily wages that/(B) the worker of this/(C) factory receive range/(D) between twenty to thirty rupees./(E) No error.

27. (A) As soon did he/(B) open the old/(C) wooden box than a rat/(D) jumped out of it./(E) No error.

28. (A) The robbers were/(B) caught just as they/(C) were about to/(D) escape from the jail./(E) No error.

29. (A) No body believed him/(B) when he said that/(C) his son was gone/(D) out of the country./(E) No error.

30. (A) Hardly did she went/(B) out of her house/(C) when the postman came/(D) with the telegram./(E) No error.

31. (A) Nihal's father advised/(B) him not to/(C) ride the motorcycle/(D) lately at night./(E) No error.

32. (A) The faster he completes/(B) the work given to/(C) him, the largest/(D) will be his profit./(E) No error.

33. (A) Rashmi's performance in the/(B) film was better than/(C) Nidhi's but not/(D) so better as Ranjna's./(E) No error.

34. (A) The boys are playing/(B) outside the house whereas/(C) the girls are sitting/(D) inside and talked loudly./(E) No error.

35. (A) They usually comes/(B) to our house/(C) whenever they pass/(D) through our home-town./(E) No error.

36. (A) She must had/(B) completed her work/(C) by now because/(D) she is very punctual./(E) No error.

37. (A) The money-lender told/(B) that he would/(C) like help us/(D) in our efforts./(E) No error.

38. (A) Tarun told me/(B) that I am/(C) ready to do/(D) any work./(E) No error.

39. (A) Ashish possesses/(B) all those good qualities/(C) which every ideal/(D) student should possesses./(E) No error.

40. (A) An immediate action/(B) has awaited/(C) in order to complete/(D) our work in time./(E) No error.

41. (A) The children observed silent/(B) just for a while/(C) before they ran/(D) to greet their leader./(E) No error.

42. (A) Some people get/(B) used to changes/(C) very easily than/(D) others do./(E) No error.

43. (A) Vijay is more studious/(B) than any other/(C) student of/(D) his age./(E) No error.

44. (A) The policemen fired all the/(B) students when/(C) they were attacked/(D) by some of them./(E) No error.

45. (A) The train was/(B) moving so fast/(C) that we could not see/(D) the places properly./(E) No error.

46. (A) Although the patient/(B) was rude with the/(C) nurses, he behaved/(D) nice with the doctor./(E) No error.

47. (A) He interrupted me when/(B) I was to about/(C) tell the truth/(D) to his father./(E) No error.

48. (A) Sanjay and Satish used/(B) to work for almost twelve/(C) hours in the factory/(D) they are working earlier./(E) No error.

49. (A) Whenever they go out/(B) for shopping, they/(C) take their/(D) pet dog with them./(E) No error.

50. (A) Although he is usually/(B) rude with everyone/(C) he behaved nice with/(D) all of us today./(E) No error.

51. (A) He ran so fastly/(B) that he reached/(C) the destination in/(D) just two minutes./(E) No error.

52. (A) The policemen started/(B) firing the crowd/(C) when the striking/(D) workers became violent./(E) No error.

53. (A) The firemen could not/(B) succeed in rescue the/(C) child although they/(D) could put out the fire./(E) No error.

54. (A) Kitti used to/(B) work for almost ten/(C) hours in the organi-sation/(D) where she has employed./(E) No error.

55. (A) Neeraj is so best/(B) a player that/(C) he would be certainly/(D) included in the team./(E) No error.

56. (A) The driver could not/(B) prevent the car from hit/(C) the child although he/(D) applied the brakes suddenly./(E) No error.

57. (A) He has not only built/(B) this big theatre but/(C) he also built a few/(D) bungalows in this city./(E) No error.

58. (A) There has not been/(B) any rainfall in this/(C) part of the country/ (D) since the last two years./(E) No error.

59. (A) Amar thought that he/ (B) would pass the examination/ (C) although he did not answer/ (D) most of the question correct./(E) No error.

60. (A) All the people/(B) living in the house/(C) including the servant/ (D) was invited there./(E) No error.

61. (A) His father promised to/(B) give him anything what he/(C) wants if he/ (D) passes in the examination./(E) No error.

62. (A) They have agreed/(B) to give him/(C) anything whatever/(D) he asks for./(E) No error.

63. (A) He is about to/(B) open the gate of/(C) the house when the/(D) dog started barking./(E) No error.

64. (A) Hardly had we/(B) all stepped out of/(C) the house when it/ (D) suddenly started raining./(E) No error.

65. (A) I advised him/(B) to do not go/ (C) abroad for/(D) further studies./ (E) No error.

66. (A) We were about to/(B) hire a taxi when/(C) Babu stopped his car/ (D) and gave us a lift./(E) No error.

67. (A) Ashu exercise/(B) everyday so/ (C) that he may/(D) keep himself healthy./(E) No error.

68. (A) Amit is as/(B) fast as or/ (C) perhaps faster/(D) than Arun./ (E) No error.

69. (A) He walked/(B) quick so that/ (C) he would not/(D) be late./(E) No error.

70. (A) The little children was/(B) quite indifferent towards/(C) the teacher who was/(D) accompanying them./(E) No error.

71. (A) After the allotted/(B) time was over/(C) they torn off all/(D) the papers which they had used./(E) No error.

72. (A) Dr. Ramesh has not only started/(B) a pathology laboratory but/ (C) also a maternity/(D) clinic in our town./(E) No error.

73. (A) Ravindar has run/(B) fastest enough to/(C) get selected for the/ (D) international sports competition./ (E) No error.

74. (A) He has a scheme/(B) of his own which/(C) he thinks perferable/ (D) than that of any other person./ (E) No error.

75. (A) No sooner did/(B) the lights went/(C) off than some/(D) boys started shouting./(E) No error.

76. (A) For the past several/(B) years, he has been/(C) trying to develop a/ (D) medicine for cancer./(E) No error.

77. (A) The Government decided/ (B) to sanction any money/(C) that was required for/(D) completing the project./ (E) No error.

78. (A) The higher we/(B) climb up the/(C) mountain the cool/(D) we feel./ (E) No error.

79. (A) One of his many/(B) good traits that/(C) come to my mind/(D) is his modesty./(E) No error.

80. (A) The chairman was force/(B) to resign as/(C) the opposition members/(D) were in majority./(E) No error.

81. (A) Did you see/(B) any of the child/(C) when you were/(D) in the garden?/(E) No error.

82. (A) Anamika's parents told/(B) her to not/(C) go to her friends,/(D) houses at night./(E) No error.

83. (A) Yesterday the thief/(B) was caught just as/(C) he is about to/(D) break open the door./(E) No error.

84. (A) Hardly had he/(B) went out of the/(C) room when people/(D) started criticising him./(E) No error.

85. (A) Jyotsna passed the/(B) examination although/(C) she did not/(D) work very hardly./(E) No error.

86. (A) The fast he finishes/(B) the construction work/(C) the larger will be/(D) his profit margin./(E) No error.

87. (A) Anjna has written no only/(B) this popular song but has/(C) also composed the/(D) music for the same./(E) No error.

88. (A) No sooner did I/(B) took the doll from/(C) the baby girl/(D) than she started crying./(E) No error.

89. (A) It being a rainy/(B) day, Rinki decided/(C) to stay indoors and/(D) do some writing./(E) No error.

90. (A) All the players of/(B) the football club, except/(C) one, was selected/(D) for the competition./(E) No error.

91. (A) Since the last several/(B) days, there has been/(C) heavy snowfall in this/(D) part of the country./(E) No error.

92. (A) The leader advised the people/(B) not to be carried away by/(C) the rumours spread/(D) in the city./(E) No error.

93. (A) He overcame with sorrow/(B) when he heard/(C) the sad news/(D) of his failure./(E) No error.

94. (A) They have requested me/(B) not take any action/(C) unless and until/(D) I don't see all the documents./(E) No error.

95. (A) He has gone/(B) to his native place/(C) with the intention/(D) of staying there./(E) No error.

96. (A) He had/(B) taken off his shirt and threw/(C) it on the floor/(D) before entering the house./(E) No error.

97. (A) Yesterday while/(B) crossing the road,/(C) he was/(D) run out by a truck./(E) No error.

98. (A) The applicant/(B) being a householder/(C) he is/(D) entitled to vote./(E) No error.

99. (A) The captain was/(B) so excited that/(C) the team members failed/(D) to held him in his seat./(E) No error.

100. (A) Every customer is/(B) entitled to pick-up/(C) a bag which is/(D) as small like this one./(E) No error.

15

ANSWERS

1. B : The words 'neatly and carefully' should be used in place of 'neat and careful', as 'neat and careful' are Adjectives and 'neatly and carefully' are Adverbs and in the given sentence, Adverbs should be used with Verb. For example :

(*i*) Asha **runs** very fast.
         ↓   ↓   ↓
        Verb Adv. Adv.

(*ii*) Jitendar **speaks** very **fluently.**
         ↓   ↓   ↓
        Verb Adv. Adv.

2. B : The word 'for' should be used in place of 'from' because the sentence is in 'Present Perfect Continous Tense' and 'a long time' indicates 'Period of Time' *Remember,* 'for' is used for 'Period of Time' and 'Since' is used for 'Point of Time', in Present Perfect, Present Perfect Continuous, Past Perfect Continuous, etc. For example :

(*i*) *Rohini has lived here for a month/since November.*
↓
Present Perfect

(*ii*) *Rohini has been living here for a month/since November.*
↓
Present Perfect Continuous

(*iii*) *Rohini had been living here for a month/since November.*
↓
Past Perfect Continuous

3. C : 'Was' should be used in place of 'were', because in this clause, 'only one' is the Subject and it is Singular. For example :

Only one of them **is** here.
    ↓   ↓

   Subject   Verb
  (Singular) (Singular)

4. A : 'And' should be used in place of 'to', because after the use of 'Between', the conjunction 'and' should be used to make the sentence meaningful and correct; For example :

Between April and June.
         ↓   ↓

Between   and

Note : The sentence can also be corrected by replacing the word 'Between' by 'From'. For example :

   From April **to** June.

   From   to

5. C : The word 'was' should be used in place of 'had' or 'had' should be followed by the word 'been', because 'was + Complement' or 'had been + Complement'. For example :

 (*i*) Mrs. Indira Gandhi was the Prime Minister of India.

         Or

 (*ii*) Mrs. Indira Gandhi had been the Prime Minister of India for many years.

Remember, when 'had' is used as 'helping verb', V_3 is used instead of had + complement.

6. D : Delete the word 'more', as Double Comparative Degree (more better is not used in the sentence. For example :

She is better these days. (and not *more better*)

7. C : Insert the word 'was' before 'cutting', as the sentence is in 'Indirect Narration' and one 'helping verb' should be used before the verb 'cutting', and in the given sentence 'was' should be the helping verb.

8. B : 'Were' should be used in place of 'was', because 'who/which/that', etc., are relative Pronouns and the Verb should be used according to Noun/Pronouns (which is called Antecedent of Relative Pronouns).

For example :

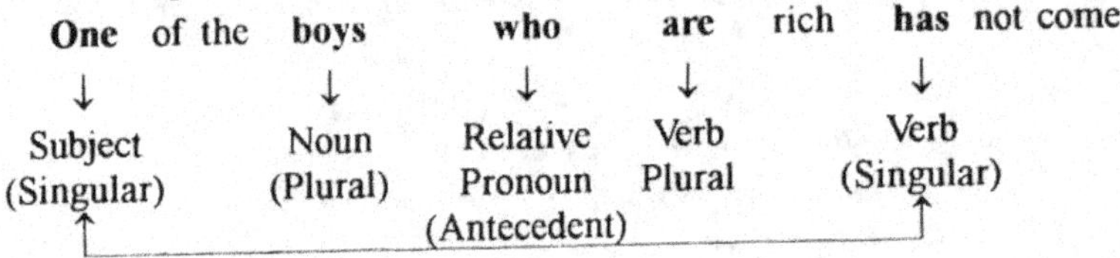

9. E : The sentence is correct.

10. A : The word 'fastest' should be replaced by 'faster', because use of 'than' indicates that construction of the sentence is comprising of 'Comparative Degree'.

11. B : Instead of 'to be included him', the words 'to include him' should be used, because 'decide to do something' is used. For example :

  It was decided **to transfer** him.

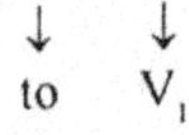

12. E : The sentence is correct.

13. B : Insert 'than' before 'there', because 'No sooner ...... than' is used together. For example :

No   sooner did Monika leave the room than the rain
         ↓   ↓
     No sooner   than
      started

14. A : Substitute 'As sooner did' with 'As soon as', because after 'As soon as' no Conjuction is used with the Main Clause and keeping this in view no conjuction has been used before 'people'. For example :

As soon as Anjana came, **the children started clapping.**
                                              ↓
                                         Main Clause

Note : No Counjuction has been used before 'Children'.

15. E : The sentence is correct.

16. A : Replace the word 'and' by 'to', because 'to' is used after 'from'. For example :

From twenty **to** thirty students have come.
       ↓   ↓
    From   to

17. A : 'Invented not only' should be used in place of the words 'not only invented', because in this sentence effort has been made to join two 'nouns' with the use of 'Not only ...... but also'.

18. D : Replace the word 'broke' with 'burst', because 'burst into tears' is 'Idiomatic'.

19. A : Replace the word 'smarter' with 'smart', because 'Positive Degree Adjective + enough' is used.

She is **good**   **enough**   to help Asha.
         ↓   ↓
      Positive   enough
      Degree
      Adjective

20. A : Replace the word 'landed' with 'land', because first form of verb (V_1) is used with 'do/does/did'. For example :

(*i*) Ajay **did/does/**not write.

(*ii*) The children **do** not **play.**
                      ↓   ↓

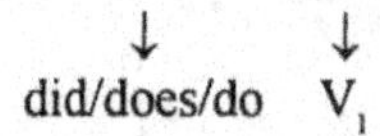
did/does/do V_1

18

Note : Alternately, the sentence can also be corrected by replacing 'did' with 'had', because third form of Verb (V_3) is used with had/has/have. For example :

   (*i*) Swati **has finished** her work.

$$\text{has} \quad V_3$$

   (*ii*) They **have gone** for lunch.

$$\text{has} \quad V_3$$

21. A : 'Not only opened' should be replaced with 'opened not only', because effort has been made to join two Nouns, by the use of 'Not only ...... but also'.

22. A : Replace the words 'to about' to read as 'about to', because to + V_1 is used together.

23. A : 'Are' should be replaced with 'have been/had been OR 'are trying' should be replaced with 'have tried', because 'for the past two years' has been used.

24. B : Were should be replaced with 'was', because 'one of' is followed by Plural Noun/Pronoun but Singular Verb. For example :

One of the **students** **was** sleeping in the class.

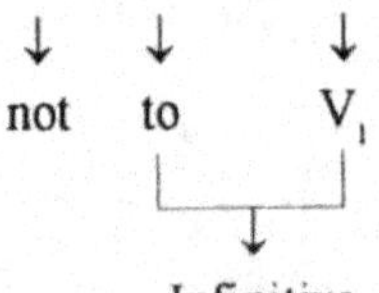

25. C : 'Not' should be used before 'to' because 'not' is used before 'Infinitive' (to + V_1). For example :

Prince is **not** **to** **purchase** this typewriter.

$$\text{not} \quad \text{to} \quad V_1$$

Infinitive

26. D : 'To' should be replaced with 'and', because Conjuction 'and' is used after 'between', For example :

   (*i*) You may come **between** 2 p.m. **and** 5 p.m.

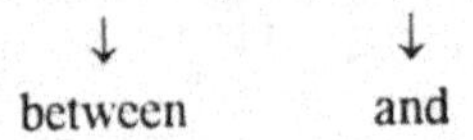

27. A : 'As soon' should be replaced with 'No sooner' because 'No sooner + did/had + Subject' is used and in part A of the sentence, did + Subject' has been used. Again in Part C, 'than' has been used, which confirms that this sentence is based on 'No sooner did ...... than'.

28. D : Delete the word 'the', because 'escape from jail' is used.

29. C : 'Was' should be replaced with 'had', because in 'Active Voice', 'to be' (is/are/am/was/were) is not used before third form of Verb (V_3). Instead 'have/has/had' is used. As 'he said' indicates Past Tense, Reported Clause should also be in Past Tense. For example :

    (*i*) Pushpa said that she **was done** some work. (Incorrect)

    (*ii*) Pushpa said that she **had done** some work. (Correct)

Note : The sentence can also be corrected by replacing 'gone' with 'going'.

30. A : 'Hardly did she went' should be replaced with 'Hardly had she gone'. *Remember*, first form of Verb (V_1) is used with do/does/did.

31. D : 'Lately' should be replaced with 'late', because 'lately' means 'recently' and 'late' means 'after the usual time'.

32. C : 'Largest' should be replaced with 'larger', because in both parts of the sentence 'Comparative Degree' is used if the construction of the sentence is parallel. For example :

The **more** he gets, **more** he wants.

      ↓   ↓

Comparative Comparative
Degree   Degree

33. D : 'Better' should be replaced with 'good', because when two persons/ things are compared in Positive Degree, 'so/as + Positive Degree + as' is used. For example :

Anu is not **so/as good as** Neetu.

       ↓   ↓   ↓

     so/as Positive as
           Degree

34. D : 'Talked' should be replaced with 'talking', because when two Principal Verbs are used with an Auxiliary Verb both Principal Verbs should be in the same form. For example :

The girls **are sitting** and **talking** loudly.

      ↓   ↓   ↓

    Aux. V_4 V_4

35. A : 'Comes' should be replaced with 'come', because Subject of the sentence 'They' is Plural.

36. A : Replace the word 'had' with 'have', because first form of Verb (V_1) is used after the word 'must'. For example :

She **must**   **go**   now.

↓   ↓

must + V_1

37. C : Insert the word 'to' before 'help', because 'like + to + V_1 is used. For example :

(*i*) Rohan **likes**   **to help** me. (Temporary Action)

↓   ↓   ↓

Verb +   to + V^1

(*ii*) Moreover, 'Like + Gerund' is also used. For example :

(*iii*) Nisha likes **swimming** (Permanent Action)

↓

Gerund

38. B : Replace the word 'am' with 'was', because when Past Tense is used in the 'Reporting Verb' : it should also be used in the 'Reported Speech' (Except Universal Truth). For example :

Shalu   **told**   me that I   **was**   ready.

↓   ↓

Past Tense   Past Tense

39. D : Replace the word 'possesses' with 'possess', because 'should + V_1' is used. For example :

The students **should come** regularly.

↓   ↓

should + V_1

40. B : As the sentence is in the 'Passive Voice', the word 'has' should be replaced by 'is' (or was). The sentence is also correct if 'been' is used after 'has', because 'has + been + V_3' is also Passive Construction.

(*i*) The result **is** awaited.

(*ii*) The result **was** awaited.

(*iii*) The result **has been** awaited.

41. A : Replace the word 'silent' by 'silence', because 'observed' has been used as 'Transitive Verb' and it should be followed by 'Object'. *Remember,* 'Noun' of 'Noun Equivalent' word is used as 'Object' and 'Adjective' or 'Adverb' should not be used in its place.

For example :
   (*i*) Isha likes **smartness**. (and not **smart**)
   (*ii*) Prince likes **friendship**. (and not **friendly**)

42. C : The word 'more' should be used in place of 'very', because 'than' has been used after the word 'easily', which indicates that the sentence is in Comparative Degree. For example :
   (*i*) Rajiv can read **more** repidly **than** other

          ↓   ↓

        more   than

43. E : The sentence is correct.

44. A : 'At' should be inserted after 'fired', because 'fire + at + somebody/ something' is used. For example :
   (*i*) Sonu **fired at** his enemy.

       ↓ ↓

     fired at

45. E : The sentence is correct.

46. D : 'Nicely' should be used in place of 'nice', because 'behaved' is 'Intransitive Verb' which should be followed by 'Adverb' and not 'Adjective'. For example :
   She **behaved nicely** with me.

      ↓   ↓

   behaved Adverb

47. B : 'To about' should be replaced with 'about to' because in the construction of the sentence :
Subject + to be (is/are/am/was/were) + to + V_1 is used.

48. D : 'Were' should be used in place of 'are', because Past Tense has been used in the beginning of the Sentence 'Sanjay and Satish used to work' and for maintaining the sequence of the sentence, it is necessary to use Past Tense in Part D also.

49. D : The sentence is correct.

50. C : 'Nicely' should be used in place of 'nice', because 'behaved' is 'Instransitive Verb' which should be followed by 'Adverb' and not 'Adjective'. For example :
   Kamlesh **behaves nicely** with me.

      ↓   ↓

   behaved Adverb

51. A : 'Fast' should be used in place of 'fastly', because there is no such word

as 'fastly'. The word 'fast' is used as 'Adjective' and 'Adverb' both.
For example :

    (*i*) Anju and Sangeeta are **fast runners**.

                    ↓   ↓

                 Adj.   Noun

    (*ii*) Geeta is **running fast**.

             ↓   ↓

         Verb Adverb

52. B : 'Firing' should be followed by 'at', because 'fire + at + somebody/ something' is used. For example :
    (*i*) Sunil **fired at** the tiger.
    (*ii*) The police started **firing at** the crowd.

53. B : 'Rescue' should be replaced with 'rescuing', because V_4, *i.e.*, Verb + Gerund (ing) is used after the Prepositions 'by/before/after/in/at/on', etc. For example :

    She aims **at achieving** the success.

             ↓   ↓

          at V_4
         (Verb + ing)

54. D : 'Has' should be replaced with 'was', because Past Tense has been used in the beginning of the sentence 'Kitti used to work' and for maintaining the sequence of the sentence, it is necessary to use Past Tense in Part D also.

55. A : 'Best' should be replaced with 'good', because when two persons/things are compared in Positive Degree, 'so/as + Positive Degree + as' is used. For example :

    Ashish is so/as good a player as ....

         ↓   ↓   ↓

     so/as Positive as
           Degree

56. B : 'Hitting' should be used in place of 'hit' because Verb + Gerund (ing) is used after the Prepositions 'by/at/in/on/after/before, etc.

57. C : Insert 'has' after 'he' because both parts of the sentence indicate the construction of the sentence as Present Perfect Tense.

58. D : 'Since' should be replaced with 'for' because 'since' is used with 'Point of Time', while as 'for' is used with 'Period of Time'.

For example:
    (*i*) Anil has been working here **for two years.**

                     ↓   ↓

                    for   Period of Time

    (*ii*) Anil has been working here **since January.**

                     ↓   ↓

                  Since   point of time

59. D : 'Correct' should be replaced with 'correctly', because 'correct' is an Adjective, while an Adverb should be used with the Verb.

For example :
    (*i*) She gave **correct answers** to all the questions.

               ↓   ↓

           Adjective Noun

    (*ii*) She **answered** all the questions **correctly**.

           ↓   ↓

       Verb   Adverb

60. D : 'Was' should be replaced with 'were' because Subject of this sentence 'All the people' is Plural.

61. B : Delete the word 'anything' or replace the word 'what' with 'that', because no 'Antecedent' is used before 'what'. Similarly, 'Relative Pronoun' 'that' is used with 'anything'. For example :
    (*i*) I will give you what you like. (and not 'anything what you like)

                      Or

    (*ii*) I will give you anything that you like. (and not 'what you like')

62. C : The use of 'anything' is superfluous, as the meaning of 'whatever' is also 'anything'. For example :
    (*i*) Take, whatever you like.
    (*ii*) Take anything that you like.

63. A : 'Was' should be used in place of 'is' because Part D of the sentence 'dog started barking' indicates that the incident relates to the **Past**.

64. D : The use of the word 'suddenly' is superfluous.

65. B : Instead of the words 'to do not go', 'not to go' should be used because 'advise somebody to do something' is used. For example :
    The teacher advised me to work hard.

        ↓   ↓ ↓

    advised somebody   to V_1

Similarly, 'advise somebody not to do something' is used. For example :

My mother advised me not to play with fire.

↓   ↓

advised   not to play

66. E : The sentence is correct.

67. A : The word 'exercise' should be replaced by 'exercises', as the Subject 'Ashu' is Singular.

68. E : The sentence is correct.

69. B : The word 'quickly' should be used in place of 'quick', Adverb should be used with the Verb 'walked' and not the Adjective, to make the sentence meaningful.

70. A : 'Were' should be used in place of 'was', as the Subject of the sentence 'The children' is 'Plural Noun', which should be followed by Plural Verb.

71. C : The word 'tore' should be used in place of 'torn', as V_2 of tear (V_1) is tore and not 'torn' (V_3).

72. A : 'Started not only' should be used in place of 'not only started', because with the use of 'not only .... but also', effort has been made to join two 'Nouns'.

73. B : The word 'fast' should be used in place of 'fastest', as 'Positive Degree + enough' is used. For example :

    (*i*) He is **kind enough** to help me.

↓   ↓

    Positive   enough

    Degree

    (*ii*) He is **intelligent enough** to understand your tricks.

↓   ↓

    Positive   enough

    Degree

74. D : Replace the word 'than' by 'to'. the word 'prefer' is followed by the Preposition 'to'. For example :

She prefers **to** take milk.

75. B : The word, 'went' (V_2) should be replaced by 'go' (V_1), because V_1

is used after the words, 'do/does/did', etc. For example :

> (*i*) **Did** she not **write** to you ?

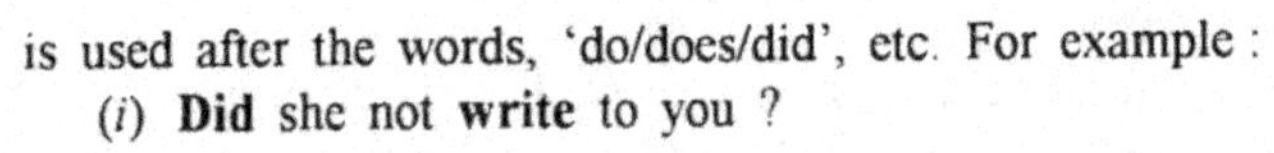

> $$Did \qquad V^1$$

> (*ii*) **Do** they **finish** their work in time ?

> $$Do \qquad V_1$$

76. E : The sentence is correct.

77. B : Replace the word 'any' with 'the' because 'money' has become **definite** with the use of 'that was required'. For example :

> **The dog that** barked at Swati did not bite her.

78. C : The word 'cool' should be replaced with 'cooler', because The + Comparative Degree is used on both parts of parallel construction. For example :

> **The higher** he climbs, **the cooler** he feels.

> the Comparative   the Comparative
> Degree   Degree

79. E : The sentence is correct.

80. A : The word 'force' should be replaced with 'forced' as the sentence is in Passive Voice and in Passive Voice, V_3 is used with the words 'is/are/am/was/were'. For example :

> She **was forced** to resign.

> $$was \quad V^3$$

81. B : 'Child' should be replaced with the word 'children', because if the word 'any of' is followed by 'countable Noun', it is used as 'Plural'. For example :

> **Any of the boys/girls/students/chairs/toys.**

> Any of   Plural Nouns

82. B : 'To not' should be replaced with the word 'not to', because to + not + V_1 is used. For example :

> (*i*) The teacher asked the students **not to make** a noise

> $$not \quad to \quad V_1$$

> (*ii*) I advised her **not to be** careless.

> $$not \; to \, V_1$$

83. C : The word 'was' should be used in place of 'is', as the sentence is in Past Tense.

84. B : The word 'gone' (V_3) should be used in place of 'went' (V_2) because V_3 is used with have/had/having. For example :

    (*i*) Anjna **has forgotten** to bring the books.

$$\downarrow \quad \downarrow$$

$$\text{has} + V^3$$

    (*ii*) Ashish **had** hardly **gone** to the village ....

$$\downarrow \qquad\qquad \downarrow$$

$$\text{had} \qquad V^3$$

85. D : Replace the word 'hardly' by 'hard', because 'hard' means 'laborious' and 'hardly' means 'rarely' or 'with difficulty'.

86. A : The word 'faster' should be used in place of 'fast' as Comparative Degree has been used in both parts of the sentence.

The **faster** they run, the **better** they do.

$$\downarrow \qquad\qquad\qquad \downarrow$$

Comparative   Comparative
Degree   Degree

87. A : 'Not only written' should be used in place of 'written not only', as the Verb 'composed' has been used after the word 'also', *e.g.* : not only **written** .... but .... also **composed**

$$\downarrow \qquad\qquad\qquad\qquad \downarrow$$

Verb   Verb

88. B : The word 'take' (V_1) should be used in place of 'took' (V_2). Do/does/did are followed by V_1. For example :

    (*i*) Hardly **does** she **come** here.

$$\downarrow \qquad \downarrow$$

$$\text{does} \qquad V^1$$

    (ii) No sooner **did** he **go** there ....

$$\downarrow \quad \downarrow$$

$$\text{did} \qquad V^1$$

89. E : The sentence is correct.

90. C : 'Were' should be used in place of 'was' as the Principal Subject of the sentence 'All the players' is Plural.

91. A : 'Since' should be replaced with the word 'For' as 'Since' is used with 'Point of time' and 'For' is used with 'Period of Time'. For example :

    (*i*) Since **November, 1994,** etc.

$$\downarrow$$

Point of Time

(*ii*) For **many years/months**.

↓

Period of Time

92. C : Replace the word 'spread' by 'spreading'. The use of Gerund (ing) with 'spread' makes the sentence clear and meaningful.

93. A : Replace the word 'overcame' by 'was overcome' because the sentence has 'Passive Construction'. For example :
   (*i*) Rahul cheated me. (Active)
   (*ii*) I was cheated by Rahul. (Passive)

94. C : Delete the word 'don't. The words 'until, unless, till, refuse, deny, lest, forbid', etc., and not followed by negative sentence. For example :
   (*i*) You should wait until I **don't** come back. (*Incorrect*)
   You should wait until I come back. (*Correct*)
   (*ii*) You will not succeed, unless and until you **don't** work hard.
   (*Incorrect*)
   You will not succeed, unless and until you work hard.
   (*Correct*)
   (*iii*) You will not do well, unless you **don't** work hard. (*Incorrect*)
   You will not do well, unless you work hard. (*Correct*)

95. E : The sentence is correct.

96. B : The word 'threw' should be replaced by 'thrown', because have/has/had + V_3 is used. For example :
   (*i*) Sunil **has met** me and **talked** to me.

   ↓   ↓   ↓

   Has V_3 V_3

97. D : The word 'run out' should be replaced by 'run over'. Because 'run out' to come to an end' and 'run over' means 'to knock down a person in riding or driving'.

98. C : The use of word 'he' is superfluous, as the Subject in the sentence is 'The applicant'.

99. D : 'Hold' should be used in place of 'held', because 'to' + V_1 is used. 'held' is the 2nd form of the Verb 'hold'.

100. D : Substitute the word 'like' with 'as', because Conjuction 'as is used after 'as'. For example :
   She is as good as you. (and not **'like'** you)

SOME FUNDAMENTAL RULES FOR CORRECTION

RULE 1 :

The words each, every, everyone, someone, somebody, everybody, anybody, nobody, anyone, are always used in Singular. In the following examples, the *italicised* words are incorrect and the words shown within the brackets are correct. For example :

1. Everybody *like* to praise his own work. (likes)
2. Every student *are* to be given free medical aid in this college. (is)
3. Each of the six boys *are* taking interest in their work. (is)

RULE 2 :

In the case of 'as well as' 'together with' alongwith, 'and not' 'in addition to', 'besides', etc., Verb relates to the first Subject instead of the second Subject.

1. Hari alongwith his father *are* going to Ambala, for purchasing some books for his studies. (is)
2. Captain along with his soldiers *were* killed in the Second World War.
   (was)
3. She besides her friends *have* decided to visit Delhi this time. (has)
4. Savita as well as her sister *are* making their programme to see the film.
   (is)
5. He and not his friends *are* expected to qualify the test. (is)

RULE 3 :

In the case of 'neither nor' 'either or', 'not only, but also', etc., the Verb relates to the second Subject *i.e.* the nearest word.

1. Not only he but also his brother *are* trying best to qualify the test. (is)
2. Either her friends or she *have* made the loss good. (has)
3. Neither the Prime Minister nor the Members of the Parliament *is* to do anything in this respect. (are)
4. Neither the principal nor the teacher *is* expected to attend the function.
   (are)

RULE 4 :

Some words : unless, till, until, refuse, deny, lest, forbid, are not followed by negative sentence.

1. He will not join the Army until he is *not* premitted by the parents.
   (Delete not)
2. Wait here till I *do not* come back. (Delete 'do not')

3.   She will not be happy unless her friends *does not* help her.

(Delete 'does not')

4.   He forbade me *not to* appear for the test. (Delete 'not')

5.   Walk fast lest you should *not* miss the train. (Delete 'not')

RULE 5 :

Double future should not be used in one sentence, in case the conditional word is found in the sentence (*i.e.* if, as and when, in case, when, provided, until, unless, till before, etc.).

1.   If she *will go* to Delhi, she will bring some gift for you. (goes)

2.   It will be better for you if you *will* study carefully. (Delete 'will')

3.   He will not have a sign of relief unless he *will qualify* the written test.

(qualifies)

4.   Please ensure that you will not waste your time on one question in case you *will* find it difficult. (Delete will)

5.   She will have left the college before you *will* reach there. (Delete will)

RULE 6 :

'Neither' can be used without 'Nor' but 'neither' is used for two persons or two things whereas 'none' is used for more than two persons or two things 'neither' and 'none' are always used in singular on the basis of 3rd person, when there is no counting of persons or things, in that case, any of the two words. (*i.e.* 'neither' and 'none') can be used *e.g.*

1.   None of the boys *want* to be arrested in the presence of their parents.

(wants)

2.   None of the assets of the company *have been* revalued so far. (has been)

3.   *Neither* of my seven friends helped me during my illness. (None)

4.   *None* of the two sisters loves each other due to some misunderstandings.

(Neither)

5.   Neither of them *have* anything to say on this point. (has)

RULE 7 :

'Either' is used for two persons or two things whereas 'any' is used for more than two *e.g.*

1.   Here are none balls, you can choose *either*. (any)

2.   Have you read *either* of the three novels written by Mr. Vijay Magon ?

(any)

3.   Do you like *any* of the two methods suggested by the principal ? (either)

RULE 8 :

Some words : insist, persist, abstain, refrain, fond, keen, succeed, prohibit and confident are used in Gerund along with Prepositions *e.g.*

1. She is confident *to speak* English even in the presence of her officers.
   (of speaking)
2. Though he was advised not to drive heavy vehicle yet he insisted *to do* so. (in doing)
3. I prohibited her *to park* her car near the police station. (from parking)
4. Everybody in this country should abstain *to speak* ill. (from speaking)
5. He acted upon my advice and succeeded *to secure* first division in Mathematics. (in securing)

RULE 9 :

In special cases, we use 'that' in place of 'who, which, where' the words—all, any, none, only, nothing, the few, the little are found in the sentence. *e.g.*
1. She spent the little money *which* she had in her pocket. (that)
2. In the meeting there was none *who* did not praise his own work. (that)
3. All *which* glitters is not gold. (that)
4. She was the only student *who* could attempt all the problem figures in the exam. (that)
5. Is there any *who* does not love her country ? (that)

RULE 10 :

Use of that of, those of e.g.
1. The goats of Tibet are more beautiful than *that of* Nepal. (those of)
2. My teaching is better *than* Jawahar. (than that of)
3. The climate of Kulu is better *than* Manali. (than that of)
4. The apples of Kashmir are better *than* Shimla. (than that of)

RULE 11 :

The words 'last', 'yesterday', 'a few days ago', are used in Past Indefinite Tense.
1. He *has sold* all his goods a few day ago. (sold)
2. She *has passed* M.A. (Final) in 1986. (passed)
3. Her mother *has come* back from tour, yesterday. (came)

RULE 12 :

Some words : stop, help, remember, avoid, reach, resemble, dislike, enjoys (is followed by first form of Verb) are used in Gerund but are not followed by any Preposition *e.g.*
1. Many girls avoid *to see* the picture with their parents. (seeing)
2. He enjoys *to play* football in the evening daily. (playing)
3. Nobody should dislike *to buy* the old books from her friends. (buying)
4. Stop *to count* the money as the time is over. (counting)
5. 'Special Book' will help *to increase* your day-to-day knowledge. (increasing)

RULE 13 :
Junior, senior inferior, superior, prior, interior, prefer are followed by 'to'. But
My senior officer, My junior officer, His prior approval, etc. are used without
'to'. These words are also not followed by any comparison word e.g.
1.   Character is preferable *than* wealth. (to)
2.   He is more *senior than* me not only in service but also in age. (senior to)
3.   Ashok is junior *from* me by four years in service. (to)
4.   My senior officer is proposing to proceed on leave next week. (No error)
5.   Ram is poorer than Mahesh. (No error)
6.   He is more careful than his brother. (No error)
Note : Comparative Degree is always followed by 'than' Superlative Degree :
1.   Vikas is the best boy in the class. (No error)
2.   Vivekanand was one of the most popular saints in India. (No error)
3.   India is one of the greatest countries. (No error)

RULE 14 :
The words : need, dare, better, rather are not followed by 'to'. *e.g.*
1.   Nobody can dare *to* challenge my authority. (Delete to)
2.   You need not *to* worry about your health. (Delete to)
3.   Something is better than nothing. (No error)

RULE 15 :
If the Principal Clause (sentence on the left hand) is given in the Past Tense,
then the Subordinate Clause must be in the Past Tense. *e.g.*
1.   The doctor asked the patient if he *can* walk on feet. (could)
2.   He worked hard so that he *may* qualify the test with distinction. (must)
3.   It was decided by the Bank that the company *will be* granted cash credit
     limit of Rs. 50 lakhs. (would be)
4.   In the meeting, it was discussed that the poor children *are* to be given
     free medical aid. (were)

RULE 16 :
Use 'that' in place of 'who' and 'which' after 'Superlative Degree' (means word
followed by 'est' or 'most'). *e.g.*
1.   Ashoka was the greatest king *who* ruled over many countries. (that)
2.   Rahul is one of the best players *who* have been-awarded certificates. (that)
3.   He is the most intelligent student *who* has got first division in Mathematics.
                                                                                  (that)
4.   'Geeta' is regarded as one of the best movies *which* have been produced
     so far by the Film Industry. (that)
5.   It is one of the most popular books *which* have been written by Tagore.
                                                                                  (that)

RULE 17 :

The word 'that' is not used with the words how, who, whether, what, where, when, whom, whose, which, why, etc. *e.g.*

1. She could not explain *that* why she did not take interest in the studies. (Delete 'that')
2. He does not know *that* how to speak Hindi with his friends. (Delete 'that')
3. It is difficult to say *that* whether she will get the job without experience.
   (Delete 'that')
4. Nothing can be said *that* when he is expected to return from his tour.
   (Delete 'that')
5. He asked me *that* why I should go there. (Delete 'that')

RULE 18 :

The word 'one of' is followed by the Plural word but is used in Singular. *e.g.*

1. One of the *proposal* made by the students is still to be viewed. (proposals)
2. One of the schemes made by the bank *are* to be launched. (is)
3. One of my friends *have* made up his mind to start his private business.
   (has)
4. Sanjay who *have* qualified the written test is one of my friends. (has)
5. Shekhar is one of those who *is* ready to die for country. (are)

Note : Serial No. 5 'one of' is not Subject. Therefore, it has not been used in Singular.

RULE 19 :

The words scenery, machinery, work, business, poor, rich, furniture, news, luggage, bread, hair, poetry, issue, fruit and fleet are used in Singular only. *e.g.*

1. The owner of the shop is going to sell all his *furnitures*. (furniture)
2. Many manufacturers use imported *machineries* just to increase the quality of their products. (machinery)
3. The *informations were* broadcast from Television. (information was)
4. The *sceneries* of Shimla *are* very charming. (scenery is)
5. Sarla has no *issues*. (issue)
6. She had gone to but *fruits*. (fruit)
7. Her *hairs are* jet black. (hair is)
8. The mother feeds the *poors*. (poor)
9. I told *these* news to my father. (this)
10. The fleet *were* destroyed by the enemy. (was)

RULE 20 :

The words : advice, mischief, abuse, alphabet, etc., are used in Singular only. *e.g.*

1. The teacher gave us many advices. (wrong)
   (a) The teacher gave us advice or piece of advice. (right)

2. My younger brother did many mischiefs. (wrong)
   (*a*) My younger brother did many acts of mischief. (right)
3. The boys were shouting abuses. (wrong)
   (*a*) The boys were shouting words of abuse. (right)
4. I have learnt the alphabets. (wrong)
   (*a*) I have learnt the letters of alphabets. (right)

RULE 21 :

The words : rupee, dozen, mile, year, food are used in Signular when used after numerical and followed by their noun. *e.g.*
1. I have a five *rupees* note. (rupee)
2. He bought two *dozens* pencils. (dozen)
3. He ran in a two *miles* race. (mile)
4. Abida is a ten *years* old girl. (year)
5. The distance is of 2 miles/kms. (no error)
6. A five *years* plan is going to be started. (year)

RULE 22 :

The words : vegetables, spectacles, trousers, Himalayas, people, orders, repairs, scissors (noun) are always used in plural. *e.g.*
1. I had gone to buy *vegetable*. (vegetables)
2. The road is closed for *repair*. (repairs)
3. The judge passed *order* for his release. (orders)
4. Very few *peoples* are hard working. (people)
5. His *spectacle is* blunt. (s) (are)
6. The *scissor is* blunt. (s) (are)
7. Your *trouser is* not loose. (s) (are)
8. The *Himalaya is* the highest mountain(s). (s) (are)

RULE 23 :

The words : fish, deer, sheep, cattle are used always in Singular for Singular and Plural purposes. *e.g.*
1. The fisherman catches many *fishes* in the pond. (fish)
2. I saw many *sheeps* and *deers* in the forest. (sheep, deer)
3. The cattle *are* returning to the village. (cattle is)

RULE 24 :

When two persons or two things are compared, use Comparative Degree. *e.g.*
1. She is braver than her sister. (No error)
2. He is taller than I by 3 inches. (No error)
3. Anup is *intelligent* than Amrik at least in English. (more intelligent)
Note : In Comparative Degree, Object will be in Subjective Case *i.e.* 'I' for me, 'He' for him 'She' for her, etc.

RULE 25 :

When two qualities of the same person are compared (Instead of comparison of two persons or two things). Use the word 'more' in place of comparative word. *e.g.*

1. She is *wiser* than honest. (more wiser)
2. He who is an officer of the Railway is *honest* than wise. (more honest)

RULE 26 :

Generally the relative words 'who' and 'which' are placed after the word for which these are used :

1. The woman/died of cholera/who lived in this cottage. (1 + 3 + 2)
2. None of the students/could qualify the test/who was intelligent.

$$(1 + 3 + 2)$$

3. It is I who *is* responsible for your bright career. (am)

RULE 27 :

The word 'call at' is used for place whereas 'call upon' or 'call on' is used for persons. *e.g.*

1. All of us *called upon* her office. (called at)
2. They *called at* us yesterday to discuss the cash credit account. (called upon)
3. I found them playing hockey when I called *on* his house. (at)
4. When I called *on* 'Subhash' residence, he had left his house. (at)

RULE 28 :

'Each other' is used for two persons and things whereas 'one another' is used for more than two. *e.g.*

1. All the five brothers were quarrelling with *each other* over their father's property. (one another)
2. They were discussing the point with each other. (No error)
3. Ambika and Sonia are fast friends and they love *one another* very much.

(each other)

RULE 29 :

The word 'who' is used for Subject whereas 'whom' is used for Object. *e.g.*

1. *Whom* do you think, will be our teacher. (who)
2. Please provide us efficient worker *who* you think honest. (whom)

RULE 30 :

We used the word 'the' before the names of oceans, rivers, mountains, sacred books, newpapers, magazines, ships, buildings, provinces, nation and communities and with the Superlative Degree *e.g.*

1. *Hindus* should not hate the Bengalis. (The Hindus)
2. Jawahar Lal was *greatest* man of the world. (the greatest)
3. *Tribune* gives us day-to-day knowledge. (The Tribune)

Note : We do not use the word 'the' before the names the of disease, persons, country and metal.

1. *The Gold* is a precious metal. (Gold)
2. He with his friend lives in *the Russia*. (Russia)
3. *The small pox* has broken out in the village. (small pox)

RULE 31 :

'Both' and 'As well as' cannot be used together in a sentence. If 'Both' is to be used, Verb will be used in Plural. If 'As well as' is to be used, Verb will be according to the 1st Subject. 'Both' is followed by 'And'. *e.g.*

1. *Both* Sanjay as well as his friends is proposing to launch a new scheme for his country. (Delete both)
2. Both Ravi *or* Shankar are going to see off their uncle. (and)
3. Both she *as well as* her sister are going to see the picture. (and)

RULE 32 :

One of the two words 'in my opinion' and 'I think' is used. *e.g.*

1. (*In my opinion*) (*I think*) he might have qualified the test. (use any one)

RULE 33 :

'Different' and 'separation' are followed by 'from' instead of other words. *e.g.*

1. Under these circumstances, I cannot bear *my sister's separation.*

(separation from my sister)

2. It is quite different *to* this. (from)

RULE 34 :

The words 'worth' and 'for' cannot be used together. *e.g.*

1. He has sold his scooter *for worth* seven thousand rupees. (for or worth)

RULE 35 :

The words 'exceed' and 'more than' are not used together. One of the two is used. *e.g.*

1. In the examination, your essay should not *exceed more than* fifteen lines.

(exceed or more than)

RULE 36 :

'It' is used for lifeless things and 'He' is used for living things. *e.g.*

1. *Being* a blind, I told him the way of his house. (he, being)
2. *Being* a cloudy day, we did not go out for a walk. (It being)
3. *It* being weak in Math, I told him this sum. (He)

RULE 37 :

'Let' and 'between' are followed by objective Clause. *e.g.*

1. Do not disclose the secret as this is between you and *I*. (me)

2. Let *she* study for the test which is to be held shortly. (her)

RULE 38 :
It two nouns denote the same meaning, both the Nouns are treated as Singular.
1. The manager and clerk of this office *are* one leave today. (is)
2. The manager and secretary of the firm *have* got the books of account audited.

    (has)
3. Both the students are going to school. (No error)
4. The secretary and treasurer was absent. (No error)
5. The secretary and the treasurer was absent. (were)

RULE 39 :
'A majority of the students' is treated as one group. 'The majority of the students' is treated as Plural *i.e.* more than one group. *e.g.*
1. The majority of the students *agrees* with the teacher on this point. (agree)
2. I large number of students *has* got through the written test. (have)

Note : 'A large number of the students' mean Plural on account of the word 'large'.

RULE 40 :
When one Noun denotes to a person and other denotes to an animal, we use 'that' in place of 'who' or 'which'. *e.g.*
1. He and his sheep *which* fell into the well, were injured. (that)
2. She and her dog *which* I saw on the road, meet with an accident. (that)

Note : 'who' is used for living person(s) and 'which' is used for animals, birds and lifeless things.

RULE 41 :
We do not use double Comparative Degree in a sentence.
1. In hockey, he is *more* better than I. (delete more)
2. She is *more* cleverer than her brother. (delete more)

RULE 42 :
'Between' is followed by 'and' whereas 'from' is following by 'to'. *e.g.*
1. The company will be granted cash credit limit between Rs. 3 lace *to e.g.*
    Rs. 5 lacs. (and)
2. We are proposing to hold a meeting today from 4.20 pm *by* 6.30 pm.

RULE 43 :
In one sentence double negative should not be used. *e.g.*
1. He has not done *nothing* wrong in this case. (anything)
2. Ramesh did not like to help *nobody*. (anybody)

RULE 44 :

The following Conjunction are used in pairs :

though	yet	hardly	when
scarcely	before or when	such	as
neither	nor	either	or
not only	but also	one	one's
whether	or	no sooner	than
lest	should		

1. Though Ram played well *still* he lost the match. (yet)
2. Hardly had he gone out *than* it started raining. (when)
3. No sooner did he *reached* the station, when *the* train whistled off.

(reach, than the)

4. Walk fast lest you should miss the train. (No error)

FILL IN THE BLANKS

This type of test is given to examine the ability of the Candidates in the use of nouns, pronouns, adjectives, adverbs, articles, prepositions, verbs and tense, etc.

In this type of test, the sentences are given with a blank and four or five alternatives are suggested. The candidates are required to choose a correct alternative from the five alternatives given below each sentence.

Directions (1-75) : *Pick out the most effective word/phrase from the given words/phrases to fill in the blank to make the sentence meaningfully correct.*

1. The union leader put the ...... of the workers before the management.
A. difficulties   B. problems
C. demands   D. feelings
E. desires

2. The prisoner escaped from the police custody ...... is bound to cause the dismissal of many policemen.
A. that   B. it
C. which   D. as
E. who

3. The prescribed medicine provided him ...... a little relief.
A. with   B. for
C. by   D. to
E. indeed

4. The elections were held peacefully barring the ...... incidents.
A. widespread   B. anticipated
C. sporadic   D. major
E. expected

5. Madhur was ...... how to use a dictionary.
A. informed   B. taught
C. learn   D. told
E. suggested

6. Ashok aims ...... starting some new work.
A. in   B. to
C. at   D. for
E. by

7. Mohit was determined ...... compromise with you.
A. for   B. to
C. by   D. in
E. at

8. Although people are doubtful, it is ...... that he would win the election.
A. certain   B. confident
C. unsure   D. infinite
E. unnecessary

9. Rashmi and her family intend to accompany us on ...... trip to Kanyakumari.
A. our   B. her
C. their   D. our's
E. its

10. The minister flew ...... the flooded areas in a helicopter.
A. along   B. over
C. in   D. at
E. about

11. Rajesh is ...... us for a ride by not keeping his promise.
A. took   B. takes
C. taking   D. taken
E. take

12. Some of the trains got delayed as a ...... of heavy rains.
A. matter   B. result
C. condition   D. fall
E. cause

13. They ...... no notice of what people say about them.
A. mind   B. keep
C. listen   D. make
E. take

14. Neelu could ...... a lot of experience by working in that organisation.
A. perform   B. know
C. maintain   D. gain
E. learn

15. A river has to be ...... to reach the temple.
A. flowed   B. cut
C. swam   D. rowed
E. crossed

16. Mr. Vijay Magon tried his best to ...... the condition of the blind.
A. improve   B. repair
C. correct   D. develop
E. raise

17. Ranjana strongly feels that she should ...... me a camera on my birthday.
A. photograph   B. give
C. sell   D. borrow
E. can

18. You must obtain first class in order to be ...... to apply for this post.
A. illegible   B. elected
C. forced   D. eligible
E. legible

19. Man ...... be happy if his basic needs are not satisfied.
A. must   B. doesn't
C. can't   D. will
E. can

20. As there was ...... all round, he could not read the book with concentration.
A. disturb   B. peace
C. troublesome   D. weather
E. noise

21. If you honestly ...... your fault, others do not take it seriously.
A. refuse   B. neglect
C. correct   D. warn
E. admit

22. Only bad people like to give ill-treatment ...... their subordinates.
A. to   B. for
C. about   D. with
E. of

23. ...... her child was not well, she did not go to office.
A. Although   B. In spite of
C. Since   D. However
E. Even if

24. We have so nicely practised that we are now confident ...... winning the match.
A. for   B. into
C. of   D. with
E. in

25. The old man has become ...... weak that he can hardly walk.
A. too   B. so

C. very   D. as
E. much

26. Satish did not work ...... so his master asked him to leave.
A. proper   B. rightly
C. properly   D. straight
E. neat

27. How much did it ...... you to reach Bombay by car ?
A. estimate   B. cost
C. price   D. pay
E. charge

28. Dinesh is unhappy with me ...... my carelessness.
A. because   B. for
C. regard   D. as
E. since

29. The waiter took the plates ...... after we had finished eating.
A. out   B. up
C. of   D. away
E. across

30. Do you know the person ...... owns that house ?
A. that   B. whom
C. which   D. who
E. to

31. Unless we go ...... once we shall miss the train.
A. now   B. so
C. for   D. that
E. at

32. I feel ill because I had been working too hard ...... months.
A. for   B. at
C. since   D. those
E. these

33. Being a sportsman is one and being a coach is ....
A. another   B. different

C. second   D. same
E. separate

34. Neeru is not happy with her present job ...... the salary is very low.
A. although   B. even if
C. in spite of D. their
E. as

35. Saveta got scared when the beggar stared ...... her.
A. over   B. on
C. about   D. at
E. to

36. Rakesh was planning to go on leave ...... he was planning to get married.
A. and   B. so
C. but   D. hence
E. as

37. In spite of her own difficulties Bhavna ...... to be helpful to her neighbours as much as possible.
A. decides   B. tries
C. agrees   D. allows
E. attempts

38. The cat was ...... by a speeding truck.
A. run over   B. crossed over
C. killed over D. moved over
E. moved over

39. Although I was doubtful, my mother was ...... that I would pass.
A. from   B. uncertain
C. decided   D. sure
E. believed

40. When I saw him in old clothes, I was ...... by surprise.
A. taken   B. took
C. takes   D. taking
E. take

41. Monika has been suffering ...... fever for the last three days.
A. in   B. from
C. with   D. for
E. against

42. Dheeraj had ...... wanted to be an engineer in his life.
A. altogether   B. almost
C. always   D. although
E. absolutely

43. The meeting was ...... and he had to stay back for a day more.
A. allowed   B. prolonged
C. waived   D. sluggish
E. stopped

44. Milan and Mahu are twins who ...... each other very much.
A. look alike   B. resemble
C. alike   D. match
E. identify

45. Much against her wishes, Veena's father ...... her to give up studies.
A. talked   B. encouraged
C. requested   D. compelled
E. advices

46. We will be ...... her on Friday at Ramesh's house.
A. talking   B. taking
C. seeing   D. meet
E. passing

47. There are ...... people living in this street.
A. many   B. much
C. lot   D. plenty
E. sufficient

48. Kaveri promised me that he would come ...... did not turn up.
A. though   B. still
C. but   D. so
E. and

49. These medicines are ...... for curing cold.
A. effective   B. powerful
C. real   D. capable
E. proper

50. Vineeta came ...... me to see the circus.
A. across   B. along
C. towards   D. together
E. after

51. The shopkeeper ...... the customer all types of toys in his shop.
A. showed   B. placed
C. called   D. saw
E. allotted

52. He ...... asleep while he was driving.
A. falls   B. fell
C. fallen   D. goes
E. went

53. We will be late if we ...... not leave now.
A. will   B. shall
C. did   D. do
E. does

54. The bus stand is directly ...... the police station.
A. around   B. about
C. towards   D. nearly
E. behind

55. The ...... has expressed his love for nature in his poem.
A. writer   B. producer
C. author   D. poet
E. journalist

56. It was a pleasant morning and we went ...... for a walk.
A. in   B. out
C. to   D. on
E. away

57. It is good that you are ...... of your faults.
A. known   B. short
C. aware   D. removing
E. approving

58. The girls complained ...... malpractice of the warden.
A. to   B. on
C. about   D. for
E. against

59. I fail to comprehend why he has developed a tendency to look down ..... his juniors.
A. at   B. on
C. upon   D. with
E. from

60. Even after his best efforts, he could not make her yield ...... his allurement.
A. before   B. for
C. in   D. to
E. by

61. You should not ...... lunch at this time because you are too late.
A. hope   B. expect
C. hope for   D. demand
E. ask for

62. We have remembered you ...... the time you parted with us.
A. till   B. since
C. for   D. up to the time
E. as

63. The bomb ...... and killed no fewer than forty people.
A. erupted   B. exploded
C. cracked   D. volleyed
E. roared

64. Since we wanted to get an experience, we have ...... such a tiring journey.
A. travelled   B. gone
C. fulfilled   D. curtailed
E. undertaken

65. The little boy ...... frightened and ran away.
A. got   B. get
C. became   D. had
E. show

66. Kapil plays tennis ...... often than Sachin does.
A. more   B. as
C. so   D. far
E. nearly

67. The crop has been ...... well after the rains.
A. grown   B. growing
C. grow   D. grows
E. grew

68. Keerti is intending to accompay them on ...... next visit abroad.
A. her   B. theirs
C. our   D. their
E. its

69. They ...... no attention to what people say about them.
A. keep   B. listen
C. pay   D. take
E. mind

70. Apparently, the disease is ...... by some mosquitoes.
A. concealed   B. conveyed
C. spread   D. speeded
E. taken

71. The train started from the station ...... and picked up speed afterwards.
A. suddenly   B. abruptly
C. feebly   D. brokenly
E. slowly

72. We became so ...... in the game that we did not notice a passenger who had got into our compartment.
A. skillful   B. absorbed
C. neglected   D. inattentive
E. meticulous

73. The exercise should not be done...... after taking food.
A. as soon as   B. much
C. as far as   D. seriously
E. immediately

74. A ...... fear of doctors persists among children.
A. universal   B. recognised
C. introduction D. threatening
E. polite

75. If I receive a ...... encouragement, it will help me.
A. few   B. least
C. some   D. most
E. little

ANSWERS

1	2	3	4	5	6	7	8	9	10
C	C	A	C	B	C	B	A	A	B

11	12	13	14	15	16	17	18	19	20
C	B	E	D	E	A	B	D	C	E

21	22	23	24	25	26	27	28	29	30
E	A	C	C	B	C	B	B	D	D

31	32	33	34	35	36	37	38	39	40
E	A	A	E	D	E	B	A	D	A

41	42	43	44	45	46	47	48	49	50
B	C	B	B	D	C	A	C	A	B

51	52	53	54	55	56	57	58	59	60
A	B	D	E	D	B	C	C	C	D

61	62	63	64	65	66	67	68	69	70
B	B	B	E	A	A	B	D	C	C

71	72	73	74	75
E	D	E	A	E

COMPREHENSION

A. Objectives

Comprehension test ascertain candidate's ability to understand the ideas contained in the prose passage. For solving the comprehension questions, the condidates should bear in mind that the various comprehension questions are set with the following objectives in view :

(*a*) To test his capability to understand the implicit as well as the explicit ideas of the passage writer.

(*b*) To test his richness and accuracy of vocabulary.

(*c*) To judge his capability to pick out the various arguments advanced by the writer for or against a certain topic.

(*d*) To test the candidate's ability to comprehend and interpret the given passage.

(*e*) To test his ability to detect the central ideas or the focal point in the passage.

(*f*) To test, though not very often, his power of appreciating critically the views contained in the passage.

B. The best way to answer the Comprehension Questions

For answering the comprehension questions correctly, constant practice is of utmost importance and is quite necessary. However, the following method will be helpful to the candidates in tackling these questions.

(*a*) First of all, the entire passage should be read carefully and quickly. This speed reading will help you to understand the gist of the passage and to remember the important details.

(*b*) Then read the passage for the second time, this time a bit slowly and steadily, concentrating your attention on the questions set below it. This second reading of the passage, with an eye of the questions, will help you to find out the correct answer to the given question.

(*c*) In third stage, make your answer in the answer sheet, as directed.

C. Few important points to remember

(*a*) Utmost care should be taken to ensure that the comprehension questions are answered within the time allotted.

(*b*) As all the questions carry equal marks, do not waste time over difficult questions. Put a cross on the serial number of the un-answered question, so as to easily identify them later on.

(*c*) If the time permits, do revision and carry out the necessary corrections.

PASSAGE 1

Directions : *Read the following passage carefully and answer the questions given below it. Certain words/ phrases have been italicised to help locate them, while answering some of the questions.*

Once upon a time there lived a merchant named Madhav who was very rich. However, as time went on, he lost all his money and became very poor. Madhav then decided to leave the city to try his luck elsewhere. He sold all he owned in order to *clear* his debts. The only item he kept was an *antique* iron beam weighing about half a ton, Madhav asked his friend Lakhan to keep the beam with him while he was away. Lakhan gladly accepted *charge* of the beam.

Years passed. Madhav travelled widely and made a lot of money. He returned to his native place as a rich man. A few days after settling down, Madhav remembered the beam. He went to see Lakhan to ask for its return. But Lakhan had no *intention* of returning the beam. "Oh, Madhav, what will I tell you !" he said in excuse. "While you were away, I kept the beam in my godown and the mice ate it. Please do foregive me for this." Madhav did not comment. When he rose to leave, he said, "Lakhan, my friend, you have been so kind in keeping the beam for me ! So I have brought you a present. Please send your son, Ramu, to *collect* it. Lakhan felt guilty. But he sent Ramu with Madhav. On reaching home, Madhav got Ramu locked up in a room.

When Ramu did not return home by evening, his father came in search of him. "Oh, I'm terribly sorry! Madhav apologised to Lakhan". "While we were coming here, a hawk flew down and carried Ramu away. I could not do anything. Please forgive me." Lakhan got *wild* on hearing this. He started quarrelling with Madhav.

The matter was finally taken to the court. The judge observed that it was not possible for a hawk to fly off with a grown-up-boy. "Yes sir, it is just as possible for a hawk to fly off with a grown-up-boy, as it is for mice to eat an iron beam weighing half a ton" explained Madhav. The judge asked what he meant and Madhav told his story. The judge ordered Lakhan to return the beam in exchange of the boy and the matter was settled.

1. What did Madhav do to pay off his debts ?

A. He sold the iron beam to Lakhan.

B. He borrowed some money from Lakhan.

C. He sought the help of his friend Lakhan.

D. He kept the iron beam with Lakhan.

E. None of these.

2. Why did Madhav go to Lakhan's house after returning to the city ?

A. He wanted to give a present to Lakhan.

B. He wanted to take Ramu to his house.

C. He wanted to keep an iron beam with Lakhan.

D. He wanted to collect a present from Lakhan.

E. He wanted to take back the iron beam from Lakhan.

3. What did Madhav do to Ramu ?

A. Madhav told Ramu to lock up the room.

B. Madhav sent him to his house.

C. Madhav took him as a present from Lakhan.

D. Madhav allowed him to be carried away by a hawk.

E. Madhav forcibly kept him in his house.

4. Lakhan went to Madhav's house to ...

A. enquire about Ramu.

B. apologise to him.

C. release Ramu from the room.

D. accept the present brought by him.

E. give back the iron beam.

5. When Lakhan went to Madhav's house, he was told that ...

A. Ramu was locked up in a room.

B. the mice had eaten up the beam.

C. Ramu had returned to his house.

D. a hawk had taken Ramu away.

E. a present has been brought for him.

6. Madhav decided to leave the city so that...

A. he could keep the iron beam with Lakhan.

B. he could pay off the debts.

C. he could try his fortune in some other place.

D. he could travel widely.

E. None of these.

7. Which of the following statements is *True* in the context of the passage ?

A. The judge ordered Lakhan to keep the iron beam with him.

B. The iron beam was not actually eaten up by mice.

C. Madhav kept the iron beam with Lakhan after coming back to his native place.

D. Lakhan did not return the iron beam because Madhav did not pay his debts.

E. None of these.

8. Which of the following statements is *Not True* in the context of the passage ?

A. Madhav brought a present for Lakhan when he returned as a rich man.

B. Lakhan was not at all interested in returning the iron beam.

C. Ramu was not at all carried away by a hawk.

D. Madhav did not quarrel with Lakhan when the iron beam was not returned to him.

E. Madhav told a lie in order to regain his iron beam.

9. When Madhav asked for the beam, Lakhan said that ...

A. he wanted to keep the beam for himself.

B. the beam was eaten up by mice.

C. he would send the beam along with Ramu.

D. the beam was lying safely in the godown.

E. a hawk flew down and carried away the iron beam.

Directions (10-13) : *Choose the word which is **most nearly the same** in meaning as the word or group of words in Capital Letters, as used in the passage.*

10. INTENTION
A. willingness   B. hope
C. ambition   D. determination
E. choice

11. CHARGE
A. duty   B. responsibility
C. care   D. receipt
E. safety

12. CLEAR
A. receive   B. sell
C. finish   D. pay
E. buy

13. WILD
A. abnormal   B. emotional
C. angry   D. impatient
E. disturbed

Directions (14-15) : *Choose the word which is **most opposite** in meaning of the words in Capital Letters, as used in the passage.*

14. COLLECT
A. gather   B. give
C. throw   D. distribute
E. take

15. ANTIQUE
A. ancient   B. pure
C. beautiful   D. clean
E. new

PASSAGE 2

Directions (1-15): *Read the following passage carefully and answer the questions given below it. Certain words in the passage have been **italicised** to help you locate them while answering some of the questions.*

Sultan Nasiruddin was a wise and *just* ruler. Everydody sang his praises. He was kind to the poor. He used to distribute money to the poor and the needy. His treasury was full of wealth. In spite of having so much wealth, he did not spend anything on himself. He earned his living by copying the holy book of the Muslims. Though a king, he felt that he must earn his own livelihood. He led a simple life. His wife was forced to do all the household chores. She had to cook her food, sweep the floor, make cothes and do many other household duties. At night, she complained of *severe* pain in her body. She *muttered* to herself, "My life is so miserable. I am tired of working from morning to evening."

One day, while cooking food, she burnt her fingers. She started weeping. On seeing her weeping, Sultan Nasiruddin asked her, "Begum, what is the matter ?" The queen started grumbling. "See, I have burnt my fingers. In spite of my being a queen, I have to work like other poor women. Why don't you employ some maid-servant ?" Sultan Nasiruddin replied, "No Begum, I earn my livelihood by copying the Koran. My income does not permit me to spend *lavishly*." The queen was annoyed. She said, "Sultan, for whom is this treasury full ? As a King, you must spend on yourself and your family. Sultan Nasiruddin disagreed. He replied, "Begum you are mistaken. I cannot touch the treasury. It is people's wealth. I am answerable to God. I must earn my livelihood." The Begum was *quiet*. She was convinced by the Sultan's argument and accepted it willingly.

1. The queen got annoyed because...
A. she had burnt her fingers.
B. of the Sultan's statement about his own income.
C. the Sultan was busy copying the holy book.
D. of the Sultan's undue concern for her.
E. the Sultan forced her to work with other poor women.

2. Why did Sultan Nasiruddin not use the money in the treasury for himself ?
A. He was afraid that his subjects would accuse him of theft.
B. He had already distributed the money to the poor.
C. He wanted to annoy his Begum.
D. He was convinced that the money belonged to the people.
E. None of these.

3. The demand of the queen was that the ......
A. Sultan should earn his own livelihood.
B. Money in the treasury should not be distributed to the poor.
C. Sultan should employ a maid servant.
D. Sultan should help her in her household duties.
E. Sultan should stop copying the holy book.

4. Why was Sultan Nasiruddin popular among his people ?
A. He was devoted to the holy Koran.

B. He was fair to all and was full of wisdom.
C. He had kept the treasury full of wealth.
D. He made his wife work like an ordinary woman.
E. None of these.

5. Which of the following statements is *true* in the context of the passage ?
A. Nobody used to praise the Sultan.
B. The wife of Nasiruddin never got tired of doing household duties.
C. The queen used to do all domestic chores.
D. The wife of Nasiruddin was from a poor family.
E. The Sultan was never God-fearing.

6. What forced the queen to do all the household chores ?
A. The simple life style of the Sultan.
B. The lack of money in the treasury.
C. The poor working of the maid servant.
D. The Sultan's greed for money.
E. None of these.

7. Why did Sultan Nasiruddin use to copy the Koran ?
A. It was the holy book of the Muslims.
B. He wanted to prove that he was religious minded King.
C. He wanted to teach his wife a lesson.
D. He wanted to learn Koran by copying it.
E. None of these.

8. What made the queen weep ?
A. The Sultan's unwillingness to use the wealth in the treasury.
B. The Sultan's lack of attention towards her.

C. The severe pain in her body.

D. The burning of her fingers.

E. None of these.

9. Which of the following statements is *Not True* in the context of the passage ?

A. The income of the Sultan did not permit him to be extravagant.

B. The queen wanted the King to spend the money in the treasury on themselves.

C. The Sultan was sympathetic to the poor and the needy.

D. The queen made the Sultan employ some servants for her.

E. The Sultan and the queen led the life of ordinary people.

10. What was the cause of the severe pain in the queen's body ?

A. The daily washing of the floor by her.

B. The burning of her body while cooking.

C. The pain was a trick to avoid domestic duties.

D. Not mentioned in the passage.

E. None of these.

Directions (11-13) : *Choose the word which is **most nearly the same** in meaning as the words in Capital Letters, as used in the passage.*

11. SEVERE

A. sad   B. serious

C. deep   D. bad

E. intense

12. QUIET

A. sorry   B. kind

C. grim   D. peaceful

E. silent

13. MUTTERED

A. apologised   B. grumbled

C. thought   D. addressed

E. reminded

Directions (14-15) : *Choose the word which is **most opposite in meaning** of the words in Capital Letters, as used in the passage.*

14. JUST

A. unbiased   B. only

C. cruel   D. unfair

E. foolish

15. LAVISHLY

A. miserly   B. minutely

C. extravagantly   D. financially

E. doubtfully

PASSAGE 3

Directions : *Read the following passage carefully and answer the questions given below it. Certain words/ phrases have been **italicised** to help you to locate them while answering some of the questions.*

This happened not so long ago in a remote village in South India. There lived in this village, a middle aged woman named Thangamma, who earned her living by selling vegetables in the market. She had a small farm near her house, where she cultivated different types of vegetables. Near her house, lived a woman named Mangamma, who owned a farm *adjacent* to Thangamma's farm. Mangamma, who was not as old as Thangamma, did not cultivate anything in her farm, but spent most of her time dreaming of getting some hidden wealth in her farm. In fact, an astrologer had once told her that she would become rich overnight. She had then gone around saying this to everyone in the village. Mangamma often *made fun of* Thangamma saying that only fool would toil so much.

One day while Mangamma was wandering over her farm, a storm *broke out* and she took shelter under a tree. As she stood there, her eyes fell upon an ordinary-looking earthen pot lying at her feet, half buried in the ground. Her curiosity aroused. She dug out the pot and with trembling fingers brushed off the mud from the lid. To her amazement, it was filled with glittering ornaments. She looked around and after ensuring that nobody was watching her, quietly took the pot home. After reaching home, she hid the pot inside a wooden box in her house. Being overjoyed at her dream coming true, she started celebrating by buying *expensive* clothes and other things for herself. In a few days she spent all the money she had. She then took out the pot and went straight to the shop of the village goldsmith to sell all the ornaments. The goldsmith after examining them carefully, threw them back to her. Mangamma asked him what he meant. The goldsmith scornfully declared that the ornaments were fake.

The fake gold ornaments were in fact the ones worn by stage actors while *portraying* mythical characters. It was none other than Thangamma who kept the pot of fake ornaments in Mangamma's farm. She did this to teach Mangamma a good lesson.

On hearing the goldsmith's words, Mangamma stood dumb-founded. She soon understood her folly and left the shop realising the merit of the old proverb. "All that glitters is not gold."

1. How did Thangamma earn her living ?
A. She worked in the farms of the villages.
B. She sold grains in the market.
C. She bought vegetables from Mangamma and sold them in the market.
D. She sold the vegetables she cultivated.
E. None of these.

2. What can be inferred from the passage regarding the age of Thangamma ?
A. She was an aged woman.
B. She was not as old as Mangamma.
C. She was of the same age as Mangamma.
D. She was older than Mangamma.
E. She was a young woman.

3. Once an astrologer had told Mangamma that she would
A. become rich at night.
B. loss all her money.
C. get a pot of ornaments in her farm.
D. become wealthy all of a sudden.
E. get some fake ornaments in her farm.

4. What did the jeweller say after examining the ornaments ?
A. He said that they were worn by stage actors.

B. He said that they were not real gold ornaments.
C. He said that he would give a few rupees for the ornaments.
D. He said that the ornaments were not shiny.
E. He said that he does not buy old ornaments.

5. Which of the following is *True* in the context of the passage ?
A. Mangamma decided to sell the ornaments although she had some money with her.
B. Mangamma wanted to cheat the goldsmith by selling the fake ornaments.
C. The astrologer did not keep the pot of ornaments in Mangamma's farm.
D. The goldsmith was responsible for teaching Mangamma a good lesson.
E. The pot of ornaments was kept in Mangamma's farm by the stage actors.

6. The ornaments kept in the pot were actually the ones
A. Worn by Thangamma when she acted in dramas.
B. Used by actors who played the role of characters from mythology.
C. Made by the goldsmith to teach Mangamma a lesson.
D. Worn by the ancient stage actors.
E. One of these.

7. What did Mangamma do with the pot of ornaments after taking it home ?
A. She took it to the goldsmith.
B. She hid it under the ground.
C. She kept it in a box.
D. She sold it to buy expensive clothes.

E. She hid it under a tree.

8. Which of the following is *Not True* in the context of the passage ?
A. Mangamma did not cultivate vegetables in her farm.
B. Mangamma tried to sell the pot of ornaments to the village goldsmith.
C. Mangamma did not tell Thangamma about the pot of ornaments.
D. Mangamma, in her dream, saw the pot of ornaments lying under the tree.
E. Mangamma often made fun of Thangamma.

9. Where did Mangamma find the pot of ornaments ?
A. Under a tree in the forest.
B. In Thangamma's farm.
C. In her own farm.
D. Near Thangamma's house.
E. Inside a wooden box in the farm.

Directions (10-12) : *Choose the word which is **most nearly the same** in meaning as the word or group of words in Capital Letters,, as used in the passage.*

10. CULTIVATED
A. marketed   B. ploughed
C. grew   D. collected
E. made

11. MADE FUN OF
A. ridiculed   B. requested
C. praised   D. advised
E. cursed

12. PORTRAYING
A. dressing   B. depicting
C. pretending   D. decorating
E. exposing

13. ADJACENT

A. joining B. distant
C. unequal D. near
E. unrelated

14. BROKE OUT

A. started B. gathered
C. vanished D. exploded
E. thundered

15. EXPENSIVE

A. attractive B. costly
C. dull D. dirty
E. cheap

PASSAGE 4

Directions : *Read the following passage carefully and answer the questions given below it. Certain words/ groups of words have been italicised to help you to locate them easily while answering some of the questions.*

King Vikramaditya was renowned for his impartial judgement. His brother-in-law, Rishiketu was very ambitious. He considered himself to be very wise; much wiser than he really was. He *used* to be *present* in the court while Vikramaditya conducted trials. Rishiketu developed a feeling that he could also give judgements like the king. Sometimes he *made* his comments *privately* to some of the courtiers who were friendly to him but his boasting reached Vikramaditya's ear. One day Vikramaditya asked Rishiketu to disguise as an old man wearing a false beard and a royal robe and to sit in his judgement seat. He announced to the courtiers, "Here is our old friend, the famous chief judge of our neighbouring kingdom. He will dispose of today's cases while I attend to some other important things. "Vikramaditya left the court but hid himself behind the screen just *close* to Rishiketu's Chair.

Rishiketu heard the first case of a thief who had stolen a hen. He ordered the thief to go and steal another hen and ordered the soldiers to follow him and arrest him immediately after his stealing the second hen. He further added that he would give his judgement only after that.

While everyone sat amazed with this *funny* trial, Vikramaditya came out and *led* Rishiketu into his private room. There he asked Rishiketu why he wanted the thief to steal one more hen. Rishiketu explained thoughtfully, "Your Majesty, a few days ago, you had fined a gold coin to a thief who had stolen two hens. In our kigndom there is no half gold coin. How can I fine half gold coin for stealing one hen ? Therefore I asked him to steal one more hen, so that I could fine him one gold coin."

1. Which of the following statements is *True* in the context of the passage ?

A. Rishiketu was not at all deserving to be a judge.
B. Rishiketu had never praised himself for his wisdom.
C. The thief had stolen another hen as per Rishiketu's order.

D. After Rishiketu heard the case, Vikramaditya fined a gold coin to the thief.

E. Rishiketu had decided to fine half gold coin to the thief.

2. Which of the following is the meaning of 'after that' as used in the last sentence of the third paragraph ?

A. After the soldiers follow the thief.

B. After carefully listening to the case of theft.

C. After Vikramaditya takes over from Rishiketu.

D. After the thief had stolen another hen.

E. After the thief was released for repeating the crime.

3. What surprised the people in the king's court ?

A. Vikramaditya's act of asking an outsider to sit in his seat.

B. Rishiketu's act of asking the thief to steal another hen.

C. Rishiketu's ordering the guards to follow and arrest the thief.

D. Rishiketu's explanation for postponement of the judgement.

E. Vikramaditya's act of giving more importance to other things than to the trials.

4. Rishiketu used to tell his courtier friends :

A. To be present in the court while he conducted trials.

B. That Vikramaditya could conduct trials very impartially.

C. Not to tell Vikramaditya his privately made comments.

D. That he was a capable of judging cases as the king.

E. None of these.

5. What did Vikramaditya do after placing Rishiketu in his judgement seat ?

A. He went out to attend to some other important things.

B. He appeared before Rishiketu in the disguise of a thief.

C. He wore a false beared and a royal robe.

D. He hid Rishiketu behind the screen, very close to the judge's seat.

E. He remained in the court without being noticed by others.

6. Vikramaditya introduced Rishiketu to his courtiers as :

A. his brother-in-law.

B. a thief who had stolen a hen.

C. the chief judge of the neighbouring kingdom.

D. a fake judge wearing a beard and a royal robe.

E. None of these.

7. After listening to Rishiketu's explanation for his judgement in the thief's case, Vikramaditya most probably would have :

A. asked him to continue in his judgement seat.

B. been pleased with his intelligence and rewarded him.

C. shown him his right place.

D. admired his ability as a judge.

E. appointed him as chief judge of his own kingdom.

Directions : (*8-12*) *Which of the following is **most nearly the same** in meaning as the words in Capital Letters, as used in the context of the passage.*

8. ADDED

A. summed   B. deposited

C. mixed
D. said
E. judged

9. LED
A. carried
B. forced
C. persuaded
D. left
E. followed

10. USED
A. utilised
B. continued
C. applied
D. liked
E. consumed

11. MADE
A. prepared
B. decided
C. expressed
D. felt
E. considered

12. FUNNY
A. happy
B. annoying
C. pleasant
D. exciting
E. ridiculous

Directions (13-15) : *Which of the following is* **most opposite in meaning** *of the words in capital letters, as used in the passage :*

13. PRESENT
A. absent
B. past
C. return
D. withdraw
E. disappear

14. CLOSE
A. open
B. away
C. disclose
D. near
E. long

15. PRIVATELY
A. lonely
B. officially
C. secretly
D. decisively
E. openly

PASSAGE 5

Directions : *Read the following passage carefully and answer the questions given below it. Certain words have been italicised to help you to locate them while answering some of the questions.*

Long ago, there lived a poor slave. One day, tired of heavy work and of the little food, he decided to run away but was caught. His master became furious and decided to punish him. He condemned the slave to a most horrible death; to be torn alive and eaten by a lion. He did this to amuse himself and his friends.

So, on the fixed day, the poor slave was dragged to the circus area and a big lion was brought in. The beast had been kept fasting for two days and so on seeing the poor man, came running towards him. But to everyone's surprise, as he drew near, he stopped and began to lick the slave's hand. It was *evident* that the beast was happy. He was wagging his tail like a dog.

The slave now started patting the lion and whispered something in his ear. Everyone was taken by surprise at the *strange* behaviour of the lion. They wondered why the beast did not *devour* the man. The master then asked the slave to give an explanation.

"It is not the first time that I attempted to run away", began the poor slave. "Once when I was the slave to another master, I had run away and had hidden myself in a cave for some days. One day this lion entered the cave limping. A big thorn had got into his right paw and caused him a lot of pain. I pulled out the thorn from his paw. From that moment, he became my friend. One day both of us were caught and *separated* by a gang of hunters. We have now come together."

The story of the poor slave *touched* everyone present there. The slave and the lion were immediately set free by the master.

1. The slave tried to run away from his present master because :

A. he wanted to meet his friend, the lion.

B. his master became furious one day.

C. he wanted to teach his master a lesson.

D. he was condemned to a horrible death.

E. he was badly treated by the master.

2. The lion did not harm the slave in the arena because :

A. the slave was the friend of the lion.

B. the slave whispered something in the lion's ear.

C. the lion had a thorn in its paw.

D. the slave started patting the lion.

E. None of these.

3. The poor slave was condemned to be eaten by a lion because :

A. he was tired of heavy work.

B. he had tried to escape.

C. there was very little food for him to eat.

D. the lion was kept fasting for two days.

E. the master wanted to test the slave's strength.

4. The poor slave hid himself in a cave after :

A. running away from the lion.

B. escaping from his present master.

C. seeing the lion in the circus arena.

D. running away from his former master.

E. removing the thorn from the lion's paw.

5. What did the slave do when the lion entered the cave ?

A. He ran away and hid himself in another cave.

B. He told something in the lion's ear.

C. He removed the thorn from the lion's paw.

D. He decided to kill it.

E. None of these.

6. Why were the spectators in the arena taken by surprise ?

A. The slave did not try to run away.

B. The lion was limping.

C. The lion came running towards the slave.

D. The lion did not harm to the slave.

E. The slave removed the thorn from the lion's paw.

7. The slave and the lion were set free by the master soon after :

A. seeing the lion limping.

B. listening to the tale of their friendship.

C. they were touched by everyone present there.

D. keeping them together in the arena.

E. the slave pulled out a thorn from the lion's paw.

8. Which of the following statements is *Not True* in the context of the passage ?

A. The slave and the lion were once caught by a group of hunters.

B. The spectators did not believe in the story narrated by the slave.

C. In the arena, the lion recognised the slave as his old friend.

D. The lion was not given food for two days before bringing it to the arena.

E. After seeing the slave in the arena, the lion started wagging its tail like a dog.

9. Which of the following statement is *True* in the context of the passage ?
A. The lion licked the slave's hand in the arena.
B. Before meeting the slave in the cave, the lion was kept fasting from two days.
C. It was the first time that the lion met the slave in the arena.
D. The lion was in pain because it was injured by a hunter.
E. The slave patted the lion as soon as it entered the cave.

Directions (10-13) : *Choose the word which is **most nearly the same** in meaning as the words in Capital Letters, as used in the passage.*

10. TOUCHED
A. contracted   B. affected
C. surprised   D. related
E. cautioned

11. STRANGE
A. unnecessary   B. kind
C. unusual   D. silly
E. mild

12. DEVOUR
A. eat   B. throw
C. punish   D. save
E. catch

13. AMUSE
A. watch   B. laugh
C. treat   D. show
E. entertain

Directions (14-15) : *Choose the word which is **most opposite in meaning** of the words Capital Letters, as used in the passage.*

14. SEPARATED
A. removed   B. added
C. invited   D. united
E. collected

15. EVIDENT
A. doubtful   B. unimportant
C. clear   D. understood
E. disagreed.

ANSWERS

Passage 1

1	2	3	4	5	6	7	8	9	10
E	E	E	A	D	C	B	A	B	A

11	12	13	14	15
B	D	C	B	E

Passage 2

1	2	3	4	5	6	7	8	9	10
B	D	C	B	C	A	E	D	D	E

11	12	13	14	15
B	E	B	D	A

Passage 3

1	2	3	4	5	6	7	8	9	10
D	D	D	B	C	B	C	D	A	C

11	12	13	14	15
A	B	B	C	E

Passage 4

1	2	3	4	5	6	7	8	9	10
A	D	B	D	E	C	C	D	A	B

11	12	13	14	15
C	E	A	B	E

Passage 5

1	2	3	4	5	6	7	8	9	10
E	A	B	D	C	D	B	B	A	B

11	12	13	14	15
C	A	E	D	A

ARRANGEMENT OF PARTS
OF SENTENCES

Now various recruits bodies have included the questions of this type with a view to test your knowledge of English Language. The sentence is broken in six parts. The first and last parts of each sentence are numbered as 1 and 6. The rest of the sentence is split into four parts and named P, Q, R and S. These four parts of the sentence are jumbled *i.e.* not given in the proper order. To recreate the original sentence from its parts, read the sentence carefully and find out which of the four combinations, given in the suggested answers, is correct.

Example 1 :

1. One of the aims
P. build character,
Q. of education is to
R. to impart some sort of moral instruction
S. and to inculcate certain traits,
6. which help a person in leading a responsible life.

A. PQRS   B. QPRS   C. RQPS   D. QRPS

The correct sentence which can be recreated from the above jumbled words is 'One of the aims of education is to build character, to impart some sort of moral instruction and to inculcate certain traits, which help a person in leading a responsible life'. Hence, the answer is QPRS which is given at (B).

Example 2 :

1. What was necessary
P. and so promises
Q. not so necessary today
R. to an individual yesterday,
S. is some how
6. are broken and forgotten.

A. SRQP   B. PQSR   C. RSQP   D. PQRS

The correct answer is 'What was necesary to an individual yesterday, is some how not so necessary today and so promises are broken and forgotten'. Hence RSQP given at answer 'C' is correct.

Directions : *In the following questions, the first and the last part of the sentence are in their proper orders. The rest of the sentence named PQR and S are not given in their proper order. Read the sentences and find out which of the four combinations is correct.*

1. 1. Voice is one
   P. which can be
   Q. controlled
   R. phycical attributes,
   S. among the
   6. cultivated and trained
   A. PRQS   B. SRQP
   C. SRPQ   D. QPRS

2. 1. The syllabus notified
   P. or, specialised study
   Q. is in broad general terms
   R. for the proper general knowledge
   S. and does not require advanced
   6. of the subject concerned.
   A. PQSR   B. RQPS
   C. QSPR   D. QRSP

3. 1. Handball is a game
   P. or, board by the players,
   Q. or, against a single wall
   R. with their hands
   S. played in a walled court
   6. to strike the ball.
   A. PQRS   B. SQPR
   C. RSQP   D. QSPR

4. 1. So still was
   P. dried autumn leaves fell
   Q. the air and
   R. that the
   S. such calm was there,
   6. straight from the tree.
   A. PSQR   B. RSPQ
   C. SPRQ   D. QSRP

5. 1. It is no secret
   P. is growing impatient
   Q. that the United States
   R. over the reluctance
   S. with Iraq
   A. RQPS   B. PQRS
   C. SRQP   D. RPQS

6. 1. A rich uncle
   P. that you spend this sum
   Q. in somewhat peculiar way
   R. has given you two hundred rupees
   S. on condition
   6. within twenty-four hours.
   A. SRPQ   B. PSRQ
   C. QRPS   D. RSPQ

7. 1. When he was a boy, Rahul,
   P. a distinguished statesman and philosopher,
   Q. in the printing office of his brother,
   R. learned his trade
   S. who afterward became
   6. who published a paper in Bombay.
   A. RPSQ   B. SPRQ
   C. PSQR   D. QPRS

8. 1. Gandhiji's elder brother had thought
   P. Gandhiji would have roaring legal practice in India
   Q. that after his return from England

R. and would become a rich and famous barrister,
S. as a qualified barrister,
6. in no time.
A. QSPR   B. SPRQ
C. RPSQ   D. PQSR

9. 1. In his whole life,
P. with an optimism,
Q. he continued
R. he had never received a letter
S. born of hope and faith, but
6. and was always the first to arrive at the post office.
A. QPRS   B. RPSQ
C. QPSR   D. PQSR

10. 1. Her two elder sisters
P. and now the youngest daughter lay,
Q. with the usual difficulties
R. in finding husbands and providing dowries
S. had been married
6. like a silent weight upon the heart of her parents.
A. RPSQ   B. SPQR
C. SQRP   D. RSPQ

11. 1. Efforts must be
P. schools in such
Q. no child may have to walk
R. made to open primary
S. a large number that
6. more than a mile.
A. PQRS   B. RQSP
C. SPQR   D. RPSQ

12. 1. The passengers
P. that there was
Q. assured them
R. were afraid
S. but the captain

6. no danger.
A. QRSP   B. SRQP
C. RSQP   D. PRQS

13. 1. It gives me
P. to this Extraordinary General Meeting,
Q. great pleasure
R. to welcome you
S. which has been convened
6. to change the name of your company.
A. QRPS   B. RPSQ
C. PSQR   D. SRPQ

14. 1. After toiling very hard,
P. period of time,
Q. he had made
R. over a long
S. he found that
6. no profit at all.
A. SRPQ   B. RPSQ
C. QSRP   D. PRSQ

15. 1. We regret to inform you
P. is left uncleared
Q. that some account
R. for a long time,
S. by you
6. despite a reminder.
A. PQRS   B. RSQP
C. QPRS   D. RPSQ

16. 1. Even today, in many countries,
P. neglected and there are far
Q. women continue to be
R. who have had the benefit of
S. fewer women than men
6. education and vocational training.
A. PRQS   B. QPSR
C. RQSP   D. SQRP

17. 1. Hobbies can fill our spare
    P. physical fatigue, and
    Q. moments with enjoyment
    R. and pleasure, they also relieve
    S. mental tiredness and
    6. corporate hinder our regular work.
    A. QRPS   B. QRSP
    C. SQPR   D. PQSR

18. 1. Certainly,
    P. who always
    Q. happy is the man,
    R. the company
    S. keeps
    6. of good books.
    A. RSQP   B. QPSR
    C. QRSP   D. SQRP

19. 1. Law should be
    P. making it compulsory
    Q. made by the parliament
    R. to undergo sterilisation
    S. for every couple
    6. after three children.
    A. RPQS   B. SRPQ
    C. QPSR   D. PSRQ

20. 1. I am also happy
    P. in the backward district of Hisar
    Q. upon a large industrialisation programme
    R. to inform you
    S. that your company is the first to embark
    6. with an investment of Rs. 3 crores.
    A. PRSQ   B. PQRS
    C. SQPR   D. RSQP

EXPLANATORY ANSWERS

1. **C :** Voice is one among the physical attributes, which can be controlled, cultivated and trained.

2. **C :** The syllabus notified is in broad general terms and does not require advanced or, specialised study for the proper general knowledge of the subject concerned.

3. **B :** Handball is a game played in a walled court or against a single wall or, board by the players, with their hands to strike the ball.

4. **D :** So still was the air and such calm was there, that the dried autumn leaves fell straight from the tree.

5. **A :** It is no secret over the reluctance that the United States is growing impatient with Iraq.

6. **D :** A rich uncle has given you two hundred rupees on condition that you spend this sum in somewhat peculiar way.

7. **B :** When he was a boy, Rahul, who afterward became a distinguished statesman and philosopher, learned his trade in the printing office of his brother, who published a paper in Bombay.

8. **A :** Gandhiji's elder brother had thought that after his return from England as a qualified barrister, Gandhiji would have roaring legal

practice in India and would become a rich and famous barrister, in no time.

9. **C :** In his whole life, he continued with an optimism, born hope and faith, but he had never received a letter and was always the first to arrive at the post office.

10. **C :** Her two elder sisters had been married with the usual difficulties in finding husbands and providing dowries and now the youngest daughter lay, like a silent weight upon the heart of her parents.

11. **D :** Efforts must be made to open primary schools in such a large number that no child may have to walk more than a mile.

12. **C :** The passengers were afraid but the captain assured them that there was no danger.

13. **A :** It gives me great pleasure to welcome you to this Extraordinary General Meeting, which has been convened to change the name of your company.

14. **B :** After toiling very hard, over a long period of time, he found that he had made no profit at all.

15. **C :** We regret to inform you that some account is left uncleared by you for a long time, despite a reminder.

16. **B :** Even today, in many countries, women continue to be neglected and there are far fewer women than men who have had the benefit of education and vocational training.

17. **B :** Hobbies can fill our spare moments with enjoyment and pleasure, they also relieve mental tiredness and physical fatigue and do not hinder our regular work.

18. **B :** Certainly, happy is the man, who always keeps the company of good books.

19. **C :** Law should be made by the parliament making it compulsory for every couple to undergo sterilisation after three children.

20. **D :** I am also happy to inform you that your company is the first to embark upon a large industrialisation programme in the backward district of Hisar with an investment of Rs. 3 crores.

———

SYNONYMS AND ANTONYMS WORDS

IMPORTANT POINTS FOR SYNONYMS AND ANTONYMS

1. Wherever possible, the question and answer words must be of the same Part of Speech. For example, if the question word is in the Passive the answer should also be in Passive. Similarly, if the question word is in the Past Tense, the answer should also be in the Past Tense and so on.
2. A favourite trick of the examiner is to include an antonym in the answer choices for a synonym question or a synonym in the answer choices for an antonym question. Be very careful about what is asked before answering a question.
3. Don't be nervous if you don't get the dictionary meaning. You are only expected to choose the best possible answer.
4. Don't ponder over a question for too long. It is better to answer those questions you know first. Then come back to those that you don't know.
5. It may be possible to choose the correct answer by rejecting those words that simply cannot be the proper choice. This is done by a process of reasoning and elimination. However, you are advised to use this process only when you are not certain of the answer, but this process is time consuming and should be used only when you are not able to choose the best possible answer.

SYNONYMS WORDS

Directions (1-100) : *Choose the word nearest in meaning to the given words.*

1. ABORTIVE
A. ineffective
B. fruitful
C. silly
D. premature
E. none

2. ABSOLVE
A. spoil
B. agree
C. acquit
D. mix
E. none

3. ABSORB
A. rub
B. remove
C. soak
D. starve
E. none

4. ACKNOWLEDGE
A. enter
B. receive
C. approve
D. admit
E. none

5. ACCUMULATE
A. buy
B. add

C. store   D. approve
E. none

6. ADHERE
A. accept   B. stick
C. fight   D. oppose
E. none

7. ADJOURN
A. postpone   B. increase
C. drop   D. record
E. none

8. ADMONISH
A. admire   B. abolish
C. warn   D. harm
E. none

9. AFFECTION
A. attraction   B. interest
C. fondness   D. attachment
E. none

10. AGILE
A. girlish   B. poor
C. dull   D. active
E. none

11. AKIN
A. cousin   B. friendly
C. foreign   D. related
E. none

12. ALLURE
A. attract   B. agitate
C. entrap   D. deceive
E. none

13. ANALOGY
A. comparison   B. linking
C. psychology   D. attitude
E. none

14. APPLAUD
A. suspend   B. agree
C. graise   D. condemn
E. none

15. ASSAIL
A. sell   B. depart
C. attack   D. invite
E. none

16. ATTEMPT
A. try   B. answer
C. explain   D. solve
E. none

17. AWE
A. dream   B. fear
C. ghost   D. lie
E. none

18. BAFFLE
A. sink   B. puzzle
C. postpone   D. mix
E. none

19. BALMY
A. irritating   B. dirty
C. soothing   D. stormy
E. none

20. BARGAIN
A. account   B. deal
C. sale   D. profit
E. none

21. BEHEST
A. battery   B. command
C. nest   D. business
E. none

22. BEHOLD
A. see   B. catch
C. chase   D. examine
E. none

23. BENEFICENT
A. kindly   B. useful
C. cheap   D. poisonous
E. none

24. BENEVOLENT
A. charitable   B. gentle

C. wealthy   D. helpful
E. none

25. BETRAY
A. tear   B. beat
C. puzzle   D. deceive
E. none

26. BID
A. command   B. befool
C. obey   D. answer
E. none

27. BITTER
A. unfriendly   B. mannerless
C. sweet   D. harsh
E. none

28. BLAST
A. storm   B. fire
C. explosion   D. furnace
E. none

29. BLEND
A. polish   B. grind
C. mix   D. dissolve
E. none

30. BLUNDER
A. foolishness   B. fall
C. accident   D. error
E. none

31. BONDAGE
A. slavery   B. bravery
C. agreement   D. hardship
E. none

32. BOOTY
A. gain   B. loss
C. footwear   D. dirty
E. none

33. BRAWL
A. noise   B. tip.
C. agitation   D. fight
E. none

34. BREACH
A. disagreement   B. violation
C. rift   D. divorce
E. none

35. BRITTLE
A. breakable   B. little
C. glassy   D. bitter
E. none

36. CALLOUS
A. unlovable   B. careless
C. hard   D. legal
E. none

37. CARESS
A. ignore   B. watch
C. inspect   D. embrace
E. none

38. CATALOGUE
A. dictionary   B. encyclopaedia
C. directory   D. list
E. none

39. CAUSTIC
A. impure   B. severe
C. bitter   D. costly
E. none

40. CELEBRATED
A. famous   B. holy
C. joyful   D. big
E. none

41. COMPENSATE
A. reward   B. compel
C. punish   D. to make up for
E. none

42. COMPREHENSIVE
A. extensive   B. annual
C. complete   D. successful
E. none

43. CONFOUND
A. comment   B. confuse

C. recover   D. discover
E. none

44. CONQUEST
A. control   B. attack
C. defence   D. victory
E. none

45. CONSPIRACY
A. enmity   B. murder
C. plot   D. mischief
E. none

46. CONVICT
A. companion   B. guard
C. supervisor   D. criminal
E. none

47. CORDIAL
A. difficult   B. neighbourly
C. sleepy   D. friendly
E. none

48. CORPORAL
A. physical   B. fat
C. concrete   D. true
E. none

49. COUNTERFEIT
A. false   B. rival
C. natural   D. opposite
E. none

50. COURTESY
A. honesty   B. simplicity
C. politeness   D. sweetness
E. none

51. CREDITABLE
A. reasonable   B. honourable
C. believable   D. desirable
E. none

52. DEARTH
A. delicacy   B. scarcity
C. want   D. necessity
E. none

53. DEBAR
A. imprison   B. prevent
C. dismiss   D. detain
E. none

54. DEFINE
A. summarise   B. expand
C. explain   D. clarify
E. none

55. DEFORMITY
A. disturbance   B. indiscipline
C. irregularity   D. ugliness
E. none

56. DELICACY
A. softness   B. freshness
C. grace   D. nicely
E. none

57. DENOUNCE
A. announce   B. decrease
C. condemn   D. auction
E. none

58. DESCEND
A. depart   B. slip
C. direct   D. fall
E. none

59. DICTATE
A. overpower   B. rule
C. direct   D. suppress
E. none

60. DISCIPLE
A. follower   B. worshipper
C. believer   D. client
E. none

61. DISGUISE
A. distort   B. spoil
C. conceal   D. deface
E. none

62. DIVERSE
A. complex   B. many

C. strange   D. various
E. none

63. DOWNRIGHT
A. straight   B. sincere
C. slippery   D. slow
E. none

64. DRENCH
A. shrink   B. trench
C. drown   D. wet
E. none

65. DROWSY
A. weak   B. stale
C. ugly   D. sleepy
E. none

66. DWELL
A. disappear   B. swell
C. stay   D. compel
E. none

67. EBB
A. fly   B. vanish
C. decline   D. rise
E. none

68. ECONOMY
A. business   B. ceapness
C. saving   D. bargain
E. none

69. EGOTISTIC
A. orthodox   B. obstinate
C. stupid   D. self-centred
E. none

70. ELAPSE
A. spend   B. cancel
C. pass   D. decrease
E. none

71. ELIGIBLE
A. qualified   B. readable
C. necessity   D. educated
E. none

72. EMERGENCY
A. importance   B. necessity
C. readable   D. educated
E. none

73. EMOLUMENT
A. gift   B. employment
C. salary   D. allowance
E. none

74. ENDORSE
A. recommend   B. approve
C. simplify   D. repeat
E. none

75. ENORMOUS
A. big   B. savage
C. multisided   D. devilish
E. none

76. ENTANGLE
A. enlarge   B. involve
C. enclose   D. rectangle
E. none

77. ENVOY
A. messenger   B. judge
C. journalist   D. writer
E. none

78. ENVY
A. neighbourer   B. rivalry
C. conspiracy   D. competition
E. none

79. EPIDEMIC
A. physical   B. circular
C. external   D. general
E. none

80. ETERNAL
A. adventurous   B. internal
C. quiet   D. everlasting
E. none

81. EVIDENT
A. clear   B. trustworthy
C. deep   D. fair
E. none

82. EXCEL
A. progress   B. rise
C. surpass   D. compete
E. none

83. EXCEPTIONAL
A. unhappy   B. signincant
C. unusual   D. critical
E. none

84. EXPEDITE
A. hasten   B. expel
C. improve   D. repeat
E. none

85. EXPENSIVE
A. latest   B. vast
C. costly   D. pretty
E. none

86. EXTRAVAGANT
A. unimportant   B. irrelevant
C. heavy   D. excessive
E. none

87. FACULTY
A. power   B. success
C. talent   D. achievement
E. none

88. FANTASTIC
A. dearest   B. high
C. whimsical D. false
E. none

89. FATAL
A. rash   B. lucky
C. quick   D. deadly
E. none

90. FICTITIOUS
A. borrowed B. harrow
C. invisible   D. false
E. none

91. FLUCTUATE
A. punctuate B. flourish
C. control   D. to rise and fall
E. none

92. FLUENT
A. sudden   B. smooth
C. fast   D. flexible
E. none

93. FRAGILE
A. personal   B. weak
C. strange   D. unseen
E. none

94. FUTILE
A. fruitful   B. delicate
C. useless   D. lenient
E. none

95. GAIETY
A. joyousness B. variety
C. honesty   D. speed
E. none

96. GIDDY
A. light   B. greedy
C. dizzy   D. speedy
E. none

97. GLOOM
A. sunset   B. darkness
C. bloom   D. glory
E. none

98. GRACE
A. addition B. beauty
C. bonus   D. birthday
E. none

99. GUILD
A. association B. crime
C. boom   D. gold
E. none

100. GUILTY
A. corrupt   B. mischievous
C. sinful   D. honest
E. none

ANSWERS

1	2	3	4	5	6	7	8	9	10
D	C	C	C	D	B	D	C	D	D

11	12	13	14	15	16	17	18	19	20
A	C	C	A	C	A	B	B	C	B

21	22	23	24	25	26	27	28	29	30
D	A	C	D	D	B	A	B	A	D

31	32	33	34	35	36	37	38	39	40
B	A	A	C	A	C	C	D	D	D

41	42	43	44	45	46	47	48	49	50
A	B	A	D	C	D	C	D	A	A

51	52	53	54	55	56	57	58	59	60
C	C	A	A	D	B	D	D	D	C

61	62	63	64	65	66	67	68	69	70
D	B	C	B	D	C	A	C	D	C

71	72	73	74	75	76	77	78	79	80
B	A	B	A	C	B	B	C	C	A

81	82	83	84	85	86	87	88	89	90
A	C	C	A	D	D	D	C	C	D

91	92	93	94	95	96	97	98	99	100
D	B	B	C	B	B	A	C	A	C

ANTONYMS WORDS

Directions (1-100) : *Each of the following words is followed by five or four words one of which is its most opposite in meaning. Mark that word which you find most opposite in meaning.*

1. ABANDON
A. to yield
B. keep
C. to leave
D. ensure

2. ABHOR
A. love
B. have
C. to regard
D. generous
E. vulgar

3. ABRUPT
A. sharp
B. hurried
C. lacking
D. gradual
E. come

4. ACCUSE
A. impeach
B. exanerate
C. to blame
D. to call
E. renounce

5. ACUTE
A. extremely   B. dull
C. sharp   D. critical
E. profound

6. ADHERE
A. to stick fast   B. to be devoted
C. locate   D. loosen
E. equip

7. ADMIRE
A. to regard   B. venerate
C. celebrate   D. display
E. despise

8. ADVERSARY
A. an opponent   B. antagonist
C. tangible   D. ally
E. unsuccessful

9. ADVERSITY
A. affliction   B. adverse fortune
C. catastrophe   D. dropping
E. prosperity

10. AFFECTION
A. simplicity
B. conspicuous
C. strenuous pursuit
D. friendliness
E. dislike

11. AFFIRM
A. to state   B. deny
C. aver   D. assert
E. mystify

12. AGILE
A. brisk   B. ready
C. dim   D. disarming
E. sluggish

13. AGREE
A. consent   B. accede
C. differ   D. coincide
E. conform

14. ALLEVIATE
A. endure   B. worsen
C. enlighten   D. manoeuvre
E. humiliate

15. ALOOF
A. at a distance   B. impartial
C. reserved   D. careless
E. involved

16. AMALGAMATE
A. equip   B. separate
C. generate   D. materialise
E. repress

17. AMASS
A. concentrate   B. rotate
C. concern   D. separate
E. recollect

18. AMBIGUITY
A. uncertainty   B. explicitness
C. equivocation   D. obscurity
E. secular

19. AMENABLE
A. obedient   B. liable
C. stubborn   D. docile
E. abnormal

20. AMICABLE
A. penetrating   B. compensating
C. unfriendly   D. zig-zag
E. unescapable

21. AMPLIFY
A. distract   B. infer
C. publicise   D. contact
E. pioneer

22. ANALYSE
A. to examine critically
B. explicate
C. synthesise
D. dissect
E. quicken

23. ANGULAR
A. unbending   B. having corners
C. inflamed   D. round
E. puzzling

24. ANIMATE
A. deceive   B. to give life
C. fortify   D. encourage
E. kill

25. ANXIOUS
A. concerned   B. confident
C. eager   D. worried
E. troubled in mind

26. APATHETIC
A. not interested   B. indifferent
C. emotional   D. thorough
E. indignant

27. APPARENT
A. discernible   B. visible
C. manifest   D. ostensible
E. obscure

28. APPEASE
A. to satisfy   B. enrage
C. to concede   D. shorten
E. urge

29. APPREHEND
A. obviate   B. set free
C. shiver   D. understand
E. contrast

30. ARROGANT
A. proud   B. insolent
C. meek   D. profound
E. angry

31. ARTLESS
A. unsophisticated
B. free from deceit
C. uncontrived
D. simple
E. cunning

32. ASCETIC
A. good-natured
B. puritan
C. one who wages
D. self-indulgent
E. one who leads simple life

33. ASSERT
A. deny
B. to state with confidence
C. predicate
D. asseverate
E. inverse

34. ASSOCIATE
A. one who shares in an enterprise
B. link
C. colleague
D. accompany
E. adversary

35. ATTAIN
A. gain   B. secure
C. miss   D. accomplish
E. reach

36. BAFFLE
A. make way   B. thwart
C. confuse   D. check
E. substitute

37. BARREN
A. unprolific   B. sterile
C. ineffective   D. fertile
E. dull

38. BENEVOLENT
A. expressing goodwill
B. cruel
C. low-necked
D. altruistic
E. humanitarian

39. BENIGN
A. gracious   B. modern
C. sinister   D. humane
E. novel

40. BIAS
A. in a diagonal manner
B. preconception   C. prejudice
D. impartiality   E. loss of mobility

41. BLATANT
A. loud   B. tasteless
C. vociferous   D. quiet
E. quick

42. BLEND
A. to mix together
B. clear
C. separate
D. harmonise
E. visualise

43. BLISS
A. heaven
B. complete happiness
C. classic
D. paradise
E. misery

44. BLEMISH
A. to accuse   B. purify
C. to destroy   D. defect
E. futile

45. BLUFF
A. heartily outspoken
B. to mislead someone
C. rough
D. subtle
E. discourteous

46. BREVITY
A. shortness of time
B. length
C. forceful
D. honesty
E. dropping

47. BRUTAL
A. unreasoning   B. cruel
C. vulgar   D. inhuman
E. human

48. CALM
A. without rough motion
B. peaceful
C. excitement
D. self-possessed
E. superior

49. CANDID
A. vague   B. secretive
C. experienced   D. anxious
E. clear

50. CAPTIVATE
A. seize   B. repel
C. to enthrall   D. subjugate
E. dangerous

51. CEREMONIAL
A. informal   B. conventional
C. formal   D. delectable
E. polished

52. COMPLEX
A. difficult
B. simple
C. perplaxing
D. interconnected parts
E. fragile

53. CONCEAL
A. withdraw from observaticn
B. prevent from divulging
C. yield
D. reveal
E. deny

54. CONFESS
A. grant   B. conceal
C. concede   D. acknowledge
E. desist

55. CRYPTIC
A. tomb-like   B. secret
C. famous   D. candid
E. coded

56. DISMAL
A. cheerless   B. puzzling
C. bankrupt   D. reserved
E. gay

57. DORMANT
A. latent   B. eternal
C. awake   D. immoral
E. headless

58. DROWSY
A. active   B. lethargic
C. sleepy   D. famous
E. incapable

59. EMOLUMENT
A. loss   B. output
C. capital   D. penalty
E. honararium

60. ETERNAL
A. permanent   B. perpetual
C. transitory   D. active
E. binding

61. EXPUNGE
A. investigate   B. perpetuate
C. cleanse   D. purge
E. delete

62. FEASIBLE
A. theoretical   B. impatient
C. constant   D. present
E. impracticable

63. FICTION
A. fabrication
B. fantasy
C. conducive
D. something feigned
E. fact

64. FLEXIBLE
A. unable   B. rigid
C. rational   D. easy
E. likeable

65. FRAGRANT
A. scented   B. aromatic
C. indecisive   D. helpless
E. foul-smelling

66. GENIOUS
A. adept   B. proficient
C. idiot   D. desperate
E. enlightened

67. GLOOMY
A. depressing   B. cheerless
C. exhilarating   D. dark
E. dim

68. GRACEFUL
A. comely   B. clumsy
C. polished   D. lovely
E. novel

69. GRAVE
A. significant   B. realistic
C. mean   D. insignificant
E. momentous

70. GREAT
A. global   B. spiritual
C. critical   D. august
E. small

71. HAPPINESS
A. contentment   B. joyous
C. gloom   D. obedience
E. renunciation

72. HARSH
A. humiliate   B. definite
C. strong   D. gentle
E. stringent

73. HATE
A. abhor   B. admire
C. concern   D. display
E. loathe

74. HIDE
A. disguise   B. suppress
C. modest   D. reveal
E. automatic

75. HUMBLE
A. soft
B. lowly

C. beautiful
D. accommodating
E. proud

76. HUMOUR
A. temperament   B. whim
C. fun   D. waggery
E. seriousness

77. HYPOCRISY
A. deceit   B. truth
C. falsehood   D. illegitimacy
E. determination

78. IDEAL
A. fancied   B. imperfect
C. beautiful   D. useful
E. visionary

79. IDENTICAL
A. similar   B. sincere
C. equivalent   D. unlike
E. alike

80. ILLUSION
A. dream   B. equivalent
C. obvious   D. farsight
E. actuality

81. IMITATE
A. impersonate   B. simulate
C. modify   D. copy
E. lacking logic

82. IMPARTIAL
A. fair   B. shrewd
C. absured   D. equitable
E. biased

83. LAWFUL
A. legal   B. illegal
C. authorised   D. errant
E. shameless

84. LAZY
A. calm   B. polished
C. transformed   D. slow
E. industrious

85. LIABLE
A. immune   B. amenable
C. frivolous   D. mean
E. responsible

86. LIFT
A. lower   B. elevate
C. inflammable   D. constructed
E. changing

87. MAD
A. sane   B. exasperated
C. demented   D. healthy
E. coward

88. MILD
A. placid   B. harsh
C. soft   D. dented
E. temperate

89. MISERABLE
A. forlorn   B. disconsolate
C. eloping   D. happy
E. fearsome

90. NEGLECT
A. care   B. oversight
C. renovate   D. quantify
E. inspire

91. NOISY
A. giant   B. interpreter
C. quiet   D. loud
E. clamorous

92. OBEDIENT
A. tractable   B. dishonourable
C. inspired   D. recalcitrant
E. complaint

93. OPPONENT
A. rival   B. enemy
C. mischievous   D. supporter
E. trusted

94. PANIC
A. alarm   B. calm

3. A. disturbing   B. harassing
   C. asking   D. enquiring
   E. worrying

4. A. waiting   B. watching
   C. standing   D. passing
   E. connecting

5. A. office   B. steps
   C. legs   D. journey
   E. way

6. A. decided   B. felt
   C. noticed   D. remembered
   E. surprised

7. A. your   B. his
   C. my   D. our
   E. fore

8. A. right   B. obvious
   C. surprising   D. clear
   E. clean

9. A. feeding   B. bestowing
   C. giving   D. hitting
   E. offering

10. A. bread   B. then
    C. so   D. change
    E. thus

2. A. distractions
   B. hardships
   C. predicaments
   D. stresses

3. A. steep   B. slow
   C. moderate   D. low

4. A. active   B. limited
   C. drastic   D. substantial

5. A. delivery   B. storage
   C. procurement   D. supply

6. A. additionally
   B. notwithstanding
   C. nevertheless
   D. besides

7. A. methods   B. modes
   C. measures   D. manners

8. A. resolution
   B. regulations
   C. determination
   D. requirement

9. A. redirection   B. distribution
   C. division   D. supply

10. A. slump   B. jump
    C. decline   D. grow

PASSAGE 3

The common people of India, whose condition always had been ..(1).. suffered great ..(2).. during world wars. There was a ..(3).. rise in the prices of all goods. There was a ..(4).. reduction in the ..(5).. of essential commodities ..(6).. all ..(7).. of control ..(8).. of price, government procurement and ..(9).. of essential supplies continued to ..(10)..

1. A. deplorable   B. neglected
   C. delectable   D. melancholy

PASSAGE 4

The human mind seems to have built in ..(1).. against original thought : for instance, we ..(2).. equipped with a wonderful ..(3).. for accepting evidence which agrees with our ..(4).. almost unconsciously allow our thinking to be ..(5).. on what we first thought, or were ..(6).. when we approached the subject. If ..(7).. man could be freed from the yoke ..(8).. this age old assumptions, prejudices, traditional imagery and ..(9).. about what is right and what is wrong ..(10).. might wake up one day to find that even the greatest and gentlest of his aspirations was possible.

1. A. interests   B. safeguards
   C. prejudices   D. ideas
2. A. have   B. had
   C. may have   D. having been
3. A. capacity   B. sense
   C. sensibility D. capability
4. A. views
   B. thoughts
   C. conceptions
   D. pre-conceptions
5. A. based   B. biased
   C. rooted   D. fixed
6. A. spoke   B. told
   C. expressed   D. said
7. A. sometimes   B. only
   C. frequently   D. when
8. A. on   B. in
   C. under   D. of
9. A. negativeness B. certainly
   C. positiveness D. negation
10. A. he   B. man
    C. men   D. they

PASSAGE 5

There is an old story told ..(1).. a man who ..(2).. into a drunken sleep. His friend stayed by him as long as he ..(3).. but being compelled to go and fearing that he might be in want, the friend hid a ..(4).. in the drunken man's garment. When the drunken man ..(5).. not knowing that his friend had ..(6).. a jewel in his garment, he wandered about ..(7).. hungry. A long time afterward the two men met again and the friend told the poorman about the jewel and advised him to look

..(8).. it. Like the drunken man of the story, people ..(9).. about suffering in this life of birth and death ..(10).. what is hidden way in their ..(11).. nature. Pure and untarnished, the priceless treasure of God.

1. A. of   B. to
   C. with   D. by
   E. that
2. A. left   B. felt
   C. fail   D. fell
   E. gone
3. A. might   B. can
   C. would   D. had
   E. could
4. A. garment   B. drink
   C. jewel   D. treasure
   E. sleep
5. A. slept   B. recovered
   C. discovered   D. drinking
   E. realised
6. A. taken   B. presented
   C. substituted D. replaced
   E. hidden
7. A. vain   B. search
   C. sleep   D. poverty
   E. pursuit
8. A. for   B. to
   C. at   D. in
   E. with
9. A. search   B. wonder
   C. wander   D. trouble
   E. unknown
10. A. conscious   B. unconscious
    C. unknowingly D. unexpected
    E. useless
11. A. hidden   B. inner
    C. obvious   D. given
    E. covered

ANSWERS

Passage 1

1	2	3	4	5	6	7	8	9	10
D	C	C	D	D	C	D	D	C	A

Passage 2

1	2	3	4	5	6	7	8	9	10
B	B	A	D	E	C	B	B	D	C

Passage 3

1	2	3	4	5	6	7	8	9	10
A	B	A	C	D	B	C	B	B	C

Passage 4

1	2	3	4	5	6	7	8	9	10
C	D	A	D	A	B	B	D	A	A

Passage 5

1	2	3	4	5	6	7	8	9	10
A	D	E	C	B	E	A	A	C	B

11
B

PRACTICE PAPER

Directions (1-10) : *Read each sentence to find out whether there is any grammatical or idiomatic error in it. The error, if any, will be in one part of the sentence. The number of that part is the answer. If there is no error, the answer is (5), i.e., No error, (Ignore the errors of punctuations, if any.)*

1. (1) We play/(2) tennis together/(3) every morning/(4) since last June/(5) No error.

2. (1) I personally feel that/(2) cleanliness in the city/(3) is one proof of the/(4) efficiently civic administration/(5) No error.

3. (1) When I/(2) last see him/(3) he was/(4) in Calcutta/(5) No error.

4. (1) During last days/(2) I was continuously trying/(3) to contact you/(4) but you were not available/(5) No error.

5. (1) The historian/(2) has been working/(3) on the project/(4) from last 12 years/(5) No error.

6. (1) A detailed inquiry/(2) in the incident/(3) has been initiated/(4) by the Central Government/(5) No error.

7. (1) The last year proved/(2) quite bad/(3) as major inustries/(4) witness lots of problems/(5) No error.

8. (1) I see you/(2) in Kanpur/(3) during my next visit/(4) in the month of May/(5) No error.

9. (1) A lot of money/(2) is wasted in/(3) the duplication of work/(4) in any organisation/(5) No error.

10. (1) According to me/(2) the Indians in general is/(3) not a vigilant/(4) and security conscious people/(5) No error.

Directions (11-17) : *Pick out the most effective word from the given words to fill-in-the-blank, to make the sentence meaningfully complete.*

11. Last year the performance of this production unit was . . . .
1. tall   2. staggard
3. fantastic   4. below
5. upwards

12. The blood donation camp was organised . . . . . . the Naval Youth Club.
1. to   2. by
3. from   4. with
5. along

13. Vinayak is the . . . . . head of the family and commands a lot of respect from the family members.
1. solely   2. strongest
3. undisputed   4. full
5. controversial

14. I am going to Bhopal today and plan to . . . . . by tomorrow evening.
1. returning   2. returned

3. have returned   4. be returning
5. return

15. We all must . . . . . that people are the most important assets of any organisation.
1. find   2. look
3. realise   4. involve
5. dispel

16. After a recent mild paralytic attack his movements are . . . . . restricted; otherwise he is still very active.
1. not   2. entirely
3. slightly   4. nowhere
5. frequently

17. . . . . . he woke up, he saw that his bag was stolen.
1. if   2. when
3. where   4. so
5. neither

Directions (18-25) : *In the following passage there are blanks, each of which has been numbered. These numbers are given below the passage and against each, five words are suggested, one of which fits the blank appropriately. Find out the appropriate word.*

Whatermelons.. (18).. to India by the 4th century AD. Sushruta, the great Indian physician,.. (19).. wrote Sushruta Samhita, mentions that watermelons were grown.. (20).. the banks of the river Indus.. (21).. are also mentioned in ancient books. Sushruta calls it as Kalinda (hence Kalingad in Marathi). It was.. (22).. to China in the 10th or 11th century and.. (23).. it is grown throughout the tropics.

Wild watermelons are.. (24).. compared to huge cultivated ones; some of which weigh up to 25 kg. The heaviest fruit weighing 118 Kg. was produced at Hope, Arkansas, USA, the State to which President Clinton.. (25)..

18. 1. came   2. go
      3. arrived   4. started
      5. grew

19. 1. did   2. when
      3. certainly   4. who
      5. whom

20. 1. above   2. outside
      3. from   4. ahead
      5. along

21. 1. It   2. They
      3. Some   4. That
      5. Those

22. 1. took   2. gave
      3. taken   4. take
      5. taking

23. 1. also   2. though
      3. now   4. tomorrow
      5. soon

24. 1. heavier   2. small
      3. thinner   4. smaller
      5. shorter

25. 1. rules   2. belongs
      3. grew   4. elects
      5. elected

Directions (26-30) : *Rearrange the following five sentences A, B, C, D and E in the proper sequence so as to form a meaningful paragraph and then answer the questions given below them.*

A. Kiran received a call to attend the interview.

B. He applied for a new job.
C. Kiran was an ambitious boy.
D. But, he was not happy there.
E. His father had put him in a clerical job.

26. Which sentence should come LAST in the paragraph ?
1. A   2. B
3. C   4. D
5. E

27. Which sentence should come FIRST in the paragraph ?
1. A   2. B
3. C   4. D
5. E

28. Which sentence should come FOURTH in the paragraph ?
1. A   2. B
3. C   4. D
5. E

29. Which sentence should come SECOND in the paragraph ?
1. A   2. B
3. C   4. D
5. E

30. Which sentence should come THIRD in the paragraph ?
1. A   2. B
3. C   4. D
5. E

Directions (31-35) : *In each of the following questions, some words are given which are denoted by the letters A, B, C, D and E. By using each of these words only once, you have to frame a meaningful and grammatically correct sentence. The correct order of the words is your answer. Choose from the five alternatives the one having the correct order of words.*

31. A. not   B. hotel
     C. comfortable   D. was
     E. the
     1. CDEBA   2. ECDAB
     3. CDAEB   4. AEBDC
     5. EBDAC

32. A. was   B. and
     C. Satish   D. kind
     E. loving
     1. CADBE   2. EBDAC
     3. CDBEA   4. AEBDC
     5. ABCDE

33. A. not   B. Hari
     C. away   D. run
     E. did
     1. ACEDB   2. CEDAB
     3. EBDCA   4. BEADC
     5. BACDE

34. A. left   B. the
     C. house   D. he
     E. suddenly
     1. ADBCE   2. BACED
     3. DEABC   4. EBCDA
     5. BDACE

35. A. I   B. immediately
     C. salary   D. my
     E. want
     1. DCAEB   2. AEDCB
     3. BEADC   4. DBCEA
     5. DEACB

Directions (36-50) : *Read the following passage carefully and answer the questions given below it.*

Yeshwant Patil—a poor farmer used to live in a village named Narasopur. He was hard-working and sincere. His father, Bhagirath, mother, Dhirubai, and younger brother, Dadu, lived with him. They were gentle and affectionate. However, Yeshwant's wife—Sonabai was a loud mouthed woman. On each and every issue she would quarrel. Yeshwant was a peace loving man. He was not much ambitious. On the other hand, Sonabai was very cunning and would not get satisfied easily. She wanted to have all luxuries of life and all household articles. Regular quarrels was a part of their family.

Sonabai in spare time used to visit neighbouring families. She would provoke other women. She would ask them to demand such things from their husbands. A lot of women started following her advice.

The farmer had a few animals including a mule. The mule would draw the small cart. The farmer used to love and take care of his animals as he knew their importance in farming. Sonabai, however, did not like this. Particularly she did not like the mule. Whenever she was required to feed the animals she would ignore the animal as far as possible. She also did not give adequate food to these animals. The animals also did not like her.

Once, Yeshwant was to go to visit his friend Kashinath. He left the house in the morning. He was to stay in that village for two-three days. Before leaving his house he patted all his animals. He instructed Sonabai to take proper care of the animals. Sonabai as usual did not pay attention to the animals. The feeding time of the animals was over but they were not fed. The mule was standing on the ground and Sonabai with great force hit him with a burning stick. The mule turned its back and kicked her furiously. Alas ! She collapsed and in a few minutes died. Messages were sent and Yeshwant returned to his village. The news of the death of Sonabai spread and people gathered in large numbers. A passing by traveller asked Devram, the elder brother of Yeshwant, "Oh, was she so popular ! Why is there so much rush ?" Someone said, "No, We are here to purchase the mule, high price is being quoted". People have not come to pay their respect for this lady. She was terrible ! She had spoiled other ladies also.

36. Why did Yeshwant love his animals ?

1. He knew that animals were partners in his progress.
2. He knew that if animals are loved people will offer more value.
3. Bhagirath had asked him to love the animals.
4. He had nothing else to offer to the animals.
5. None of these.

37. Why did people offer high price for the mule ?

1. It was very strong.
2. The cost of feeding this mule was negligible.

3. It was capable of protecting the house.
4. It was considered to be very lucky.
5. None of these.

38. People turned in large numbers to meet Yeshwant . . . . . .
1. as this was a normal practice of the villagers.
2. as they were shocked and in grief.
3. to purchase the mule.
4. to console the parents of Kashinath.
5. to take care of the mule and other animals.

39. What activity Sonabai used to do in her free time ?
1. Look after the animals.
2. Visit Kashinath's house.
3. Help the neighbours.
4. Not given in the passage.
5. None of these.

40. Who among the following does not belong to Patil's family ?
1. Dadu
2. Bhagirath
3. Dhirubai
4. Kashinath
5. Devram

41. Why did Sonabai not give sufficient food to the animals ?
1. As per instructions of Yeshwant.
2. There was shortage of animal fodder.
3. The animals were lazy.
4. Not given in the passage.
5. Dhirubai did not like the animals.

42. Sonabai had succeeded in . . . . .
1. creating a group of followers. selling the mule.

3. taking care of the animals.
4. commanding love and respect of the villagers.
5. controlling her behaviour.

43. Why did the mule attack Sonabai ?
1. She had beaten all the animals on that day.
2. Sonabai did not allow the mule to pull the cart.
3. Sonabai used to harass the family members.
4. It would not allow anyone to touch except Yeshwant.
5. None of these.

44. Which of the following correctly describes the behaviour of Sonabai ?
1. She would quarrel only occasionally.
2. She was ambitious and strong willed.
1. Only 'a'
2. Only 'b'
3. Either 'a' or 'b'
4. Neither 'a' nor 'b'
5. Both 'a' and 'b'.

Directions (45-47) : *Choose the word which is most nearly the SAME in meaning as the word in Capital Letters, as used in the passage.*

45. DRAW
1. ride
2. push
3. run
4. pull
5. sketch

46. REGULAR
1. big
2. large
3. frequent
4. systematic
5. disciplined

47. PART
1. piece   2. feature
3. sign   4. whole
5. separate

Directions (48-50) : *Choose the word which is most OPPOSITE in meaning of the word in Capital Letters, as used in the passage.*

48. GREAT
1. short   2. unknown
3. weak   4. powerful
5. ordinary

49. LIKE
1. similar   2. hate
3. differ   4. calm
5. refuse

50. FOLLOWING
1. ignoring   2. leading
3. beginning   4. closing
5. observing

EXPLANATORY ANSWERS

1. (1) Replace the words, 'We play' by 'We have been playing' to make it meaningfully correct.
In 'Present Perfect Continunous Tense', the construction of the sentence should be as follows :

Subject + have/has + been + V_4 (Verb + ing) + for/since + time

She   has been   playing   cricket   since January 95

2. (4) Replace 'efficiently' by 'efficiency of the' or 'efficient'.
The word 'efficiently' should not be used as it is an Adverb, which does not express the quality of Noun, while as 'efficient' is an Adjective, which makes the sentence meaningful.

3. (2) Replace 'see' by 'saw', as the incident has happened in the past.

4. (1) Replace 'last days' by 'the last few days'

5. (4) Replace 'from last' by 'for' the last', because the sentence is in 'Present Perfect Continuous Tense' and 'last 12 years' indicates 'Period of Time'.
Remember : 'for' is used for 'Period of Time' and 'since' is used for 'Point of Time', in 'Present Perfect', 'Present Perfect Continuous', 'Past Perfect Continuous', etc. For example :

(i) Saveta has lived here for a month / since January.

Present Perfect   for Period   since Point of
                 of Time   Time

(*ii*) Saveta has been living here for a month / since January.

| | Present Perfect Continuous | | for | Period of Time | since | Point of Time |

(*iii*) Saveta had been living here for a month / since January.

| | Present Perfect Continuous | | for | Period of Time | since | Point of Time |

6. (2) The words 'into' should be used in place of 'in', before 'inquiry' is followed by 'into'.

7. (4) The word 'wintnessed' should be used in place of 'witness', as the sentence indicates 'Past Tense'.

8. (1) The words 'I will see you' should be used in place of 'I see you', as the sentence indicates 'Future Tense'.

9. (2) The Preposition 'on' should be used in place of 'in' 'waste' is followed by 'on'.

10. (2) The Verb 'are' should be used in place of 'is', as the Subject 'the Indians' is Plural.

For example :

(*i*)   He   is playing in the field.

    Subject   Verb
    (Singular) (Singular)

(*ii*)   They   are playing in the field.

    Subject   Verb
    (Plural)   (Plural)

11	12	13	14	15	16	17	18	19	20
(3)	(2)	(3)	(5)	(3)	(3)	(2)	(1)	(4)	(5)
21	22	23	24	25	26	27	28	29	30
(2)	(3)	(3)	(4)	(2)	(1)	(3)	(2)	(5)	(4)
31	32	33	34	35	36	37	38	39	40
(5)	(1)	(4)	(3)	(2)	(1)	(5)	(3)	(5)	(4)
41	42	43	44	45	46	47	48	49	50
(4)	(1)	(5)	(2)	(4)	(3)	(2)	(3)	(2)	(1)

PREVIOUS TEST PAPERS
(*Based on Memory*)

ENGLISH LANGUAGE

PAPER-1

Directions (1-5) : *Read each sentence to find out whether there is any grammatical/idiomatic error in it. The error, if any, will be in one part of the sentence. The letter of that part is the answer. If there is no error, the answer is 'E'. (Ingnore the errors of punctuation, if any).*

1. (A) In spite of the difficulties/(B) on the way/(C) they enjoyed their/(D) trip to Gangothri/(E) No error.

2. (A) We decided not tell to/(B) the patient about/(C) the discease he was/(D) suffering from/E. No error.

3. (A) No sooner did he/(B) got up from bed/(C) than he was sent/(D) to the diary/(E) No error.

4. (A) Even after being requested/(B) he did not/(C) tell us that how/(D) he solved the problem/(E) No error.

5. A. We never thought/(B) that Mahesh is/(C) oldest than the other/(D) players in the team/(E) No error.

Directions (6-10) : *Pick out the most effective word from the given words to fill in the blank to make the sentence meaningfully complete.*

6. The lights .... just as we sat down to watch the movie on television.
A. went off   B. shut out
C. put out   D. blew down
E. gone off

7. The villagers have not .... over the shock of losing everything in the earthquake.
A. got   B. made
C. forgotten   D. freed
E. felt

8. Since Vivek stays far away from our place, we do not meet each other ....
A. rarely   B. shortly
C. timely   D. frequently
E. momentarily

9. Since the priest did not arrive in time, the ceremony was .... late.
A. beings   B. begun
C. began   D. beginning
E. begin

10. He succeeded in getting possession .... his land after a long court case.
A. to   B. against
C. of   D. with
E. for

Directions (11-20) : *Read the following passage carefully and answer the questions given below it. Certain words/ phrases are printed in italic to help you locate them while answering some of the questions.*

Morning and afternoon, all the young girls and maidens used to *gather* around the village well with their water pots. There they exchanged pleasantries, chatted and discussed. Lakshmi was the prettiest girl at the well. But, she was an orphan.

One day, a well built man came to Lakshmi's house. He brought with him the richest clothes and jewels as presents for her. "I am your dead father's brother", he told the astonished girl. "You have not seen me before because I have been staying abroad. You must come and live with me now." Lakshmi believed his sweet words and in a short time, locked up her little house and set out with the man.

But a terrible surprise was in store for poor Lakshmi when she got to her new found uncle's home. The man locked her in a room. "I am not your uncle, but a robber. And I am going to marry you," he told her, Lakshmi howled and wept when she heard this. Saying he would be back in a day or two after making arrangements for the wedding, the man went away. Lakshmi continued sobbing for a while and then stopped. "I must think of a plan to escape," she told herself. Lakshmi guessed that the robber would try to enter her room. So she kept near her bed a sharp krife which she could find in the room.

One night the robber did enter her room but Lakshmi did not make any sound. She just kept a tight hold of the knife and pretended to be sound asleep. When the robber was near her bed, she stood up suddenly, brandishing the knife. The robber was taken aback and with a loud cry, he ranout. Lakshmi *gave chase* and he climbed up the nearest tall tree. Lakshmi then gathered some dry twigs and sticks around the foot of the tree and set them on fire. On seeing the rising flames, the robber gave a mighty yell and jumped down. But it was such a long way to the ground that he broke a couple of bones and was unable to move away from the place he fell.

In the meantime, the police was informed by someone about the robber. Very soon they reached the spot and arrested the robber. The people who had gathered at the spot were all praise for Lakshmi's courage and presence of mind.

11. Which of the following is most nearly the SAME in meaning as the phrase, *gave chase* as used in the passage ?

A. escaped   B. continued
C. followed   D. prevented
E. raced

12. The reason given by the man for his inability to meet Lakshmi earlier was that :

A. he was not knowing where she lived.
B. he was not in friendly terms with her father.

C. he was living in a foreign country.
D. he was not sure whether she would recognise him.
E. he was staying in another village, for away from her place.

13. Why did Lakshmi go with the man ?
A. She was convinced that the man was her uncle.
B. She wanted to accompany him and then get him arrested by the police
C. She intended to teach him a good lesson.
D. She wanted the man to marry her.
E. She felt it necessary to verify his claim by accompanying him.

14. How was the robber injured ?
A. Lakshmi stabbed him with the sharp knife.
B. He fell down accidentally while climbing the tree.
C. He was beaten by Lakshmi and his bones were broken.
D. He jumped down from the tree to save his life.
E. He got burnt in the rising flames.

15. Why did the robber run out of the room ?
A. He was stabbed by Lakshmi.
B. He got scared of the rising flames.
C. Lakshmi told him to go out as fast as possible.
D. He was afraid that Lakshmi would strike him with the knife.
E. He ran out to catch hold of Lakshmi and bring her back.

16. Which of the following is *True* in the context of the passage ?
A. Lakshmi told the robber to climb up the tall tree.

B. At night, the robber entered Lakshmi's room with a knife.
C. Lakshmi had no near relatives and she stayed alone.
D. The robber started running after jumping from the tree.
E. The people who had gathereed at the spot set fire to the tree.

17. Which of the following is most OPPOSITE in meaning of the word 'gather' as used in the passage ?
A. collect   B. reduce
C. distribute   D. break
E. disperse

18. Which of the following statements is *Not True* in the context of the passage ?
A. The police was summoned by Lakshmi herself.
B. The well built man was not the real brother of Lakshmi's father.
C. When the robber entered the room at night, Lakshmi was awake.
D. Lakshmi used to go to the village well to collect water.
E. Lakshmi's guess regarding the robber turned out to be correct.

19. "But a terrible surprise was in store ______ uncle's home". What is the "terrible surprise" that is being referred to ?
A. The man told her that her father was dead.
B. The man refused to marry her.
C. The man took away her ornaments and locked her in a room.
D. The man told her that he was her real uncle.

E. The man turned out to be a robber interested in marrying her.

20. Where did the robber apparently go after locking up Lakshmi ?

A. He went to her house to loot all the things.
B. He went out to bring a sharp knife.
C. He went away to bring clothes and jewels for her.
D. He went away to make preparations for his marriage.
E. He went out to bring the priest for performing the wedding ceremony.

Directions (21-25) : *Rearrange the following six sentences a, b, c, d, e and f in the proper sequence so as to form a meaningful paragraph; then answer the questions given below them :*

a. A taxi was summoned and Venu was taken to Lifeline Hospital.
b. While hurrying home from school, Venu was hit by a car.
c. Since they did not succeed, they decided to take him to a hospital.
d. When Venu opened his eyes, he found himself surrounded by doctors and nurses.
e. Some people rushed towards him and tried to bring him to his senses.
f. He was thrown a couple of feet away and lost consciousness.

21. Which sentence should come LAST (*i.e.* sixth) in the paragraph ?
A. b   B. c   C. a
D. d   E. e

22. Which sentence should come FIRST in the paragraph ?
A. d   B. f   C. b
D. e   E. c

23. Which sentence should come SECOND in the paragraph ?
A. e   B. a   C. d
D. c   E. f

24. Which sentence should come THIRD in the paragraph ?
A. f   B. b   C. e
D. a   E. d

25. Which sentence should come FOURTH in the paragraph ?
A. c   B. e   C. f
D. b   E. a

Directions (26-30) : *In each of the following questions, six words are given which are denoted by a, b, c, d, e and f. By using all the six words, each only once, you have to frame a meaningful and grammatically correct sentence. The correct order of the words is your answer. Choose from the five alternatives the one having the correct order of words.*

26. a. the   b. near
        c. theatre   d. met
        e. they   f. him

A. edafbc   B. bacfed
C. fbaced   D. bedacdf
E. edfbac

27. a. there   b. while
        c. he   d. sick
        e. fell   f. staying

A. cfabed   B. bfaced
C. caebfd   D. bcfaed
E. afbced

28. a. on   b. keep
        c. table   d. the
        e. things   f. those

A. afcbde   B. bdeafc
C. dcbafe   D. bfcadc
E. debafc

29.	a. playing	b. students	30.	a. seen	b. to
	c. many	d. seen		c. talking	d. he
	e. were	f. football		e. somebody	f. was
	A. cebdaf	B. bedacf		A. efadcb	B. dfcbea
	C. cbedaf	D. bafedc		C. dafcbe	D. dfacbe
	E. beadcf			E. efacbd	

EXPLANATORY ANSWERS

1. E : The answer is correct.

2. A : 'not to tell' to appears in place of 'not tell to'.

3. B : 'get up' to come in place of 'got up' because after 'did' usually the 1st form of Verb is applicable.

4. C : Remove 'that' before 'how'.

5. C : 'Oldest of all the other' should come in place of Oldest than the other.

6	7	8	9	10	11	12	13	14	15
A	A	D	B	C	C	C	A	D	D
16	**17**	**18**	**19**	**20**	**21**	**22**	**23**	**24**	**25**
C	E	A	E	D	D	C	E	C	A
26	**27**	**28**	**29**	**30**					
E	B	D	C	D					

PAPER - 2

Directions (1-10) : *In each of the questions you will find a word followed by four alternative words. You will have to find out alternatives, the word which means the same as the first word.*

1. DESTRUCTION
A. restoration   B. ruin
C. renovation   D. replacement

2. LENIENT
A. cruel   B. rough
C. kind   D. harsh

3. ROBUST
A. weak   B. useless
C. able   D. stupid

4. GENUINE
A. correction   B. germinate
C. separate   D. proper

5. IRRELEVANT
A. irregular   B. illegible
C. not connected   D. immature

6. GENERATE
A. prefer   B. pace
C. command   D. produce

7. LATENT
A. hand   B. concealed
C. visible   D. display

8. ACUTE
A. rice   B. accidental
C. sever   D. curious

9. PLEASURE
A. happiness
B. disappointment
C. grief
D. anxiety

10. RIVAL
A. friend   B. partner
C. associate   D. opponent

Directions (11-20) : *In the sentences given below the italicised words are grammatically incorrect. You will have to correct them. Following each sentence, there are four possible corrections, only one of which will correctly replace the incorrect part of the sentence. For each incorrect sentence choose the correct word.*

11. I have full confidence *on* you.
A. over   B. with
C. in   D. towards

12. There is no alternative *of* the plan.
A. to   B. for
C. towards   D. against

13. She is very much fond *for* music
A. of   B. towards
C. at   D. with

14. Ram could not go to school *for* fever
A. on account of   B. for
C. on   D. because

15. He should not have told this *at* his face.
A. in   B. on
C. to   D. before

16. A man who does not stick *at* his principles can never prosper.
A. in   B. with
C. to   D. into

92

17. I have no interest *of* cinema.
A. at B. about
C. for D. in

18. He has no faith *on* you.
A. over B. at
C. towards D. in

19. He has no ambition *of* learning.
A. about B. for
C. towards D. to

20. He has a passion *of* music
A. with B. for
C. to D. on

Directions (21-30) : *In each question here five words (marked as A, B, C, D and E) are given. Of these five words only one has been wrongly spelt. Find out correct word.*

21. A. Regiment B. Enunciate
C. Envelope D. Marvell
E. Materialism

22. A. Allmighty
B. Ballot
C. Desend
D. Compartment
E. Allocate

23. A. Gallon B. Idiom
C. Interfere D. Sovereign
E. Fillament

24. A. Ballon B. Obsolete
C. Stumble D. Deliberate
E. Forestall

25. A. Begining B. Inject
C. Gleaming D. Optimism
E. National

26. A. Mechanic B. Shackel
C. Pneumonia D. Rumble
E. Synthesis

27. A. Unwholesome
B. Erchant
C. Memoir
D. Galary
E. Unwining

28. A. Pretending
B. Unpronounceable
C. Comissionors
D. Patience
E. Allure

29. A. Topsyturvy B. Varsetile
C. Salvage D. Segregate
E. Jealous

30. A. Toothache B. Spurious
C. Insuportable D. Courage
E. Oppressive

Directions (31-40) : *Here you will have to spot errors in sentences. Read each sentence to find out whether there is any error in any of the under lined parts. If you find that there is an error in an underlined part of the sentence, note the index of the underlined part (i.e., A or B or C or D).*

31. (A)/In the high school girls often do/(B) as good as boys,/(C) if not better/(D) than the boys./(E) No error

32. (A)/The Selection Board will call only/(B) those candidates/(C) whom have the/(D) proper qualifications./(E) No error

33. (A)/Due to the explosion/(B) the walls/(C) bursted apart and the roof/(D) was blown off./(E) No error.

34. (A)/No employee are permitted to/ (B) act on behalf of the company/ (C) in financial/(D) matters./(E) No error

35. (A)/The authorities states that the students/(B) are responsible for the/(C) lack of discipline in/(D) the colleges./(E) No error.

36. (A)/We are fortunate in/(B) being able to visit Puri because there/(C) is many who cannot/(D) go there./ (E) No error.

37. (A)/If a man joins a post and do not work/(B) he is asked/(C) to resign/(D) the post./(E) No error.

38. (A)/There will be increased emphasis /(B) on heavy industry/ (C) in the seventh five year/(D) plan./(E) No error.

39. (A)/Us may/(B) stay in Darjeeling/ (C) until the monsoon/(D) starts./ (E) No error.

40. (A)/After Independence many people have/(B) say many things/ (C) about the/ (D) national language./(E) No error.

Directions (41-45) : *Read the passage carefully and answer the related questions.*

Aldinga reef is a watery paradise, a teeming sea jungle, a happy hunting ground for under-water spear-fisherman like myself. Forty of us each in black rubber suit and flippers, glasswindowed face mask and spear-fishing gun were waiting for the reference's nine O'clock whistle to announce that the annual South Australian skin diving and spear-fishing championship competition has begun. Each of us would have five hours to bring into the judge the biggest bag, reckoned both by total weight and by number of different species of fish. My own chances looked good. I have owned the 1961-62 championship and I had been runner-up the next session. I had promised Kay that this would be my last competition. I meant to clinch to the title and then retire in glory, diving thenceforth only for fun, when Kay and I might both want to.

Lesser sharks—like the Bronze whaler and Grey nurse—are familiar to skin divers and have not proved aggressive. Fortunately the dreaded white hunter or 'white death' sharks, caught by professional fisherman in the open ocean, are rarely seen by the skin divers. But as a precaution two high powered patrol boats criss-crossed our hunting area keeping a wary lookout.

41. To protect the skin divers from the 'white death' the authority :

A. took no measure at all.

B. provided them with the safety measures such as glass mask, black rubber suit and spear-fishing gun.

C. provided patrol boats for searching the place and protecting them.

D. arranged the competition in such an area of the sea where the' white deaths' are rarely seen.

42. The competitors were evaluated in terms of the :

A. amount of time spent under the water.

B. number of sharks killed.
C. total weight and number of different types of fishes.
D. number of fishes caught.

43. The author was so optimistic about his success due to the fact that :
A. he was a good swimmer.
B. he was a good sportsman.
C. he was one of the competitors of South Australian skin diving and spear-fishing championship.
D. he won championship last year and was runner-up for the next session.

44. Aldinga reef is a paradise for those who :
A. love to take bath in the sea.
B. love swimming.
C. like spear-fishing in underground water.
D. like to contest for the skin diving championship.

45. The most suitable title for the passage would be :
A. Dangers under the sea.
B. Shark and the swimmer.
C. Story about spear-fishing championship.
D. None of these.

EXPLANATORY ANSWERS

1	2	3	4	5	6	7	8	9	10
B	C	C	D	C	D	B	C	A	D

11	12	13	14	15	16	17	18	19	20
C	A	A	A	B	C	D	D	B	B

21. D : The correct word is : 'Marvel'

22. A : The correct word is : 'Almighty'

23. E : The correct word is : 'Filament'

24. A : The correct word is : 'Balloon'

25. A : The correct word is : 'Beginning'

26. B : The correct word is : 'Shackle'

27. E : The correct word is : 'Unwinning'

28. C : The correct word is : 'Commissioners'

29. B : The correct word is : 'Versatile'

30. C : The correct word is : 'Insupportable'

31. B : Replace 'as good as' with 'as well as'.

32. C : Replace 'Whom' with 'who'.

33. C : Replace 'bursted' with 'burst'.

34. **A** : Replace 'are' with 'is' because 'No employee' in Singular.
35. **A** : Replace 'states' with 'state'.
36. **C** : Replace 'is' with 'are'.
37. **A** : Replace 'do not' with 'does not' because 'man' in Singular.
38. **A** : 'will be' should be followed by 'an'.
39. **A** : 'us' should be replaced by 'we'.
40. **B** : 'say' should be replaced by 'said'.

QUANTITATIVE APTITUDE

NUMBERS

A number tells us how many times a unit is contained in a given quantity. It therefore signifies one or more units, or denotes one or more distinct objects of the same kind. For example, *one* rupee, *six* pencils, *nine* cats, *thirty* paise, etc. The words in italics denote numbers.

Whole Numbers: The numbers 0, 1, 2, 3, 4, 5, 6, 7, 8, 9, 10, 11, ... are called whole numbers or integers. So 84 is an integer while 6¼ is not an integer.

Even Numbers: The numbers, which are divisible by two are called even numbers. *For example,* 2, 4, 6, 8, 10, 12, 28, 36, etc.

Odd Numbers: The numbers, which cannot be divided by two are called odd numbers. *For example,* 1, 3, 5, 7, 9, 11, 13, 15, 17, 19, etc.

Prime Numbers: The numbers, which are divisible only by themselves and one are called prime numbers. *For example,* 2, 3, 5, 7, 11, 13, etc.

Composite Numbers: The numbers, which are not prime called composite numbers. Thus, the prime numbers and composite numbers make up the set of natural numbers.

Consecutive Numbers: A collection of numbers is consecutive if each number is the successor of the number which precedes it. *For example,* 4, 5, 6, 7, 8 and 9 are consecutive, but 4, 5, 6, 8, 10 are not. 6, 8, 10, 12 are consecutive even numbers. 11, 13, 17, 19 are consecutive prime numbers.

> **Any whole number can be written as a product of factors which are prime numbers.**

How to write a number as a product of prime factors?
   (*i*) Divide the number by 2 if possible; continue to divide by 2 until the factor you get, is not divisible by 2.
   (*ii*) Divide the result from (i) by 3 if possible; continue to divide by 3 until the factor you get, is not divisible by 3.
   (*iii*) Divide the result from (ii) by 5 if possible; continue to divide by 5 until the factor you get, is not divisible by 5.
   (*iv*) Continue this procedure by dividing by 7, 11, 13, and so on; until all the factors are prime.

EXAMPLES :

Example 1. *Express 2310 as a product of prime factors.*

Solution.

2	2310
2	1155
5	385
7	77
	11

$\therefore$ $2310 = 2 \times 3 \times 5 \times 7 \times 11.$

Example 2. *Resolve 1026 into prime factors.*

Solution.

2	1026
3	513
3	171
3	57
	19

$\therefore$ $1026 = 2 \times 3 \times 3 \times 3 \times 19$

A number n is a common multiple of two other numbers a and b if it is a multiple of each of them. For example, 24 is a common multiple of 2 and 3, since $2 \times 12 = 24$ and $3 \times 8 = 24$. But 21 is not a common multiple of 3 and 6, because 21 is not a multiple of 6.

> **A number x is a common factor of two other numbers a and b if x is a factor of a and x is a factor of b.**

L.C.M.: The least common multiple of two numbers is the smallest number which is a common multiple of both numbers.

How to find the least common multiple of two numbers a and b?

(i) Write a and b as products of *primes* separately.

(ii) If there are any common factors delete them in one of the products.

(iii) Multiply the remaining factors to get L.C.M.

PROPERTIES OF NUMBERS

1. The product of any two consecutive numbers is divisible by 2

For example,	$2 \times 3 = 6$	is divisible by 2
	$3 \times 4 = 12$	is divisible by 2
	$4 \times 5 = 20$	is divisible by 2
	$15 \times 16 = 240$	is divisible by 2

2. The product of any three consecutive numbers is divisible by 6.
For example,

$$2 \times 3 \times 4 = 24 \qquad \text{is divisible by 6}$$
$$3 \times 4 \times 5 = 60 \qquad \text{is divisible by 6}$$
$$4 \times 5 \times 6 = 120 \qquad \text{is divisible by 6}$$
$$10 \times 11 \times 12 = 1320 \quad \text{is divisible by 6}$$
$$40 \times 41 \times 42 = 68880 \text{ is divisible by 6}$$

3. The product of any four consecutive numbers is divisible by 24.
For example,

$$2 \times 3 \times 4 \times 5 = 120 \qquad \text{is divisible by 24.}$$
$$4 \times 5 \times 6 \times 7 = 24 \times 5 \times 7$$
$$6 \times 7 \times 8 \times 9 = 3 \times 2 \times 7 \times 8 \times 9$$
$$= 24 \times 2 \times 7 \times 9$$
$$10 \times 11 \times 12 \times 13 = 2 \times 5 \times 11 \times 12 \times 13$$
$$= 24 \times 5 \times 11 \times 13$$

4. The product of any five consecutive numbers is divisible by 120.
For example,

$$2 \times 3 \times 4 \times 5 \times 6 = 120 \times 6$$
$$3 \times 4 \times 5 \times 6 \times 7 = 120 \times 21$$
$$4 \times 5 \times 6 \times 7 \times 8 = 120 \times 56$$

5. Every square number is a multiple of 3 or exceeds of multiple of 3 by unity.
For example,

$$3^2 = 9 = 3 \times 3$$
$$4^2 = 16 = 3 \times 5 + 1$$
$$5^2 = 25 = 3 \times 8 + 1$$
$$6^2 = 36 = 3 \times 12$$
$$7^2 = 49 = 3 \times 16 + 1$$

6. Difference of the squares of any two odd numbers is always divisible by 8.
For example,

$$5^2 - 3^2 = 25 - 9 = 16 = 8 \times 2$$
$$7^2 - 5^2 = 49 - 25 = 24 = 8 \times 3$$
$$9^2 - 5^2 = 81 - 25 = 56 = 8 \times 7$$
$$11^2 - 3^2 = 121 - 9 = 112 = 8 \times 14$$

7. A number is exactly divisible by 11 when the difference between the sums of the digits in the odd and even places respectively is zero or a multiple of 11.
For example, Consider the number 1569942

Sum of the odd digits $= 1 + 6 + 9 + 2 = 18$
Sum of the even digits $= 5 + 9 + 4 = 18$

Difference between the sums of the odd and even digits
$$= 18 - 18 = 0$$
Hence, 1569942 is divisible by 11.

8. The product of two consecutive odd or even numbers increased by unity is a perfect square.

For example,
$$3 \times 5 + 1 = 16 = 4^2$$
$$4 \times 6 + 1 = 25 = 5^2$$
$$5 \times 7 + 1 = 36 = 6^2$$
$$6 \times 8 + 1 = 49 = 7^2$$

9. The sum of any two consecutive numbers is equal to the difference of their squares.

For example,
$$3 + 4 = 7 = 4^2 - 3^2 = 7$$
$$5 + 4 = 9 = 5^2 - 4^2 = 9$$
$$7 + 6 = 13 = 7^2 - 6^2 = 13$$

10. The sum of the cubes of any three consecutive numbers is divisible by the sum of the numbers themselves.

For example, $2^3 + 3^3 + 4^3 = 8 + 27 + 64 = 99 = (2 + 3 + 4)\ 11$
$$4^3 + 5^3 + 6^3 = 64 + 125 + 216 = 405$$
$$= (4 + 5 + 6)\ 27$$

EXERCISE

1. 2, 4, 6, 8, 10, ... are:
A. prime numbers
B. odd numbers
C. even numbers
D. natural numbers

2. 1, 2, 3, 4, ... are :
A. Natural numbers
B. Odd numbers
C. Prime numbers
D. Composite numbers

3. 1, 2, 3, 4, 5, 7, 11 and 13 are:
A. even numbers
B. odd numbers
C. prime numbers
D. natural numbers

4. The prime numbers between 1 to 100 are:
A. 20   B. 22
C. 25   D. 30

5. The only even prime number is:
A. 2   B. 67
C. 79   D. 98

6. Which of the following is not a prime number?

79, 83, 87, 97

A. 79   B. 83
C. 87   D. 97

7. Which of the following is a prime number?

117, 147, 149, 159

A. 117   B. 147
C. 149   D. 159

8. The next number in the sequence
1, 7, 3, 9, 5, 11, ... is :
A. 7   B. 13
C. 15   D. 17

9. In the sequence 4, 9, ...25, 36, the missing number is :
A. 14   B. 16
C. 20   D. 21

10. In the sequence 17, ..., 18, 15, 19, 14, 20, 13, the missing number is:
A. 5   B. 10
C. 12   D. 16

Directions. *For questions 11 to 14, let* * *means add the first number to twice the second number.*

11. The value of 5*4 is:
A. 20   B. 9
C. 11   D. 13

12. The value of 7*0 is:
A. 7   B. 9
C. 14   D. 0

13. The value of [1*2] * 3 is:
A. 5   B. 7
C. 9   D. 11

14. The value of 3* [0*6] is:
A. 18   B. 23
C. 27   D. 29

Directions. *For questions 15 to 17, let* Δ *means square the first number and add the second.*

15. The value of 2 Δ 10 is:
A. 12   B. 14
C. 27   D. 102

16. The value of 6 Δ 7 is:
A. 42   B. 43
C. 54   D. 59

17. The value of [3 × 2] Δ 9 is :
A. 42   B. 45
C. 87   D. 91

Directions. *For questions 18 to 20, let* ** *means increase the first number by 2 and then multiply by the second number.*

18. The value of 5** 3 is :
A. 15   B. 25
C. 21   D. 17

19. The value of [3**3]**4 is:
A. 68   B. 60
C. 54   D. 36

20. The value of [5**0]**3 is :
A. 0   B. 6
C. 15   D. 21

21. The smallest whole number which is divisible by 3 and also by the next two greater prime number is:
A. 15   B. 21
C. 60   D. 105

22. A number is called perfect, when it is equal to the sum of all its divisions excluding the number itself, e.g., 6 = 1 + 2 + 3. The other perfect number less than 32 is:
A. 8   B. 12
C. 16   D. 28

23. The smallest number of four digits is:
A. 1001   B. 0001
C. 0010   D. 1000

24. The largest number of four digits is:

    A. 1000   B. 9000

    C. 9009   D. 9999

25. If 'a' is an odd number, 'b' is an even number and 'c' is odd then, $a + b + c$ is:

    A. odd number

    B. even number

    C. prime number

    D. any number

26. The product of two prime numbers is a :

    A. prime number

    B. even number

    C. odd number

    D. composite number

27. Prime factors of a number are 2, 2, 3, 7. The number is :

    A. 14   B. 41

    C 48   D. 84

28. The largest number which is a factor of 56 as well as 84 is :

    A. 2   B. 7

    C. 14   D. 28

29. H.C.F. of 72, 108, 56 is :

    A. 3   B. 4

    C. 6   D. 8

30. L.C.M. of 6, 9, 12, 18 is :

    A. 28   B. 36

    C. 38   D. 42

31. If 'x' and 'y' are both odd numbers, which of the following numbers must be an even number?

    A. $x + y$

    B. $x \times y$

    C. $xy + 2$

    D. $2x + y$

32. 'a' is less than 'b', which of the following numbers is greater than 'a' and less than 'b' :

    A. $\dfrac{a+b}{2}$ B. $\dfrac{ab}{2}$

    C. $b^2 - a^7$ D. ab

33. $a + b + c + d$ is a positive number, a minimum of 'x' of the numbers a, b, c and d must be positive, where 'x' is equal to :

    A. 1   B. 2

    C. 3   D. 4

34. Which of the following is largest?

$[2 + 2 + 2]^2$, $[(2 + 2)^2]^2$,

$[2 \times 2 \times 2]^2$, $[4]^2$

    A. $[2 + 2 + 2]^2$

    B. $[(2 + 2)^2]^2$

    C. $[2 \times 2 \times 2]^2$

    D. $[4]^2$

35. The sum of two numbers is 84. If one of them exceeds the other by 12, the numbers are :

    A. 62, 22   B. 36, 24

    C. 48, 36   D. 35, 47

36. Take a number. Double it and add 15 to it. If the result is 81, the number is :

    A. 30   B. 32

    C. 33   D. 66

37. Take a number, find its square root and add 20 to it. If the result is 30, the number is :

    A. 5   B. 1

    C. 20   D. 100

38. There are four numbrs A, B, C and D. Average of the first three, i.e., A, B and C is 15 and that of

B, C and *D* is 16. If the last number, i.e. *D* is 19, then the first number is:

A. 15   B. 16
C. 17   D. 18

39. Think of a number, divide it by 9 and add 9 to it, if the result is 27, the number is :

A. 18   B. 21
C. 100   D. 162

40. Of the three numbers, the first is twice the second and thrice the third. If the average of three is 22, the three numbers are:

A. 12, 18, 36   B. 18, 12, 36
C. 36, 12, 18   D. 36, 18, 12

41. The number which when added to itself 10 times gives 264. The number is:

A. 20   B. 22
C. 24   D. 26

42. If a person is standing on the sixth number in the queue from both the ends, the total persons in the queue are:

A. 9   B. 11
C. 12   D. 13

43. A number increased by itself and 5 gives 17. The number is :

A. 2   B. 3
C. 5   D. 6

44. Consider a number '*x*'. Divide it by 4 and add 9. If the result is 15, the value of '*x*' is :

A. 20   B. 24
C. 23   D. 28

45. A number '*x*' when multiplied by 5 and added to three times its

own gives 64, the number is:

A. 8   B. 12
C. 14   D. 18

46. If the sum of two numbers '*x*' and '*y*' is equal to twice the first number, the second number '*y*' is:

A. $> x$
B. $< x$
C. $= x$
D. negative number

47. The excess of thrice a certain number over 11 is 19. The number is:

A. 8   B. 9
C. 10   D. 11

48. The difference between the squares of two consecutive numbers is 25. The numbers are:

A. 13, 12   B. 12, 13
C. 15, 14   D. 14, 13

49. The sum of two digits of a number is 15. If 9 is added to the number, the digits are reversed. The number is :

A. 78   B. 87
C. 69   D. 96

50. A number which when multiplied by 11 is as much above 180 as it was originally below it. The number is:

A. 25   B. 30
C. 40   D. 45

51. Divide ₹ 53 among *X, Y, Z* so that *X* may receive ₹ 7 more than *Y*, and *Y* may receive ₹ 8 more than *Z*.

A. 10, 15, 18   B. 18, 10, 25
C. 20, 12, 27   D. 25, 18, 10

EXPLANATORY ANSWERS

1. C : The numbers divisible by 2 are called even numbers since, 4, 6, 8, 10, are divisible by 2, hence these are even numbers.

2. A : The numbers written in natural sequence are natural numbers.

3. C : The numbers which are not divisible by 2, 3, 5, 7, 11 and 13 (*i.e.*, by any numbers except themselves and one) are called prime numbers.

4. C : To find out prime numbers between 1 and 100, write all numbers between 1 to 100.

✳	②	③	4	⑤	6	⑦	8	9	10
⑪	12	⑬	14	15	16	⑰	18	⑲	20
21	22	㉓	24	25	26	27	28	㉙	30
㉛	32	33	34	35	36	㊲	38	39	40
㊶	42	㊷	44	45	46	㊼	48	49	50
51	52	㊾	54	55	56	57	58	㊾	60
㊶	62	63	64	65	66	67	68	69	70
71	72	73	74	75	76	77	78	79	80
81	82	83	84	85	86	87	88	89	90
91	92	93	94	95	96	97	98	99	100

(*i*) Cross out 1 which is not a prime number.

(ii) Cross out all numbers divisible by 2, except 2 which is a prime number.

(*iii*) Cross out all numbers divisible by 3, except 3 itself.

(*iv*) Cross out all numbers divisible by 5, except 5 itself.

(*v*) Cross out all numbers divisible by 7, except 7 itself.

The numbers remaining are the prime numbers between 1 and 100 which are circled and are 25 in all.

5. A : 2 is the only even prime number.

6. C : 87 is divisilble by 3, therefore it is not a prime number.

7. C : 149 is not divisible by any number, therefore it is a prime number.

8. A : In the sequence 1, 7, 3, 9, 5, 11..... the alternate numbers differ by 2, i.e., first and third number differ by 2, similarly the difference of second and fourth number is 2. Thus, next number in the series should be 5 + 2 = 7.

9. **B** : The sequence 4, 9, ..., 25, 36 contains the square of natural numbers, *i.e.*, 2^2, 3^2, 4^2, 5^2, 6^2. Thus the missing number is 4^2, *i.e.*, 16.

10. **D** : In the sequence 17, ..., 18, 15, 19, 14, 20, 13, the next alternate number is one more than the previous alternate number, i.e., 17 + 1 = 18, 18 + 1 = 19, 19 + 1 = 20. Also the second number and fourth number differ by 1, i.e., 13 + 1 = 14, 14 + 1 = 15, 15 + 1 = 16 is the required missing number).

   [*means add the first number to the twice of the second number*].

11. **D** : 5 + [2 × 4] = 5 + 8 = 13

12. **A** : 7 + [2 × 0] = 7 + 0 = 7.

13. **D** : [1 * 2]* 3 = [1 + 2 × 2]* 3 = 5* 3 = 5 + 3 × 2 = 11.

14. **C** : 3 * [0 * 6] = 3 *[0 + 2 × 6] = 3* 12 = 3 + 2 × 12 = 27

   [Δ *means square the first number and add the second number.*]

15. **B** : 2 Δ 10 = 2 × 2 + 10 = 14

16. **B** : 6 Δ 7 = 6 × 6 + 7 = 43

17. **B** : [3 × 2] Δ 9 = 6 Δ 9 = 6 × 6 + 9 = 45

   [** *means increase the first number by 2 and then multiply by the second number*].

18. **C** : 5**3 = [5 + 2] × 3 = 21

19. **A** : [3**3]**4 = [(3 + 2) × 3]**4 = 15**4 = [15 + 2] × 4 = 68

20. **B** : [5**0]**3 = [(5 + 2) × 0] = **3 = 0**3 = [0 + 2] × 3 = 6

21. **D** : The number should be divisible by 3, 5, and 7. Thus L.C.M. of 3, 5, 7 is equal to 105 which is the required number.

22. **D** : 28 is multiple of 1, 2, 4, 7, 14.
   Also 1 + 2 + 4 + 7 + 14 = 28

23. **D.** 24. **D.**

25. **A** : Out of *a, b, c* ; a is odd and *c* is odd while b is even. The sum of two odd numbers is even, *i.e.*, a + c = even = d. Also the sum of two even numbers is even, i.e., d + b = even.
   ∴ a + b + c = Even number.

26. **D** : Product of two prime numbers is not a prime number but it is always composite number.

27. **D** : The number is equal to the product or prime factors.
   ∴ 2 × 2 × 3 × 7 = 84 is the required number.

28. **D** : Find H.C.F. of 56, 84 which is equal to 28.

29. **B.**

30. B.

31. A : Since the sum of two odd numbers is always even number, therefore, $x + y$ is even number.

32. A : Average of two different numbers is always between the two numbers.

33. A : If all the numbers were not positive, then the sum could not be positive. If a, b, c were all -1 and d were 5, then $a + b + c + d$ would be positive, so B, C, D are incorrect.

34. B :
$$(2 + 2 + 2)^2 = 6^2 = 36$$
$$[(2 + 2)^2]^2 = [4^2]^2 = [4 \times 4]^2 = 16 \times 16 = 256$$
$$[2 \times 2 \times 2]^2 = (8)^2 = 64$$
$$(4)^2 = 4 \times 4 = 16.$$

35. C : Let the numbers be x and y
$$x + y = 84$$
$$x + (x + 12) = 84, \text{ or } 2x = 84 - 12 = 72,$$

or
$$x = \frac{72}{2} = 36$$
$$y = x + 12 = 36 + 12 = 48.$$

36. C : Let the number be x
$$\therefore \quad 2x + 15 = 81, \text{ or } 2x = 81 - 15 = 66$$
$$\therefore \quad x = \frac{66}{2} = 33.$$

37. D : Let the number be x
$$\therefore \quad \sqrt{x} + 20 = 30, \text{ or } \sqrt{x} = 30 - 20 = 10$$
$$\therefore \quad \left(\sqrt{x}\right)^2 = (10)^2, \text{ or } x = 100.$$

38. B :
$$\frac{A+B+C}{3} = 15, \text{ or, } A + B + C = 15 \times 3 = 45 \qquad \text{...(i)}$$
$$\frac{B+C+D}{3} = 16, \text{ or } B + C + D = 48 \qquad \text{... (ii)}$$
$$D = 19$$
$$\therefore \quad B + C + 19 = 48 \text{ or, } B + C = 48 - 19 = 29$$
But, $A + B + C = 45$

Putting the value of $B + C = 29$ in the above equationi (i), we get
$$A + 29 = 45$$
$$\therefore \quad A = 45 - 29 = 16$$

39. D : Let the number be x.

$$\therefore \qquad \frac{x}{9} + 9 = 27 \text{ or, } \frac{x}{9} = 27 - 9 = 18$$

$$\therefore \qquad x = 18 \times 9 = 162$$

40. D : Let the third number $= x$

$$\therefore \qquad \text{First number} = 3x, \text{ Second number} = \frac{3x}{2}$$

$$\therefore \qquad \frac{1}{3}\left[x + 3x + \frac{3x}{2}\right] = 22 \text{ or, } \frac{11}{2}\,x = 66$$

$$\text{or, } \qquad x = \frac{66 \times 2}{11} = 12 = \text{Third number,}$$

$$12 \times 3 = 36 = \text{First number,}$$

$$\frac{12 \times 3}{2} = 18 = \text{Second number.}$$

41. C : Let the number be x.
Then, $\qquad x + 10x = 264$

$$\text{or, } \qquad 11x = 264, \quad \therefore \ x = \frac{264}{11} = 24$$

42. B : If the person is standing at sixth number in the queue from both sides, that means there are five persons ahead and five persons behind him. Hence, total number of person in the queue is $5 + 1 + 5 = 11$.

43. D : Let the number is x.

$$\therefore \qquad x + x + 5 = 17, \text{ or } 2x = 17 - 5 = 12$$

$$\therefore \qquad x = \frac{12}{2} = 6$$

44. B :

$$\frac{x}{4} + 9 = 15$$

$$\frac{x}{4} = 15 - 9 = 6$$

$$\therefore \qquad x = 6 \times 4 = 24.$$

45. A : $5 \times x + 3x = 64$ or, $8x = 64$, $\qquad \therefore \ x = \frac{64}{8} = 8$

46. C : $\qquad x + y = 2x$

$$\therefore \qquad y = 2x - x = x$$

47. C : Let the number be x.

$$\therefore \quad 3x - 11 = 19, \quad \text{or } 3x = 19 + 11 = 30$$

$$\therefore \quad x = \frac{30}{3} = 10.$$

48. A : Let the numbers are x and $(x + 1)$

$$\therefore \quad (x + 1)^2 - x^2 = 25$$

or, $\quad x^2 + 1 + 2x - x^2 = 25$

or, $\quad 2x + 1 = 25$

or, $\quad 2x = 25 - 1 = 24, \quad \therefore x = \frac{24}{2} = 12$

$$\therefore \quad x + 1 = 12 + 1 = 13$$

Hence, the numbers are 12, 13.

49. A : Let x be the digit in units place. Digit in ten's place is then $15 - x$.

$\therefore$ The number $= 10(15 - x) + x$

The new number with reserve digits $= 10 \times x + (15 - x)$

$\therefore \quad 10(15 - x) + x + 9 = 10x + 15 - x$

$\quad 150 - 10x + x + 9 = 9x + 15$

or, $\quad 18x = 144, \quad \therefore x = \frac{144}{18} = 8$

The digit of ten's place $= 15 - 8 = 7$

$\therefore$ The required number $= 78$

50. B : Let the number is x

$$\therefore \quad 180 - x = 11x - 180$$

or, $\quad 180 + 180 = 11x + x, \ 360 = 12x,$

or, $\quad x = \frac{360}{12} = 30$

51. D : Let Y receives ₹ a.

Then X receives ₹ $a + 7$ and Z receives ₹ $a - 8$.

But, $a + 7 + a + a - 8 = ₹ 53$

or, $\quad 3a - 1 = 53, \ 3a = 53 + 1$

$\therefore \ 3a = 54, \ \text{or}, \ a = \frac{54}{3}$

$\quad = ₹ 18. = Y\text{'s share}$

X's share $= a + 7 = 18 + 7 = ₹ 25,$

Z's share $= a - 8 = 18 - 8 = ₹ 10.$

FRACTIONS AND DECIMALS

A fraction is a number that represents a ratio or division of two whole numbers. A fraction is written in the form x/y, the number on the top, 'x' is called numerator; the number on the bottom, 'y' is called denominator. The denominator tells how many equal parts there are; and the numerator tells how many of these equal parts are taken.

> **Sets of equal fractions can be obtained by multiplying, or dividing, the numerator and denominator by the same number.**

For example,

$$\frac{3}{4} = \frac{3 \times 2}{4 \times 2} = \frac{3 \times 2 \times 2}{4 \times 2 \times 2} = \frac{3 \times 3}{4 \times 3} = \frac{3 \times 4}{4 \times 4}$$

Mixed Numbers: A mixed number consists of a whole number and a fraction.3¼ is a mixed number, it means 3 + ¼.

How to change mixed number into fraction?

(*i*) Multiply the whole number by the denominator of the fraction.

(*ii*) Add the numerator of the fraction to the result of step (*i*)

(*iii*) Use the result of step (*ii*) as the numerator and use the denominator of the fractional part of the mixed number as the denominator. This fraction is equal to the mixed number.

> **In calculations involving mixed numbers, always change the mixed numbers into fractions.**

Multiplication of Fractions: While multiplying, two fractions multiply their numerators and divide this by the product of their denominators.

Note: In word problems, **of** *always indicates multiplication.*

Division of Fractions: This can be done either by multiplying by the L.C.M. of the denominators of the fractions, or by multiplying by such a number which can make the denominator 1.

It may be noted that one fraction is a reciprocal of another if their product is 1. So $\frac{1}{3}$ and 3 are reciprocals. To find the reciprocal of a fraction, simply interchange the numerator and deno-minator. This is known as inverting fractions. To divide one fraction by another fraction, invert the divisor and multiply. *For example :*

$$\frac{3}{8} \div \frac{1}{2} = \frac{3}{8} \times 2 = \frac{6}{8} = \frac{3}{4}$$

Addition of Fractions: If the fractions have same denominator, then the denominator is called a common denominator. In such cases, add the numerators and use this sum as the new numerator with the common denominator as the denominator of the sum. *For example,*

$$\frac{3}{15} + \frac{7}{15} = \frac{3+7}{15} = \frac{10}{15} = \frac{2}{3}$$

If the fractions have different denominators, then L.C.M. is called the least common denominator and as has been said for the case when the fractions had the same denominator, *For example,*

$$\frac{1}{3} + \frac{9}{4} + \frac{3}{5} = ?$$

In this case, common denominator is L.C.M. of 3, 4, 5, which is equal to 60,

$$\frac{1}{3} = \frac{20}{60}, \frac{9}{4} = \frac{135}{60}, \frac{3}{5} = \frac{36}{60}$$

$$= \frac{20}{60} + \frac{135}{60} + \frac{36}{60} = \frac{191}{60}$$

Subtracting Fractions: When the fractions have the same denominator, subtract the numerators and place the result over the denominator.
For example,

$$\frac{5}{8} - \frac{3}{8} = \frac{5-3}{8} = \frac{2}{8}$$

When the fractions have different denominators,
(*i*) First of all, find the common denominator:
(*ii*) Express the fractions as equivalent fractions with the same denominator.
(*iii*) Subtract as has been said above, *for example,*

$$\frac{5}{8} - \frac{1}{5} = ?$$

Common denominator in this case is 40,

$$\frac{5}{8} = \frac{25}{40}, \frac{1}{5} = \frac{8}{40}$$

$$\frac{25}{40} - \frac{8}{40} = \frac{25-8}{40} = \frac{17}{40}$$

Equivalent Fractions: Two fractions may be equivalent or equal if they represent the same ratio of number. *For example,*

$$\frac{2}{5} = \frac{4}{10} = \frac{6}{15} = \frac{20}{50}$$

Combined Operations: Sometimes in simplifying fractions, we may come across the following signs :

   (i) Brackets – ( ), { }, [ ]

   (ii) Of – means multiplication

while dealing with such problems,

   (i) first of all brackets should be removed,

   (ii) then *of* followed by,

   (iii) division and multiplicaiton, then

   (iv) addition and subtraction.

Note: Terms enclosed within brackets are to be treated as one quantity.

When an expression within a bracket is preceded by the sign (+), the bracket may be removed without making any change in the sign of the quantities or terms within the bracket.

When an expression within a bracket is preceded by the sign (–), the bracket may be removed only after changing the sign of every term within it.

Complex Fractions: A fraction whose numerator and denominator are themselves fractions is called a complex fraction.

For example, $\dfrac{3/8}{4/5}$

It can be simplified by dividing the fractions. Thus,

$$\frac{3/8}{4/5} = \frac{3}{8} \div \frac{4}{5} = \frac{3}{8} \times \frac{5}{4} = \frac{15}{32}$$

DECIMALS

A collection of digits after a period (decimal point) is called decimal fraction. *For example,* .513, .317, .219, .6, etc. Every decimal represents a fraction.

How to find a fraction represented by decimal?

    (i) Take a fraction whose denominator is 10, and whose numerator is the first digit to the right of decimal point.

    (ii) Take the fraction whose denominator is 100, and whose numerator is the second digit to the right of decimal point.

    (iii) Continue the procedure untill all the digits to the right of the decimal point have been used up. The denominator in each case is 10 times the denominator in the previous step.

(*iv*) The sum of the fractions obtained in (i), (ii) and (iii) is the fraction represented by the decimal point. For example, the fraction represensed by 0.317 may be found out as follows:

$$\frac{3}{10}+\frac{1}{100}+\frac{7}{1000}=\frac{300}{1000}+\frac{10}{1000}+\frac{7}{1000}=\frac{317}{1000}$$

> **Any number of zeros may be added to the right of a decimal fraction without changing its value.**

Addition and Subtraction of Decimals: While adding decimals we put decimal under decimal, units under units, tens under tens and hundreds under hundreds.

For example, 23.4621 + 102.019 + 0.961 =?

$$\begin{array}{r} 23.4621 \\ 102.0190 \\ 0.9610 \\ \hline 126.4421 \\ \hline \end{array}$$

Multiplicaiton of Decimals: When we multiply the decimal fractions by 10, the hundredths become tenths ($10 \times 1/100 = 1/10$), the tenths become units ($10 \times 1/10 = 1$) and the units become tens ($1 \times 10 = 10$) and so on.

For example, $2.45 \times 10 = 24.5$.

Decimals are multiplied like whole numbers. The decimal point of the product is placed in such a way that the number of decimal places in the product is equal to the total of the number of decimal places in all the numbers multiplied.

Division of Decimals: While dividing one decimal by another decimal :

(*i*) Move the decimal point in the divisor to the right until there is no decimal fraction in the divisor.

(*ii*) Move the decimal point in the dividend the same number of places to the right as you moved the decimal point in step (*i*).

(*iii*) Divide the result of (*ii*) by the result of (*i*).

(*iv*) The number of decimal places in the result should be equal to the number of decimal places in the result of step (*ii*).

For example, $66.957 \div 0.11$

$$=\frac{66.957}{0.11}=\frac{66.957\times100}{0.11\times100}=\frac{6695.7}{11}=608.7$$

Relation between Decimal Fraction and Normal Fraction: A fraction can be converted into a decimal fraction by dividing the numerator by denominator. *For example,* $1/2 = 1.0/2 = 0.5$.

$$\frac{1}{5}=\frac{1.0}{5}=0.2, \qquad\qquad \frac{1}{10}=\frac{1\cdot0}{10}=0\cdot1$$

$$\frac{1}{4} = \frac{1\cdot00}{4} = 0\cdot25, \qquad \frac{1}{100} = \frac{1\cdot00}{100} = 0\cdot01$$

$$\frac{3}{4} = \frac{3\cdot00}{4} = 0\cdot75, \qquad \frac{1}{1000} = \frac{1\cdot000}{1000} = 0.001$$

$$\frac{1}{20} = \frac{1\cdot00}{20} = 0.05, \qquad \frac{3}{8} = \frac{3.000}{8} = 0\cdot375$$

$$\frac{1}{16} = \frac{1\cdot0000}{16} = 0\cdot0625, \qquad \frac{7}{8} = \frac{7\cdot000}{8} = 0\cdot875$$

EXERCISE

1. Which of the following is equivalent to $\dfrac{15}{25}$?

   A. $\dfrac{150}{25}$ B. $\dfrac{15}{250}$

   C. $\dfrac{3}{5}$ D. $\dfrac{60}{75}$

2. Which of the following is not equivalent to $\dfrac{13}{20}$?

   A. $\dfrac{26}{40}$ B. $\dfrac{130}{200}$

   C. $\dfrac{39}{60}$ D. $\dfrac{52}{60}$

3. If $\dfrac{9*3}{3*7}$ is equivalent to $\dfrac{9}{7}$, the sign * is replaced by :

   A. ÷ B. ×
   C. + D. −

4. $\dfrac{5}{6}$ of an hour is equal to :

   A. half an hour B. 40 minutes
   C. 50 minutes D. 55 minutes

5. An aircraft uses 2/5 of its fuel in flying 1,250 kilometres. The distance travelled on remaining fuel is :

   A. 1875 km B. 2125 km
   C. 250 km D. 475 km

6. If $\dfrac{4}{3}*\dfrac{3}{4}=\dfrac{16}{9}$, then * means :

   A. + B. −
   C. × D. ÷

7. If $\dfrac{3}{15}*\dfrac{17}{5}=\dfrac{51}{75}$, then * means :

   A. + B. −
   C. × D. ÷

8. If $5x = 1$, then x is equal to :

   A. .20 B. .02
   C. $\dfrac{1}{2}$ D. 5

9. Which of the following is the largest fraction?

   A. $\dfrac{3}{15}$ B. $\dfrac{5}{20}$

   C. $\dfrac{8}{64}$ D. $\dfrac{25}{1000}$

10. Which of the following is the smallest fraction?

A. $\dfrac{1}{10}$ B. $\dfrac{1}{100}$

C. $\dfrac{9}{1000}$ D. $\dfrac{500}{10000}$

11. Six times x increased by 12 is equal to :

A. $\dfrac{x}{2}$ B. $2x$

C. $6x + 12$ D. $12x + 6$

12. Five times y diminished by 20 is equal to :
A. $5y - 20$ B. $5y + 20$
C. $y/4$ D. $4y$

13. The number less than 15 by 7 is:
A. $15x - 7$ B. $15/7$
C. 15   D. 8

14. The excess of thrice a certain number over 16 is 32. The number is :
A. 17   B. 16
C. 12   D. 10

15. If 21 is added to four times a number, the result is 57. The number is :
A. 7   B. 8
C. 9   D. 10

16. A number, the sum of whose fourth and fifth parts exceeds their third part by 28, is :
A. 120   B. 240
C. 220   D. 160

17. Which fraction should be added to the sum of $5\dfrac{3}{4}$, $4\dfrac{4}{5}$ and $7\dfrac{3}{8}$ to make the result a whole number?

A. $\dfrac{1}{40}$ B. $\dfrac{2}{40}$

C. $\dfrac{3}{40}$ D. $\dfrac{4}{40}$

18. $\dfrac{1}{15} + \dfrac{3}{15} + \dfrac{5}{15} + \dfrac{6}{15} = ?$

A. $\dfrac{10}{15}$ B. $\dfrac{3}{5}$

C. $\dfrac{4}{5}$ D. 1

19. A number one-sixth of which exceeds its one-ninth by 100 is :
A. 600   B. 900
C. 1500   D. 1800

20. The sum of $\dfrac{1}{2}, \dfrac{1}{4}$ and $\dfrac{1}{8}$ of a number is 28. The number is :
A. 28   B. 32
C. 36   D. 42

21. The sum of $\dfrac{1}{9}, \dfrac{1}{3}, \dfrac{1}{6}$ and $\dfrac{7}{18}$ of a number is 150. The number is :
A. 120   B. 130
C. 140   D. 150

22. Which is the greatest? .999, .1011, .1995, .9985
A. .999   B. .1011
C. .1995   D. .9985

23. In decimal system, $9\dfrac{1}{8}$ may be represented as:
A. 9.18   B. 9.125
C. 9.025   D. 9.225

24. $2.205 \div 0.15 = ?$
A. 1.47   B. 14.7
C. 147   D. 0.147

25. G.C.M. of .24, 3.2 and 16.0 is :
A. 80   B. 8
C. .8   D. .08

26. L.C.M. of .24, 3.2 and 16.0 is :
A. .48   B. 4.8
C. 48   D. 480

27. A pole has 0.5 of its length in mud, 0.25 of its length in water and 2 metres above water. The total length of the pole is :
A. 8 metres   B. 5 metres
C. 4 metres   D. 2 metres

28. $\sqrt{1/3}$ is equal to :
A. 0.57   B. 0.35
C. 0.30   D. 3.00

29. How many times does 2/3 of 1/2 go into half of one third?
A. 2   B. 1/2
C. 1/3   D. 2/3

30. The eleventh part of $990\dfrac{990}{990}$ is:
A. 99.0   B. 99.99
C. 90   D. 90.9

31. A train started from Delhi at 6.00 A.M. On the next (second) station 1/3 passengers got down and 96 got in. On the next (third) station, 1/2 of the total passengers present in the train got down and 12 came in. Now there were 248 passengers in the train. When the tain started from Delhi, total number of passengers were :
A. 435   B. 564
C. 654   D. 736

32. $1 \div [1 + 1 \div \{1 + 1 \div 1(1 + 1 \div 2)\}]$ is equal to:
A. 1   B. 2
C. $\dfrac{5}{8}$ D. zero

33. L.C.M. of 6, 7, 8 and 10 is equal to :
A. 840   B. 830
C. 820   D. 800

34. By how much does $\dfrac{6}{7/8}$ exceed $\dfrac{6/7}{8}$:
A. $6\dfrac{2}{3}$ B. $6\dfrac{3}{4}$
C. $7\dfrac{1}{2}$ D. $8\dfrac{3}{4}$

35. $\dfrac{.03}{1000}$ is equal to :
A. 3×10^5 B. 3×10^{-3}
C. 3×10^{-6} D. 3×10^{-5}

36. $10\dfrac{1}{25}$ is equal to :
A. 10.25   B. 10.125
C. 10.04   D. 10.025

37. $1.25 \times 1.25 + 2.75 \times 2.75 + 2 \times 1.25 \times 2.75$ is equal to :
A. 4.000   B. 16.000
C. 26.1250   D. 28.3250

38. What fraction of an hour is a second ?
A. $\dfrac{1}{24}$ B. $\dfrac{1}{60}$
C. $\dfrac{1}{120}$ D. $\dfrac{1}{3600}$

39. G.C.M. of 1.6 and 0.72 is equal to :
A. 8   B. .8
C. .08   D. .008

40. $\dfrac{4}{5}$ of 0.025 is equal to :
A. 0.0002   B. 0.002
C. 0.02   D. 0.2

EXPLANATORY ANSWERS

1. **C :** $\dfrac{15}{25} = \dfrac{3 \times 5}{5 \times 5} = \dfrac{3}{5}$.

2. **D :** $\dfrac{26}{40} = \dfrac{2 \times 13}{2 \times 20} = \dfrac{13}{20}, \dfrac{39}{60} = \dfrac{13 \times 3}{20 \times 3} = \dfrac{13}{20}$

   $\dfrac{130}{200} = \dfrac{13 \times 10}{20 \times 10} = \dfrac{13}{20}, \dfrac{52}{60} = \dfrac{13 \times 4}{20 \times 3} = \dfrac{13}{20} \times \dfrac{4}{3}$

   Hence, $\dfrac{52}{60}$ is not equal to $\dfrac{13}{20}$.

3. **B :** $\dfrac{9*3}{3*7} = \dfrac{9}{7}$, or, $\dfrac{9 \times 3}{7 \times 3} = \dfrac{9}{7}$, $\therefore$ The sign * is $\times$.

4. **C :** $\dfrac{5}{6}$ of 1 hr = $\dfrac{5}{6} \times 60$ minutes = 50 minutes.

5. **A :** Remaining fuel = $1 - \dfrac{2}{5} = \dfrac{5-2}{5} = \dfrac{3}{5}$

   Distance flown by $\dfrac{2}{5}$ of fuel = 1250 km.

   Distance flown by full fuel = $\dfrac{1250}{2/5} = \dfrac{1250 \times 5}{2}$ km.

   Distance flown by $\dfrac{3}{5}$ of fuel = $\dfrac{1250 \times 5 \times 3}{2 \times 5} = 1875$ km.

6. **D.**   7. **C.**

8. **A :** $5x = 1$, $\therefore x = \dfrac{1}{5} = .20$.

9. **B :** $\dfrac{3}{15} = \dfrac{1}{5}, \dfrac{8}{64} = \dfrac{1}{8}$, $\dfrac{5}{20} = \dfrac{1}{4}, \dfrac{25}{1000} = \dfrac{1}{40}$,

   $\dfrac{1}{5}, \dfrac{1}{4}, \dfrac{1}{8}, \dfrac{1}{40}$, $\dfrac{16,\ 20,\ 10,\ 2}{80}$

   $\therefore$ The largest fractin is $\dfrac{1}{4} = \dfrac{5}{20}$.

10. C : $\dfrac{1}{10} = .1$, $\dfrac{9}{1000} = .009$

$\dfrac{1}{100} = .01$. $\dfrac{500}{10000} = \dfrac{5}{100} = .05$

The smallest of these quantities is $.009 = \dfrac{9}{1000}$.

11. C : $x \times 6 + 12 = 6x + 12$.

12. A : $5 \times y - 20 = 5y - 20$.

13. D : $15 - 7 = 8$.

14. B : Let the number be x

$$3x - 16 = 32$$

$\therefore$ $\qquad 3x = 32 + 16 = 48$, or $x = \dfrac{48}{3} = 16$.

15. C : Let the number is x

$\therefore 4x + 21 = 57$ or, $4x = 57 - 21 = 36$, or, $x = \dfrac{36}{4} = 9$.

16. B : Let the number is x.

$$\therefore \dfrac{x}{4} + \dfrac{x}{5} = \dfrac{x}{3} + 28, \ \dfrac{9x}{20} = \dfrac{x}{3} + 28, \text{ or, } \dfrac{9x}{20} - \dfrac{x}{3} = 28$$

or, $\dfrac{27x - 20x}{60} = 28$ or, $7x = 28 \times 60$ $\therefore$ $x = \dfrac{28 \times 60}{7} = 240$.

17. C : $5\dfrac{3}{4} + 4\dfrac{4}{5} + 7\dfrac{3}{8} = \dfrac{23}{4} + \dfrac{24}{5} + \dfrac{59}{8} = \dfrac{717}{40}$

717/40 becomes whole number when 3/40 is added to it, i.e.,

$\dfrac{717}{40} + \dfrac{3}{40} = \dfrac{720}{40} = 18$ which is a whole number.

18. D : $\dfrac{1}{15} + \dfrac{3}{15} + \dfrac{5}{15} + \dfrac{6}{15} = \dfrac{1+3+5+6}{15} = \dfrac{15}{15} = 1$.

19. D : Let the number is x.

$\dfrac{x}{6} = \dfrac{x}{9} + 100$ or, $\dfrac{x}{6} - \dfrac{x}{9} = 100$, or, $\dfrac{x}{18} = 100$

or, $x = 100 \times 18 = 1800$.

20. B : Let the number is x.

$$\therefore \ \frac{x}{2}+\frac{x}{4}+\frac{x}{8}=28, \ \text{or,} \ \frac{7x}{8}=28 \ \therefore \ 7x=28\times 8 \ \text{or,} \ x=\frac{28\times 8}{7}=32.$$

21. D : Let the number is x.

$$\therefore \ \frac{x}{9}+\frac{x}{3}+\frac{x}{6}+\frac{7x}{18}=150 \quad \text{or,} \quad \frac{2x+6x+3x+7x}{18}=150 \Rightarrow \frac{18x}{18}=150$$

$$\text{or,} \ x=\frac{150\times 18}{18}=150.$$

22. A : .999 is the greatest.

23. B : $9\dfrac{1}{8}=9+\dfrac{1}{8}=9+.125=9.125$.

24. B : $2.205\div 0.15=\dfrac{2.205}{0.15}=\dfrac{2205}{1000}\times\dfrac{100}{15}=\dfrac{2205}{150}=14.7$.

25. D : G.C.M. of .24, 3.2 and 16.0

$$=\text{G.C.M. of} \ \frac{24, \ 320 \ \text{and} \ 1600}{100}=\frac{8}{100}=0.08.$$

26. C : L.C.M. of .24, 3.2 and 16.0 = L.C.M. of

$$\frac{24, \ 320 \ \text{and} \ 1600}{100}=\frac{4800}{100}=48.$$

27. A : Let total length of the pole $= x$

Pole above water $= x - [0.5x + 0.25x] = 0.25x$;

$0.25x = 2$ metres

$$\therefore \ x=\frac{2\times 100}{25}=8 \ \text{metres}.$$

28. A : $\sqrt{\dfrac{1}{3}}=\dfrac{\sqrt{1}}{\sqrt{3}}=\dfrac{1}{\sqrt{3}}=\dfrac{1}{1.732}=\dfrac{1000}{1732}=0.57$.

29. B : $\dfrac{2}{3}$ of $\dfrac{1}{2}=\dfrac{2}{3}\times\dfrac{1}{2}=\dfrac{1}{3}, \ \dfrac{1}{2}$ of $\dfrac{1}{3}=\dfrac{1}{6} \ \therefore \ \dfrac{1}{6}\div\dfrac{1}{3}=\dfrac{1}{6}\times\dfrac{3}{1}=\dfrac{1}{2}$.

30. C : Eleventh part of $990\dfrac{990}{990}=990\dfrac{990}{990}\div 11=\dfrac{991}{11}=90.09.$

31. B : When train started from Delhi let number of passengers was x. On next station, 1/3 got down and 96 got in.

Now passengers in train $= x - \dfrac{x}{3} + 96 = \dfrac{2x}{3} + 96$

On next station 1/2 of it got down and 12 got in, i.e.,

$\dfrac{1}{2}\left[\dfrac{2x}{3} + 96\right]$ got down and 12 got in

Now passengers in train $= \dfrac{2x}{3} + 96 - \left[\dfrac{x}{3} + 48\right] + 12$

$= \dfrac{2x}{3} - \dfrac{x}{3} + 96 - 48 + 12 = 248 \quad \therefore x = [248 - 60] \times 3 = 188 \times 3 = 564.$

32. C.

33. A : The L.C.M. of 6, 7, 8 and 10 is calculated as follows :

2	6,	7,	8,	10
3	3,	7,	4,	5
4	1,	7,	4,	5
5	1,	7	1,	5
7	1,	7,	1,	1
	1,	1,	1,	1

L.C.M. $= 2 \times 3 \times 4 \times 5 \times 7 = 840.$

34. B : $6 \div \dfrac{7}{8} = \dfrac{6}{1} \times \dfrac{8}{7} = \dfrac{48}{7}$ or $\dfrac{6}{7} \div 8 = \dfrac{6}{7} \times \dfrac{1}{8} = \dfrac{3}{28}$

$\dfrac{48}{7} - \dfrac{3}{28} = \dfrac{192 - 3}{28} = \dfrac{189}{28} = 6\dfrac{21}{28} = 6\dfrac{3}{4}.$

35. D.   **36. C.**

37. B : Put $1.25 = a$ and $2.75 = b$, then,
$1.25 \times 1.25 + 2.75 \times 2.75 + 2 \times 1.25 \times 2.75$
$= a^2 + b^2 + 2ab = (a + b)^2 = (1.25 + 2.75)^2 = (4)^2 = 16.000.$

38. D.   **39. C.**

40. C : $\dfrac{4}{5} \times 0.025 = \dfrac{4}{5} \times \dfrac{25}{1000} = \dfrac{1}{50} = 0.02$.

3

POWERS, EXPONENTS
AND ROOTS

If 'x' is any number and 'n' is a whole numbr greater than 0, x^n means that the product of n factors each of which is equal to x. Thus,

$$x^n = x \cdot x \cdot x \cdot x \,............\,x \; n \text{ times}$$
$$2^4 = 2 \times 2 \times 2 \times 2 = 16$$
$$3^5 = 3 \times 3 \times 3 \times 3 \times 3 = 243$$

$$\left(\frac{x}{y}\right)^n = \frac{x^n}{x^n}$$

$$\left(\frac{3}{7}\right)^2 = \frac{3 \times 3}{7 \times 7} = \frac{9}{49}.$$

In the expression x^n, x is called the base and n is called the exponent. The laws of exponents are :

$$x^n \times x^m = x^{n+m}$$
$$\frac{x^n}{x^m} = x^{n-m}$$
$$(x^m)^n = x^{mn}$$
$$(xy)^m = x^m y^m$$

Negative Exponents: $x^0 = 1$, for any non-zero number x. By one of the law of exponents,

$$x^n \times x^0 = x^{n+0} = x^n$$

i.e., $\qquad\qquad x^0 = 1$

Also, $\qquad\qquad x^{-n} = \dfrac{1}{x^n}$

Roots : If a number 'x' is raised to nth power and the result is 'a', then 'x' is called the *nth* root of 'a', which is usually written as $\sqrt[n]{a} = x$, *For example,*

$$2^4 = 16, \quad \text{or} \quad \sqrt[4]{16} = 2$$

The second root is called the square root, the third root is called the cube root.

or,

$$x^{1/n} \times y^{1/n} = (x.y)^{1/n}$$

$$\sqrt[n]{x \times y} = \sqrt[n]{x} \times \sqrt[n]{y}$$

> **A number which is a prfect square must end in one or another of the digits 0, 1, 4, 5, 6, 9.**

It may be noted that the square of,

1 & 9 both end in 1.

2 & 8 both end in 4.

3 & 7 both end in 9.

4 & 6 both end in 6.

5 end in 5.

(1, 9); (2, 8); (3, 7); (4, 6); (5, 5) are pairs of complementary digits, i.e., the sum of the digits in each pair is 10.

> **If two numbers end in complementary digits, their squares will have the same final digit.**

> **If a number end in zero, its square should contain 2 zero and if a number ends in 2 zeros, its square should end in 4 zeros, and so on.**

> **A number ending in an odd number of zeros cannot be a perfect square.**

EXERCISE

1. $\sqrt{\dfrac{1}{3}} = ?$

A. 0.30

B. 0.57

C 0.89

D. 3.00

2. $\dfrac{6^4}{3^3} = ?$

A. 24

B. 42

C 48

D. 2

3. $\left(\dfrac{1}{2}\right)^{-1} = ?$

A. $-\dfrac{1}{2}$

B. $+\dfrac{1}{2}$

C. -2

D. $+2$

4. $125° = ?$

A. 125 B. 1

C. 1250 D. 12.5

5. $8^{1/3} = ?$

  A. $\dfrac{8}{3}$ B. $\dfrac{3}{8}$

  C. 4   D. 2

6. $4^4 \times 4^{17} = ?$

  A. 8^{17} B. 4^{21}

  C. 8^{21} D. 4^{13}

7. $\dfrac{10x^8}{5x^4} = ?$

  A. $2x^4$ B. $2x^2$

  C. $2x^8$ D. $2x^{12}$

8. $2^{3^2} = ?$

  A. 2^6 B. 2^9

  C. 2^5 D. 8^4

9. $(2^3)^2 = ?$

  A. 8   B. 64

  C. 312   D. 512

10. $(36)^{1/2} = ?$

  A. 18   B. 9

  C. 6   D. 3

11. $x^{3/4} \cdot x^{3/4} = ?$

  A. $2x^{3/1}$ B. $x^{9/16}$

  C. $x^{6/8}$ D. $x^{3/2}$

12. $(x^{3/4})^{1/2} = ?$

  A. $x^{3/8}$ B. $x^{4/6}$

  C. $x^{2/5}$ D. $x^{3/2}$

13. $\sqrt{32} = ?$

  A. 4   B. $2\sqrt{4}$

  C. $4\sqrt{2}$ D. $2^3\sqrt{2}$

14. $5\sqrt{3} = ?$

  A. $\sqrt{75}$ B. $\sqrt{50}$

  C. $\sqrt{25}$ D. $\sqrt[3]{5}$

15. $x^{b-c} \times X^{c-a} \times X^{a-b} = ?$

  A. x^{a+b+c} B. x^{a-b-c}

  C. $x^{2a-2b-2c}$ D. 1

16. When 16000 is expressed as a product of powers of 4 and 10, then it equals :

  A. $4^2 \times 10^2$ B. $4^2 \times 10^3$

  C. $4^3 \times 10^3$ D. $4^2 \times 10^4$

17. When 1800 is expressed as a product of powers of prime numbers, then it equals :

  A. $2 \times 9 \times 10^2$ B. $2 \times 3^2 \times 10^2$

  C. $2 \times 3^2 \times 5^2$ D. $2^3 \times 3^2 \times 5^2$

18. 27×243 is equal to :

  A. 3^8 B. 3^9

  C. 3^{10} D. 3^{11}

19. The sum of the squares of two numbers is 26 and difference is 8. The numbers are :

  A. 9, 17   B. 3, 17

  C. $9, \sqrt{17}$ D. $3, \sqrt{17}$

20. $\left[\left(\dfrac{x}{y} \right)^3 \right]^{-2} = ?$

  A. $\left(\dfrac{x}{y} \right)^{-6}$ B. $\left(\dfrac{x}{y} \right)^{1}$

  C. $\left(\dfrac{x}{y} \right)^{6}$ D. $\left(\dfrac{x}{y} \right)^{5}$

21. $(x^4)^3$ is equal to :

  A. x^{6+2} B. x^{12}

  C. $x^{4/13}$ D. x^{4-3}

22. $(27)^{-4/3}$ is equal to :

  A. 81   B. 54

  C. $\dfrac{1}{21}$ D. $\dfrac{1}{81}$

23. $x^{1/8} \div x^{3/4}$ is equal to :

  A. $x^{5/8}$ B. $x^{2/4}$

  C. $x^{2/3}$ D. $\dfrac{1}{x^{5/8}}$

24. $\left[27^{-2/3}\right]^{1/2}$ is equal to :

   A. $\dfrac{27}{54}$ B. $\dfrac{2}{3}$

   C. $\dfrac{1}{3}$ D. $\dfrac{1}{9}$

25. $\sqrt{72}$ is equal to :

   A. $6\sqrt{2}$

   B. $4\sqrt{6}$

   C. $9\sqrt{6}$

   D. $2\sqrt{6}$

EXPLANATORY ANSWERS

1. B : $\sqrt{\dfrac{1}{3}} = \sqrt{0.3333} = 0.57$.

2. C : $\dfrac{6^4}{3^3} = \dfrac{6\times6\times6\times6}{3\times3\times5} = 2\times2\times2\times6 = 48$.

3. D : $\left(\dfrac{1}{2}\right)^{-1} = (2)^{+1} = 2$.

4. B : Any number raise to power zero = 1.

5. D : $(8)1/3 = (\sqrt[3]{8})^1 = \sqrt[3]{8} = 2$.

6. B : Since, $a^x \times a^x = a^{x+y}$

    $\therefore$ $4^4 \times 4^{17} = 4^{4+17} = 4^{21}$.

7. A : $\dfrac{10x^8}{5x^4} = \dfrac{2x^8}{x^4} = 2x^8 \times x^{-4} = 2x^{8-4} = 2x^4$.

8. B : $2^{3^2} = 2^{3\times3} = 2^9$.

9. B : $(2^3)^2 = (2\times2\times2)^2 = 2\times2\times2\times2\times2\times2 = 64$.

10. C : $(36)^{1/2} = \sqrt{36} = 6$.

11. D : $x^{3/4}.x^{3/4} = x^{3/4+3/4} = x^{6/4} = x^{3/2}$.

12. A : $(x^{3/4})^{1/2} = x^{3/4.1/2} = x^{3/8}$.

13. C : $\sqrt{32} = \sqrt{4\times4\times2} = \sqrt{(4)^2.2} = 4\sqrt{2}$.

14. A : $5\sqrt{3} = \left(\sqrt{5}\right)^2.\sqrt{3} = \sqrt{5}.\sqrt{5}.\sqrt{3} = \sqrt{5.5.3} = \sqrt{75}$.

15. D : $x^{b-c} \cdot x^{c-a} \cdot x^{a-b} = x[b - c + c - a + a - b] = x^0 = 1.$

16. B : $16000 = 16 \times 1000 = (4)^2 \times (10)^3 = 4^2 \times 10^3.$

17. D : The prime factors of 1800 are, $2 \times 2 \times 2 \times 3 \times 3 \times 5 \times 5$
$= 2^3 \times 3^2 \times 5^2.$

18. A : $27 \times 243 = [3 \times 3 \times 3] \times [3 \times 3 \times 3 \times 3 \times 3] = 3^3 \cdot 3^5 = 3^8.$

19. D : Let the numbers are x and y

$$\therefore \qquad x^2 + y^2 = 26 \qquad \qquad ...(i)$$
$$x^2 - y^2 = 8 \qquad \qquad ...(ii)$$

Adding (i) and (ii), we get
$$2x^2 + y^2 - y^2 = 26 + 8 = 34$$

or, $\qquad 2x^2 = 34,\qquad$ or $\qquad x^2 = \dfrac{34}{2} = 17$

$\therefore \qquad\qquad\qquad x = \sqrt{17}$

Since, $\qquad\qquad x^2 + y^2 = 26$

or, $\qquad\qquad 17 + y^2 = 26$

$\therefore \qquad\qquad\qquad y^2 = 26 - 17 = 9$

$\therefore \qquad\qquad\qquad y = \sqrt{9} = 3$

Hence, the numbers are 3 and $\sqrt{17}$.

20. A : $\left[\left(\dfrac{x}{y}\right)^3\right]^{-2} = \left(\dfrac{x}{y}\right)^{3\times-2} = \left(\dfrac{x}{y}\right)^{-6}$

21. B : $(x^4)^3 = x^4 \cdot x^4 \cdot x^4 = x^{4+4+4} = x^{12}.$

22. D : $(27){-4/3} = \dfrac{1}{(27)^{4/3}} = \dfrac{1}{\sqrt[3]{(27)^4}} = \dfrac{1}{3^4} = \dfrac{1}{3\times3\times3\times3} = \dfrac{1}{81}.$

23. D :
$$x^{1/8} \div x^{3/4}$$
or $\qquad\qquad\qquad x^{1/8 - 3/4}$

or $\qquad\qquad\qquad x^{-5/8} = \dfrac{1}{x^{5/8}}.$

24. C : $[27^{-2/3}]^{1/2} = 27^{-2/3 \times 1/2} = 27^{-1/3} = \dfrac{1}{27^{1/3}} = \dfrac{1}{3}.$

25. A : $\sqrt{72} = \sqrt{36\times2} = \sqrt{6\times6\times2} = 6\sqrt{2}.$

———

4

PERCENTAGE

Percent, or per centum means 'for every hundred'. A percentage is a fraction expressed with 100 as its denominator and the rate per cent as its numerator. Thus, 5 per cent means 5 out of 100, or it can be expressed as $5/100 = 1/20$. The symbol % is used to denote the term 'per cent'.

A decimal is converted to percentage by multiplying the decimal by 100, or by moving the decimal point two places to the right.

A percentage can be converted into decimal by dividing it by 100, or by moving the decimal point two places to the left.

For example, $12.5\% = 0.125$

and, $25\% = .25$

A fraction can be converted into a percentage by changing the fraction to a decimal and then changing the decimal to a percentage. A percentage can be changed into a fraction by first converting the percentage into a decimal and then changing the decimal to a fraction. *For example,*

$$1\% = .01 = 1/100, \quad 100\% = 1.0 = 1$$
$$2\% = .02 = 2/100, \quad 120\% = 1.2 = 12/10$$
$$5\% = .05 = 1/20, \quad 12.5\% = 0.125 = 1/8$$

Remember :

1. To change a fraction or mixed number to a per cent; multiply the fraction or mixed number by 100. Reduce, if possible and add % sign.
2. To remove a % sign attached to a decimal and to keep it as decimal, divide the decimal by 100.
3. To remove a % sign attached to a decimal and to change the number to a fraction; divide the decimal by 100, change the result to a fraction, and reduce if necessary.
4. To remove a % sign attached to a fraction or mixed number and to keep it as fraction, divide the fraction or mixed number by 100.
5. To remove a % sign attached to a fraction or mixed number and to change the number to a decimal; divide the fraction by 100 and change the result to decimal.
6. In percentage problems, the whole is 100%. *For example,* if a problem involves 20% of a quantity, the rest of the quantity is $100 - 20 = 80\%$.

EXERCISE

1. 20% is equal to :

   A. $\dfrac{1}{3}$ B. $\dfrac{1}{4}$

   C. $\dfrac{1}{5}$ D. $\dfrac{2}{5}$

2. 5/8 may be expressed as:
   A. 50/80%
   B. 62.5%
   C. 55.5%
   D. 70.5%

3. 15% of ₹ 50 is equal to:
   A. ₹ 25 B. 12.50
   C. ₹ 9.50 D. 7.50

4. What rate per cent is one minute 12 seconds to an hour?
   A. 2% B. 3%
   C. 4% D. 5%

5. A student has to secure 40 per cent marks to pass. If he gets 20 marks and fails by 20 marks, the maximum marks are:
   A. 20 B. 40
   C. 80 D. 100

6. A person spends 75% of his salary and saves ₹ 150 per month. His monthly salary is:
   A. ₹ 750 B. ₹ 600
   C. ₹ 400 D. ₹ 300

7. Standard gold contains 22 parts of pure gold to 2 parts of alloy. The percentage of alloy in a sovereign which is made of standard gold is:
   A. 11% B. 12%

   C. $8\dfrac{1}{3}\%$ D. $11\dfrac{1}{3}\%$

8. The catalogue price of an article is ₹ 250. A reduction of 12% is made for cash purchase. The case price is:
   A. ₹ 250
   B. ₹ 220
   C. ₹ 200
   D. ₹ 180

9. 20% of ₹ 5 is :
   A. Re. 1 B. ₹ 2
   C. ₹ 3 D. ₹ 4

10. 15% of 3 metres is :
    A. 30 cm
    B. 45 cm
    C. 60 cm
    D. 25 cm

11. 5% of a number is 15. The number is :
    A. 150 B. 200
    C. 250 D. 300

12. 75% of what area is 15 square metres?
    A. 10 square metres
    B. 15 square metres
    C. 20 square metres
    D. 25 square metres

13. What per cent of ₹ 30 is ₹ 10?
    A. 30% B. 33.3%
    C. 35% D. 40%

14. What per cent of 6.25 is 1.25?
    A. 10% B. 15%
    C. 20% D. 25%

15. What per cent of 3 metres is 75 cm?
    A. 10% B. 15%
    C. 20% D. 25%

16. 62.5% may be written as :

A. $\dfrac{3}{8}$ B. $\dfrac{4}{8}$

C. $\dfrac{5}{8}$ D. $\dfrac{6}{8}$

17. 125% may be expressed in fractions as :

A. $\dfrac{4}{5}$ B. $\dfrac{5}{4}$

C. $\dfrac{3}{5}$ D. $\dfrac{6}{5}$

18. 97% of students were present in a school and 18 students were absent. The total number of students in the school is:
A. 400 B. 450
C. 500 D. 600

19. The population of a town increased from 50,000 to 52,000. The increase per cent is:
A. 4%
B. 3%
C. 2%
D. 1%

20. At a clearance sale, goods were sold at a reduction of 20 per cent. A student purchased a pen for ₹ 12 at the clearance sale. The usual price of the pen was:
A. ₹ 12
B. ₹ 13
C. Rs 14
D. ₹ 15

21. In a college election, a candidate who got 40% of total votes was defeated by his rival by 160 votes.

the total number of votes polled was:
A. 900 B. 800
C. 700 D. 600

22. In an election, 4000 votes were polled. One of the candidates got 40% votes. He was defeated by:
A. 2400 votes
B. 1600 votes
C. 800 votes
D. 600 votes

23. The selling price of a certain commodity was reduced by 25%. As a result of it, the sales increased by 30%. What was the effect of it on cash collected by daily sales?
A. 5% increase
B. 5% decrease
C. 2.5% increase
D. 2.5 decrease

24. If the price of kerosine be raised by 10%, find by how much per cent a house holder must reduce his consumption of kerosine so that not to increase his expenditure?
A. 10%
B. 9.09%
C. 9.0%
D. 8.25%

25. A towel was 50 cm broad and 100 cm long. When bleached, it was found to have lost 20% of its length and 10% of breadth. The percentage of decrease in area is:
A. 28%
B. 20%
C. 10.08%
D. 10%

EXPLANATORY ANSWERS

1. C : $20\% = \dfrac{20}{100} = \dfrac{1}{5}$.

2. B : $\dfrac{5}{8} \Rightarrow \dfrac{5}{8} \times 100 = \dfrac{500}{8} = 62.5\%$.

3. D : 15% of ₹ $50 = \dfrac{15}{100} \times$ ₹ $50 = $ ₹ 7.50.

4. A : 1 minute 12 seconds = 60 + 12 = 72 second

1 hour = 60 × 60 = 3600 seconds

$$\therefore \qquad \dfrac{72 \times 100}{3600} = 2\%.$$

5. D : Marks required to pass = 40% = 20 + 20

$$\therefore \qquad \text{Maximum marks} = \dfrac{100 \times 40}{40} = 100.$$

6. B : Saving = 100% − 75% = 25% = ₹ 150

$$\therefore \qquad \text{Total salary} = \dfrac{100}{25} \times 150 = \text{₹ } 600.$$

7. C : Total parts = 22 parts + 2 parts = 24 parts; 24 parts contain 2 parts alloy

$$\therefore \ 100 \text{ parts contain } \dfrac{2}{24} \times 100 = \dfrac{25}{3} = 8\dfrac{1}{3}\%.$$

8. B : Reduction at 12% on ₹ $250 = \dfrac{12}{100} \times 250 = $ ₹ 30

$$\therefore \qquad \text{Cash price} = \text{Catalogue price} - \text{Reduction}$$
$$= \text{₹ } 250 - \text{₹ } 30 = \text{Rs. } 220.$$

9. A : 20% of ₹ $5 = \dfrac{20}{100} \times 5 = \text{Re. } 1$.

10. B : 15% of 3 metres = 15% of 300 cm $= \dfrac{15}{100} \times 300 = 45$ cm.

11. D : Let the number $= x$

$\therefore$ 5% of x $= 15$

or, $\dfrac{5}{100} \times x = 15$

$\therefore$ $x = \dfrac{15 \times 100}{5} = 300.$

12. C : Let the area $= x$ m^2

$\therefore$ 75% of $x = 15$ sq. m

or $\dfrac{75}{100} \times x = 15$

$\therefore$ $x = \dfrac{15 \times 100}{75} = 20$ sq. m.

13. B : $\dfrac{10}{30} \times 100 = 33.3\%.$

14. C : $\dfrac{1.25}{6.25} \times 100 = 20\%.$

15. D : $\dfrac{75}{300} \times 100 = 25\%.$

16. C : $62.5\% = \dfrac{62.5}{100} = \dfrac{625}{1000} = \dfrac{5}{8}.$

17. C : $125\% = \dfrac{125}{100} = \dfrac{5}{4}.$

18. D : Number of students absent $= 100\% - 97\% = 3\% = 18$

$\therefore$ $100\% = \dfrac{18 \times 100}{3} = 600.$

19. A : Increase in population $= 52{,}000 - 50{,}000 = 2000$

$\therefore$ % increase $= \dfrac{2000}{50{,}000} \times 100 = 4\%.$

20. D : S.P. $= ₹\ 12 = 80\%$ of usual price

$\therefore$ Usual price $= \dfrac{100}{80} \times 12 = ₹\ 15.$

21. B : Candidate who won the election got $100 - 40 = 60\%$ votes;

Difference of votes $= 60\% - 40\% = 20\% = 160$

$\therefore$ Total votes polled $= \dfrac{160}{20} \times 100 = 800$.

22. C : Candidates who lost election got 40% of 4000

$$= \dfrac{40}{100} \times 4000 = 1600 \text{ votes}$$

Candidates who won the election got 60% of 4000

$$= \dfrac{60}{100} \times 4000 = 2400 \text{ votes}$$

Difference of votes $= 2400 - 1600 = 800$ votes.

23. D : Selling price $= 100 - 25 = 75\%$, Daily sales $= 100 + 30 = 130\%$;

$0.75 \times 1.30 = 0.975 = $ Cash collected $= 97.5\%$;

$100\% - 97.5\% = 2.5\%$ decrease.

24. B : Raised price of kerosine is 110/100 of the original price. Hence, the consumption should become 100/110 of the original consumption so as to keep the expenditure same.

$\therefore$ Reduction $= \left(1 - \dfrac{100}{110}\right)$ of original consumtion

$$= \dfrac{10}{110} \text{ of original consumption}$$

Reduction $\% = \dfrac{10}{110} \times 100 = 9.09\%$.

25. A : Original area $= 100 \times 50 = 5000$ sq. cm.

Reduced length $= 80\%$ of 100 cm $= 80$ cm.

Reduced breadth $= 90\%$ of 50 cm. $= 45$ cm.

Reduced area $= 80 \times 45 = 3600$ sq. cm.

Reduction in area $= 5000 - 3600 = 1400$ sq. cm.

$\therefore$ $\%$ Reduction $= \dfrac{1400}{5000} \times 100 = 28\%$.

———

5

RATIO AND PROPORTION

Ratio: The relation which one quantity bears to another quantity of the same kind, showing the number of times one quantity is contained in another, is called ratio between the two quantities. Thus, the relation between ₹ 48 and ₹ 6 is the same as the relation between ₹ 8 and Re. 1. This relation or the ratio is written as 8 : 1.

Since, a ratio is a fraction, it is not altered if both of its terms are divided or multiplied by the same number.

For example,

$$\frac{2}{3} = \frac{4}{6} = \frac{8}{12} = \frac{20}{30}$$

Both the quantities are called the terms of the ratio. The quantity in the numerator is called *antecedent* and the quantity in the denominator is called *consequent.*

Inverse Ratio: When antecedent and consequent of one ratio become respectively the consequent and antecedent of the other, the second ratio is called the inverse or reciprocal ratio of the first.

For example, 3/5 or 3 : 5 is the inverse ratio of 5/3 or 5 : 3.

Compound Ratio: When the antecedents and consequents of two or more ratios are multiplied to get a new antecedent and a new consequent, the new ratio formed is called their compound ratio.

For example,
the compound ratio of 2 : 3, 3 : 4, 5 : 6 is

$$\frac{2}{3} \times \frac{3}{4} \times \frac{5}{6} = \frac{5}{12} \text{ or } 5 : 12$$

Proportion: Four quantities may be in proportion when the ratio of first to the second is the same as the ratio of third to the fourth. Thus the ratio 2 : 5 and 12 : 30 are equal and the four numbers 2, 5, 12 and 30 are in proportion and are writen as 2 : 5 : :12 : 30

> **If four quantities are in proportion, the product of the extremes is equal to the product of the means.**

EXERCISE

1. The ratio between two numbers is 3 : 4 and their sum is 490. The numbers are:
   A. 200 and 290
   B. 210 and 280
   C. 220 and 270
   D. 230 and 260

2. The ratio between two numbers is 3 : 4 and the sum of their squares is 625. The numbers are:
   A. 6 and 8   B. 15 and 20
   C. 18 and 24   D. 20 and 25

3. Which of the following is greatest?
   3 : 4, 4 : 5, 5 : 6, 6 : 7
   A. 3 : 4   B. 4 : 5
   C. 5 : 6   D. 6 : 7

4. In an examination, 25 students out of 70 scored less than 50% marks. The ratio of number of students who scored 50% marks or more to the number of students who scored less than 50% marks is:
   A. 1 : 2   B. 3 : 5
   C. 9 : 5   D. 5 : 7

5. The fraction that bears the same ratio to 4/9 that 3/11 does to 5/33 is:
   A. 4 : 5   B. 5 : 6
   C. 6 : 5   D. 7 : 5

6. If the consequent be 15 and the value of the ratio 3/5, then the value of antecedent is:
   A. 7   B. 8
   C. 9   D. 10

7. If A : B = 5 : 7 and B : C = 9 : 11, then A : C = ?
   A. 9 : 11   B. 45 : 77
   C. 45 : 66   D. 39 : 77

8. Three numbers are in the ratio of 2 : 3 : 4 and the sum of the squares of the numbers is 116. The numbers are:
   A. 4 : 6 : 8
   B. 5 : 6 : 7
   C. 6 : 9 : 12
   D. 8 : 12 : 16

9. Sides of two squares are in the ratio of 3 : 4. Their perimeters are in the ratio of:
   A. 3 : 4   B. 7 : 8
   C. 5 : 6   D. 6 : 7

10. Two cubical boxes made of card-board have their edges in the ratio of 3 : 4. The ratio of the amounts of card-board in each of them is:
    A. 3 : 4   B. 5 : 6
    C. 6 : 7   D. 9 : 16

11. The angles of a triangle are in the ratio of 1 : 2 : 3. The largest angle is of:
    A. 30°   B. 60°
    C. 90°   D. 120°

12. The salaries of two persons are in the ratio of 4 : 7. Both of them spend 80 per cent of salaries and save rest of the money. The ratio of their savings is:
    A. 8 : 2
    B. 4 : 7
    C. 7 : 5
    D. 5 : 3

13. The mean proportion between 9 and 25 is:
   A. 10   B. 12
   C. 15   D. 17

14. The third proportional to 12 and 30 is:
   A. 40   B. 45
   C. 50   D. 75

15. The fourth proportional to 3, 4 and 15 is:
   A. 20   B. 18
   C. 17   D. 15

16. $75 : 15 = x : 7$, the value of x is:
   A. 25   B. 35
   C. 40   D. 45

17. $x : 7.5 = 7 : 17.5$, the value of x is:
   A. 1.0   B. 2.5
   C. 3.0   D. 3.5

18. The mean proportional to 5 and 125 is:
   A. 10   B. 15
   C. 20   D. 25

19. The inverse ratio of 12 to 18 is:
   A. $\dfrac{3}{2}$ B. $\dfrac{2}{3}$
   C. $\dfrac{1}{3}$ D. $\dfrac{3}{1}$

20. Two numbers are in the ratio of 2 : 3 and if 8 is added to each of them, they become in the ratio of 3 : 4. The number are:
   A. 2 and 3
   B. 4 and 6
   C. 8 and 12
   D. 16 and 24

21. If $x : y = 3 : 2$, then $(x + y) : (x - y) = ?$
   A. 1 : 5   B. 5 : 1
   C. 3 : 5   D. 5 : 2

22. If $x : y = y : z$, then $x = ?$
   A. z B. $\dfrac{z}{y^2}$
   C. $\dfrac{y^2}{z}$ D. $\dfrac{y}{z}$

EXPLANATORY ANSWERS

1. B : Ratio is 3 : 4, sum = 490

If sum is 7, the numbers are 3 and 4.

If sum is 490, the numbers are $\dfrac{3}{7} \times 490$ and $\dfrac{4}{7} \times 490$ *i.e.*, 210 and 280.

2. B : Ratio is 3 : 4. Sum of the squares of 3 and 4 is $9 + 16 = 25$. If sum of the squares is 25, the squares of numbers are 9 and 16.

If sum of the squares is 625, the squares of numbers are $\dfrac{9}{25} \times 625$ and $\dfrac{16}{25} \times 625$ *i.e.*, 225 and 400.

Hence, the numbers are $\sqrt{225}$ and $\sqrt{400}$, *i.e.*, 15 and 20.

3. D : $\dfrac{3}{4}, \dfrac{4}{5}, \dfrac{5}{6}, \dfrac{6}{7}$

$\dfrac{315,\ 336,\ 350,\ 360}{420}$. Hence, the ratio 6 : 7 is the greatest.

4. C : Total students = 70.

Number of students scoring less than 50% marks = 25; Number of students scoring 50% or more than 50% marks = 70 − 25 = 45.

∴ The ratio of number of students who scored 50% marks or more to the number of students who scored less than 50% marks

$$= 45 : 25 = 9 : 5.$$

5. A : Let the required fraction is x. Then

$$\frac{x}{4/9} = \frac{3/11}{5/33} = \frac{3}{11} \times \frac{33}{5} = \frac{9}{5}$$

∴
$$x = \frac{9}{5} \times \frac{4}{9} = \frac{4}{5}, \text{ or } , 4 : 5.$$

6. C :
$$\text{Ratio} = \frac{3}{5} = \frac{\text{Antecedent}}{\text{Consequent}} = \frac{x}{15}$$

∴
$$x = 9, \text{ only then } \frac{9}{15} = \frac{3}{5}$$

7. B : $A : B = 5 : 7; B : C = 9 : 11; A : C = ?$

$$\frac{A}{B} = \frac{5}{7}, \ \frac{B}{C} = \frac{9}{11}, \ \frac{A}{C} = x$$

$$\frac{A}{B} \times \frac{B}{C} = \frac{5}{7} \times \frac{9}{11}, \text{ or, } \frac{A}{C} = \frac{45}{77}$$

∴
$$A : C = 45 : 77$$

8. A : Ratio of numbers = 2 : 3 : 4.

Ratio of squares of numbers = 4 : 9 : 16

If sum of the squares is 29, the squares of the numbers are 4, 9, 16.

If sum of the squares is 116, the squares of the numbers are

$$\frac{4}{29} \times 116, \ \frac{9}{29} \times 116, \ \frac{16}{29} \times 116 = 16, 36, 64$$

∴ The numbers are $\sqrt{16}, \sqrt{36}, \sqrt{64} = 4, 6, 8.$

9. A : Let the sides of two squares are $3x$ and $4x$.
Their perimeters are $4(3x)$ and $4(4x) = 12x$ and $16x$.
Ratio of permieters $= 12x : 16x = 3 : 4$.

10. D : Let the sides of two cubes are $3x$ and $4x$. Surface areas of two cubes are $6(3x)^2$ and $6(4x)^2$.
Ratio of surface areas $= 6(3x)^2 : 6(4x)^2 = 54x^2 : 96x^2 = 9 : 16$.

11. C : Ratio of the angles of triangle $= 1 : 2 : 3$

Sum of the angles of triangle $= 180°$

$$\text{Largest angle} = \frac{3}{6} \times 180 = 90°$$

12. B : Let the salaries be $4x$ and $7x$.
Savings are $100 - 80 = 20\%$
Ratio of savings $= 20\%$ of $4x : 20\%$ of $7x$

$$= \frac{20}{100} \times 4x : \frac{20}{100} \times 7x = 4 : 7$$

13. C : The mean proportion between any two numbers is equal to the square root of their product.
Let x be the mean proportion between 9 and 25.

$\therefore \qquad\qquad 9 : x = x : 25$

or, $\qquad\qquad x^2 = 25 \times 9$, or, $x = \sqrt{25 \times 9} = \sqrt{225} = 15$.

14. D : Let x be the third proportional to 12 and 30.

Then, $\qquad\qquad 12 : 30 = 30 : x$

or, $\qquad\qquad 12x = 30 \times 30$

$$\therefore \qquad\qquad x = \frac{30 \times 30}{12} = 75.$$

15. A : Let x be the fourth proportional to 3, 4, 15.

Then, $3 : 4 = 15 : x$

Since, product of the extremes $=$ Product of the means

$$\therefore \qquad\qquad 3x = 15 \times 4, \text{ or, } x = \frac{15 \times 4}{3} = 20.$$

16. B : $\qquad\qquad 75 : 15 = x : 7$

$$75 \times 7 = 15 \times x \text{ or, } x = \frac{75 \times 7}{15} = 35.$$

17. C :
$$x : 7.5 = 7 : 17.5$$
$$x \times 17.5 = 7.5 \times 7.0$$
$$\therefore \qquad x = \frac{7.5 \times 7.0}{17.5} = 3.0.$$

18. D : Let x be the mean proportional to 5 and 125.

Then, $5 : x = x : 125$ or, $x^2 = 125 \times 5$
$$\therefore \qquad x = \sqrt{125 \times 5} = \sqrt{625} = 25.$$

19. A : The inverse ratio of $12 : 18$ *i.e.*,

$\dfrac{12}{18}$ is $\dfrac{18}{12} = \dfrac{3}{2}$.

20. D : Let the numbers be $2x$ and $3x$.

Then we have, $\dfrac{2x+8}{3x+8} = \dfrac{3}{4}$, or, $8x + 32 = 9x + 24$

or, $\qquad 9x - 8x = 32 - 24$, or, $x = 8$

$\therefore$ The numbers are 2×8 and 3×8 *i.e.*, 16 and 24

21. B : $\qquad x : y = 3 : 2,\ x + y = 3 + 2$

and $\qquad x - y = 3 - 2$

$\therefore \qquad (x + y) : (x - y) = 5 : 1$

22. C : $\qquad x : y = y : z$, or, $\dfrac{x}{y} = \dfrac{y}{z}$

$$\therefore \qquad x = \frac{y}{z} \cdot y = \frac{y^2}{z}$$

___

6

PROFIT AND LOSS

Profit and Loss: The terms profit and loss are largely used in business. When the selling price (S.P.) is greater than cost price (C.P.) there is always some profit. When the selling price is less than the cost price, there is always loss.

> **It should be noted that profit or loss is calculated on the cost price, generally in the form of per cent.**

For example, a man buys an article for ₹ 50 and sells it for ₹ 65. The gain per cent is calculated as follows:

$$\text{Profit} = \text{Selling Price} - \text{Cost Price}$$
$$= ₹\ 65 - ₹\ 50 = ₹\ 15$$

$$\%\ \text{Profit} = \frac{15}{50} \times 100 = 30\%$$

When cost price and profit or loss % are given, then

$$\text{S.P.} = \frac{[100 + \text{gain}\%]}{100} \times \text{C.P.}$$

or $$\text{S.P.} = \frac{[100 - \text{Loss}\%]}{100} \times \text{C.P.}$$

When selling price and profit or loss % are given,

$$\text{C.P.} = \frac{\text{S.P.} \times 100}{100 + \text{Gain}\%} \quad \text{or} \quad \text{C.P.} = \frac{\text{S.P.} \times 100}{100 - \text{Loss}\%}$$

(i) To find the cost price when the selling price and the % profit based on cost price is given:

Establish a relation between S.P. and C.P. and solve it to find C.P.

For example, an article is sold for Rs.10 which is a 10% profit of C.P.

In this case, S.P. = ₹ 10 = C.P. + 10% of C.P. (Profit)

∴ S.P. = 100% of C.P.

or, $$\text{C.P.} = ₹\ \frac{10 \times 100}{110} = ₹\ 9.09.$$

(ii) To find the S.P. when the profit based on S.P. is given:

Establish a relation between the S.P. and C.P. and solve it to find the S.P.

43

For example, a person buys a book for ₹ 27 and sells it at a profit of 10% of S.P. Find the S.P.

$$₹ \ 27 + \text{Profit} = \text{S.P.}$$

Since, profit is 10% of S.P., the C.P. must be 90% of S.P.

$$∴ \qquad ₹ \ 27 = 90\% \text{ of S.P.}$$

$$∴ \qquad \text{S.P.} = \frac{27 \times 100}{90} = ₹ \ 30.$$

(iii) To find S.P. when the % loss on the S.P. is given:

Establish a relation between C.P. and S.P. and solve it to find S.P.

For example, an article was bought for ₹ 10. Due to some breakage, it was sold for 25% loss on the S.P. Find the S.P. of the article.

$$₹ \ 10 - \text{Loss} = \text{S.P.}$$

Since, the loss is 25% of the S.P., the C.P. must be 125% of S.P.

$$∴ \qquad ₹ \ 10 = 125\% \text{ of S.P.}$$

$$∴ \qquad \text{S.P.} = \frac{\text{Rs. } 10 \times 100}{125} = ₹ \ 8.$$

(iv) To find S.P. when the list price and % discount are given:

Multiply the list price by % discount to find the discount in terms of money and subtract it from the list price.

For example, the list price of an article is ₹ 90. Find its selling price if it is sold at 10% discount.

$$\text{List price} = ₹ \ 90.00, \text{ Discount} = 10\% \text{ of } ₹ \ 90.00$$

$$= \frac{10 \times 90}{100} = ₹ \ 9.00$$

$$∴ \qquad \text{Selling price} = ₹ \ 90.00 - ₹ \ 9.00 = ₹ \ 81.00$$

(v) To find S.P. when list price and a series of discounts are given:

(a) Multiply the list price by first % discount.

(b) Subtract it from the list price.

(c) Multiply the remainder by second discount.

(d) Subtract the product from the remainder.

(e) Continue the same procedure if more discounts are given.

For example, find the selling price of an article listed at ₹ 200 on which there are discounts of 10% and 20%.

$$\text{First discount} = 10\% \text{ of } ₹ \ 200$$

$$= \frac{10 \times 200}{100} = ₹ \ 20$$

$$\text{First selling price} = ₹ \ 200 - ₹ \ 20 = ₹ \ 180.$$

Second discount = 20% of ₹ 180

$$= \frac{20 \times 180}{100} = ₹\ 36$$

Second selling price = ₹ 180 – ₹ 36 = ₹ 144

(vi) *To find the single equivalent discount of a series of discounts* :

   (a) Add first two discounts.

   (b) Multiply first two discounts.

   (c) Subtract this product from the sum to find the equivalent discount of the first two discounts.

   (d) If there is third discount, add the equivalent of first two discounts to the third.

   (e) Multiply the equivalent of first two discounts by third.

   (f) Subtract this product from the sum to find the equivalent of the three discounts.

   (g) Continue the same procedure, if there are more discounts.

For example, what is the single discount equivalent to discount series 10%, 20%, 30%.

$$10\% + 20\% = 0.1 + 0.2 = 0.3$$
$$10\% \times 20\% = 0.1 \times 0.2 = 0.02$$
$$0.30 - 0.02 = 0.28$$
$$0.28 + 30\% = 0.28 + 0.3 = 0.580$$
$$0.28 \times 30\% = 0.28 \times 0.3 = 0.084$$
$$0.580 - 0.084 = 0.496 = 49.6\%$$

Hence, the single equivalent discount of 10%, 20% and 30%, is 49.6%.

EXERCISE

1. A man buys an article for ₹ 25 and sells it for ₹ 30. His profit is:
   A. 16.67%   B. 20%
   C. 25.5%   D. 25.67%

2. If an article is sold at 10% profit, then the selling price in terms of cost price is:
   A. 10/11   B. 11/10
   C. ₹ 110   D. ₹ 90

3. If an article is sold at gain of x%, the cost price in terms of selling price is:

   A. $\dfrac{100}{100 + x}$ B. $\dfrac{100 + x}{100}$

   C. $\dfrac{100}{100 - x}$ D. $\dfrac{100 - x}{100}$

4. If an article is sold at gain of y%, the selling price in terms of cost price is:

   A. $\dfrac{100}{100 - y}$ B. $\dfrac{100 - y}{100}$

   C. $\dfrac{100}{100 + y}$ D. $\dfrac{100 + y}{100}$

5. If an article is sold at a loss of 25%, the selling price in terms of cost price is:

A. $\dfrac{1}{2}$ B. $\dfrac{2}{3}$

C. $\dfrac{3}{4}$ D. $\dfrac{4}{5}$

6. If an article is sold at a loss of 50%, the cost price in terms of selling price is:

A. $\dfrac{1}{2}$
B. 2
C. 2.5
D. None of the above

7. If S.P. of an article is 4/3 of C.P., the profit is:

A. $\dfrac{1}{3}\%$ B. $33\dfrac{1}{3}\%$

C. $25\dfrac{1}{5}\%$ D. $20\dfrac{1}{2}\%$

8. If C.P. of an article is 3/2 of S.P., the profit or loss percentage is:

A. $33\dfrac{1}{3}\%$ loss   B. $33\dfrac{1}{3}\%$ profit

C. $33\dfrac{1}{8}\%$ loss   D. $33\dfrac{1}{8}\%$ profit

9. If S.P. of an article is 6 times the loss, the loss percentage is:

A. $14\dfrac{5}{9}\%$ B. $15\dfrac{2}{8}\%$

C. $16\dfrac{3}{5}\%$ D. $14\dfrac{2}{7}\%$

10. If gain is 1/4 of C.P., the profit percentage is:
A. 4%   B. 25%
C. 50%   D. 75%

11. If loss is 1/3 of S.P., the loss percentage is:
A. 33%   B. 25%
C. 20%   D. 17%

12. A man bought certain articles at 8 for ₹ 7 and sold them at 6 for ₹ 5. The gain or loss percentage is:

A. $4\dfrac{16}{21}\%$ gain

B. $4\dfrac{16}{21}\%$ loss

C. No profit no loss
D. None of the above

13. A man bought a number of oranges at 3 for a rupee and an equal number at 2 for a rupee. At what price per dozen should be sell them to make a profit of 20%?
A. ₹ 4   B. ₹ 5
C. ₹ 6   D. ₹ 7

14. A machine was bought for ₹ 9000. For how much should it be sold to gain 15%?
A. ₹ 10,150   B. ₹ 10,250
C. ₹ 10,300   D. ₹ 10,350

15. Find the selling price if a fountain pen costing ₹ 6.20 is sold at a loss of 10%?
A. ₹ 6.92   B. ₹ 5.58
C. ₹ 6.00   D. ₹ 5.92

16. A carpet is sold for ₹ 585 at a loss of 10%. The cost price is:
A. ₹ 650   B. ₹ 640
C. ₹ 630   D. ₹ 620

17. A machine is sold at a profit of 20%. If it had been sold at a profit of 25%, it would have fetched ₹ 35 more. The cost price of the machine is:

A. ₹ 650   B. ₹ 700

C. ₹ 750   D. ₹ 800

18. By selling a book for ₹ 31 a person loses 7% of his outlay. If he sells the same book for ₹ 35, the bargain is:

A. 4% loss   B. 4% profit

C. 5% loss   D. 5% profit

19. The cost price of 12 articles is equal to the selling price of 9 articles. The gain per cent is:

A. 25.0%   B. 33.3%

C. 30.0%   D. 67.7%

20. At a clearance sale, the prices had been reduced by 20%. If a transistor was being sold at ₹ 150 before reduction, the price at clearance sale was:

A. ₹ 130

B. ₹ 125

C. ₹ 120

D. ₹ 115

EXPLANATORY ANSWERS

1. B : Profit = ₹ 30 – ₹ 25 = ₹ 5, % Profit = $\dfrac{5}{25} \times 100 = 20\%$.

2. B : If the profit is 10%, then S.P. = 110% of C.P. = $\dfrac{110}{100}$ of C.P. = $\dfrac{11}{10}$ of C.P.

3. A : Gain = $x\%$, S.P. = $[100 + x]$ % of C.P. $\therefore$ C.P. $= \dfrac{100}{100 + x}$ S.P.

4. D : Gain = $y\%$, S.P. = $[100 + y]$ % of C.P.

$$\text{S.P.} = \dfrac{100 + y}{100} \times \text{C.P.}$$

5. C : Loss = 25%, C.P. = 100, S.P. = 100 – 25 = 75

or, S.P. = 75% of C.P. = $\dfrac{3}{4}$ of C.P.

6. B : Let C.P. = 100, Loss = 50%, S.P. = 100 – 50 = 50%;

or, S.P. = 50% of C.P. or, C.P. = 200% of S.P. or, C.P. = 2 × S.P.

7. B : C.P. = 1, S.P. = $\dfrac{4}{3}$, Profit = $\dfrac{4}{3} - 1 = \dfrac{1}{3}$

% Profit = $100 \times \dfrac{1}{3} = 33\dfrac{1}{3}\%$.

8. A : C.P. = 1, S.P. = $\dfrac{2}{3}$ of C.P., Loss = $1 - \dfrac{2}{3} = \dfrac{1}{3}$.

% Loss = $\dfrac{1}{3} \times 100 = 33\dfrac{1}{3}\%$.

9. D :   S.P. = 6 times the Loss or, Loss = $\dfrac{1}{6}$ of S.P.

$$\text{C.P.} = \text{S.P.} + \text{Loss} = \text{S.P.} + \dfrac{1}{6} \text{ of S.P.} = \dfrac{7}{6} \text{ of S.P.}$$

or,   S.P. = $\dfrac{6}{7}$ of C.P.   ∴ Loss = $1 - \dfrac{6}{7}$ of C.P. = $\dfrac{1}{7}$ of C.P.

$$\% \text{ Loss} = 100 \times \dfrac{1}{7} = 14\dfrac{2}{7}\%$$

10. B : C.P. = 1, Gain = $\dfrac{1}{4}$ of C.P. = $\dfrac{1}{4} \times 1 = \dfrac{1}{4}$

$$\% \text{ Gain} = \dfrac{1}{4} \times 100 = 25\%.$$

11. B : Loss = $\dfrac{1}{3}$ of S.P.

$$\text{C.P.} = \text{S.P.} + \text{Loss} = \text{S.P.} + \dfrac{1}{3} \text{ of S.P.} = \dfrac{4}{3} \text{ of S.P.}$$

or,   S.P. = $\dfrac{3}{4}$ of C.P.   ∴ Loss = $\dfrac{1}{4}$ of C.P.

$$\% \text{ Loss} = \dfrac{1}{4} \times 100 \text{ of C.P.} = 25\% \text{ of C.P.}$$

12. B : C.P. of one article = ₹ $\dfrac{7}{8}$, S.P. of one article = ₹ $\dfrac{5}{6}$

$$\text{Loss} = \text{C.P.} - \text{S.P.} = \dfrac{7}{8} - \dfrac{5}{6} = \dfrac{1}{24}$$

$$\% \text{ Loss} = \dfrac{1}{24} \times \dfrac{8}{7} \times 100 = \dfrac{100}{21} = 4\dfrac{16}{21}\%$$

13. C : Let 1 dozen oranges were bought at 3 for a rupee and one dozen oranges were bought at 2 for a rupee.

∴   C.P. of 1 dozen = ₹ 4

C.P. of 1 dozen = ₹ 6

C.P. of 2 dozens = ₹ 6 + ₹ 4 = ₹ 10

% Profit 20% = 20% of ₹ 10 = ₹ 2

∴   S.P. = C.P. + Profit = ₹ 10 + ₹ 2

= ₹ 12

S.P. of 2 dozen oranges = ₹ 12

∴   S.P. of 1 dozen oranges = ₹ $\dfrac{12}{2}$ = ₹ 6

14. **D :** C.P. = ₹ 9000, Gain = 15% of ₹ 9000 = $\dfrac{15}{100} \times 9000$ = ₹ 1350.

$\therefore$ S.P. = ₹ 9000 + ₹ 1350 = ₹ 10,350.

15. **B :** C.P. = ₹ 6.20, Loss = 10% of C.P. = 10% of ₹ 6.20

$$= \dfrac{10}{100} \times 6.20 = 62 \text{ paise}$$

S.P. = C.P. – Loss = ₹ 6.20 – 62 paise

$$= ₹ 5.58$$

16. **A :** S.P. = ₹ 585, Loss = 10% of C.P.

$$\text{C.P.} = \dfrac{\text{S.P.} \times 100}{\left[100 - \text{Loss\%}\right]} = \dfrac{585 \times 100}{100 - 10} = \dfrac{585 \times 100}{90} = ₹ 650.$$

17. **B :** Let, C.P. = ₹ 100

Ist S.P. = ₹ 120, IInd S.P. = ₹ 125

Difference = ₹ 125 – ₹ 120 = ₹ 5

If difference is ₹ 5, C.P. = ₹ 100

If difference is ₹ 35, C.P. = $\dfrac{100}{5} \times 35$ = ₹ 700

18. **D :** S.P. = ₹ 31, Loss = 7%

$$\therefore \quad \text{C.P.} = \dfrac{31 \times 100}{93} = ₹ \dfrac{100}{3}$$

IInd S.P. = ₹ 35, Profit = ₹ 35 – ₹ $\dfrac{100}{3}$ = ₹ $\dfrac{5}{3}$

$$\therefore \ \% \text{ Profit} = \dfrac{5}{3} \times \dfrac{3}{100} \times 100 = 5\%.$$

19. **B :** Let C.P. of one article = ₹ 1

$\therefore$ C.P. of 12 articles = ₹ 12

C.P. of 12 articles = S.P. of 9 articles = ₹ 12

$$\therefore \text{S.P. of 12 articles} = \dfrac{12}{9} \times 12 = ₹ 16$$

Profit = ₹ 16 – ₹ 12 = ₹ 4

$$\% \text{ Profit} = \dfrac{4}{12} \times 100 = 33.3\%$$

20. **C :** S.P. before reduction = ₹ 150

S.P. after reduction = 100 – 20 = 80% of ₹ 150

$$= \dfrac{80}{100} \times 150 = ₹ 120.$$

7

INTEREST

Interest is the sum which is paid for the use of other's money. If it is payable yearly, it is called rate per cent per annum. Thus, 6% per annum means ₹ 6 paid as interest on each ₹ 100 for one year. The money borrowed is called *Principal.* The sum of the principal and interest is called *Amount.*

In the Case of Simple Interest:

$$\text{Simple Interest} = \frac{\text{Principal} \times \text{Rate\%} \times \text{Time (in years)}}{100}$$

$$\text{Amount} = \text{Principal} + \text{Interest}$$

When time, rate% and interest are given,

$$\text{Principal} = \frac{\text{Interest} \times 100}{\text{Rate} \times \text{Time (in years)}}$$

When principal, interest and time are given,

$$\text{Rate} = \frac{\text{Interest} \times 100}{\text{Principal} \times \text{Time}}$$

When principal, interest and rate are given,

$$\text{Time} = \frac{\text{Interest} \times 100}{\text{Principal} \times \text{Rate}}$$

Example 1. A sum of money amounts to ₹ 6000 in 2 years. If the interest on the sum for that time is ₹ 1000. Find the rate of simple interest.

Solution. Amount = ₹ 6000, Interest = ₹ 1000

Principal = ₹ 6000 – ₹ 1000 = ₹ 5000

Time = 2 years

$$\text{Rate} = \frac{\text{Interest} \times 100}{\text{Principal} \times \text{Time}} = \frac{1000 \times 100}{5000 \times 2} = 10\%$$

Example 2. What principal with yield ₹ 600 as simple interest at 12% per annum in 1 year?

Solution. Interest = ₹ 600, Rate = 12%, Time = 1 year

$$\text{Principal} = \frac{\text{Interest} \times 100}{\text{Rate} \times \text{Time}} = \frac{\text{Rs. } 600 \times 100}{12 \times 1} = ₹\ 5000.$$

50

Example 3. At what time will the interest on a sum of money will equal to the principal at 10% per annum?

Solution. Let, Principal $= x$, $\therefore$ Interest $= x$, Rate $= 10\%$

$$\text{Time} = \frac{\text{Interest} \times 100}{\text{Principal} \times \text{Rate}} = \frac{x \times 100}{x \times 10} = 10 \text{ years.}$$

Example 4. Three years back, a sum of money was remitted in a bank at 12% per annum S.I. The accounts are now cleared, the bank paying a sum of ₹ 6,800. What was the sum originally invested?

Solution. Interest for 3 years $= 3 \times 12 = 36\%$ of the principal. The amount in 3 years $= 100 + 36 = 136\%$ of the principal $=$ ₹ 6800.

$$\therefore \quad \text{Original sum invested} = \frac{6800 \times 100}{136} = ₹\ 5000.$$

In the Case of Compound Interest:

$$\text{Amount} = \text{Principal} \left[1 + \frac{\text{Rate}}{100} \right]^{\text{Time(in year)}}$$

If rate of compound interest differs from year to year, then

$$\text{Amount} = \text{Principal} \left[1 + \frac{\text{Rate}_1}{100} \right] \left[1 + \frac{\text{Rate}_2}{100} \right] \left[1 + \frac{\text{Rate}_3}{100} \right] \cdots\cdots$$

Example 5. Find the compound interest on ₹ 2000 for 2 years at 10%.

Solution. $\text{Amount} = \text{Principal} \left[1 + \frac{\text{Rate}}{100} \right]^2$

$$= ₹\ 2000 \left[1 + \frac{10}{100} \right]^2 = ₹\ 2000 \times \frac{11}{10} \times \frac{11}{10}$$

$$= ₹\ 2420$$

Compound Interest $= ₹\ 2420 - ₹\ 2000 = ₹\ 420$

Example 6. Find the compound interest on ₹ 4000 for 1.5 years at 10% interest payable half- yearly.

Solution. (In such cases, double the time and half the rate)

$$\text{Amount} = 4000 \left(1 + \frac{5}{100} \right)^3$$

$$= ₹\ 4000 \times \frac{21}{20} \times \frac{21}{20} \times \frac{21}{20} = ₹\ 4630.50$$

Compound Interest $= ₹\ 4630.50 - ₹\ 4000 = ₹\ 630.50$

Example 7. In what time ₹ 12000 will amount to ₹ 13230 at 5% C.I.?

Solution. Principal $\left[1+\dfrac{\text{Rate}}{100}\right]^{n}$ = Amount

$$\therefore \quad ₹\ 13230 = ₹\ 12000 \left[1+\frac{5}{100}\right]^{n}$$

$$\therefore \quad \left[1+\frac{5}{100}\right]^{n} = \frac{\text{Rs. }13230}{\text{Rs. }12000}$$

$$\text{or,} \quad \left[\frac{21}{20}\right]^{n} = \frac{441}{400} = \frac{21}{20}\times\frac{21}{20} = \left[\frac{21}{20}\right]^{2}$$

$$\therefore \quad n = 2 \text{ years}$$

When interest is calculated half-yearly, halve the rate and double the time. When interest is calculated quarterly, divide the rate by 4 and multiply the time by 4.

EXERCISE

1. S.I. on ₹ 5000 for 5 years at 10% p.a. is equal to:
   A. ₹ 250   B. ₹ 2000
   C. ₹ 2500   D. ₹ 2800

2. What principal will yield ₹ 120 as S.I. at 6% p.a. in 10 years?
   A. ₹ 100   B. ₹ 125
   C. ₹ 150   D. ₹ 200

3. In how many years will the sum of money double itself at 10% per annum S.I.?
   A. 4 years   B. 5 years
   C. 8 years   D. 10 years

4. What sum of money will produce an interest of ₹ 80 in 5 years at the rate of 5% per annum?
   A. ₹ 320   B. ₹ 380
   C. ₹ 420   D. ₹ 500

5. If S.I. on ₹ 5000 in 2 years is ₹ 500, the amount is:
   A. ₹ 4500   B. ₹ 5500
   C. ₹ 5575   D. ₹ 6000

6. The simple interest on a certain sum of money is ₹ 49 and the rate per cent is equal to the number of years. The rate per cent is:
   A. 10%   B. 9%
   C. 7%   D. 6%

7. If the rate of interest is 2 paise per rupee per month, then the interest on ₹ 200 in one year will be:
   A. ₹ 4   B. ₹ 24
   C. ₹ 48   D. ₹ 50

8. What annual payment will discharge a debt of ₹ 440 due in 5 years? Simple interest reckoned at 5%.
   A. ₹ 80   B. ₹ 90
   C. ₹ 100   D. ₹ 105

9. Compound interest on ₹ 2000 for 3 years at 5% p.a. is:
   A. ₹ 300   B. ₹ 315.25
   C. ₹ 325.50   D. ₹ 333.75

10. Find the compound interest on ₹ 1000 is one year at 5% per annum when the interest is calculated half-yearly?
A. ₹ 50.20   B. ₹ 50.62
C. ₹ 50.82   D. ₹ 55.62

11. The difference between C.I. and S.I. on ₹ 2500 for 2 years at 4% p.a. is:
A. ₹ 2   B. ₹ 3
C. ₹ 4   D. ₹ 5

12. What sum lent at C.I. at 5% p.a. will amount to ₹ 441 in 2 years?
A. ₹ 200   B. ₹ 250
C. ₹ 450   D. ₹ 400

13. For a sum of ₹ 1000, during same time at the same rate, highest quantity will be:
A. S.I.   B. C.I.
C T.D.   D. B.G.

14. S.I. is equal to C.I. for a certain sum when:
A. rate is same
B. time is same
C. interest is computed annually and time is one year
D. None of the above

15. Simple interest on the sum due of a bill for the time from when the bill is discounted to the due date of bill is called:
A. Simple Interest
B. Compound Interest
C. True Discount
D. Banker's Discount

16. A sum becomes double in 15 years at simple interest. It will become triple in:
A. 20 years   B. 30 years
C. 35 years   D. 40 years

17. In 5 years the interest on certain sum amounts to one-fourth of the sum. The rate of interest per annum is:
A. 4%   B. 5%
C. 6%   D. 10%

EXPLANATORY ANSWERS

1. C : $\text{S.I.} = \dfrac{\text{Principal} \times \text{Time} \times \text{Rate}}{100} = \dfrac{5000 \times 5 \times 100}{100} = ₹\ 2500.$

2. D : $\text{Principal} = \dfrac{\text{S.I.} \times 100}{\text{Time} \times \text{Rate}} = \dfrac{120 \times 100}{6 \times 10} = ₹\ 200$

3. D : Let Principal $= x$

∴   Amount $= 2x$, Hence, Interest $= 2x - x = x$

$\text{Rate} = 10\%,\ \text{Time} = \dfrac{\text{Interest} \times 100}{\text{Principal} \times \text{Rate}} = \dfrac{x \times 100}{x \times 10} = 10 \text{ years.}$

4. A : Principal $= \dfrac{\text{Interest} \times 100}{\text{Rate} \times \text{Time}} = \dfrac{80 \times 100}{5 \times 5} =$ ₹ 320.

5. B : Amount = ₹ 5000 + ₹ 500 = ₹ 5500.

6. C : Let the Principal = ₹ 100, Time = x years, Rate = $x\%$

$$\text{S.I.} = \frac{100 \times x \times x}{100} = x^2 = ₹\ 49$$

$$\therefore \qquad x = \sqrt{49} = 7 = 7\%$$

7. C : Rate of interest = 2% per month

$$= 24\% \text{ per year}$$

$$\therefore \qquad \text{Interest} = \frac{200 \times 24 \times 1}{100} = ₹\ 48$$

8. A.

9. B :

$$\text{Amount} = ₹\ 2000 \left(1 + \frac{5}{100}\right)^3$$

$$= ₹\ 2315.25$$
$$\text{C.I.} = \text{Amount} - \text{Principal} = 2315.25 - 2000$$
$$= ₹\ 315.25.$$

10. B : When interest is calculated half-yearly, convert 1 year into 2 half years and take half of the rate.

Thus, $\qquad$ rate = 2.5%, $n = 2$

$$\text{Amount} = ₹\ 1000 \left(1 + \frac{2.5}{100}\right)^2$$

$$= ₹\ 1050.62$$
$$\text{Interest} = 1050.62 - 1000 = ₹\ 50.62.$$

11. C. $\qquad$ **12. D.** $\qquad$ **13. B.** $\qquad$ **14. C.** $\qquad$ **15. D.** $\qquad$ **16. B.**

17. B : Let sum = x, $\therefore$ Interest = $x/4$,

$$\text{Time} = 5 \text{ years,}$$

$$\text{Rate} = \frac{\text{Interest} \times 100}{\text{Sum} \times \text{Time}} = \frac{x/4 \times 100}{x \times 5} = 5\%.$$

8

DISCOUNT

Discount in the general term is the reduction or an allowance made from the amount of a bill in lieu of its immediate cash payment. The reduction made in consideration of making immediate payment is called discount or true discount. The immediate cash payment or cash equivalent is called present worth or present value.

$$\text{Sum Due} = \text{Present Worth} + \text{True Discount}$$
$$\text{True Discount} = \text{Sum Due} - \text{Present Worth}$$
$$\text{True Discount on Sum Due} = \text{Interest on Present Worth}$$
$$\text{Present Worth} = \frac{100 \times \text{Sum Due}}{100 + [\text{Rate} \times \text{Time}]}$$
$$\text{True Discount} = \frac{\text{Sum Due} \times \text{Rate} \times \text{Time}}{100 + [\text{Rate} \times \text{Time}]}$$

Example. *Find the present worth and true discount on ₹ 6000 due 2 years at 10% per annum S.I.*

Solution.

$$\text{P.W.} = \frac{100 \times \text{Sum Due}}{100 + [\text{Rate} \times \text{Time}]}$$

$$= \frac{100 \times 6000}{100 + [10 \times 2]} = \frac{100 \times 6000}{120} = ₹\ 5000$$

$$\text{T.D.} = \frac{\text{Sum Due} \times \text{Rate} \times \text{Time}}{100 + [\text{Rate} \times \text{Time}]}$$

$$= \frac{6000 \times 10 \times 2}{100 + [10 \times 2]} = \frac{6000 \times 10 \times 2}{120} = ₹\ 1000.$$

Banker's Discount: In business when a trader buys goods from a wholesaler, the payment is generally made by a bill of exchange which is a kind of undertaking in writing to pay for the goods after a certain time. When the wholesaler wants money at earlier date, in such case, the bill is sold to the banker for ready money and it is said to be discounted and the amount which the banker deducts is called Banker's discount.

Banker's Discount (B.D.) is the same as the simple interest on the amount of bill for the number of days the bill has yet to run.

$$\text{Banker's Gain (B.G.)} = \text{Banker's Discount} - \text{True Discount}$$
$$\text{Banker's Discount} = \text{True Discount} + \text{Interest on True Discount}$$
$$\text{Sum Due} = \frac{\text{B.D.} \times \text{T.D.}}{\text{B.D.}-\text{T.D.}}$$
$$\text{T.D.} = \sqrt{\text{P.W.} \times \text{B.G.}}$$

Example 1. *True discount on a certain sum of money due 1 year hence is ₹ 48 and interest on the same sum for the same time is ₹ 50. Find the sum and the rate per cent.*

Solution.
$$\text{Sum} = \frac{\text{Interest} \times \text{Discount}}{\text{Interest} - \text{Discount}}$$
$$= \frac{\text{Rs. } 50 \times \text{Rs. } 48}{\text{Rs. } 50 - \text{Rs. } 48} = ₹ \frac{50 \times 48}{2} = ₹ \ 1200$$

Now, ₹ 50 is the interest on ₹ 1200 in one year,

$$\therefore \qquad \text{Rate} = \frac{50 \times 100}{1200 \times 1} = 4\frac{1}{6}\%$$

Example 2. The banker's discount and true discount on a certain sum of money at 5% S.I. are ₹ 30 and ₹ 25 respectively. Find the sum.

Solution.
$$\text{Sum} = \frac{\text{B.D.} \times \text{T.D.}}{\text{B.D.} - \text{T.D.}} = \frac{30 \times 25}{30 - 25} = ₹ \ 150$$

Example 3. *Find the banker's discount and banker's gain on a bill of ₹ 4000 at 10% if it is cashed 3 months in advance.*

Solution.
$$\text{Banker's discount} = \frac{\text{Rs. } 4000 \times 10 \times 3}{12 \times 100} = ₹ \ 100$$
$$\text{Cash received by the bill holder} = ₹ \ 4000 - ₹ \ 100 = ₹ \ 3900$$
$$\text{Interest on } ₹ \ 100 = ₹ \ 2.50$$
$$\text{Amount} = ₹ \ 100 + ₹ \ 2.50 = ₹ \ 102.50$$

If amount is ₹ 102.50, $\qquad \text{T.D.} = ₹ \ 2.50$

If amount is ₹ 4000, $\qquad \text{T.D.} = \frac{2.50}{102.50} \times 4000 = ₹ \ 97.56$

B.G. = B.D. – T.D. = ₹ 100 – ₹ 97.56 = ₹ 2.44.

Example 4. *Banker's gain on a bill is ₹ 18 whose present worth is ₹ 450. Find true discount.*

Solution.
$$\text{T.D.} = \sqrt{\text{P.W.} \times \text{B.G.}}$$
$$= \sqrt{450 \times 18} = \sqrt{8100} = ₹ \ 90.$$

Example 5. *True discount on a bill of ₹ 5400 is ₹ 900. Find the banker's discount and also banker's gain.*

Solution.

$$\text{Amount} = ₹\ 5400, \ \text{T.D.} = ₹\ 900,$$
$$\text{P.W.} = \text{Amount} - \text{T.D.} = ₹\ 5400 - ₹\ 900$$
$$= ₹\ 4500$$
$$\text{S.I. on } ₹\ 4500 = ₹\ 900$$
$$\therefore \quad \text{S.I. on } ₹\ 5400 = ₹\ \frac{900 \times 5400}{4500} = ₹\ 1080$$
$$\therefore \quad \text{B.D.} = ₹\ 1080$$
$$\therefore \quad \text{B.G.} = \text{B.D.} - \text{T.D.} = ₹\ 1080 - ₹\ 900 = ₹\ 180.$$

EXERCISE

1. Present worth of a money is equal to:

   A. $\dfrac{100 \times \text{Sum Due}}{100 + \text{Rate} + \text{Time}}$

   B. $\dfrac{100 \times \text{Sum Due}}{(100 + \text{Rate})\ \text{Time}}$

   C. $\dfrac{100 + (\text{Rate} \times \text{Time})}{100 \times \text{Sum Due}}$

   D. $\dfrac{100 \times \text{Sum Due}}{100 + (\text{Rate} \times \text{Time})}$

2. Find the present worth of ₹ 1248 due 2 years hence at 2% per annum simple interest

   A. ₹ 1200   B. ₹ 1210
   C. ₹ 1220   D. ₹ 1242

3. Find the present worth of ₹ 460 due 3 years hence at 5% per annum S.I.

   A. ₹ 450   B. ₹ 420
   C. ₹ 410   D. ₹ 400

4. Find the discount on ₹ 1010 due 3 months hence at 4% p.a. S.I.

   A. ₹ 8   B. ₹ 9
   C. ₹ 10   D. ₹ 12

5. Find the reduction made on a bill of ₹ 1150 paid 1.25 years before it is due when the rate of interest is 12%

   A. ₹ 100   B. ₹ 150
   C. ₹ 200   D. ₹ 225

6. Find the difference between S.I. and T.D. on ₹ 5100 for half-year at 4% p.a.

   A. Re. 0.50   B. Re. 1.00
   C. ₹ 1.50   D. ₹ 2.00

7. If the true discount on a bill due 2 years hence at 5% p.a. is ₹ 25, the amount of the bill is:

   A. ₹ 125   B. ₹ 220
   C. ₹ 250   D. ₹ 275

8. If the present worth of a bill of ₹ 660 due 2 years hence is ₹ 600, the rate per cent per annum is:

   A. 4%   B. 5%
   C. 6%   D. 10%

9. The true discount on a sum of money due 1 year is ₹ 100 and banker's discount on the same sum and for the same time is ₹ 104. The sum is:

   A. ₹ 2500   B. ₹ 2550
   C. ₹ 2600   D. ₹ 2700

10. The true discount on a sum of money due 12 months is ₹ 200 and banker's discount on the same sum and for the same time is ₹ 208. The rate of interest is:
A. 4%   B. 5%
C. 6%   D. 7%

11. The true discount on a certain sum of money for 2 years is 3/4 the banker's discount. The rate of interest is:
A. 15%   B. 16.67%
C. 20%   D. 20.33%

12. The T.D. on a bill is 5/6 of B.D. and the rate is 4%. The time is:
A. 5 years   B. 4 years
C. 3 years   D. 2 years

13. A trader's terms are 20% discount for cash payment and interest is charged after one year. What rate of interest per annum does the customer get on his money for cash payment?
A. 15%   B. 20%
C. 25%   D. 30%

14. The T.D. on a bill due 1 year hence at 5% p.a. is ₹ 40. The amount is:
A. ₹ 840   B. ₹ 900
C. ₹ 950   D. ₹ 1000

15. The interest on ₹ 5000 is equal to the true discount on ₹ 5050 at 4% p.a. The latter is due after:
A. 3 months   B. 4 months
C. 5 months   D. 6 months

EXPLANATORY ANSWERS

1. D : $\text{P.W.} = \dfrac{100 \times \text{S.D.}}{100 + (\text{Rate} \times \text{Time})}$.

2. A : $\text{P.W.} = \dfrac{100 \times \text{S.D.}}{100 + (\text{Rate} \times \text{Time})} = \dfrac{100 \times 1248}{100 + (2 \times 2)} = \dfrac{100 \times 1248}{104} = ₹\ 1200.$

3. D : $\text{P.W.} = \dfrac{100 \times \text{S.D.}}{100 + (\text{Rate} \times \text{Time})} = \dfrac{100 \times 460}{100 + (3 \times 5)} = \dfrac{100 \times 460}{115} = ₹\ 400.$

4. C : $\text{T.D.} = \dfrac{\text{Sum} \times \text{Rate} \times \text{Time}}{100 + (\text{Rate} \times \text{Time})} = \dfrac{1010 \times 1/4 \times 4}{100 + (1/4 \times 4)} = \dfrac{1010}{101} = ₹\ 10$

5. B : $\text{Reduction} = \text{T.D.} = \dfrac{1150 \times 12 \times 5/4}{100 + (12 \times 5/4)} = \dfrac{1150 \times 15}{115} = ₹\ 150.$

6. D : $\text{S.I.} = \dfrac{5100 \times 4 \times 1/2}{100} = ₹\ 102$

$\text{T.D.} = \dfrac{5100 \times 4 \times 1/2}{100 + (4 \times 1/2)} = \dfrac{5100 \times 2}{102} = ₹\ 100$

$\text{S.I.} - \text{T.D.} = ₹\ 102 - ₹\ 100 = ₹\ 2.$

7. D : Let P.W. = ₹ 100

S.I. on ₹ 100 at 5% for 2 years $= \dfrac{100 \times 5 \times 2}{100} = ₹\ 10$

Amount = 100 + 10 = ₹ 110,

₹ 10 is the T.D. on ₹ 110

If T.D. is ₹ 10, amount = ₹ 110

If T.D. is ₹ 25, amount = $\dfrac{110}{10} \times 25$ = ₹ 275.

8. B : P.W. = ₹ 600, Interest = ₹ 660 – ₹ 600 = ₹ 60,

Time = 2 years, Rate = $\dfrac{60 \times 100}{600 \times 2}$ = 5%.

9. C : Sum = $\dfrac{\text{B.D.} \times \text{T.D.}}{\text{B.D.} - \text{T.D.}} = \dfrac{104 \times 100}{104 - 100} = \dfrac{104 \times 100}{4}$ = ₹ 2600.

10. A : Sum = $\dfrac{\text{B.D.} \times \text{T.D.}}{\text{B.D.} - \text{T.D.}} = \dfrac{208 \times 200}{208 - 200} = \dfrac{208 \times 200}{8}$ = ₹ 5200.

Now, ₹ 208 is the interest on ₹ 5200 for 1 year.

$\therefore$ Rate = $\dfrac{208 \times 100}{5200 \times 1}$ = 4%.

11. B : If B.D. = x, T.D. = 3/4x, Sum = $\dfrac{x \times 3/4\,x}{x - 3/4\,x}$ = 3x,

Since, B.D. is the interest on sum due, $\therefore$ Rate = $\dfrac{x \times 100}{3x \times 2} = \dfrac{100}{6}$ = 16.67%.

12. A : If, B.D. = x, T.D. = 6/5x, Sum = $\dfrac{x \times 5/6x}{x - 5/6x}$ = 5x

Since, B.D. is the interest on sum due, $\therefore$ Time = $\dfrac{x \times 100}{5x \times 4}$ = 5 years.

13. C : Let amount of Bill = ₹ 100, Discount for cash payment = 20% = ₹ 20

$\therefore$ Cash price = ₹ 100 – ₹ 20 = ₹ 80

i.e., ₹ 20 is interest earned on ₹ 80 for one year.

$\therefore$ Rate = $\dfrac{20 \times 100}{80 \times 1}$ = ₹ 25%.

14. A : T.D. = Interest on P.W. = ₹ 40

Time = 1 year, Rate = 5% P.W. = $\dfrac{40 \times 100}{5 \times 1}$ = ₹ 800.

$\therefore$ Amount = 800 + 40 = ₹ 840

15. A : Interest on P.W. = T.D. on amount

Now, Interest on ₹ 5000 = T.D. on ₹ 5050

$\therefore$ ₹ 5000 is the P.W. of ₹ 5050 due at 4%

$\therefore$ Interest on ₹ 5000 = Sum due – P.W. = ₹ 5050 – ₹ 5000 = ₹ 50

$\therefore$ Time = $\dfrac{50 \times 100}{5000 \times 4} = \dfrac{1}{4}$ year = 3 months

9

TIME, WORK AND WAGES

While dealing with problems of time and work, it should be kept in mind that,

(*i*) If a man can do a piece of work in 5 days, It is evident that in one day he will finish 1/5 of his whole work; and vice versa.

(*ii*) If the number of persons engaged to do a certain job be increased in a certain ratio, the time required to do the same job will be decreased in the same ratio, and vice-versa. Thus, if the number of persons be changed in the ratio of 3 : 5, the time required to finish the job will be changed in the ratio of 5 : 3.

(*iii*) If A is twice as good workman as B, then A will take one-half of the time taken by B to do the same job.

(*iv*) While dealing with problems on wages, it may be kept in mind that the money obtained is always divided in the ratio of the work done by each person.

In the problems based on time and work, it is always assumed that a person works at uniform rate, unless and until specified in the problem.

Example. *A can do a piece of work in 4 days and B can do the same work in 6 days. How long will A and B take to do the work together?*

Solution.   A's work in one day $= \dfrac{1}{4}$ of the total work

B's Work in one day $= \dfrac{1}{6}$ of the total work

$(A + B)$'s work in one day $= \dfrac{1}{4} + \dfrac{1}{6} = \dfrac{5}{12}$ of the total work

$\therefore$ Number of days taken by A + B to finish the work $= \dfrac{12}{5} = 2.4$ days.

EXERCISE

1. A can do a certain job in 6 days and B can finish the same job in 10 days. A and B together will finish the same job in:
   A. less than 10 days but more then 6 days
   B. more than 10 days
   C. less than 6 days
   D. 2 days

2. A can make a table in 3 days while his friend can make it in 6 days. A and his friend together

will make the table in:
A. 3 days 　　　 B. 2 days
C. 1 day 　　　 D. 1/2 days

3. X and Y together can do a certain job in 10 days while X alone can do the same job in 15 days. Y alone will do the same job in:
A. 15 days 　　 B. 20 days
C. 25 days 　　 D. 30 days

4. Amit can do 1/2 of a piece of work in 8 days, while Aslam can do 1/3 of the same work in 8 days. In how many days can both do it together?
A. 9.6 days 　　 B. 10.5 days
C. 11.2 days 　 D. 16.0 days

5. X, Y and Z together can do a piece of work in 8 days while X and Z together can do it in 12 days. Y alone will do the same work in:
A. 16 days 　　 B. 20 days
C. 24 days 　　 D. 28 days

6. 24 persons can assemble a machine in 12 days. In how many days 36 persons will assemble the same machine?
A. 8 days 　　　 B. 12 days
C. 16 days 　　 D. 20 days

7. X, Y and Z can do a certain job in 8, 10 and 8 days respectively. How long would they take to complete the same job when all work together?
A. $2\frac{1}{7}$ days 　 B. $2\frac{3}{7}$ days
C. $2\frac{5}{7}$ days 　 D. $2\frac{6}{7}$ days

8. If m men can do $1/n$ of a piece of work in P days, find the expression for the number of persons required to do the whole work in q days?
A. mn/pq 　　 B. mnq/p
C. mnp/q 　　 D. mp/nq

9. In the above Q. No. 8 if $m = 15$, $n = 4$, $p = 12.5$ and $q = 20$, then the number of persons required to do the same work is:
A. 38 　　　　 B. 34
C. 30 　　　　 D. 26

10. A piece of work can be done by 6 men and 5 women in 6 days or 3 men and 4 women in 10 days. In how many days can it be done by 9 men and 15 women?
A. 1 day 　　　 B. 2 days
C. 3 days 　　　 D. 4 days

11. X and Y undertook a contract to do a certain job for ₹ 4200. X alone could do the job in 3 weeks and Y alone in 4 weeks. If both of them finished the job working together, in what ratio should money be divided (X : Y)?
A. 3 : 4 　　　 B. 4 : 3
C. 1 : 1 　　　 D. 2 : 3

12. X and Y did a piece of work together and received ₹ 300. If X alone can do that piece of work in 2 weeks and Y alone in 3 weeks, how should the money be divided between them?
A. X = ₹ 180, Y = ₹ 120
B. X = ₹ 120, Y = ₹ 180
C. X = ₹ 150, Y = ₹ 150
D. X = ₹ 200, Y = ₹ 100

13. A, B and C did a work together and earned ₹ 195. If the ratio of work of A : B : C be as 4 : 6 : 3, the money obtained by C is:
A. ₹ 90   B. ₹ 60
C. ₹ 45   D. ₹ 30

14. To finish a certain job X takes twice as long as Y and Z together and Z three times as long as X and Y together. If X, Y and Z working together complete the job in 6 days, how long would X take to complete the work alone?
A. 16 days   B. 18 days
C. 24 days   D. 28 days

15. In the above question, how long would Z take to complete the work alone?
A. 16 days   B. 18 days
C. 20 days   D. 24 days

SOME SELECTED EXPLANATORY ANSWERS

1. C : Work done by A in one day $= \dfrac{1}{6}$

Work done by B in one day $= \dfrac{1}{10}$

Work done by (A + B) in one day $= \dfrac{1}{6} + \dfrac{1}{10} = \dfrac{8}{30}$

∴   A + B together will finish the work in $\dfrac{30}{8}$ days $= 3\dfrac{6}{8}$ days

which is less than 6 days.

2. B : Work done by A and his friend in one day $= \dfrac{1}{3} + \dfrac{1}{6} = \dfrac{3}{6}$

∴ Both will finish the work in $\dfrac{6}{3} = 2$ days

3. D : Work done by X + Y in one day $= \dfrac{1}{10}$

Work done by X alone in one day $= \dfrac{1}{15}$

Work done by Y alone in one day $= \dfrac{1}{10} - \dfrac{1}{15} = \dfrac{1}{30}$

∴ Y alone will finish the work in 30 days.

4. A : Amit alone can do the whole work in $8 \times 2 = 16$ days

$\therefore$ Work done by Amit in one day $= \dfrac{1}{16}$

Aslam alone can do the whole work in $8 \times 3 = 24$ days

$\therefore$ Work done by Aslam in one day $= \dfrac{1}{24}$

Work done by Amit and Aslam in one day $= \dfrac{1}{16} + \dfrac{1}{24} = \dfrac{5}{48}$

$\therefore$ Amit and Aslam will finish the work in $\dfrac{48}{5} = 9.6$ days.

5. C : Work done by X + Y + Z in one day $= \dfrac{1}{8}$

Work done by X + Z in one day $= \dfrac{1}{12}$

Work done by Y in one day $= \dfrac{1}{8} - \dfrac{1}{12} = \dfrac{1}{24}$

$\therefore$ Y alone will finish the work in 24 days.

6. A : $\because$ 24 persons can assemble in 12 days.

$\therefore$ 1 person can assemble in 12×24 days

$\therefore$ 36 persons can assemble in $\dfrac{12 \times 24}{36} = 8$ days

7. D : Work done by X + Y + Z in one day $= \dfrac{1}{8} + \dfrac{1}{10} + \dfrac{1}{8} = \dfrac{7}{20}$

$\therefore$ X + Y + Z will complete the work in $\dfrac{20}{7} = 2\dfrac{6}{7}$ days.

8. C : m men can do $1/n$ of work in p days

$\therefore$ Number of men required to do the work in one day $= mnp$

Hence, number of men required to do the whole work in q days $= mnp/q$.

9. A : $mnp/q = \dfrac{15 \times 4 \times 12.5}{20} = 38.$

64

10. C :

$$6 \text{ days} \to 6\,m + 5\,w$$
$$1 \text{ day} \to 36\,m + 30\,w$$

Similarly,

$$10 \text{ days} \to 3\,m + 4\,w$$
$$1 \text{ day} \to 30\,m + 40\,w$$
$$36\,m + 30\,w = 30\,m + 40\,w$$

or, $\qquad 6\,m = 10\,w$

or, $\qquad 1\,m = \dfrac{5}{3}\,w$

Therefore, $\quad 6\,m + 5\,w = 15\,w$

and $\qquad 9\,m + 15\,w = 30\,w$

The problem now reduce to

$$15\,w \to 6 \text{ days}$$

$\therefore \qquad 30\,w \to 6 \times \dfrac{15}{30} = 3 \text{ days}$

11. B : Ratio of working capacity of X and Y is 4 : 3

$\therefore$ Ratio of money to be divided = 4 : 3

12. A : Ratio of working capacity of X and Y is 3 : 2

$\therefore \qquad$ X's share $= \dfrac{3}{5} \times 300 = ₹\ 180,$

$\qquad$ Y's share $= \dfrac{2}{5} \times 300 = ₹\ 120.$

13. C : Money obtained by C $= \dfrac{3}{13} \times 195 = ₹\ 45.$

14. B : 2 times X's daily work = (Y + Z)'s daily work

Adding X's daily work to both sides we get

3 times X's daily work = (X + Y + Z)'s daily work = 1/6

$\therefore$ X's daily work $= \dfrac{1}{6} \times \dfrac{1}{3} = \dfrac{1}{18}$

$\therefore$ X alone can finish the work in 18 days.

15. D : 3 times Z's daily work = (X + Y)'s daily work

Adding Z's daily work to both sides, we get

4 times Z's daily work = (X + Y + Z)'s daily work = 1/6

$\therefore$ Z's daily work $= \dfrac{1}{6} \times \dfrac{1}{4} = \dfrac{1}{24}$

$\therefore$ Z alone can finish the work in 24 days.

10

SPEED, TIME AND DISTANCE

Important Formulae :

$$\text{Distance} = \text{Speed} \times \text{Time}$$

$$\text{Speed} = \frac{\text{Distance}}{\text{Time}}$$

$$\text{Time} = \frac{\text{Distance}}{\text{Speed}}$$

EXERCISE

1. Speed of a moving car is 36 km/hr. Its speed in metres per second is:
   A. 10 m/s   B. 15 m/s
   C. 20 m/s   D. 25 m/s

2. Two trains start at the same time from two stations X and Y, 900 km apart; and proceed towards each other at an average speed of 38 and 22 km per hour respectively. They will meet after
   A. 12 hours   B. 13 hours
   C. 14 hours   D. 15 hours

3. A scooterist completes a journey in 10 hours, the first half at the rate of 21 km/hr and the second half at the rate of 24 km/hr. The total distance travelled is :
   A. 256 km   B. 224 km
   C. 204 km   D. 192 km

4. A train 100 m long is running at the speed of 60 km per hour. Time taken by the train to pass a telegraph post is:
   A. 4 sec   B. 5 sec
   C. 6 sec   D. 3 sec

5. A train 150 m long is running at the speed of 90 km/hr. Time taken by the train to pass through a tree is :
   A. 3 sec   B. 4 sec
   C. 6 sec   D. 8 sec

6. A train 100 m long is running at the speed of 65 km/hr. Time taken by the train to pass through a man walking at the rate of 5 km/hr in the direction of the train is :
   A. 8 sec   B. 6 sec
   C. 4 sec   D. 2 sec

7. A train 100 m long is running at the rate of 55 km/hr. Time taken by the train to pass through a man walking at the rate of 5 km/hr moving in opposite direction is :
   A. 10 sec   B. 8 sec
   C. 6 sec   D. 4 sec

(1335) Math-5

8. Two persons start from the same place and walk in the opposite directions at 5 km and 4 km per hour respectively. At the end of 3 hours, distance between them is
A. 12 km B. 15 km
C. 27 km D. 30 km

9. A person starts from a place P at 6 A.M. and walks to Q at 3 km per hour. Another person starts from P at 8 A.M. and follows the first on bicycle at 6 km per hour. Both of them reach Q at the same time. The distance from P to Q is:
A. 12 km B. 10 km
C. 8 km D. 6 km

10. A person can row at the rates of x km/hr up a stream and at the rate of y km/hr down the stream. The rate in still water is:
A. $x + y$ B. $x - y$
C. $\dfrac{x - y}{2}$ D. $\dfrac{x + y}{2}$

11. In Q. 10, the rate of flow of stream is :
A. $x + y$ B. $x - y$
C. $y - x$ D. $\dfrac{y - x}{2}$

12. A person can row down a stream at 6 km/hr and up the same stream at 3 km/hr. His rate in still water is :
A. 9 km/hr B. 4.5 km/hr
C. 1.5 km/hr D. 1.0 km/hr

13. In Q. 12, the rate of flow of the stream is :
A. 1.5 km/hr B. 2.5 km/hr
C. 4.5 km/hr D. 18.0 km/hr

14. A man can row at the rate of 9 km per hr in still water. At what rate can he row against a stream flowing 7 km per hour?
A. 8 km/hr B. 7 km/hr
C. 2 km/hr D. –2 km/hr

15. To walk one kilometre A takes m minutes and B, n minutes. In one hour, the difference of distance travelled by A and B is:
A. $m - n$ B. $60m - 60n$
C. $\dfrac{60}{m} - \dfrac{60}{n}$ D. $\dfrac{60}{mn}$

$$\boxed{\textbf{EXPLANATORY ANSWERS}}$$

1. A : Speed $= \dfrac{36 \text{ km}}{1 \text{ hr}} = \dfrac{36000 \text{ m}}{3600 \text{ sec}} = 10$ m/s.

2. D : Distance covered by two trains in 1 hour $= 38 + 22 = 60$ km.

$$\text{Distance} = 900 \text{ km}$$

$$\text{Time taken} = \dfrac{900}{60} = 15 \text{ hours.}$$

3. B : Let distance $= x$ km.

Time taken in travelling $\dfrac{x}{2}$ km at the rate of 21 km/hr

$$= \frac{1}{21} \times \frac{x}{2} = \frac{x}{42} \text{ hr.}$$

Time taken in travelling $\frac{x}{2}$ km at the rate of 24 km/hr

$$= \frac{1}{24} \times \frac{x}{2} = \frac{x}{48} \text{ hr}$$

But

$$\frac{x}{42} + \frac{x}{48} = 10$$

$$\frac{8x + 7x}{336} = 10$$

$$15x = 3360$$

$$\Rightarrow \qquad x = 224 \text{ km.}$$

4. C : Distance = 100 m

$$\text{Speed} = \frac{60 \text{ km}}{1 \text{ hr}} = \frac{60000 \text{ m}}{3600 \text{ sec}} = \frac{50}{3} \text{ m/sec}$$

$$\text{Time} = \frac{\text{Distance}}{\text{Speed}} = \frac{100}{50/3} = \frac{100 \times 3}{50} = 6 \text{ sec.}$$

5. C :

$$\text{Speed} = \frac{90 \text{ km}}{1 \text{ hr}} = \frac{90000 \text{ m}}{3600 \text{ sec}} = 25 \text{ m/sec.}$$

Distance = 150 m.

$$\text{Time} = \frac{\text{Distance}}{\text{Speed}} = \frac{150}{25} = 6 \text{ sec.}$$

6. B : Net speed = Speed of train – speed of man = 65 – 5 = 60 km/hr

$$\text{Speed} = \frac{60 \text{ km}}{1 \text{ hr}} = \frac{60000 \text{ m}}{3600 \text{ sec}} = \frac{50}{3} \text{ m/s}$$

$$\text{Time} = \frac{\text{Distance}}{\text{Speed}} = \frac{100}{50/3} = \frac{100 \times 3}{50} = 6 \text{ sec.}$$

7. C : Net speed = speed of train + speed of man = 55 + 5 = 60 km/hr

For rest of the answer see Q. 6.

8. C : Since, both the persons are moving in opposite direction and start from the same place, distance them after one hour = 5 + 4 = 9 km.

∴ Distance after 3 hours = 9 × 3 = 27 km.

9. A : Let distance from P to $Q = x$ km

Speed of first person = 3 km/hr

$$\text{Time taken} = \frac{x}{3} \text{ hr}$$

Speed of second person = 6 km/hr

$$\text{Time taken} = \frac{x}{6} \text{ hr}$$

According to problem, $\quad \dfrac{x}{3} - \dfrac{x}{6} = 2$

$$\frac{2x - x}{6} = 2$$

$$x = 12$$

$\therefore$ Distance from P to $Q = 12$ km.

10. D : Rate in still water $= \dfrac{x+y}{2}$.

11. D : Rate of flow of stream $= \dfrac{y-x}{2}$.

12. B : Rate of still water $= \dfrac{6+3}{2} = 4.5$ km/hr.

13. A : Rate of flow of stream $= \dfrac{6-3}{2} = 1.5$ km/hr.

14. C : Rate of rowing against flowing water

= Rate of rowing of man – Rate of flow of the stream

= 9 – 7 = 2 km/hr.

15. C : Distance travelled by A in 1 hour $= \dfrac{60}{m}$ km

Distance travelled by B in 1 hour $= \dfrac{60}{n}$ km

$\therefore$ Difference of distance travelled by A and B in 1 hour $= \dfrac{60}{m} - \dfrac{60}{n}$.

———

11

AVERAGE

EXERCISE

1. The heights of 5 students (in cm) are 140, 135, 142, 138, 140. Their average height is :
   A. 136
   B. 138
   C. 139
   D. 140

2. Marks obtained by 10 students are 22, 35, 37, 38, 29, 27, 34, 36, 28, 34. The average marks are :
   A. 30   B. 31
   C. 32   D. 34

3. Average of class I to class V is 29. Average of class I to class III is 31. Average of class IV to class V is:
   A. 25   B. 26
   C. 27   D. 28

4. The average age of a group of 13 boys is 13 years. When two more boys joined the group, the average rose by 2 years. The sum of the ages of the two new boys is :
   A. 50 years
   B. 30 years
   C. 56 years
   D. 26 years

5. A boy of height 165 cm is replaced by another, which decreases the average height of the group of 34 boys by 1 cm. The height of the new boy is :
   A. 132 cm   B. 129 cm
   C. 130 cm   D. 131 cm

6. The average of five consecutive even numbers, starting with 2, is:
   A. 4   B. 6
   C. 7   D. 5

7. The average of 4, 5, 3.5, 7.5, 9.5 and 6.5 is :
   A. 6.0   B. 5.2
   C. 5.5   D. 5.0

8. The average of 8 numbers is 12. If each number is increased by 2, the average of the new set of numbers is:
   A. 14   B. 12
   C. 15   D. 13

9. The weights of 5 balls in gms are as under 50, 54, 53, 56, 52. The average weight is :
   A. 53   B. 54
   C. 52   D. 51

10. The lengths of 5 pieces of a string in cms are : 5, 5.2, 6.3, 7.2, 6.3. The average length of a piece is:
    A. 5.8   B. 6.0
    C. 6.1   D. 6.2

70

EXPLANATORY ANSWERS

1. C : Average height $= \dfrac{140+135+142+138+140}{5} = \dfrac{695}{5} = 139.$

2. C : Average marks $= \dfrac{22+35+37+38+29+27+34+36+28+34}{10}$

$$= \dfrac{320}{10} = 32.$$

3. B : Total students in class I to V $= 29 \times 5 = 145$

Total students in class I to III $= 31 \times 3 = 93$

Total students in class IV and V $= 145 - 93 = 52$

Average of class IV and V $= \dfrac{52}{2} = 26.$

4. C : Total age of 13 boys $= 13 \times 13 = 169$ years

Total age of 15 boys $= 15(13 + 2) = 15 \times 15 = 225$ years

Total age of two new boys $= 225 - 169 = 56$ years.

5. D : Average decrease in height of 34 boys $= 1$ cm

Total decrease in height of 34 boys $= 34 \times 1 = 34$ cm

$\therefore$ Height of the new boy $= 165 - 34 = 131$ cm.

6. B : Sum of five consecutive even numbers starting with 2

$$= 2 + 4 + 6 + 8 + 10 = 30$$

Average $= 30 \div 5 = 6.$

7. A.

8. A : New average $= 12 + 2 = 14.$

9. A : Average weight $= \dfrac{50+54+53+56+52}{5} = \dfrac{265}{5} = 53.$

10. B : Average length $= \dfrac{5+5.2+6.3+7.2+6.3}{5} = \dfrac{30.0}{5} = 6.0.$

12

PARTNERSHIP

EXERCISE

1. *X*, *Y* and *Z* invested in a common business. *X* invested ₹ 6000 for 2 months, *Y* invested ₹ 7000 for 4 months and *Z* invested ₹ 6400 for 5 months. Out of a profit of ₹ 900, *X*'s share is:
   A. ₹ 400   B. ₹ 350
   C. ₹ 150   D. ₹ 110

2. *X*, *Y* and *Z* invested ₹ 2400, ₹ 3600 and ₹ 4800 in a business. Out of a profit of ₹ 1260, *X*'s share is :
   A. ₹ 280   B. ₹ 420
   C. ₹ 560   D. ₹ 140

3. *A*, *B* and *C* invested in a common business. *A* invested ₹ 5000 for 2 months, *B* invested ₹ 6000 for 3 months and *C* invested ₹ 4000 for 5 months. Out of a profit of ₹ 960, *A*'s share is:
   A. ₹ 360   B. ₹ 200
   C. ₹ 400   D. ₹ 300

4. *A*, *B* and *C* invested in a common business. *A* invested ₹ 10000 for 3 months, *B* invested ₹ 15000 for 4 months and *C* invested ₹ 12000 for 5 months. Out of a profit of ₹ 1020, *A*'s share is :
   A. ₹ 204   B. ₹ 408
   C. ₹ 612   D. ₹ 816

5. *X*, *Y* and *Z* invested in a common business. *X* invested ₹ 4000 for 2 months, *Y* invested ₹ 2500 for 4 months and *Z* invested ₹ 3000 for 6 months. Out of a profit of ₹ 1800, *X*'s share is :
   A. ₹ 400   B. ₹ 500
   C. ₹ 800   D. ₹ 900

6. *X*, *Y* and *Z* invested ₹ 4800, ₹ 7200 and ₹ 9600 in a business. Out of a profit of ₹ 2520, *Z*'s share is:
   A. ₹ 280   B. ₹ 560
   C. ₹ 840   D. ₹ 1120

7. *A*, *B* and *C* invested ₹ 600, ₹ 900 and ₹ 1200 in a business. Out of a profit of ₹ 549, *A*'s share is:
   A. ₹ 61   B. ₹ 122
   C. ₹ 183   D. ₹ 244

8. *A*, *B* and *C* invested in a common business. *A* invested ₹ 2000 for 5 months, *B* invested ₹ 1200 for 6 months and *C* invested ₹ 2500 for 3 months. Out of a profit of ₹ 494, A's share is :
   A. ₹ 144   B. ₹ 200
   C. ₹ 150   D. ₹ 300

9. *X*, *Y* and *Z* invested ₹ 10000, ₹ 7200 and ₹ 7500 in a common business. Out of a profit of ₹ 988, *X*'s share is :
   A. ₹ 400   B. ₹ 288
   C. ₹ 300   D. ₹ 247

71

10. *A*, *B* and *C* invested ₹ 1200, ₹ 1800 and ₹ 2400 in a common business. Out of a profit of ₹ 1098, *A*'s share is :
A. ₹ 244 B. ₹ 586
C. ₹ 488 D. ₹ 366

11. *A* and *B* invested ₹ 30000 and ₹ 34000 in a common business. Out of a profit of ₹ 1600, *A*'s share is :
A. ₹ 800 B. ₹ 750
C. ₹ 850 D. ₹ 900

12. Mohan and Ramesh invested ₹ 8000 and ₹ 1000 respectively in a common business. Out of a profit of ₹ 9630, Mohan's share is:
A. ₹ 3210 B. ₹ 4280
C. ₹ 5350 D. ₹ 6420

13. *X*, *Y* and *Z* invested ₹ 2880, ₹ 3600 and ₹ 1800 in a common business. Out of a profit of ₹ 9600, *X*'s share is :
A. ₹ 3360 B. ₹ 4200
C. ₹ 2100 D. ₹ 6300

14. *A*, *B* and *C* invested ₹ 2400, ₹ 3600 and ₹ 4800 in a common business. Out of a profit of ₹ 981, *A*'s share is :
A. ₹ 109 B. ₹ 218
C. ₹ 327 D. ₹ 436

EXPLANATORY ANSWERS

1. C : *X*'s investment for 1 month = ₹ 6000 × 2 = ₹ 12000
Y's investment for 1 month = ₹ 7000 × 4 = ₹ 28000
Z's investment for 1 month = ₹ 6400 × 5 = ₹ 32000

$$12000 \quad : \quad 28000 \quad : \quad 32000$$
$$3 \quad : \quad 7 \quad : \quad 8$$

Sum of ratio = 3 + 7 + 8 = 18

X's share in the profit = $\dfrac{3}{18} \times 900$ = ₹ 150.

2. A :

$$X \qquad\qquad Y \qquad\qquad Z$$
$$₹\ 2400 \quad : \quad ₹\ 3600 \quad : \quad ₹\ 4800$$
$$2 \quad : \quad 3 \quad : \quad 4$$

Sum of ratio = 2 + 3 + 4 = 9

X's share in the profit = $\dfrac{2}{9} \times 1260$ = ₹ 280.

3. B : *A*'s investment for 1 month = ₹ 5000 × 2 = ₹ 10000
B's investment for 1 month = ₹ 6000 × 3 = ₹ 18000
C's investment for 1 month = ₹ 4000 × 5 = ₹ 20000

$$\text{Ratio} = \quad 10000 \quad : \quad 18000 \quad : \quad 20000$$
$$5 \quad : \quad 9 \quad : \quad 10$$

Sum of ratio = 5 + 9 + 10 = 24

A's share in the profit = $960 \times \dfrac{5}{24}$ = ₹ 200.

4. A : A's investment = ₹ 10000 × 3 = ₹ 30000

B's investment = ₹ 15000 × 4 = ₹ 60000

C's investment = ₹ 12000 × 5 = ₹ 60000

Ratio = 30000 : 60000 : 60000

1 : 2 : 2

Sum of ratio = 1 + 2 + 2 = 5

A's share in the profit = ₹ $1020 \times \dfrac{1}{5}$ = ₹ 204.

5. A : X's investment = ₹ 4000 × 2 = ₹ 8000

Y's investment = ₹ 2500 × 4 = ₹ 10000

Z's investment = ₹ 3000 × 6 = ₹ 18000

$X : Y : Z$ = 8000 : 10000 : 18000

4 : 5 : 9

Sum of ratio = 4 + 5 + 9 = 18.

X's share in the profit = $\dfrac{4}{18} \times 1800$ = ₹ 400.

6. D :

X		Y		Z
4800	:	7200	:	9600
2	:	3	:	4

Sum of ratio = 2 + 3 + 4 = 9

Z's share in the profit = $\dfrac{4}{9} \times 2520$ = ₹ 1120.

7. B :

A		B		C
600	:	900	:	1200
2	:	3	:	4

Sum of ratio = 2 + 3 + 4 = 9

A's share in the profit = $\dfrac{2}{9} \times 549$ = ₹ 122.

8. b : A's investment = ₹ 2000 × 5 = ₹ 10000

B's investment = ₹ 1200 × 6 = ₹ 7200

C's investment = ₹ 2500 × 3 = ₹ 7500

Ratio = 10000 : 7200 : 7500

100 : 72 : 75

Sum of ratio = 100 + 72 + 75 = 247

A's share in the profit = $\dfrac{100}{247} \times 494$ = ₹ 200.

9. A :

	X		Y		Z
	10000	:	7200	:	7500
	100	:	72	:	75

Sum of ratio = 100 + 72 + 75 = 247

X's share in the profit = $\dfrac{100}{247} \times 988$ = ₹ 400.

10. A :

	A		B		C
	1200	:	1800	:	2400
	2	:	3	:	4

Sum of ratio = 2 + 3 + 4 = 9

A's share in the profit = $\dfrac{2}{9} \times 1098$ = ₹ 244.

11. B :

	A		B
	30000	:	34000
	15	:	17

Sum of ratio = 15 + 17 = 32

A's share in the profit = $\dfrac{15}{32} \times 1600$ = ₹ 750.

12. B : Mohan's investment = ₹ 8000

Ramesh's investment = ₹ 10000

Ratio = 8000 : 10000 = 4 : 5

Sum of ratio = 4 + 5 = 9

Mohan's share in the profit = $\dfrac{4}{9} \times$ Rs.9630 = ₹ 4280.

13. A :

	X		Y		Z
	2880	:	3600	:	1800
	8	:	10	:	5

Sum of ratio = 9 + 10 + 5 = 23

X's share in the profit = $\dfrac{8}{23} \times 9660$ = ₹ 3360.

14. B :

	A		B		C
	2400	:	3600	:	4800
	2	:	3	:	4

Sum of ratio = 2 + 3 + 4 = 9

A's share in the profit = $\dfrac{2}{9} \times 981$ = ₹ 218.

———

MIXTURE AND ALLIGATION

1. Rule of Alligation:

$\dfrac{\text{Amount of Cheaper ingredient}}{\text{Amount of Dearer ingredient}}$	$=$	$\dfrac{\text{Cost price of Dearer} - \text{Mean Price}}{\text{Mean Price} - \text{Cost Price of Cheaper}}$

Here cost price of unit quantity of the mixture is called the *Mean Price*. The above rule may be represented schematically as under:

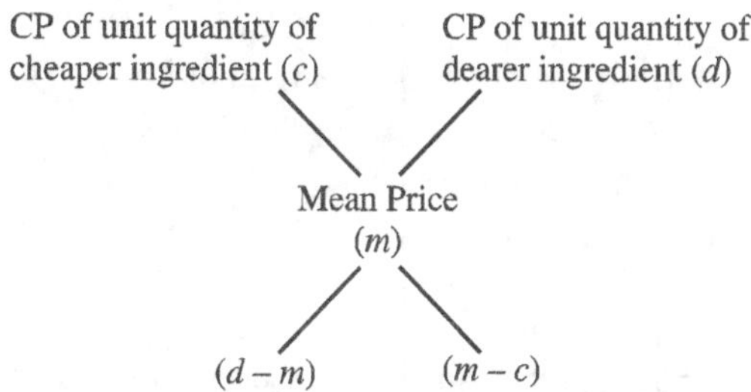

(Cheaper quantity) : (Dearer quantity) = $(d - m) : (m - c)$

This relationship is very helpful in solving problems on mixture involving percentage values, rates, prices, speeds etc.

2. m gm of sugar solution has x % sugar in it. To increase the sugar content in the solution to y %,

quantity of sugar need to be added $= \dfrac{m(y - x)}{100 - y}$

3. A vessel contains x litres of liquid A. y litres are withdrawn and replaced by liquid B. Next y litres of the mixture is withdrawn and again replaced by liquid B.

This operation is repeated n times.

$$\frac{\text{Quantity of liquid A left after } n\text{th operation}}{\text{Whole quantity of liquid A initially present}} = \left(\frac{x - y}{x}\right)^n \text{ or } \left(1 - \frac{y}{x}\right)^n$$

EXERCISE

1. Two vessels A and B contain mixture of milk and water in the ratio 4 : 1 and 9 : 11 respectively. They are mixed in the ratio of 3 : 2. Find the ratio of milk : water in the resulting mixture.
   A. 34 : 16   B. 33 : 17
   C. 16 : 34   D. 17 : 33

2. In what ratio must water be added to spirit to gain 25% by selling it at cost price?
   A. 1 : 4   B. 4 : 1
   C. 3 : 4   D. 4 : 3

3. A person has ₹ 5000. He invests a part of it at 3% per annum and the remainder at 8% per annum simple interest. His total income in 3 years is ₹ 750. Find the sum invested at different rates of interest.
   A. ₹ 2000 and ₹ 3000
   B. ₹ 2500 and ₹ 2500
   C. ₹ 3000 and ₹ 2000
   D. ₹ 2750 and ₹ 2250

4. A person covers a distance of 100 kms in 10 hours, partly by walking at 7 km/hr and rest by running at 12 km/hr. Find the distance covered in each part.
   A. 48 kms   B. 72 kms
   C. 108 kms   D. 124 kms

5. A vessel contains 80 litres of milk. 16 litres of milk was taken out of the vessel and replaced by water. Then 16 litres of mixture was withdrawn and again replaced by water. The operation was repeated for third time. How much milk is now left in the vessel?
   A. 96.40 litres
   B. 50.36 litres
   C. 40.96 litres
   D. 32.76 litres

6. If 4 kg of an alloy made of 1/4th iron and rest is mixed with 6 kg of another alloy made of 2/3rd iron and rest tin, find the ratio of iron to tin in the resultant mixture.
   A. 1 : 1   B. 2 : 1
   C. 1 : 2   D. 3 : 2

7. In a courtyard there are many chickens and goats. If heads are counted, it comes to 100 but when legs are counted, it comes to 320. Find the number of chickens and goats in the courtyard.
   A. 20, 50   B. 30, 70
   C. 40, 60   D. 50, 50

8. A container is full of milk. One-third of milk is taken out of it and replaced by same quantity of water. Then again one-third of the mixture is taken out of it and replaced by the same quantity of water. The process is repeated 4 times. If 16 litres of milk is left in the container at the end of 4th operation, find the capacity of the container.
   A. 76 litres   B. 81 litres
   C. 82 litres   D. 85 litres

9. The cost of type-I rice is ₹ 15 per kg and type-II is ₹ 20 per kg. If both type I and type II are mixed in the ratio of 2 : 3, then find the price per kg of the mixed variety.
A. ₹ 19.50
B. ₹ 19
C. ₹ 18.50
D. ₹ 18

10. A cask full of wine from which 8 litres are drawn and is then filled with water. This operation is performed three more times. The ratio of quantity of wine left in the cask to that of the water is 16 : 81. How much wine did the cask hold originally?
A. 42 litres   B. 32 litres
C. 24 litres   D. 18 litres

EXPLANATORY ANSWERS

1. B: Fraction is

	Milk	Water
A :	$\dfrac{4}{5}$	$\dfrac{1}{5}$
B :	$\dfrac{9}{20}$	$\dfrac{11}{20}$

$$(3A + 2B) = A \text{ and } B : \left(\frac{12}{5}+\frac{9}{10}\right)\ \left(\frac{3}{5}+\frac{11}{10}\right)$$

$$\frac{33}{10} \qquad \frac{17}{10}$$

So, Ratio of milk : water in the resulting mixture = 33 : 17.

2. A: Let cost price of spirit be Re. 1 per litre.

Then SP of mixture = Re. 1 per litre

Gain = 25%

So,   CP of mixture $= 1 \times \dfrac{100}{125} = $ Re. $\dfrac{4}{5}$

We assume that CP of water is zero.

Using alligation rule on cost price,

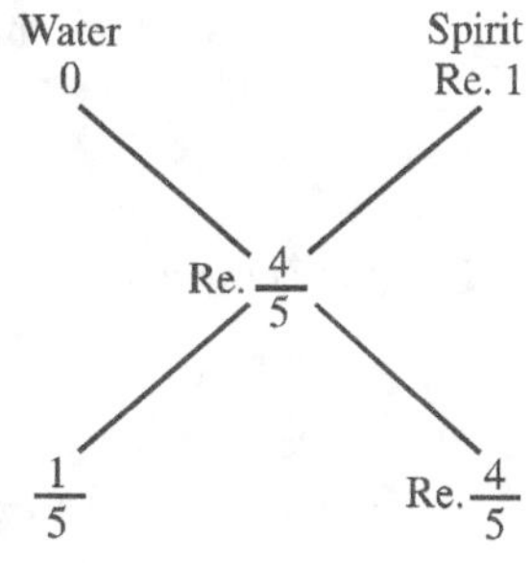

Water should be mixed to spirit in the ratio $\dfrac{1}{5}$: $\dfrac{4}{5}$ or 1 : 4.

3. C: Average rate of interest $= \dfrac{100 \times 750}{5000 \times 3} = 5\%$ per annum

Investment at 3% per annum

$= \dfrac{3}{3+2} \times 5000 = ₹\,3000$

Investment at 8% per annum

$= \dfrac{2}{3+2} \times 5000 = ₹\,2000.$

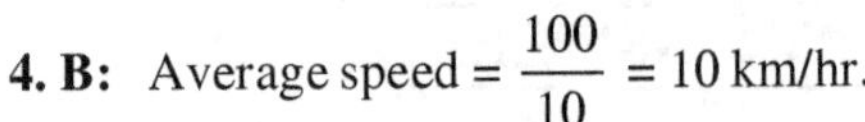

4. B: Average speed $= \dfrac{100}{10} = 10$ km/hr.

Ratio of time taken at 7 km/hr to 12 km/hr $= 2:3$

Time taken at 7 km/hr $= \dfrac{2}{2+3} \times 10 = 4$ hrs.

Distance covered at 7 km/hr $= 7 \times 4 = 28$ km.

Distance covered at 12 km/hr $= 100 - 28 = 72$ km.

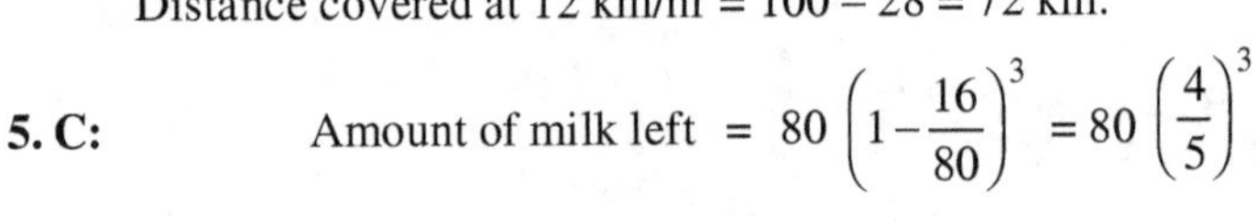

5. C: Amount of milk left $= 80 \left(1 - \dfrac{16}{80}\right)^3 = 80 \left(\dfrac{4}{5}\right)^3$

$$80 \times \dfrac{64}{125} = 40.96 \text{ litres.}$$

6. A: Total quantity of iron $= 4\left(\dfrac{1}{4}\right) + 6\left(\dfrac{2}{3}\right) = 1 + 4 = 5$ kg.

Total quantity of tin $= (4+6) - 5$

$= 5$ kg.

In the resultant mixture, iron : tin $= 5:5$ or $1:1$.

7. C: Average no. of legs per head

$= \dfrac{320}{100} = \dfrac{16}{5}$

or, $\qquad 3:2$

No. of goats $= \dfrac{3}{3+2} \times 100 = 60$

No. of chickens $= 100 - 60 = 40.$

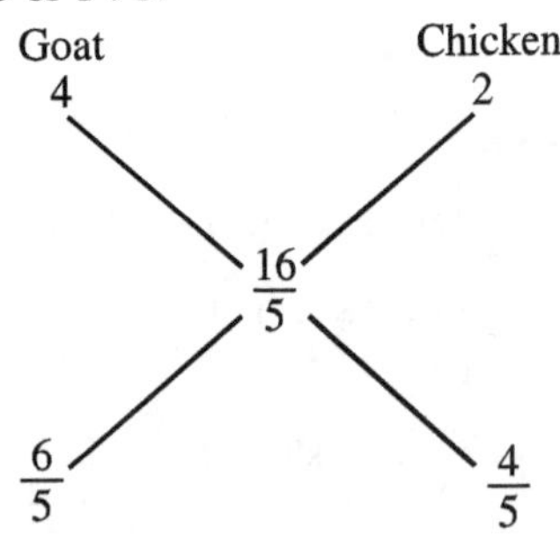

8. B: Let capacity of the container be x litre; then

$$x(1 - 1/3)^4 = 16 \Rightarrow x\left(\frac{2}{3}\right)^4 = 16 \Rightarrow x \times \frac{16}{81} = 16 \quad \therefore x = 81 \text{ litres}$$

9. D: Let the price per kg of mixed variety be ₹ x; then

By the rule of alligation,

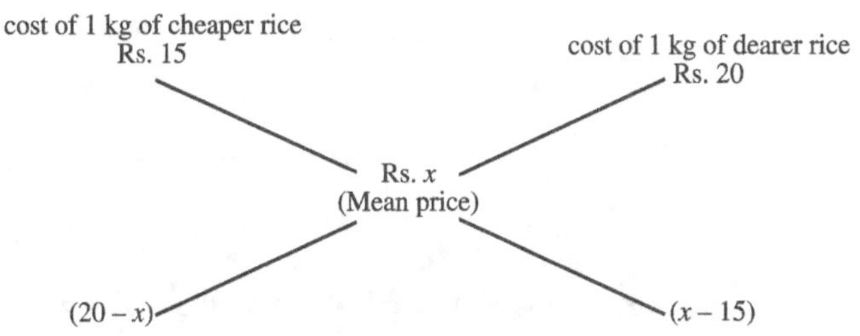

Now, $\dfrac{20-x}{x-15} = \dfrac{2}{3} \qquad \Rightarrow 60 - 3x = 2x - 30 \qquad \Rightarrow 5x = 90 \therefore x = ₹ \ 18$

10. C: Let x litres wine cask hold originally, then

$$\frac{x\left(1-\dfrac{8}{x}\right)^4}{x} = \frac{16}{81} \Rightarrow \left(1-\frac{8}{x}\right)^4 = \left(\frac{2}{3}\right)^4 \Rightarrow \left(1-\frac{8}{x}\right) = \frac{2}{3}$$

$$\Rightarrow \frac{8}{x} = 1 - \frac{2}{3} \Rightarrow \frac{8}{x} = \frac{1}{3} \quad \therefore x = 24 \text{ litres}$$

14

MENSURATION

Triangle

1. Perimeter = 3 × side (Equilateral triangle)

2. Area = $\dfrac{1}{2} \times$ base $\times$ height , or

$$\text{Area} = \sqrt{s(s-a)(s-b)(s-c)}$$

where a, b, c, are the lengths of the sides of triangle and $s = \dfrac{a+b+c}{2}$

Equilateral Triangle : All three sides are equal in length and all three angles are equal to 60°.

$$\text{Area} = \frac{\sqrt{3}}{4} \times (\text{Side})^2$$

Isosceles Triangle : Two sides are equal in lengths.

1. Area = $\dfrac{b}{4}\sqrt{4a^2 - b^2}$

   where a = lengths of equal sides $\qquad$ b = length of unequal side

2. In an isosceles right triangle,

   (a) Hypotenuse = $\sqrt{2} \times$ congruent side (a)

   (b) Area = $\dfrac{1}{2} \times a^2$

   (c) Perimeter = $\sqrt{2} \times a\left(\sqrt{2} + 1\right)$

Rectangle :

1. Area = length(l) × breadth(b)
2. Perimeter = 2(l + b)
3. Diagonal = $\sqrt{l^2 + b^2}$

80

Square :
1. Area = (Side)^2
2. Perimeter = 4 × side
3. Diagonal = side × $\sqrt{2}$

Parallelogram: Area = Base × Height.

Trapezium : Area = $\dfrac{1}{2}$ × Height × (Sum of parallel sides). Here, height is the distance between the two parallel sides.

Rhombus :

1. Area = $\dfrac{1}{2}$ × Product of diagonals

2. Side = $\sqrt{\left(\dfrac{d_1}{2}\right)^2 + \left(\dfrac{d_2}{2}\right)^2}$, where d_1 and d_2 are diagonals

3. Perimeter = 4 × side

Quadrilateral : Area = $\dfrac{1}{2}$ × One diagonal × (Sum of perpendicular to it from the opposite vertices) = $\dfrac{1}{2} \times d \times (a+b)$

Circle :
1. Diameter = 2 × Radius

2. Area = $\pi r^2 = \dfrac{\pi}{4} d^2$; where d = diameter = $\sqrt{\dfrac{4A}{\pi}}$

3. Circumference = $2\pi r = \pi d$

4. Radius = $\dfrac{\text{Circumference}}{2\pi} = \dfrac{\sqrt{\text{Area}}}{\pi}$

5. Length of an Arc = $\dfrac{\theta}{360°} \times 2\pi r$

6. Area of sector = $\dfrac{\theta}{360°} \times \pi r^2 = \dfrac{1}{2} \times \text{Arc} \times r$

Polygon :
1. Interior angle + Exterior angle = 180°

2. Each interior angle = $\left(\dfrac{2n-4}{n}\right) \times 90°$

where n = number of sides

3. Sum of Exterior angles = 360°
4. Perimeter = Number of sides × Length of side.
5. For an equilateral triangle of side 'a'

(a) radius of inscribed circle $=\dfrac{a}{2\sqrt{3}}$

and side of the triangle = $2\sqrt{3}r$,

(b) radius of circumcircle $=\dfrac{a}{\sqrt{3}}$

6. Area of regular polygon $=\dfrac{1}{2}$(No. of sides) (Radius of the inscribed circle)

7. Area of regular hexagon $=\dfrac{3\sqrt{3}}{2}(\text{side})^{2}=2.598\ (\text{side})^{2}$

8. Area of a regular octagon $=2\left(\sqrt{2}+1\right)(\text{side})^{2}=4.828\ (\text{side})^{2}$

9. Area of quadrilateral, A $=\sqrt{s(s-a)(s-b)(s-c)(s-d)}$

where, $s=\dfrac{a+b+c+d}{2}$

VOLUME AND SURFACE AREA OF SOLIDS

Cuboid : A cuboid has six faces, each one a ractangle. It has 12 edges. For example, a rectangular brick.

Let Length = l, Breadth = b and Height = h, then,

1. Volume = (Length × Breadth × Height)
2. Whole Surface Area = $2(lb + bh + lh)$
3. Diagonal = $\sqrt{l^{2}+b^{2}+h^{2}}$
4. Area of 4 walls of a room = $2 \times h\ (l + b)$

Cube : In a cube, Length = Breadth = Height

1. Volume = $(l)^{3}$
2. Length = $\sqrt[3]{\text{Volume}}$
3. Whole Surface Area = $6\ l^{2}$
4. Diagonal = $l \times \sqrt{3}$
5. Lateral Surface Area = $4\ l^{2}$

Cylinder :

1. Volume $= \pi r^2 h$
2. Curved Surface Area $= 2\pi rh$
3. Total Surface Area $= 2\pi r(r + h)$
   where r = radius, h = height

Spherical Cell :

1. Volume $= \dfrac{4}{3}\pi\left(R^3 - r^3\right)$
2. Total Surface Area$= 4\pi(R^2 - r^2)$
   where   R = Outer radius
               r = Inner radius

Sphere :

1. Volume $= \dfrac{4}{3}\pi r^3$
2. Surface Area $= 4\pi r^2$

Semi-sphere :

1. Volume $= \dfrac{2}{3}\pi r^3$
2. Curved surface area $= 2\pi r^2$
3. Total surface area $= 3\pi r^2$

Cone :

1. Slant height $(l) = \sqrt{r^2 + h^2}$
2. Volume $= \dfrac{1}{3}\pi r^2 h$
3. Curved surface area $= \pi r l$
4. Total surface area $= \pi r\,(l + r)$
5. If the depth of the frustum of a cone be k and the radii of its ends are r_1 and r_2, then

   (i) Slant height of the frustum of a cone
   $$= \sqrt{k^2 + (r_1 - r_2)^2}$$

   (ii) Curved surface of the frustum $= \pi(r_1 + r_2)\,l.$

   (iii) Volume $= \dfrac{\pi k}{3}\left(r_1^2 + r_1 r_2 + r_2^2\right)$

EXERCISE

1. What is the area of a circle whose radius is equal to the side of a square whose perimeter is 112 metres?
   A. 176 sq m
   B. 2504 sq m
   C. 284 sq m
   D. None of these

2. The sum of the circumference of a circle and the perimeter of a rectangle is 132 cm. The area of the rectangle is 112 sq cm and breadth of the rectangle is 8 cms. What is the area of the circle?
   A. 616 sq cm
   B. 540 sq cm
   C. 396 sq cm
   D. Cannot be determined

3. The total area of a circle and a rectangle is equal to 1166 sq cm. The diameter of the circle is 28 cm. What is the sum of the circumference of the circle and the perimeter of the rectangle if the length of the rectangle is 25 cm?
   A. 186 cm
   B. 182 cm
   C. 184 cm
   D. Cannot be determined

4. What would be the cost of laying a carpet on a floor which has its length and breadth in the respective ratio of 32 : 21 and where its perimeter is 212 feet, if the cost per square foot of laying the carpet is ₹ 2.5?
   A. ₹ 6,720
   B. ₹ 5,420
   C. ₹ 7,390
   D. None of these

5. A triangle's perimeter is 25 cms. Which of the following may be true or is a possibility?
   (*a*) The sides are 7 cms., 7 cms. and 11 cms.
   (*b*) It is an equilateral triangle.
   (*c*) The value of sides can be in integer only.
   A. Only (*a*)
   B. Only (*a*) and (*b*)
   C. Only (*c*)
   D. Only (*b*) and (*c*)

6. What will be the cost of building a fence around a circular field with area equal to 18,634 sq. metres; if the cost of building the fence per metre is ₹ 365?
   A. ₹ 1,76,660   B. ₹ 68,01,410
   C. ₹ 2,43,250   D. ₹ 56,60,220

7. The area of a square is 196 sq cms whose side is half the radius of a circle. The circumference of the circle is equal to breadth of a rectangle. If perimeter of the rectangle is 712 cm. What is the length of the rectangle?
   A. 196 cm   B. 186 cm
   C. 180 cm   D. 190 cm

8. The circumference of a circular plot is 484 metres Find out the area of that circular plot—
   A. 15246 metre^2
   B. 18634 metre^2
   C. 20328 metre^2
   D. 13552 metre^2

9. A room measures 22 dm by 16 dm. I wish to buy a carpet for the floor leaving an uncarpeted margin 2 dm wide along each of the shorter sides of the room and a margin 0.5 dm wide along each of the longer sides of the room. If the price of the carpet is ₹ 500 per sq. metre, what is the cost of the whole carpet required?

A. ₹ 500 B. ₹ 2700
C. ₹ 2000 D. ₹ 1350

10. A paper is in the form of a rectangle ABCD where AB = 22 cm and BC = 14 cm. A semi-circular portion with segment BC as a diameter is cut off. Find the area of remaining paper.

A. 231 cm^2 B. 213 cm^2
C. 321 cm^2 D. 200 cm^2

11. How many plants can be put in a circular flower bed whose circumference is 880 dm allowing 35 dm^2 for each plant?

A. 880 B. 1760
C. 1000 D. 1500

12. An athletic track 14 m wide consists of two straight sections 120 m long joining semi-circular ends whose inner radius is 35 m. Calculate the area of the track :

A. 5670 m^2 B. 7065 m^2
C. 5670 m^2 D. 7056 m^2

13. A square park has each side of 100 m. At each corner of the park, there is a flower bed in the form of a quadrant of radius 14 m. Then the area of the remaining part of the park is :

A. 9384 m^2 B. 9834 m^2
C. 9000 m^2 D. 8900 m^2

14. The length of minute hand of a clock is 14 cm. Then the area swept by the minute hand in one minute.

A. 10 m^2 B. 12.26 m^2
C. 20.26 m^2 D. 10.26 m^2

15. Find the area of ring between two concentric circles whose circumference are 77 cm and 55 cm.

A. 770 cm^2 B. 321 cm^2
C. 231 cm^2 D. 230 cm^2

16. A rectangle water reservoir is 10.8 metres long and 3.75 metres wide at base. Water flows into it at the rate of 18 m per sec. through the pipe having the cross section 7.5 cm × 4.5 cm. Then the height to which the water will rise in the reservoir in 30 minutes is :

A. 7.2 m B. 2.7 m
C. 3.7 m D. 7.3 m

17. A rectangular sheet of 44 cm × 18 cm is rolled along its length and a cylinder is formed. Then the volume of cylinder is :

A. 7227 cm^2 B. 7272 cm^2
C. 2727 cm^2 D. 2772 cm^2

18. How many metres of cloth 5 metre wide will be required to make a conical tent, the radius of whose base is 7 metre and height is 24 metre?

A. 100 m B. 110 m
C. 550 m D. 55 m

19. The surface area of a sphere whose volume is 4851 cubic metres is :
A. 1386 m^2 B. 1380 m^2
C. 1286 m^2 D. 3186 m^2

20. A hollow sphere of external and internal diameter 4 cm and 2 cm respectively, is melted into a cone of base diameter 8 cm. Then the height of the cone is :
A. 12 cm   B. 14 cm
C. 20 cm   D. 24 cm

21. The diamensions of a metallic rod are 19 cm × 4 cm × 2 cm and each side of a metallic cube is 4 cm. Both are melted and recast into a new cube. Find the length of edge of cube so formed.
A. 4 cm   B. 5 cm
C. 6 cm   D. 7 cm

22. An agricultural field is in the form of a rectangle of length 35 metres and width 15.4 metres. A pit 5.5 metres long, 4 metres wide and 2.5 metres deep is dug in the corner of the field and the earth taken out of the pit is spread uniformly over the remaining area of the field. The extent to which the level of the field has been raised is :
A. 16.6 cm   B. 10.6 cm
C. 16.1 cm   D. 6.10 cm

23. The side of a square exceeds the side of the another square by 4 cm and the sum of areas of two squares is 400 sq. cm. Find the dimensions of the square.

A. 8 cm, 12 cm
B. 10 cm, 14 cm
C. 12 cm, 16 cm
D. 14 cm, 18 cm

24. The cost of levelling a rectangular field at the rate of 85 paise per square metre is ₹ 624.75. Then the perimeter of the field if its sides are in the ratio of 5 : 3 is :
A. 35 m   B. 21 m
C. 112 m   D. 49 m

25. The diagonal of a rectangular field is 15 m and its area is 108 sq. m. What will be the total expenditure in fencing the field at the rate of ₹ 5 per metre?
A. ₹ 441   B. ₹ 420
C. ₹ 210   D. ₹ 120

26. The minute hand of a clock is 10 cm long. The area of the face of the clock described by the minute hand between 9 AM and 9.35 AM is :
A. 140 cm^2 B. 183.3 cm^2
C. 180 cm^2 D. 175.3 cm^2

27. The length of a rectangular plot is 60% more than its breadth. If the difference between the length and the breadth of that rectangle is 24 cm, what is the area of that rectangle?
A. 2400 sq. cm
B. 2480 sq. cm
C. 2560 sq. cm
D. Data inadequate

28. The area of a rectangle is 460 square metres. If the length is 15% more than the breadth, what is the breadth of the rectangular field?

A. 15 metres
B. 26 metres
C. 34.5 metres
D. None of these

29. The ratio between the length and the breadth of a rectangular field is 3 : 2. If only the length is increased by 5 metres, the new area of the field will be 2600 sq. metres. What is the breadth of the rectangular field?

A. 40 metres
B. 60 metres
C. 65 metres
D. Cannot be determined

30. If the length and breadth of a rectangular plot be increased by 50% and 20% respectively, then how many times will its area be increased?

A. $1\frac{1}{3}$
B. 2
C. $3\frac{2}{5}$
D. None of these

31. The length of a rectangle is decreased by $r\%$, and the breadth is increased by $(r + 5)\%$. Find r, if the area of the rectangle is unaltered.

A. 5
B. 8
C. 10
D. 20

32. The length and breadth of the floor of the room are 20 feet and 10 feet respectively. Square tiles of 2 feet length of different colours are to be laid on the floor. Black tiles are laid in the first row on all sides. If white tiles are laid in the one-third of the remaining and blue tiles in the rest, how many blue tiles will be there?

A. 16
B. 24
C. 32
D. 48

33. A park square in shape has a 3 metre wide road inside it running along its sides. The area occupied by the road is 1764 square metres. What is the perimeter along the outer edge of the road?

A. 576 metres
B. 600 metres
C. 640 metres
D. Data inadequate

34. What will be the length of the diagonal of that square plot whose area is equal to the area of a rectangular plot of length 45 metres and breadth 40 metres?

A. 42.5 metres
B. 60 metres
C. 75 metres
D. Data inadequate

35. The length of one pair of opposite sides of a square is increased by 5 cm on each side; the ratio of the length and the breadth of the newly formed rectangle becomes 3 : 2. What is the area of the original square?

A. 25 sq. cm
B. 81 sq. cm
C. 100 sq. cm
D. 225 sq. cm

36. What will be the ratio between the area of a rectangle and the area of a triangle with one of the sides of the rectangle as base and a vertex on the opposite side of the rectangle?

A. 1 : 2
B. 2 : 1
C. 3 : 1
D. None of these

37. A cow is tethered in the middle of a field with a 14 feet long rope. If the cow grazes 100 sq. ft. per day, then approximately what time will be taken by the cow to graze the whole field?

A. 2 days   B. 6 days
C. 18 days   D. 24 days

38. A circular ground whose diameter is 35 metres, has a 1.4 m broad garden around it. What is the area of the garden in square metres?

A. 160.16
B. 176.16
C. 196.16
D. None of these

39. The cost of the paint is ₹ 36.50 per kg. If 1 kg of paint covers 16 square feet, how much will it cost to paint outside of a cube having 8 feet each side?

A. ₹ 692   B. ₹ 768
C. ₹ 876   D. ₹ 972

40. The capacity of a cylindrical tank is 246.4 litres. If the height is 4 metres, what is the diameter of the base?

A. 1.4 m   B. 2.8 m
C. 14 m   D. 28 m

$$\boxed{\textbf{EXPLANATORY ANSWERS}}$$

1. D: $\because$ Radius of the circle $= \dfrac{112}{4} = 28$ m

$\therefore$ Area of the circle $= \dfrac{22}{7} \times 28 \times 28 = 2464$ m^2.

2. A: Length of the rectangle $= \dfrac{112}{8} = 14$ cm.

$\therefore$ Perimeter of the rectangle $= 2(14 + 8) = 44$ cm.
$\therefore$ Circumference of the circle $= 132 - 44 = 88$ cm.

$\therefore \qquad r = \dfrac{88 \times 7}{2 \times 22} = 14$ cm

$\therefore \quad$ Area of the circle $= \dfrac{22}{7} \times 14 \times 14 = 616$ sq cm.

3. B: From question—

∵ Diameter of the circle = 28 cm.

$$\Rightarrow \text{Area of the circle} = \frac{22}{7} \times (14)^2 = 616 \text{ cm}^2$$

∴ Area of the rectangle = 1166 − 616 = 550 cm²

$$\Rightarrow \text{Breadth of the rectangle} = \frac{550}{25} = 22 \text{ cm.}$$

∴ Required sum $= 2 \times \dfrac{22}{7} \times (14) + 2(25 + 22)$

$$= 88 + 94 = 182 \text{ cm.}$$

4. A: Length of the floor $= \dfrac{212 \times 32}{2 \times (32 + 21)} = 64$ ft.

and breadth the floor $= \dfrac{64 \times 21}{32} = 42$ ft.

∴ Area of the floor = 64 × 42 = 2688 sq. ft.

∴ Reqd. cost = ₹ 2688 × 2.5 = ₹ 6720.

5. A: Only statement A may be true or possibility.

6. A: Area of the circular field = 18634 m²

∴ $\pi r^2 = 18634$

∴ $r^2 = 18634 \times \dfrac{7}{22} = 5929$

∴ $r = 77$ m

∴ Length of the fence $= 2 \times \dfrac{22}{7} \times 77 = 484$ m

∴ Total cost = 484 × 365 = ₹ 176660.

7. C: One side of the square $= \sqrt{196} = 14$ cm

∴ Radius of the circle = 28 cm

∴ Circumference of the circle $= 2 \times \dfrac{22}{7} \times 28 = 176$ cm

∴ Breadth of the rectangle = 176 cm

∴ Length of the rectangle $= \dfrac{712}{2} - 176 = 356 - 176 = 180$ cm.

8. B: Let r be the radius of the circular plot then from problem,

$\because$ The circumference of the circular plot = 484 m

$\Rightarrow \qquad 2\pi r = 484$

$$r = 484 \times \frac{7}{22} \times \frac{1}{2} = 77 \text{ metres}$$

$\therefore$ Area of the circular plot $= \pi r^2 = \dfrac{22}{7} \times (77)^2 = 18634 \text{ m}^2.$

9. D.

10. A: Area of the whole paper ABCD $= 22 \times 14 = 308 \text{ cm}^2$

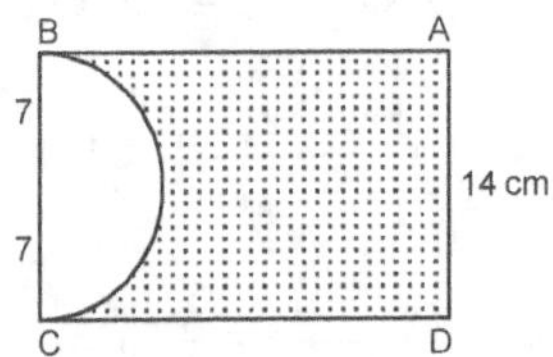

Radius of the semi-circle $= \dfrac{1}{2} \times 14$ cm = 7 cm

$\therefore$ Area of the semi-circle $= \dfrac{1}{2}\pi r^2 = \dfrac{1}{2} \times \dfrac{22}{7} \times 7 \times 7 = 77 \text{ cm}^2$

$\therefore$ Area of the remaining part of the paper

$$= 308 \text{ cm}^2 - 77 \text{ cm}^2 = 231 \text{ cm}^2.$$

11. B: Circumference of flower bed = 880 dm

$\Rightarrow \qquad 2\pi r = 880$ dm

$$\Rightarrow \qquad r = \frac{880}{2\pi} \text{ dm} = \frac{880 \times 7}{2 \times 22} = 140 \text{ dm}$$

Area of flower bed $= \pi r^2 = \dfrac{22}{7} \times (140)^2 \text{ dm}^2$

$\therefore$ Required number of plants

$$= \frac{\dfrac{22}{7} \times 140 \times 140}{35} \text{ dm}^2$$

$$= \frac{22}{7} \times \frac{140 \times 140}{35} = 1760.$$

12. D.

13. A: Area of each quadrant $= \dfrac{\theta}{360} \times \pi r^2$

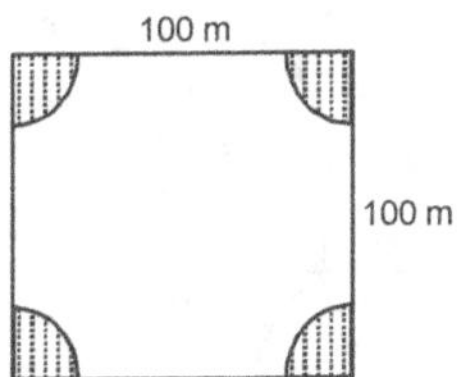

$$= \dfrac{90}{360} \times \dfrac{22}{7} \times 14 \times 14 \ \text{m}^2 = 154 \ \text{m}^2$$

$\therefore$ Area of 4 quadrants $= 154 \times 4 \ \text{m}^2 = 616 \ \text{m}^2$

Area of park $= (100)^2 = 10{,}000 \ \text{m}^2$

Hence area of the remaining part of the park

$$= 10{,}000 - 616 = 9{,}384 \ \text{m}^2.$$

14. D: Length of minute hand of clock $= r = 14 \ \text{cm}$

Central angle covered in 1 minute $= \dfrac{360}{60} = 6°$

$\therefore$ Area swept in one minute $=$ Area of sector with central angle $6°$

$$= \dfrac{\theta}{360} \times \pi r^2 \ = \ \dfrac{6}{360} \times \dfrac{22}{7} \times 14 \times 14$$

$$= \dfrac{154}{15} \ = 10.26 \ \text{cm}^2.$$

15. C: Let R be the radius of outer circle and r the radius of inner circle.

Circumference of outer circle $= 77 \ \text{cm}$

$$\therefore \ 2\pi R = 77 \Rightarrow R = \dfrac{77}{2\pi} = \dfrac{77 \times 7}{2 \times 22} = \dfrac{49}{4} \ \text{cm}$$

Circumference of inner circle $= 55 \ \text{cm}$

$$\therefore \qquad 2\pi r = 55 \qquad \Rightarrow r = \dfrac{55}{2\pi} = \dfrac{55 \times 7}{2 \times 22} = \dfrac{35}{4} \ \text{cm}$$

$$\therefore \qquad \text{Area of ring} = \pi(R^2 - r^2)$$

$$= \dfrac{22}{7} \times \left(\dfrac{49}{4} + \dfrac{35}{4}\right)\left(\dfrac{49}{4} - \dfrac{35}{4}\right) = 231 \ \text{cm}^2$$

16. B: Volume of water that flows in one second
$$= (18 \times 0.075 \times 0.045) \text{ m}^3$$
Volume of water that flows in 30 minutes
$$= 18 \times 0.075 \times 0.045 \times 30 \times 60$$
$$= 109.35 \text{ m}^3.$$
Area of the base of the reservoir $= 10.8 \times 3.75 \text{ m}^2$

$\therefore$ Height of water $= \dfrac{109.35}{10.8 \times 3.75} = 2.7$ metres.

17. D: Let r cm be the radius of the base and h cm be the height.
Then, $h = 18$ cm.
Now, circumference of the base = Length of the sheed
$\Rightarrow$ Circumference $= 44$ cm
$\Rightarrow$ $2\pi r = 44$
$\Rightarrow$ $2 \times \dfrac{22}{7} \times r = 44$
$\Rightarrow$ $r = 7$ cm
Volume of the cylinder $= \pi r^2 h$ cm^3
$$= \dfrac{22}{7} \times (7)^2 \times 18 \text{ cm}^3$$
$$= 2772 \text{ cm}^3$$

18. B: Slant height, $l = \sqrt{r^2 + h^2}$
$$= \sqrt{7^2 + 24^2} = 25 \text{ metres}$$
Area of curved surface of cone $= \pi r l$
$$= \dfrac{22}{7} \times 7 \times 25 = 550 \text{ m}^2$$
$\therefore$ Area of the cloth required $= 550 \text{ m}^2$

$\therefore$ Length of the cloth $= \dfrac{550}{5} = 110$ metres.

19. A.
20. B.

21. C: Volume of the metallic rod $= 19 \times 4 \times 2 = 152$ cu.cm.
Volume of the cube $= 4^3 = 64$ cu. cm.

Total volume of both after melting them
$$= 152 + 64 = 216 \text{ cu.cm.}$$
$\therefore$ Volume of new cube $= 216$ cu. cm.
$\Rightarrow \qquad$ Side $= 6$ cm.

22. B.

23. C: Let S_1 and S_2 be the two squares. Let the side of the square S_1 be x cm. Then the side of the square $S_2 = (x + 4)$ cm.

$\therefore \qquad$ Area of square $S_1 = x^2$

and, $\qquad$ Area of square $S_2 = (x + 4)^2$

$\therefore$ From question,

$\Rightarrow \qquad x^2 + (x + 4)^2 = 400$

Solving the equation,

$\Rightarrow \qquad x = -16 \text{ and } 12$

But x cannot be negative

$\therefore \qquad$ Side of the square $S_1 = 12$ cm

$\therefore \qquad$ that of square $S_2 = x + 4 = 12 + 4 = 16$ cm.

24. C: $\qquad$ Area of the field $= \left(\dfrac{\text{Total cost}}{\text{Rate/metre}^2} \right)$

$$= \dfrac{624.75}{0.85} = 735 \text{ sq. metres}$$

Let the length and breadth of the field be $5x$ and $3x$ metres respectively. Then, its area $= 5x \times 3x = 15x^2$ sq. metres

$\therefore \qquad 15x^2 = 735$

$\Rightarrow \qquad x^2 = \dfrac{735}{15} = 49$

$\Rightarrow \qquad x = 7$

$\therefore \qquad$ Length $= 5x = 5 \times 7 = 35$ metres

and $\qquad$ breadth $= 3x = 3 \times 7 = 21$ metres

$\therefore \qquad$ Perimeter $= 2 (35 + 21) = 112$ metres.

25. C.

26. B: Angle described by minute hand in 60 minutes $= 360°$

Angle described by minute hand in 35 minutes $= \dfrac{360}{60} \times 35 = 210°$

$\therefore$ The required area swept by the minute hand = Area of sector $r = 10$ cm

and, $\qquad \theta = 210°$

$$= \frac{22}{7} \times 10 \times 10 \times \frac{210}{360}$$

$$= 183.3 \text{ cm}^2.$$

27. C: Let breadth = x cm. Then, length = $\left(\frac{160}{100}x\right)$ cm = $\frac{8}{5}x$ cm.

So, $\frac{8}{5}x - x = 24 \quad \Rightarrow \quad \frac{3}{5}x = 24$

$\Rightarrow \quad x = \left(\frac{24 \times 5}{3}\right) = 40.$

$\therefore$ Length = 64 cm, Breadth = 40 cm.

Area = (64×40) cm^2 = 2560 cm^2.

28. D: Let breadth = x metres. Then, length = $\left(\frac{115x}{100}\right)$ metres.

$$\therefore \quad x \times \frac{115x}{100} = 460 \quad \Rightarrow \quad x^2 = \left(\frac{460 \times 100}{115}\right) = 400$$

$\Rightarrow \quad x = 20.$

29. A: Let length = $(3x)$ metres and breadth = $(2x)$ metres.

Then, $\quad (3x + 5) \times 2x = 2600$

$\Rightarrow \quad 6x^2 + 10x - 2600 = 0$

$\Rightarrow \quad 3x^2 + 5x - 1300 = 0$

$\Rightarrow \quad (3x + 65)(x - 20) = 0$

$\Rightarrow \qquad\qquad\qquad x = 20.$

$\therefore \qquad$ Breadth = $2x$ = 40 m.

30. D:

31. D: Let original length = x and original breadth = y.

Then, original area = xy.

$$\text{New area} = \left[\frac{(100 - r)}{100} \times x\right]\left[\frac{(105 + r)}{100} \times y\right]$$

$$= \left[\left(\frac{10500 - 5r - r^2}{10000}\right)xy\right]$$

$$\therefore \left(\frac{10500 - 5r - r^2}{10000} \right) xy = xy \quad \Rightarrow \quad r^2 + 5r - 500 = 0$$

$$\Rightarrow \quad (r + 25)(r - 20) = 0 \quad \Rightarrow \quad r = 20.$$

32. A: Area left after laying black tiles = $[(20 - 4) \times (10 - 4)$ sq. ft = 96 sq. ft.

Area under white tiles = $\left(\frac{1}{3} \times 96 \right)$ sq. ft = 32 sq. ft

Area under blue tiles = $(96 - 32)$ sq. ft = 64 sq. ft

Number of blue tiles = $\dfrac{64}{(2 \times 2)}$ = 16.

33. B: Let the length of the outer edge be x metres. Then, length of the inner edge = $(x - 6)$ m.

$$\therefore \qquad x^2 - (x - 6)^2 = 1764$$
$$\Rightarrow \quad x^2 - (x^2 - 12x + 36) = 1764$$
$$\Rightarrow \qquad\qquad 12x = 1800$$
$$\therefore \qquad\qquad x = 150.$$
$$\therefore \qquad \text{Required perimeter} = (4x) \text{ m} = (4 \times 150) \text{ m}$$
$$= 600 \text{ m}.$$

34. B: Area = (45×40) m^2 $\quad \Rightarrow \quad \dfrac{1}{2} \times (\text{diagonal})^2 = 1800$

$\Rightarrow \quad$ diagonal = 60 m.

35. C: Let original length of each side = x cm.

Then, its area = (x^2) cm^2.

Length of rectangle formed = $(x + 5)$ cm and its breadth = x cm.

$$\therefore \quad \frac{x+5}{x} = \frac{3}{2} \quad \Rightarrow \quad 2x + 10 = 3x \quad \Rightarrow \quad x = 10.$$

$\therefore$ Original length of each side = 10 cm and its area = 100 cm^2.

36. B: Area of rectangle = lb sq. units.

Area of the triangle = $\dfrac{1}{2} lb$ sq. units.

$\therefore$ Required ratio = $lb : \dfrac{1}{2} lb$ = 2 : 1.

37. B: Area of the field grazed $= \left(\dfrac{22}{7} \times 14 \times 14\right)$ sq. ft

$$= 616 \text{ sq. ft.}$$

Number of days taken to graze the field $= \dfrac{616}{100}$ days $= 6$ days (approx.).

38. D: Radius of the ground $= 17.5$ m.

Radius of inner circle $= (17.5 - 1.4)$ m $= 16.1$ m.

Area of the garden $= \pi \times [(17.5)^2 - 16.1)^2]$ m^2

$$= \left[\dfrac{22}{7} \times (17.5 + 16.1)(17.5 - 16.1)\right] \text{m}^2$$

$$= \left(\dfrac{22}{7} \times 33.6 \times 1.4\right) \text{m}^2 = 147.84 \text{ m}^2.$$

39. C: Surface area of the cube $= (6 \times 8^2)$ sq. ft $= 384$ sq. ft.

Quantity of paint required $= \left(\dfrac{384}{16}\right)$ kg $= 24$ kg.

$\therefore$ Cost of painting $= ₹ \,(36.50 \times 24) = ₹ \,876.$

40. D: Volume of the tank $= 246.4$ litres $= 246400$ cm^3.

Let the radius of the base be r cm. Then,

$$\left(\dfrac{22}{7} \times r^2 \times 400\right) = 246400 \;\Rightarrow\; r^2 = \left(\dfrac{246400 \times 7}{22 \times 400}\right) = 196 \;\Rightarrow\; r = 14.$$

$\therefore$ Diameter of the base $= 2r = 28$ cm.

15

ALGEBRAIC IDENTITIES

It is the branch of mathematics that uses letters and symbols to represent variable quantities and numbers, and to express generalizations about them.

SOME IMPORTANT FORMULAE

A. $a^2 - b^2 = (a + b)(a - b)$

B. $(a + b)^2 = a^2 + 2ab + b^2$

C. $(a - b)^2 = a^2 - 2ab + b^2$

D. $a^3 + b^3 = (a + b)(a^2 - ab + b^2)$

E. $a^3 + b^3 = (a + b)^3 - 3ab(a + b)$

F. $a^3 - b^3 = (a - b)(a^2 + ab + b^2)$

G. $a^3 - b^3 = (a - b)^3 + 3ab(a - b)$

H. $(a + b)^2 = (a - b)^2 + 4ab$

I. $(a - b)^2 = (a + b)^2 - 4ab$

J. $a^3 + b^3 + c^3 - 3abc = (a + b + c)(a^2 + b^2 + c^2 - ab - bc - ca)$

K. If $a + b + c = 0$, then $a^3 + b^3 + c^3 = 3abc$

EXERCISE

1. If $x = 12$ and $y = 4$, the value of $(x + y)^{x/y}$ will be:

  A. 4096   B. 3896

  C. 4196   D. 5086

2. If $x = 9$, $y = \sqrt{17}$, then the value of $\left(x^2 - y^2\right)^{-1/2}$ will be:

  A. 2^{-4} B. 2^2

  C. 3^{-3} D. 2^{-3}

3. If $x + y = 2z$, then the value of $\left(\dfrac{x}{x - z} + \dfrac{z}{y - z}\right)$ will be:

  A. 1   B. 4

  C. 3/2   D. 2

4. If $x + y + z = 0$, then the value of $\dfrac{(x + y)(y + z)(z + x)}{xyz}$ will be:

  A. -3 B. -2

  C. 0   D. -1

5. If $x + \dfrac{1}{x} = 3$, the value of $x^4 + \dfrac{1}{x^4}$ will be:

  A. 49   B. 47

  C. 37   D. 42

6. If $x^2 + y^2 + z^2 = 115$ and $xy + yz + zx = 27$, then the value of $x + y + z$ will be:

  A. ± 15 B. ± 13

  C. ± 17 D. ± 19

7. If $x = 17$, $y = 15$ and $z = 13$, then the value of $x^2 + y^2 + z^2 - 2xy - 2xz - 2yz$ will be:

A. 111   B. 109

C. 121   D. 120

8. If $x + y = 1$, then the value of $x^3 + y^3 + 3xy$ will be:

A. 1   B. 4

C. 3   D. 7

9. What will be the value of $x^3 + y^3 + z^3 - 3xyz$ if $x + y + z = 16$ and $xy + yz + zx = 78$?

A. 352   B. 452

C. 342   D. 360

10. Which of the following is equivalent to $(x^4 + y^4)(x^2 + y^2)(x + y)(x - y)$?

A. $x^8 - y^8$

B. $x^{10} - y^{10}$

C. $x^6 - y^6$

D. $x^{12} - y^{12}$

11. If $x^2 = y + z$, $y^2 = z + x$ and $z^2 = x + y$, then the value of $\left(\dfrac{1}{x+1} + \dfrac{1}{y+1} + \dfrac{1}{z+1} \right)$ will be?

A. 4   B. 3

C. 1   D. 2

12. If $2x = a + 3$, then what will be the value of $8x^3 - 18ax$?

A. $a^3 + 27$ B. $a^3 - 27$

C. $a^3 + 25$ D. $a^3 - 36$

13. If $x + y = 8$ and $x - y = 2$, then the value of $x^2 + y^2$ will be:

A. 38   B. 40

C. 42   D. 34

14. If $a^2 + b^2 = 30$ and $a - b = 6$, then the value of ab will be:

A. −3   B. −5

C. 2   D. −6

15. If $a + b + c = 15$ and $a^2 + b^2 + c^2 = 77$, the what will be the value of $ab + bc + ca$?

A. 22   B. 74

C. 20   D. 18

EXPLANATORY ANSWERS

1. A: $(x + y)^{x/y} = (12 + 4)^{12/4} = (16)^3 = 4096.$ $[\because x = 12, y = 4]$

2. D: $\left(x^2 - y^2\right)^{-1/2} = (81 - 17)^{-1/2}$

$$= (64)^{-1/2} = \frac{1}{\sqrt{64}} = \frac{1}{8} = 2^{-3}.$$

3. A: $\because x + y = 2z \Rightarrow x - z = z - y = -(y - z)$

$$\therefore \frac{x}{x-z} + \frac{z}{y-z} = \frac{x}{-(y-z)} + \frac{z}{y-z} = \frac{z-x}{y-z} = 1. \quad [\because x - z = z - y]$$

4. D: $\because$ $x + y + z = 0$ $\Rightarrow$ $x + y = -z$

             $x + y + z = 0$ $\Rightarrow$ $y + z = -x$

   and $x + y + z = 0$ $\Rightarrow$ $z + x = -y$

$$\therefore \quad \frac{(x+y)(y+z)(z+x)}{xyz} = \frac{-z.-x.-y}{xyz} = -1.$$

5. B:

6. B: $\because (x + y + z)^2 = x^2 + y^2 + z^2 + 2(xy + yz + zx)$

$$\therefore (x + y + z)^2 = 115 + 2 \times 27$$
$$= 115 + 54 = 169$$

$$\therefore (x + y + z) = \sqrt{169} = \pm 13.$$

7. C: The given expression is equivalent to $(x - y - z)^2$

$$\therefore \quad (x - y - z)^2 = (17 - 15 - 13)^2$$
$$= (-11)^2 = 121.$$

8. A: $\because \quad (x + y)^3 = x^3 + y^3 + 3xy(x + y)$

$$\therefore \quad (1)^3 = x^3 + y^3 + 3xy \times 1$$
$$\therefore \quad 1 = x^3 + y^3 + 3xy.$$

9. A: $\because (x + y + z) = 16 \Rightarrow (x + y + z)^2 = (16)^2$

$$= x^2 + y^2 + z^2 + 2(xy + yz + zx) = 256$$
$$\therefore x^2 + y^2 + z^2 + 2 \times 78 = 256 \Rightarrow x^2 + y^2 + z^2$$
$$= 256 - 156 = 100$$
$$\therefore x^3 + y^3 + z^3 - 3xyz = (x + y + z)[(x^2 + y^2 + z^2) - (xy + yz + zx)]$$
$$= 16[100 - 78]$$
$$= 16 \times 22 = 352.$$

10. A: $\because (x^4 + y^4)(x^2 + y^2)(x + y)(x - y)$

$$= (x^4 + y^4)(x^2 + y^2)(x^2 - y^2)$$
$$= (x^4 + y^4)(x^4 - y^4)$$
$$= x^8 - y^8.$$

11. C:

12. A: $\because 2x = a + 3$

$$\Rightarrow \quad (2x)^3 = (a + 3)^3$$
$$\therefore \quad 8x^3 = a^3 + 27 + 3 \times a \times 3(a + 3)$$
$$= a^3 + 9a^2 + 27a + 27$$

and $\quad 18ax = 9a \times 2x$

$$= 9a \times (a + 3) = 9a^2 + 27a$$
$$\therefore \quad 8x^3 - 18ax = a^3 + 9a^2 + 27a + 27 - 9a^2 - 27a$$
$$= a^3 + 27.$$

13. D: $\because x^2 + y^2 = \dfrac{(x+y)^2 + (x-y)^2}{2}$

$$= \frac{(8)^2 + (2)^2}{2} = \frac{64 + 4}{2} = \frac{68}{2} = 34.$$

14. A: $\because$ $\qquad (a - b)^2 = a^2 + b^2 - 2ab$

$\Rightarrow \qquad ab = \dfrac{a^2 + b^2 - (a-b)^2}{2}$

$$= \dfrac{30 - (6)^2}{2}$$

$$= \dfrac{30 - 36}{2} = \dfrac{-6}{2} = -3.$$

15. B: $\because \ (a + b + c)^2 = a^2 + b^2 + c^2 + 2(ab + bc + ca)$

$\therefore \qquad ab + bc + ca = \dfrac{(a+b+c)^2 - \left(a^2 + b^2 + c^2\right)}{2}$

$$= \dfrac{(15)^2 - 77}{2} = \dfrac{225 - 77}{2}$$

$$= \dfrac{148}{2} = 74.$$

16
SURDS

Given a number, it is not always possible to find some whole number which when multiplied by itself will give the given number. In other words all given numbers are not perfect square numbers. For example, square root of 9, *i.e.,* $\sqrt{9}$ is 3, which is a whole number. But square root of 15, *i.e.,* $\sqrt{15} = 3.873$, which is not a whole number.

Hence square roots of natural numbers which are not perfect squares are not rational numbers. These are irrational numbers and are called **Surds**. For example, $\sqrt{3}, \sqrt{7}, 2+\sqrt{11}, 4+\sqrt{13}$ ..... etc. are **Surds**.

Given below are a few formulas which are quite helpful in solving the problems related to surds:

1. $\sqrt{a} \times \sqrt{a} = a$

2. $\sqrt{a} \times \sqrt{b} = \sqrt{ab}$

3. $\left(\sqrt{a} + \sqrt{b}\right)^2 = a + b + 2\sqrt{ab}$

4. $\left(\sqrt{a} - \sqrt{b}\right)^2 = a + b - 2\sqrt{ab}$

5. $x\sqrt{a} + x\sqrt{b} = x\left(\sqrt{a} + \sqrt{b}\right)$

6. $\dfrac{1}{\sqrt{a}+\sqrt{b}} = \dfrac{1}{\sqrt{a}+\sqrt{b}} \times \dfrac{\sqrt{a}-\sqrt{b}}{\sqrt{a}-\sqrt{b}} = \dfrac{\sqrt{a}-\sqrt{b}}{a-b}$

7. $\dfrac{1}{\sqrt{a}-\sqrt{b}} = \dfrac{1}{\sqrt{a}-\sqrt{b}} \times \dfrac{\sqrt{a}+\sqrt{b}}{\sqrt{a}+\sqrt{b}} = \dfrac{\sqrt{a}+\sqrt{b}}{a-b}$

8. $a + \sqrt{b} = c + \sqrt{d} \Rightarrow a = c$ and $b = d$

9. $\sqrt{2} = 1.41421, \sqrt{3} = 1.73205, \sqrt{5} = 2.23607,$

   $\sqrt{6} = 2.4494$

   $\sqrt{7} = 2.64575, \sqrt{8} = 2.82842, \sqrt{10} = 3.16227,$

   $\sqrt{11} = 3.31662$

EXERCISE

1. What will be the value of $\dfrac{1}{\sqrt{3}}$ upto 3 decimal places?
   A. 0.577
   B. 0.477
   C. 0.673
   D. 0.575

2. If $\sqrt{2} = 1.4122$, the value of $\dfrac{1}{2}\left(\dfrac{\sqrt{2}-1}{\sqrt{2}+1}\right)$ is:
   A. .0768
   B. .0658
   C. .0858
   D. .0458

3. If $\sqrt{1936} = 44$, the value of $\sqrt{19.36} + \sqrt{0.1936} + \sqrt{.001936}$ upto 3 decimal places will be:
   A. 5.679
   B. 4.884
   C. 9.884
   D. 6.778

4. Value of $\dfrac{\sqrt{2}-1}{\sqrt{2}+1}$ upto 3 decimal places will be:
   A. 0.172
   B. 0.158
   C. 0.176
   D. 0.188

5. $\sqrt[3]{8^4}$ is equivalent to:
   A. 15
   B. 9
   C. 16
   D. 25

6. If $\sqrt{6} = 2.45$, the value of $\sqrt{\dfrac{2}{3}} + 3\sqrt{3/2}$ will be equivalent to:
   A. 3.942
   B. 4.492
   C. 4.942
   D. 9.345

7. $\sqrt{72}$ is equivalent to:
   A. $3\sqrt{5}$
   B. $6\sqrt{2}$
   C. $8\sqrt{2}$
   D. $7\sqrt{3}$

8. What will be the value of $\left(\sqrt{80} + 3 \times \sqrt{245} - \sqrt{125}\right)$?
   A. $18\sqrt{5}$
   B. $20\sqrt{5}$
   C. $22\sqrt{5}$
   D. $28\sqrt{2}$

9. Value of $\left(\dfrac{\sqrt{5}+\sqrt{3}}{\sqrt{5}-\sqrt{3}}\right)$ will be equivalent to :
   A. $4 + \sqrt{15}$
   B. $3 - \sqrt{15}$
   C. $2 + \sqrt{15}$
   D. $4 - \sqrt{15}$

10. The expression $\left(\dfrac{\sqrt{7}+\sqrt{5}}{\sqrt{7}-\sqrt{5}}\right)$ is equivalent to:
    A. $6 - \sqrt{35}$
    B. $2 + \sqrt{35}$
    C. $4 - \sqrt{35}$
    D. $6 + \sqrt{35}$

EXPLANATORY ANSWERS

1. A: $\because \dfrac{1}{\sqrt{3}} = \dfrac{1}{\sqrt{3}} \times \dfrac{\sqrt{3}}{\sqrt{3}} = \dfrac{\sqrt{3}}{3} = \dfrac{1.732}{3} = 0.577$.

2. C: $\because \dfrac{1}{2}\left(\dfrac{\sqrt{2}-1}{\sqrt{2}+1}\right) = \dfrac{1}{2} \times \dfrac{\sqrt{2}-1}{\sqrt{2}+1} \times \dfrac{\sqrt{2}-1}{\sqrt{2}-1} = \dfrac{1}{2} \times \dfrac{\left(\sqrt{2}-1\right)^2}{\left(\sqrt{2}\right)^2 - 1^2}$

$$= \frac{1}{2} \times \frac{2+1-2\sqrt{2}}{2-1} = \frac{1}{2} \times \frac{3-2\sqrt{2}}{1} = \frac{1}{2} \times (3 - 2 \times 1.4142)$$

$$= \frac{1}{2} \times 0.1716 = .0858$$

3. B: $\because \sqrt{1936} = 44 \Rightarrow \sqrt{19.36} = 4.4$

$$\Rightarrow \sqrt{0.1936} = 0.44$$

$$\Rightarrow \sqrt{.001936} = .044$$

$$\therefore \sqrt{19.36} + \sqrt{0.1936} + \sqrt{.001936}$$
$$= 4.4 + 0.44 + .044 = 4.884.$$

4. A: $\because \dfrac{\sqrt{2}-1}{\sqrt{2}+1} = \dfrac{\sqrt{2}-1}{\sqrt{2}+1} \times \dfrac{\sqrt{2}-1}{\sqrt{2}-1} = \dfrac{\left(\sqrt{2}-1\right)^2}{\left(\sqrt{2}\right)^2 - (1)^2} = \dfrac{2+1-2\sqrt{2}}{2-1}$

$$= \frac{3-2\sqrt{2}}{1} = 3 - 2 \times 1.414 = 0.172.$$

5. C: $\sqrt[3]{8^4} = (8)^{\frac{4}{3}} = \left(2^3\right)^{\frac{4}{3}} = 2^{3 \times \frac{4}{3}} = 2^4 = 16 \cdot$

6. B: $\because \sqrt{\dfrac{2}{3}} + 3\sqrt{\dfrac{3}{2}} = \dfrac{\sqrt{2}}{\sqrt{3}} \times \dfrac{\sqrt{3}}{\sqrt{3}} + 3 \times \dfrac{\sqrt{3}}{\sqrt{2}} \times \dfrac{\sqrt{2}}{\sqrt{2}}$

$$= \frac{\sqrt{6}}{3} + \frac{3\sqrt{6}}{2} = \sqrt{6}\left[\frac{1}{3} + \frac{3}{2}\right] = \sqrt{6} \times \frac{11}{6} = \frac{11}{6} \times 2.45 = 4.492 \, .$$

7. B: $\because \sqrt{72} = \sqrt{6 \times 6 \times 2} = \sqrt{6^2 \times 2} = 6\sqrt{2} \cdot$

8. B: $\because \sqrt{80} + 3 \times \sqrt{245} - \sqrt{125}$

$$= \sqrt{16 \times 5} + 3 \times \sqrt{49 \times 5} - \sqrt{25 \times 5}$$

$$= 4\sqrt{5} + 21\sqrt{5} - 5\sqrt{5} = 20\sqrt{5} \cdot$$

9. A: $\because \quad \dfrac{\sqrt{5}+\sqrt{3}}{\sqrt{5}-\sqrt{3}} = \dfrac{\sqrt{5}+\sqrt{3}}{\sqrt{5}-\sqrt{3}} \times \dfrac{\sqrt{5}+\sqrt{3}}{\sqrt{5}+\sqrt{3}}$

$$= \dfrac{\left(\sqrt{5}+\sqrt{3}\right)^2}{\left(\sqrt{5}\right)^2 - \left(\sqrt{3}\right)^2} = \dfrac{5+3+2\sqrt{15}}{5-3}$$

$$= \dfrac{8+2\sqrt{15}}{2} = 4+\sqrt{15}$$

10. D: $\because \quad \dfrac{\sqrt{7}+\sqrt{5}}{\sqrt{7}-\sqrt{5}} = \dfrac{\sqrt{7}+\sqrt{5}}{\sqrt{7}-\sqrt{5}} \times \dfrac{\sqrt{7}+\sqrt{5}}{\sqrt{7}+\sqrt{5}}$

$$= \dfrac{\left(\sqrt{7}+\sqrt{5}\right)^2}{\left(\sqrt{7}\right)^2 - \left(\sqrt{5}\right)^2}$$

$$= \dfrac{7+5+2\sqrt{35}}{7-5} = \dfrac{12+2\sqrt{35}}{2} = 6+\sqrt{35}.$$

———

17

Triangles and its Various Kinds

Properties of geometrical figures:

(*i*) **Equilateral triangle:** All sides are equal.

(*ii*) **Isosceles triangle:** Two sides are equal.

(*iii*) **Rhombus:** All sides are equal and no angle is a right angle, but diagonals are at right angles and unequal.

(*iv*) **Square:** All sides are equal and each angle is right angle. The diagonals are also equal.

(*v*) **Parallelogram:** Opposite sides are parallel and equal, diagonals bisect each other.

(*vi*) **Rectangle:** Opposite sides are equal and each angle is a right angle, diagonals are equal.

Co-ordinates of standard points:

(*i*) *Centroid of a triangle:*

The point is the intersection of the medians. This point divides each median in the ratio 2 : 1, its co-ordinates are

$$G_1\left(\frac{x_1+x_2+x_3}{3}, \frac{y_1+y_2+y_3}{3}\right)$$

(*ii*) *Incentre of a triangle:*

This is the centre of the circle which touches the sides of a given triangle, it is the point of intersection of the internal bisectors of the angles of the triangle, its co-ordinates are given by the formula

$$I = (x, y) \text{ where } x = \frac{ax_1+bx_2+cx_3}{a+b+c}$$

$$y = \frac{ay_1+by_2+cy_3}{a+b+c}$$

where (a, b, c) are the lengths of the triangle

105

(*iii*) *Orthocentre of a triangle:*

The point *H* is the intersection of the altitudes.

(*iv*) The points *O, G, H* are collinear and *G* divides *OH* in the ratio 1 : 2.

EXERCISE

1. The points *A* (12, 8), *B*(–2, 6) and *C* (6, 0) are vertices of :
   A. right angled triangle
   B. isosceles triangle
   C. equilateral triangle
   D. None of these

2. The points (1, 1) (–1, –1) and $(-\sqrt{3}, \sqrt{3})$ are the angular points of a triangle, then the triangle is:
   A. right angled
   B. isosceles
   C. equilateral
   D. None of these

3. Two vertices of a triangle are the points (1, 4) and (7, 2). Its centroid is the point (5, 3), then the third vertex is :
   A. (3, 7)
   B. (7, 3)
   C. (1, 1)
   D. (0, 0)

4. Let the vertices of a triangle be (0, 0), (3, 0) and (0, 4), then its orthocentre is :
   A. (0, 0)
   B. $\left(1, \dfrac{4}{3}\right)$
   C. $\left(\dfrac{3}{2}, 2\right)$
   D. None of these

5. Distance of (2, 3) from origin is:
   A. 2
   B. 5
   C. –1
   D. $\sqrt{13}$

6. Find the values of *y* for which the distance between the points P(2, –3) and Q(10, *y*) is 10 units.
   A. 8, 2
   B. –9, 3
   C. –9, 5
   D. –8, 2

7. The centroid of the triangle whose vertices are A(4, –6), B(3, –2) and C(5, 2) is :
   A. 3, 2
   B. 4, 1
   C. 4, –2
   D. 4, 3

8. If (7, 3), (6, 1), (8, 2) and (P, 4) are the vertices of a parallelogram taken in order then the value of P is :
   A. 4
   B. 6
   C. 7
   D. 9

9. If the vertices of rhombus are (3, 0), (4, 5), (–1, 4) and (–2, –1) taken in order then area of rhombus is :
   A. 20 square units
   B. 24 square units
   C. 22 square units
   D. 26 square units

10. Find the value of P for which the points A(–1, 3), B(2, P) and C(5, –1) are collinear :
    A. 3
    B. 1
    C. 2
    D. 4

EXPLANATORY ANSWERS

1. A: $BC^2 + CA^2 = AB^2$.

2. C: $BC^2 = CA^2 = AB^2$.

3. B: $5 = \dfrac{\Sigma x}{3}$, $3 = \dfrac{\Sigma y}{3}$.

4. A: The two altitudes *i.e.*, x-axis and y-axis of ΔOAB meet at origin.

5. D:

$$A \overset{(0,\,0)}{\rule{6cm}{0.4pt}} \overset{(2,\,3)}{} B$$

$$AB = \sqrt{(2-0)^2 + (3-0)^2} = \sqrt{4+9} = \sqrt{13}$$

6. B: $\because$ PQ $= 10$

$$\Rightarrow \sqrt{(10-2)^2 + (y+3)^2} = 10$$

$$\sqrt{64 + y^2 + 9 + 6y} = 10$$

Squaring both sides,

$y^2 + 6y - 27 = 0$

$\Rightarrow y^2 + 9y - 3y - 27 = 0$

$\Rightarrow y(y + 9) - 3(y + 9) = 0$

$\Rightarrow (y + 9)(y - 3) = 0$

$\Rightarrow y = -9, y = 3$

$\therefore y = -9, 3$

7. C:

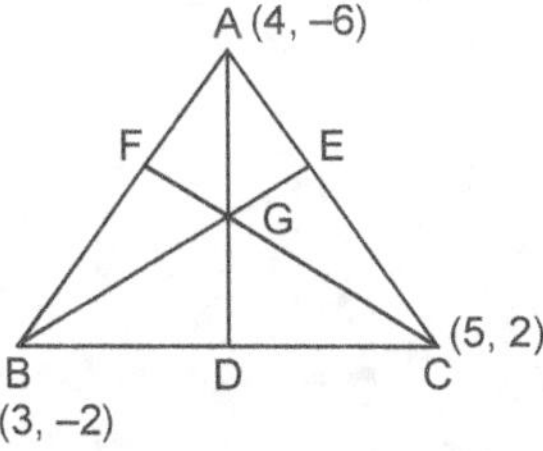

The centroid of the triangle G(x, y)

$$= G\left(\dfrac{4+3+5}{3}, \dfrac{-6-2+2}{3}\right)$$

$$= G(4, -2)$$

8. D:

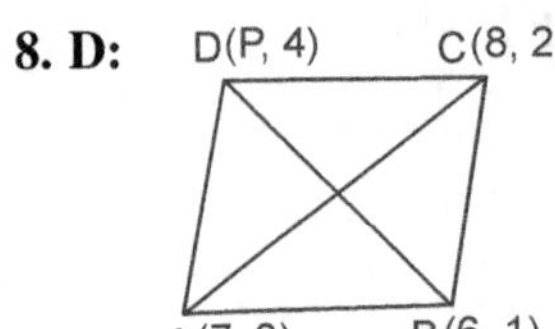

We know that the diagonals of a parallelogram bisect each other. Mid-point of AC and BD coincide.

Hence, $\left(\dfrac{7+8}{2}, \dfrac{3+2}{2}\right) = \left(\dfrac{6+P}{2}, \dfrac{1+4}{2}\right)$

$\Rightarrow \left(\dfrac{6+P}{2}, \dfrac{5}{2}\right) = \left(\dfrac{15}{2}, \dfrac{5}{2}\right)$

Equating the x-co-ordinate, we get

$\dfrac{6+P}{2} = \dfrac{15}{2} \Rightarrow P = 9$

9. B: We know that area of rhombus

$= \dfrac{1}{2} \times AC \times BD = \dfrac{1}{2} \times \sqrt{(-1-3)^2 + (4-0)^2} \times \sqrt{(-2-4)^2 + (-1-5)^2}$

$= \dfrac{1}{2}\sqrt{32} \times \sqrt{72} = \dfrac{1}{2} \times 4\sqrt{2} \times 6\sqrt{2}$

$= \dfrac{1}{2} \times 48 = 24$ square units.

10. B: Points A, B, C are collinear

$\Rightarrow$ Area of $\triangle ABC = 0$

$\dfrac{1}{2} [-1\,(P + 1) + 2(-1 - 3) + 5(3 - P) = 0$

$\Rightarrow \dfrac{1}{2} [-6P + 6] = 0 \Rightarrow 3P = 3 \Rightarrow P = 1.$

18

SIMILARITY OF TRIANGLES

Two triangles are said to be similar, if

(*i*) their corresponding angles are equal and

(*ii*) their corresponding sides are in the same ratio (*i.e.* proportional).

Also, we know that :

(*i*) If corresponding angles of two triangles are equal, then they are known as equiangular triangles.

(*ii*) Two line segments are divided proportionally when the ratio of the lengths of the segments of one of them is equal to the ratio of the lengths of the segments of the other.

EXERCISE

1. Two similar triangles have
A. equal sides
B. equal areas
C. equal angles
D. None of these

2. Two congruent triangles have
A. proportional sides
B. equal sides
C. equal corresponding sides
D. equal corresponding angles

3. Which of the following is false for two congruent triangles
A. Corresponding angles are equal.
B. Two sides and included angles are equal.
C. Corresponding sides are equal.
D. Two angles and one side are equal.

4. If the sides of a triangle are 8 cm, 12 cm and 15 cm then the angle is
A. Right angle
B. Obtuse angle
C. Acute angle
D. None of these

5. If two triangles are on the same base and between the parallel lines then they will be
A. equilaterals
B. right angled
C. equal in area
D. congruent

6. If the three heights of a traingle are equal then it is
A. right angled triangle
B. obtuse angled triangle
C. equilateral triangle
D. None of these

7. If two corresponding sides and the angle between them of a traingle are equal to another triangle. Then the angles are :
A. congruent but not similar
B. similar but not congruent
C. neither congruent nor similar
D. congruent and similar.

8. Ratio of areas of two similar triangles is equal to :
A. ratio of squares of the corresponding altitudes
B. ratio of squares of corresponding medians.
C. Either (A) or (B)
D. (A) and (B) both

9. If the areas of two similar triangles are equal then the triangles :
A. are congruent
B. have equal length of corresponding sides
C. (A) and (B)
D. None of these

10. Two isosceles triangles have equal vertical angles and their areas are in the ratio of 9 : 25 then the ratio between their corresponding heights is :
A. 5 : 3   B. 25 : 9
C. 3 : 5   D. 16 : 9

EXPLANATORY ANSWERS

1. C: equal angles
2. C: equal corresponding sides
3. D: Two angles and one side are equal.
4. C: Acute angle
5. C: equal in area
6. C: equilateral triangle
7. C: neither congruent nor similar
8. D: (A) and (B) both
9. C. (A) and (B)
10. C: According to equestion

$$\angle A = \angle D \text{ and } \frac{ar\,(\triangle ABC)}{ar\,(\triangle DEF)} = \frac{9}{25}$$

Since,   AB = AC (given)   ....(i)
DE = DF (given)   ....(ii)

Dividing (i) by (ii)

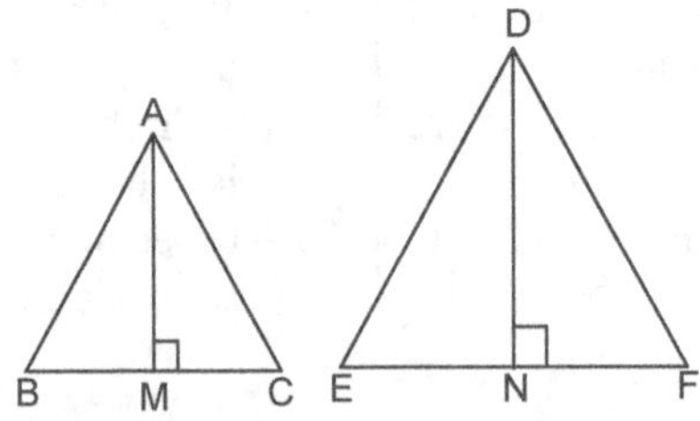

$$\frac{AB}{DE} = \frac{AC}{DF} \qquad \qquad \text{...(iii)}$$

Hence, $\triangle ABC \sim \triangle DEF$ $\qquad$ [By SAS criterion of similar $\triangle s$]

In $\triangle AMC$ and $\triangle DNF$

$$\angle AMC = \angle DNF = 90°$$

$$\angle C = \angle F \qquad \qquad \text{(because } \triangle ABC \sim \triangle DEF)$$

$\therefore \angle AMC \sim DNF$ (By AA Criterion of similar $\triangle s$)

$$\therefore \qquad \frac{AC}{DF} = \frac{AM}{DN}$$

and, $\qquad \dfrac{ar\,(\triangle ABC)}{ar\,(DEF)} = \dfrac{AC^2}{DF^2} = \dfrac{AM^2}{DN^2}$

$$\therefore \qquad \frac{AM^2}{DN^2} = \frac{9}{25} \Rightarrow \frac{AM}{DN} = \frac{3}{5}$$

Hence required ratio = 3 : 5

19

CIRCLE AND TANGENTS

A circle is a set of those points in a plane that are at a given constant distance from a given fixed point in the plane. The fixed point is called the **centre of the circle** and the constant distance of every point on the circle from its centre of called the **radius of the circle**.

The fixed point O is called its centre and the constant distance r is called the radius.

Diameter is the longest chord of the circle.

Secant

A line which interesects a circle in two distinct points is called a **secant** of the circle. In the fig. the line l intersects the circle in two distinct points A and B. The line l is a secant to the circle.

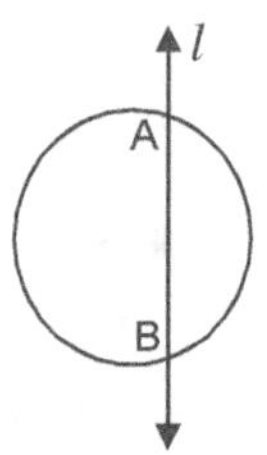

Tanget

A tangent to a circle is a line that intersects the circle at exactly one point.

The point at which it meets the circle is called its point of contact and the line (tangent) is said to touch the circle at this point. In the figure, the line l meets the circle at only point A. Here A is the point of contact.

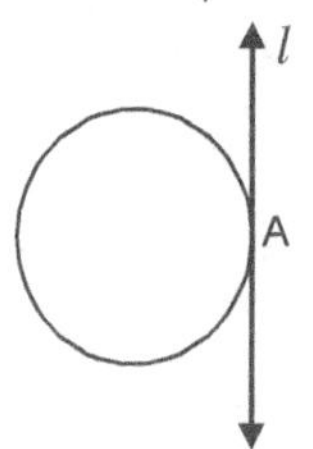

EXERCISE

1. PQ is a diameter and PQRS is a cyclic quadrilateral. If $\angle$PSR = 150°, then measure of $\angle$RPQ is :

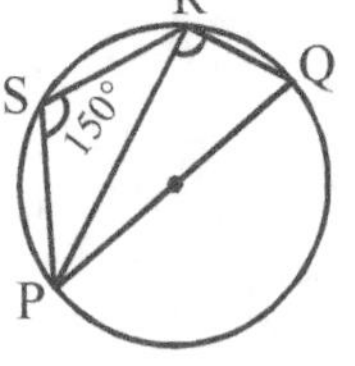

A. 90°

B. 60°

C. 30°

D. None of these

2. Determine the value of x in the figure given below.

A. 35°

B. 25°

C. 30°

D. 60°

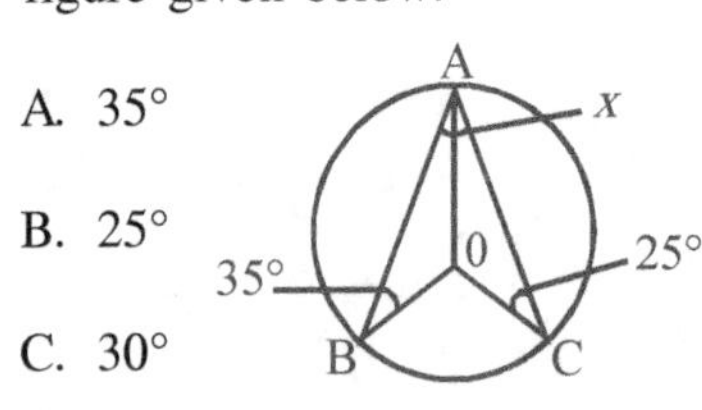

3. O is the centre of the circle. If ∠OAB = 30° and ∠OCB = 40°, find ∠AOC.

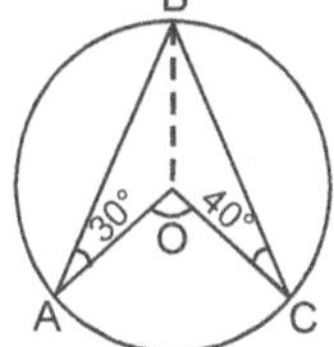

A. 120°

B. 140°

C. 110°

D. 130°

4. In fig. if ∠ACB = 40°, ∠DPB = 120°, then find y.

A. 10°

B. 20°

C. 15°

D. 25°

5. In the fig. if ∠BDC = 30°, ∠CBA = 110°, then find BCA.

A. 20°

B. 40°

C. 35°

D. 60°

6. From a point Q, the length of the tangent to a circle is 24 cm and the distance from the centre is 25 cm. The radius of the circle is

A. 7 cm   B. 12 cm

C. 15 cm   D. 24.5 cm

7. In the given figure, if TP and TQ are the two tangents to a circle with centre O and that ∠POQ = 110°, then ∠PTQ is equal to

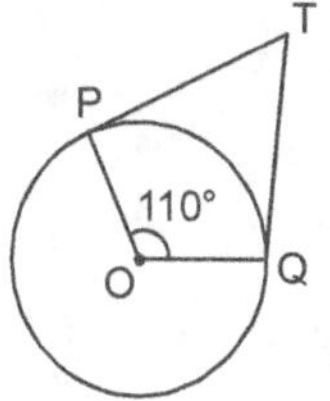

A. 60°

B. 70°

C. 80°

D. 90°

8. If tangents PA and PB from a point P to a circle with centre O are inclined to each other at angle of 80°, then ∠POA is equal to

A. 50°

B. 60°

C. 70°

D. 80°

9. In Fig., a circle touches all the four sides of a quadrilateral ABCD whose sides AB = 6 cm, BC = 7 cm and CD = 4 cm. Find AD

A. 2 cm

B. 5 cm

C. 3 cm

D. 4 cm

10. If AB, AC, PQ are tangents in the figure and AB = 5 cm. The perimeter of ΔAPQ is

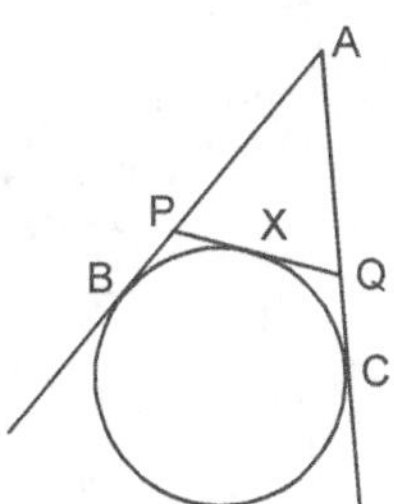

A. 8 cm

B. 6 cm

C. 10 cm

D. 5 cm

EXPLANATORY ANSWERS

1. B: $\angle PQR = 180° - 150° = 30°$

$\angle PRQ = 90°$ (Angle of a semicircle)

$\angle RPQ + 90° + 30° = 180°$

$\Rightarrow \angle RPQ = 60°$

2. D: $\angle OAB = \angle OBA\ (\because OA = OB)$

$\angle OAB = 35°$

Similarly, $\angle AOC = 25°$

$\therefore\quad \angle x = 35° + 25° = 60°$

3. B: O is the centre of the circle,

$\angle OAB = 30°$, $\angle OCB = 40°$. join OB

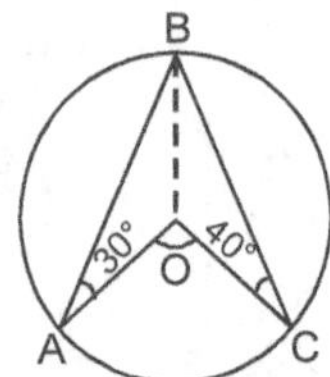

In $\triangle OAB$,

$\therefore$ OA = OB (radii of the same circle)

$\therefore \angle OBA = \angle OAB = 30°$ ($\angle s$ opp. to equal sides of a $\triangle$) ...(*i*)

Similarly, $\angle OBC = \angle OCB = 40°$ ...(*ii*)

Adding equations (*i*) and (*ii*), we get

$\angle OBA + \angle OBC = 30° + 40°$

$\Rightarrow \angle ABC = 70°$

$\because\ \overset{\frown}{AC}$ subtends $\angle AOC$ at the centre and

$\triangle ABC$ at any point on the circumference

$\angle AOC = 2 \times \angle ABC$

$\qquad = 2 \times 70° = 140°$

4. B: $\angle D = \angle C$ [$\because \angle s$ in the same segment of a circle are equal]

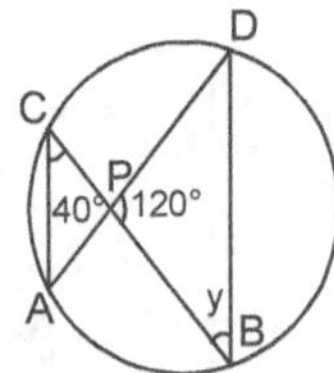

But $\angle C = 40°$ (Given)

$\therefore$ $\angle C = 40°$

In $\triangle$ BPD, we have

$\angle BPD + \angle D + \angle B = 180°$ $[\because$ sum of three $\angle s$ of a $\triangle = 180°]$

$\Rightarrow 120° + 40° + y = 180°$

$\Rightarrow y = 180° - 160° = 20°.$

5. B: $\angle BAC = \angle BDC$ ($\angle s$ in the same segment)

   $= 30°$ (given)

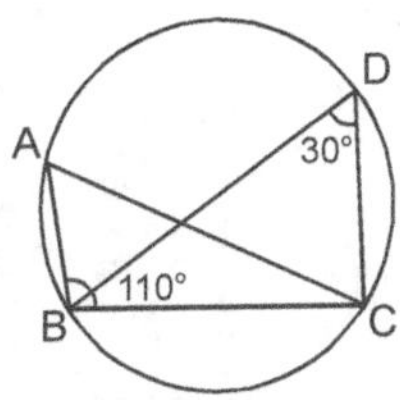

$\angle BAC + \angle CBA + \angle BCA = 180°$ ($\angle s$ of $\triangle ABC$)

$\Rightarrow 30° + 110° + \angle BCA = 180°$

$\Rightarrow \angle BCA = 180° - 30° - 110° = 40°$

6. A: In rt. $\angle d$ $\triangle OTQ,$

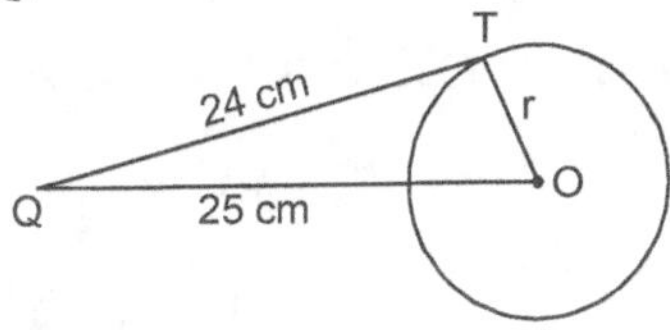

$OT = \sqrt{OQ^2 - OT^2}$

   $= \sqrt{25^2 - 24^2} = \sqrt{625 - 576}$

   $= \sqrt{49} = 7$ cm.

7. B: Since $\angle POQ + \angle PTQ = 180°$ $[\because \angle OPT = 90°, \angle OQT = 90°]$

$\Rightarrow 110° + \angle PTQ = 180°$

$\Rightarrow \angle PTQ = 180° - 110° = 70°.$

8. A: Since $\angle APB = 80°$

        $\angle AOB = 180° - 80° = 100°$

        $\angle PAO = \angle PBO = 90°$

Since OP bisects $\angle AOB$

116

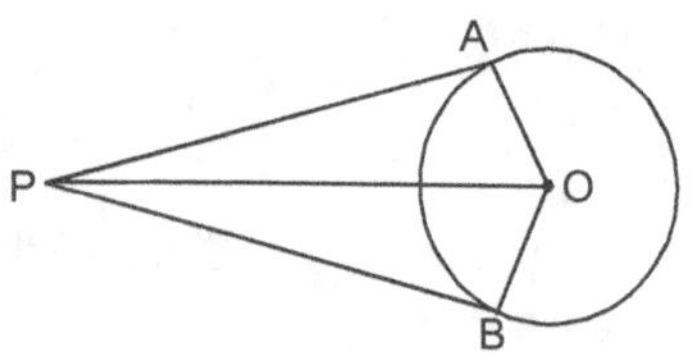

$$\angle AOP = \frac{1}{2}(100°) = 50°$$

i.e. $\angle POA = 50°.$

9. C: AD = AS + DS = AP + DR   [∵ AS = AP and DS = DR]

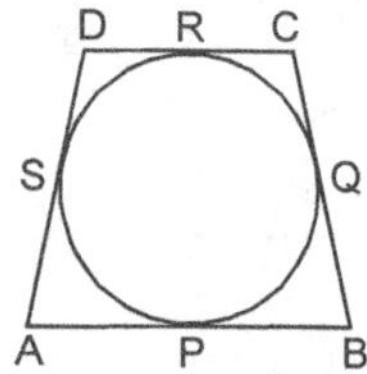

= (AB − BP) + (CD − RC)

= AB + CD − (BP + RC)

= AB + CD − (BQ + CQ)   [∵ BP = BQ, RC = CQ]

= AB + CD − BC = 6 + 4 − 7 = 3 cm.

10. C: Since AB and AC are the tangents from the same point A

∴ AB = AC = 5 cm

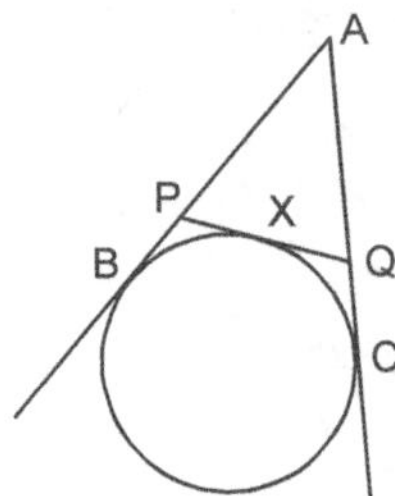

Similarly, BP = PX and XQ = QC

Perimeter of △APQ = AP + AQ + PQ

= AP + AQ + (PX + XQ)

= (AP + PX) + (AQ + XQ)

= (AP + BP) + (AQ + QC)

= AB + AC = 5 + 5 = 10 cm.

20

TRIGONOMETRY

Trigonometric Ratios of Angles

There are six trigonometric ratios — sine, cosine, tangent, cotangent, secant and cosecant—upon which trigonometry is based.

$\triangle ABC$ is a right- angled triangle in which $\angle ACB = \theta$. The side AB is opposite to an angle θ and is called **opposide side**. BC is the **adjacent side** in relation to angle θ; AC is the **hypotenuse**.

The six trigonometric ratios of the acute angle θ are defined as follows :

$$\sin\theta = \frac{p}{h} = \frac{AB}{AC} \qquad\qquad \cos\theta = \frac{b}{h} = \frac{BC}{AC}$$

$$\tan\theta = \frac{p}{b} = \frac{AB}{BC} \qquad\qquad \cot\theta = \frac{b}{p} = \frac{BC}{AB}$$

$$\sec\theta = \frac{h}{b} = \frac{AC}{BC} \qquad\qquad \operatorname{cosec}\theta = \frac{h}{p} = \frac{AC}{AB}$$

$$\boxed{\textbf{IMPORTANT FORMULAE}}$$

A. (*i*) $\tan\theta = \dfrac{\sin\theta}{\cos\theta} = \dfrac{1}{\cot\theta}$ 　　　(*ii*) $\cot\theta = \dfrac{\cos\theta}{\sin\theta} = \dfrac{1}{\tan\theta}$

(*iii*) $\sec\theta = \dfrac{1}{\cos\theta}$ 　　　(*iv*) $\operatorname{cosec}\theta = \dfrac{1}{\sin\theta}$

B. (*v*) $\sin^2\theta + \cos^2\theta = 1$

$\sin^2\theta = 1 - \cos^2\theta \Rightarrow \sin\theta = \sqrt{1-\cos^2\theta}$

$\cos^2\theta = 1 - \sin^2\theta \Rightarrow \cos\theta = \sqrt{1-\sin^2\theta}$

(*vi*) $1 + \tan^2\theta = \sec^2\theta$

$\sec^2\theta - \tan^2\theta = 1$

$\sec^2\theta - 1 = \tan^2\theta$

(vii) $1 + \cot^2\theta = \text{cosec}^2\theta$

$\text{cosec}^2\theta - \cot^2\theta = 1$

$\text{cosec}^2\theta - 1 = \cot^2\theta$

C. $(viii)$ $\sin(90 - \theta) = \cos\theta$

(ix) $\cos(90 - \theta) = \sin\theta$

(x) $\tan(90 - \theta) = \cot\theta$

(xi) $\cot(90 - \theta) = \tan\theta$

(xii) $\sec(90 - \theta) = \text{cosec}\theta$

$(xiii)$ $\text{cosec}(90 - \theta) = \sec\theta$

D. (i) $\sin(A \pm B) = \sin A \times \cos B \pm \cos A \times \sin B$

(ii) $\cos(A \pm B) = \cos A \times \cos B \mp \sin A \times \sin B$

E. (i) $\sin 2\theta = 2\sin\theta \cdot \cos\theta$

(ii) $\cos 2\theta = \cos^2\theta - \sin^2\theta$

$= 1 - 2\sin^2\theta = 2\cos^2\theta - 1$

(iii) $\tan 2\theta = \dfrac{2\tan\theta}{1 - \tan^2\theta}$

F. (i) $\sin 3\theta = 3\sin\theta - 4\sin^3\theta$

(ii) $\cos 3\theta = 4\cos^3\theta - 3\cos\theta$

T-Ratios of Standard Angles

θ	$0°$	$30°$	$45°$	$60°$	$90°$
$\sin\theta$	0	$\dfrac{1}{2}$	$\dfrac{1}{\sqrt{2}}$	$\dfrac{\sqrt{3}}{2}$	1
$\cos\theta$	1	$\dfrac{\sqrt{3}}{2}$	$\dfrac{1}{\sqrt{2}}$	$\dfrac{1}{2}$	0
$\tan\theta$	0	$\dfrac{1}{\sqrt{3}}$	1	$\sqrt{3}$	∞
$\cot\theta$	∞	$\sqrt{3}$	1	$\dfrac{1}{\sqrt{3}}$	0
$\sec\theta$	1	$\dfrac{2}{\sqrt{3}}$	$\sqrt{2}$	2	∞
$\text{cosec}\theta$	∞	2	$\sqrt{2}$	$\dfrac{2}{\sqrt{3}}$	1

HEIGHT AND DISTANCE

Our common use for trigonometry is to measure heights and distance that are either awkward or impossible to measure by ordinary means. One of the biggest triumphs of trigonometry is being able to find the size of an object or the distance to an object (such as the moon) without going to the object. In trigonometry, we develop methods for measuring sides and angles as well as for solving related applied problems. Because of the extensive use of these concepts, trigonometry is considered one of the most practical and relevant branches of mathematics.

The Angle of Elevation

If a person is looking up at an object, the acute angle measured from the horizontal to a line of sight observation of the object is called the angle of elevation.

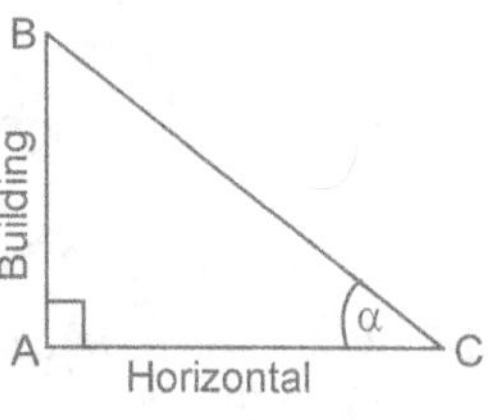

In the given figure, α is the angle of elevation.

The Angle of Depression

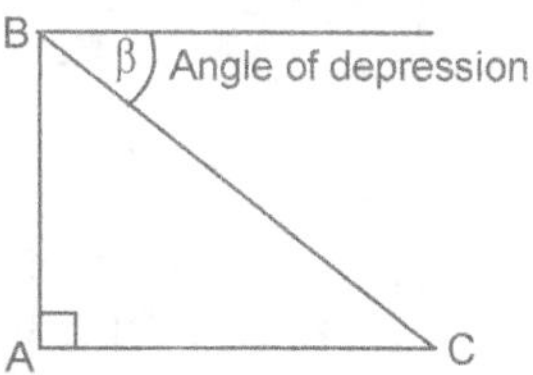

The angle β for a point below a horizontal line is the angle formed by the horizontal line and the observer's line of sight through the point. In the following figure, β is the angle of depression.

EXERCISE

1. If $2 \tan \theta = 1$, find the value of
$$\frac{3\cos\theta + 2\sin\theta}{2\cos\theta - \sin\theta}$$

  A. $\dfrac{8}{3}$ B. $\dfrac{5}{3}$

  C. $\dfrac{2}{3}$ D. 2

2. $\cos^2 72° + \cos^2 18° = ?$
  A. 0   B. 1
  C. −1   D. 2

3. $3 \tan^2 30° + \sec^4 45° - \tan^2 60°$
  is equal to :
  A. 0   B. 1
  C. 2   D. 3

4. The value of $\dfrac{\sin 10°}{\cos 80°}$ is :
  A. 0   B. 1
  C. 2   D. 3

5. If $\theta = 45$ then $\dfrac{2\tan\theta}{1+\tan^2\theta}$ is :
  A. 1   B. 0
  C. 2   D. 3

6. If $\theta = 30°$ then $\cos 2\theta$ is :
  A. 0   B. 1
  C. $\dfrac{1}{2}$ D. $\dfrac{\sqrt{3}}{2}$

7. What is the value of $\sin^2 35° + \sin^2 55°$?

   A. 0   B. 1

   C. $\dfrac{1}{2}$ D. 2

8. The value of $\tan 45° \times \cot 45°$ is :

   A. 0   B. 1

   C. 2   D. $\dfrac{1}{2}$

9. The value of $\sin(90° - \theta)$ is :

   A. $\cos \theta$ B. $\sin \theta$

   C. $-\cos \theta$ D. None of these

10. What is the value of $\sin 30° \times \text{cosec } 30°$

   A. 1   B. 0

   C. $\dfrac{1}{2}$ D. 2

11. $\sin \theta + \cos \theta = 1$ where $\theta = $ ......

   A. 30°   B. 45°

   C. 60°   D. 90°

12. $\tan 45° \times \tan 82°$ is

   A. 1   B. 0

   C. 2   D. 3

13. The angle of elevation of the top of a tower from a point on the ground, which is 30 m away from the foot of the tower is 30°. The height of the tower is :

   A. $8\sqrt{3}$ m   B. $9\sqrt{3}$ m

   C. $10\sqrt{3}$ m   D. $12\sqrt{3}$ m

14. A kite is flying at a height of 60 m above the ground. The string attached to the kite is temporarily tied to a point on the ground. The inclination of the string with the ground is 60°. Find the length of the string, assuming that there is no slack in the string.

   A. $40\sqrt{3}$ m   B. $30\sqrt{3}$ m

   C. $20\sqrt{3}$ m   D. $10\sqrt{3}$ m

15. From a point on the ground, the angles of elevation of the bottom and top of a transmission tower fixed at the top of a 20 m high building are 45° and 60° respectively. The height of the tower is :

   A. $25(\sqrt{3}-1)$ m

   B. $20(\sqrt{3}-1)$ m

   C. 20 m

   D. 10 m

16. Two poles of equal heights are standing opposite to each other on either side of a road, which is 100 metres wide. From a point between them on the road, the angles of elevation of their tops are 30° and 60°. The height of each pole is

   A. 44 m   B. 43.25 m

   C. 50 m   D. 40.5 m

17. The angle of elevation of the top of a hill at the foot of a tower is 60° and the angle of elevation of top of the tower from the foot of the hill is 30°. If the tower is 50 m high, then the height of the hill is :

   A. 148 m   B. 150 m

   C. 152 m   D. 160 m

18. The angles of elevation of the top of a tower from two points a and b from the base and in the same straight line with it are complementary. The height of the tower is :

A. ab B. $\sqrt{ab}$

C. a^2b^2 D. None of these

19. The angles of elevation of the top of a tower from two points at the distances of 4 m and 9 m from the base of the tower and in the same straight line with it are complementary. The height of the tower is :

A. 8 m   B. 5 m

C. 6 m   D. 4 m

20. The value of $\dfrac{\tan 49°}{\cot 41°}$ is :

A. 1   B. 2

C. 0   D. 3

EXPLANATORY ANSWERS

1. A: $\dfrac{3\cos\theta + 2\sin\theta}{2\cos\theta - \sin\theta} = \dfrac{3\dfrac{\cos\theta}{\cos\theta} + 2\dfrac{\sin\theta}{\cos\theta}}{2\dfrac{\cos\theta}{\cos\theta} - \dfrac{\sin\theta}{\cos\theta}}$

[Dividing both the numerator and denominator by cos θ]

$= \dfrac{3 + 2\tan\theta}{2 - \tan\theta} = \dfrac{3 + 2\times\dfrac{1}{2}}{2 - \dfrac{1}{2}}$ [Given 2 tan θ = 1 $\therefore$ tan θ = $\dfrac{1}{2}$]

$= \dfrac{3+1}{3/2} = 4\times\dfrac{2}{3} = 2\dfrac{2}{3}.$

2. B: $\cos^2 72° + \cos^2 18° = \cos^2(90 - 18°) + \cos^2 18°$

$= \sin^2 18° + \cos^2 18° = 1.$

3. C: $3\left(\dfrac{1}{\sqrt{3}}\right)^2 + \left(\sqrt{2}\right)^2 - \left(\sqrt{3}\right)^2$

$= 3\times\dfrac{1}{3} + 4 - 3 = 2.$

4. B: $\dfrac{\sin 10°}{\cos(90° - 10°)} = \dfrac{\sin 10°}{\sin 10°} = 1.$

5. A: $\dfrac{2\tan 45°}{1 + \tan^2 45°} = \dfrac{2\times 1}{1 + 1} = \dfrac{2}{2} = 1.$

6. C: $\cos 2(30°) = \cos 60° = \dfrac{1}{2}$.

7. B: $\sin^2 35° + \sin^2(90° - 35°)$

$= \sin^2 35° + \cos^2 35° = 1.$ $\qquad\qquad$ $[\because \sin^2\theta + \cos^2\theta = 1]$

8. B: $\tan 45° \times \cot 45° = 1 \times 1 = 1.$

9. A: $\sin(90° - \theta) = \cos\theta.$

10.A: $\sin 30° \times \operatorname{cosec} 30° = \dfrac{1}{2} \times \dfrac{2}{1} = \dfrac{1}{1} = 1.$

11.D: Put $\theta = 90°$ then $\sin\theta + \cos\theta = \sin 90° + \cos 90° = 1 + 0 = 1.$

12.A: $\tan 45° \times \tan 8° \cdot \tan(90° - 8°)$

$= \tan 45° \times \tan 8° \times \cot 8° = 1 \times 1 = 1.$

13.C: Let AB be the tower. The angle of elevation of the top A of the tower from a point C on the ground which is 30 metres away from the foot of the tower is 30°.

$\therefore \qquad\qquad \angle ACB = 30°$

and $\qquad\qquad\quad BC = 30$ m.

From right $\triangle ABC$, we have

$$\dfrac{AB}{BC} = \tan 30°$$

$\Rightarrow \qquad\qquad AB = BC \tan 30° = 30 \times \dfrac{1}{\sqrt{3}} = 10\sqrt{3}$ m.

14.A: Let AB = height of kite = 60 m and the inclination of the string AC is 60°.

From right-angled $\triangle ABC$, we have

$$\dfrac{AC}{AB} = \operatorname{cosec} 60°$$

$\Rightarrow \qquad\qquad \dfrac{AC}{60} = \dfrac{2}{\sqrt{3}} \Rightarrow AC = 60 \times \dfrac{2}{\sqrt{3}} = 40\sqrt{3}$ m.

15.A: Let AB = 20 m be the building and AC be the transmission tower fixed at the top of building. From a point D on the ground, the angle of elevation of the bottom and top of transmission tower are 45° and 60°.

$\therefore \angle ADB = 45°$ and $\angle CDB = 60°$

From right $\triangle ABD$, we have

$$\frac{AB}{BD} = \tan 45° = 1$$

$$\therefore \qquad AB = BD$$

$$\Rightarrow \qquad BD = 20 \text{ m} \qquad [\because AB = 20 \text{ m}]$$

From right-angled $\triangle CBD$, we have

$$\frac{BC}{BD} = \tan 60°$$

$$\Rightarrow \qquad BC = BD \tan 60°$$

$$= 20 \times \sqrt{3} = 20\sqrt{3} \text{ m}$$

Now $\qquad AC = BC - AB = 20\sqrt{3} - 20$

$$= 20(\sqrt{3} - 1) \text{ m}.$$

Hence the height of the tower $= 20(\sqrt{3} - 1) \text{ m}.$

16.B: Let AB and CD be the two poles of equal height h metres standing on either side of the road $AC = 100$ metres.

Let M be the point at which the poles AB, CD subtend angles of $30°$ and $60°$ respectively.

Let $CM = x$ metres so that

$AM = (100 - x)$ metres

In right-angled $\triangle MCD$, $\dfrac{h}{x} = \tan 60°$

$$\Rightarrow \qquad h = x\sqrt{3} \qquad \qquad ...(i)$$

In right-angled $\triangle MAB$,

$$\frac{h}{100 - x} = \tan 30° \Rightarrow \frac{h}{100 - x} = \frac{1}{\sqrt{3}}$$

$$\Rightarrow \qquad h\sqrt{3} = 100 - x \Rightarrow (x\sqrt{3})\sqrt{3} = 100 - x$$

$$3x = 100 - x$$

$$4x = 100; \ x = 100 \div 4 = 25 \text{ m}$$

$\therefore$ From (i), $h = x\sqrt{3} = 25 \times 1.73 = 43.25 \text{ m}$

Hence, distance of point M from C $= 25$ m and distance of point from A $= (100 - 25)$m $= 75$ m. Height of each pole $= 43.25$ m.

124

17.B: Let AB be the hill and CD the tower.

$$\angle BDA = 60° \text{ and } \angle DBC = 30°$$
$$CD = 50 \text{ m.}$$

Let AB = h metres

In right-angled $\triangle ADC$,

$$\frac{CD}{BD} = \tan 30°$$

$$\Rightarrow \qquad BD = \frac{CD}{\tan 30°}$$

$$= CD \cot 30°$$

$$\Rightarrow \qquad BD = 50\sqrt{3} \text{ metres}$$

Now in right-angled $\triangle ABD$, we have

$$\frac{AB}{BD} = \tan 60° \Rightarrow AB = BD \tan 60°$$

$$\Rightarrow AB = \left(50\sqrt{3}\right)\sqrt{3} = 150 \text{ m.}$$

Hence, height of the hill is 150 m.

18.B: Let AB be the tower and C and D be the two points such that BD = a and BC = b.

If $\angle BDA = \theta$, then $\angle BCA = 90° - \theta$

Now in right-angled $\triangle ABD$,

$$\frac{AB}{BD} = \tan \theta \Rightarrow \frac{h}{a} = \tan \theta$$

$$\therefore \qquad h = a \tan \theta \qquad \qquad ...(i)$$

In right-angled $\triangle ABC$,

$$\frac{AB}{BC} = \tan (90° - \theta) = \cot \theta$$

$$\Rightarrow \qquad \frac{h}{b} = \cot \theta \Rightarrow h = b \cot \theta \qquad \qquad ...(ii)$$

multiplying (i) and (ii), we get

$$h^2 = ab \tan \theta \cot \theta = ab \tan \theta \times \frac{1}{\tan \theta} = ab.$$

$$\therefore \qquad h = \sqrt{ab}.$$

19.C: Let AB be the tower and C and D be the two points such that BD = 4 m and BC = 9 m.

If $\angle BDA = \theta$, then $\angle BCA = 90° - \theta$

Now in right-angled $\triangle ABD$,

$$\frac{AB}{BD} = \tan\theta \Rightarrow \frac{h}{4} = \tan\theta$$

$\therefore \qquad h = 4\tan\theta \quad ...(i)$

In right-angled $\triangle ABC$,

$$\frac{AB}{BC} = \tan(90° - \theta) = \cot\theta$$

$$\Rightarrow \qquad \frac{h}{9} = \cot\theta \Rightarrow h = 9\cot\theta \qquad\qquad ...(ii)$$

multiplying (i) and (ii), we get

$$h^2 = 36\tan\theta\cot\theta = 36\tan\theta \times \frac{1}{\tan\theta} = 36.$$

$\therefore \qquad h = \pm\sqrt{36} = 6$ m.

20.A: $\dfrac{\tan 49°}{\cot 41°} = \dfrac{\tan(90° - 41°)}{\cot 41°} = \dfrac{\cot 41°}{\cot 41°} = 1 \qquad [\because \tan(90° - \theta) = \cot\theta]$

21

DATA TABLES

TABLES

Tables are often used in reports, magazines and newspaper to present as set of numerical data. It is one of the easiest and most accurate ways of presenting data. One of the main purposes of tables is to make complicated information easier to understand. Hence, the advantage of presenting data in a table is that one can see the information at a glance. We present below an example of tabular presentation of annual expenditure of 5 families for last 5 years.

Annual Expenditure of 5 families (in ₹ Thousands)

Years → Families ↓	2008	2009	2010	2011	2012
A	35	50	55	60	70
B	40	60	65	75	80
C	45	50	70	80	95
D	30	40	45	50	75
E	50	55	60	70	90

Essentials of a Tables:

(*i*) **Title:** Heading of the table

(*ii*) **Stub:** The section of the table containing row headings in called Stub.

(*iii*) **Column Captions :** The heading of each column is designated as column caption.

(*iv*) **Body**

(*v*) **Footnotes**

(*vi*) **Source**

EXERCISE

Directions (Qs. 1 to 4) : *Study the table below to answer these questions.*

Rate of Interest, Dividend Payout Ratio and the Retained Earnings of Five Companies

Company	Interest (₹ 000)	Rate of Interest (%)	Dividend Payout Ratio (%)	Retained Earnings (₹ lakh)
A	234	18	22.50	155
B	576	24	19.60	402
C	129.6	16	8.75	365
D	144	9	32.50	270
E	180	15	28.00	216

Profit earned is either paid out as dividend or ploughed back in business as retained earnings. Interest is paid on borrowings.

1. What is the sum of profits made by Companies A & B?
   A. ₹ 700 lakh   B. ₹ 500 lakh
   C. ₹ 600 lakh   D. None of these

2. What is the sum of the borrowings of all five companies?
   A. ₹ 14.6 crore
   B. ₹ 146 lakh
   C. ₹ 14.6 lakh
   D. None of these

3. By how much do the borrowings of Company B exceed that of Company A?
   A. ₹ 1,000,000
   B. ₹ 1,210,000
   C. ₹ 1,320,000
   D. ₹ 1,100,000

4. By how much does the dividend paid by Company D exceed the dividend paid by Company B?
   A. ₹ 320 lakh
   B. ₹ 23 lakh
   C. ₹ 32 lakh
   D. ₹ 230 lakh

Directions (Qs. 5 to 9) : *Study the following table to answer these questions.*

Average Hourly Wage (in ₹) by Age Group

Years	18 – 20 years		21 – 23 years	
	Male	Female	Male	Female
2007	15.1	15.1	29.7	25.1
2008	12.4	13.4	21.0	19.1
2009	10.0	13.8	14.7	16.9
2010	11.0	13.4	18.0	20.5
2011	21.2	16.3	29.1	32.7
2012	15.0	21.0	32.1	33.9

5. In 2011, for the 21-23 years age group, the wages for the females was approximately what per cent of that of the males?
   A. 220   B. 30
   C. 85   D. 110

6. What was the difference between the average wages of males and of females for the 21 – 23 years age group?
   A. 0.80   B. 0.60
   C. 0.40   D. 0.20

7. In how many years was the wage for the females higher than that of males in both the age groups?
A. Three   B. Four
C. Two   D. One

8. In the age group of 18–20 years, in which year was the wage-disparity maximum?
A. 2010   B. 2011
C. 2009   D. 2012

9. In the age group of 21–23 years, in which year was the wage-disparity minimum?
A. 2008   B. 2012
C. 2009   D. 2007

Directions (Qs. 10 to 15) : *Answer these questions on the basis of the data given in the following table indicating the trend in sales of four companies. The amounts given are in lakhs of rupees :*

Year	Name of the Company			
	Dowby	Alpha	Baron	Celia
2004	12.00	2.00	18.50	12.00
2005	10.00	5.00	15.00	16.00
2006	18.00	7.50	16.50	15.00
2007	20.00	11.50	14.50	36.00
2008	25.00	15.00	50.00	48.00

10. Which company has shown consistently an increasing sales average?
A. Alpha   B. Baron
C. Celia   D. Dowby

11. The cumulative sales of all the companies put together in 2005 was how much of the sales of 2008?

A. $\dfrac{3}{7}$ B. $\dfrac{2}{5}$

C. $\dfrac{1}{4}$ D. $\dfrac{1}{3}$

12. What was the average sales of Baron over the 5 years?
A. 22.90   B. 21.90
C. 23.90   D. 20.90

13. Which company faced a decline in sales in 2007 over its previous year?
A. Alpha   B. Baron
C. Celia   D. Dowby

14. The ratio of the highest turnover of any company in any year to the lowest turnover of any company in any year is
A. 25   B. 15
C. 2.5   D. 0.25

15. How many companies had the same turnover in the same year?
A. 1   B. 2
C. 3   D. 4

EXPLANATORY ANSWERS

1. A:

2. D:

3. D: Required difference = 2400000 – 1300000 (From solutions of 179)
= ₹ 1100000

4. C: Dividend paid by company B = $\dfrac{402}{80.4} \times 19.6$ = ₹ 98 lakh

Dividend paid by company D $= \dfrac{270}{67.5} \times 32.5 = ₹$ 130 lakh

Their difference $= 130 - 98 = ₹$ 32 lakh.

5. D: Required percentage $= \dfrac{32.7}{29.1} \times 100 = 112.37 \approx 110\%$.

6. B:

7. A:

Year	Wage for male 18-20 years + 21-23 years	Wage for female 18-20 years + 21 – 23 years
2007	₹ 44.8	₹ 40.2
2008	₹ 33.4	₹ 32.5
2009	₹ 24.7	₹ 30.7
2010	₹ 29.0	₹ 33.9
2011	₹ 50.3	₹ 49.0
2012	₹ 47.1	₹ 54.9

Hence, in three years the wage of females was higher than that of male.

8. D: In 2012 wage for male (18-20 years) was ₹ 15.0 white wage for female was ₹ 21.0. Obviously it is maximum wage disparity.

9. B: In 2012 wage for male (21-23 years) was ₹ 32.1 white wage for female was ₹ 33.9. Obviously it is minimum wage-disparity.

10. A: Of course, Alpha has shown consistently increasing sales average.

11. C:

Year	Total Sales of all the Companies	Cumulative Sales
2004	44.50	44.50
2005	46.00	90.50
2006	57.00	147.50
2007	82.00	229.00
2008	138.00	367.50

Let, $\quad 90.50 = K \times 367.50$

$\Rightarrow \quad K = \dfrac{90.50}{367.50} = \dfrac{181}{735} \approx \dfrac{1}{4}$.

12. A: $\dfrac{18.50 + 15.00 + 16.50 + 14.50 + 50.00}{5} = \dfrac{114.50}{5} = 22.90$.

13. B: Obviously, Baron faced a decline in sales.

14. A: $\dfrac{50}{2} = 25$

15. B: In 2004, Celia and Dowby.

22

BAR GRAPHS

BAR GRAPHS

Given quantity of a bar graph can be compared by the height or length. A bar graph can have either vertical or horizontal bars. You can compare different quantities or the same quantity at the different times. The bars may be placed adjacent to each other or may be separated from each other by spaces depending upon the problem.

For Illustration:

Registration of New Vehicles in Delhi (in thousands)

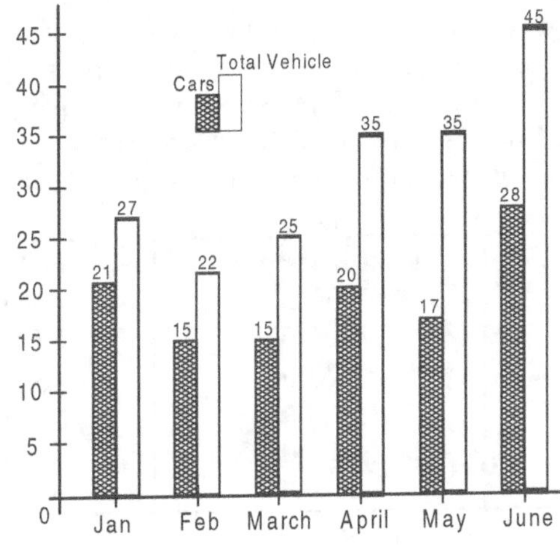

CUMULATIVE GRAPH

These are usually bar or line graphs where the height of the bar or line is divided up proportionally among various quantities presented in the graph. The representation of quantities may be done in terms of either percentage of the total or in absolute figures. These are also called sub-divided graphs. Thus, cumulative graph may be conveniently used for making comparisons.

For Illustration:

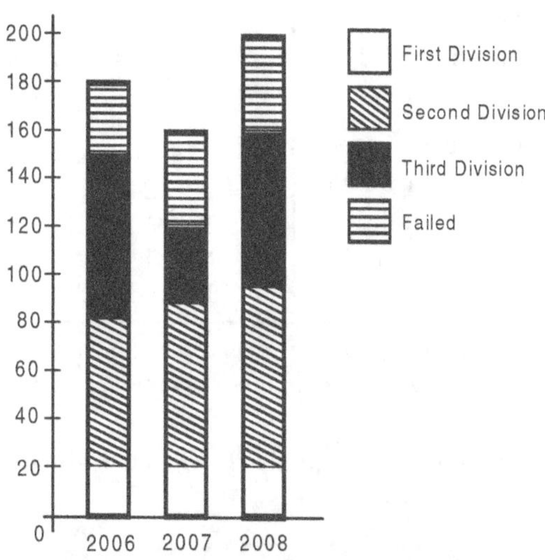

EXERCISE

Directions (Qs. 1 to 4) : *Study the following bar graph giving Economic Indices for the period 1961-62 to 2001-02 to answer these questions.*

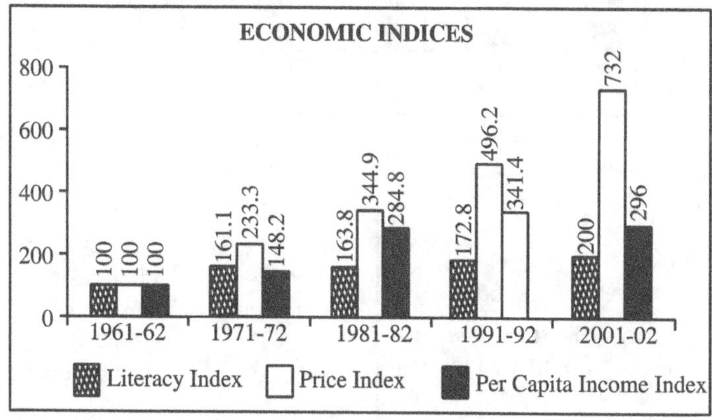

1. What is the average annual percentage increase in literacy index from 1961-62 to 2001-02?
   A. 25%   B. 15.8%
   C. 18.3%   D. 4.9%

2. Of the three economic indices which index for which period shows the maximum percentage increase as compared to the previous period?

A. Literacy, 1971-72

B. Price, 2001-02

C. Per capita income, 1981-82

D. Price, 1971-72

3. In which period the per capita income index increases at a faster rate than the price index as compared to the preceding period?

A. 1971-72   B. 2001-02
C. 1981-82   D. 1991-92

4. What are the respective indices of literacy, price and per capita income for 2001-02 taking 1971-72 as the base period?
A. 124.1, 313.8, 200
B. 313.8, 124, 201
C. 313.8, 124.1, 190
D. 124.1, 313.8, 194

Directions (Qs. 5 to 9) : *The following bar graph indicates the production of sugar (in lakh tonnes) by three different sugar companies P, Q and R over the years 2003 to 2007.*

Production of Sugar by Companies P, Q and R during 2003–2007.

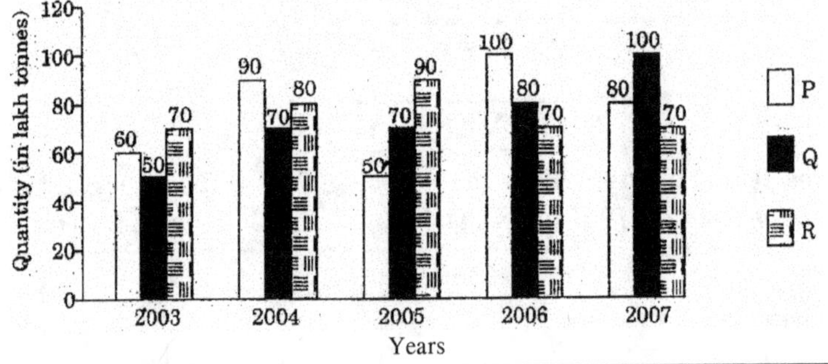

5. The percentage of production of Company R to production of Company Q is the maximum in the year
A. 2005   B. 2004
C. 2003   D. 2006

6. The ratio of the average production of Company P during the years 2005 to 2007 to the average production of Company Q for the same period is
A. 15 : 17   B. 23 : 25
C. 27 : 29   D. 9 : 11

7. The percentage increase in production of Company Q from the year 2003 to the year 2007 is
A. 60%   B. 80%
C. 90%   D. 100%

8. The average production over the years 2003–2007 was maximum for the Company(ies)
A. R   B. Q
C. P   D. None of these

9. The percentage rise or fall in production of Company Q as compared to the previous year is the maximum in the year
A. 2006   B. 2005
C. 2004   D. 2007

Directions (Qs. 10 to 13) : *Study the following graph to answer these questions.*

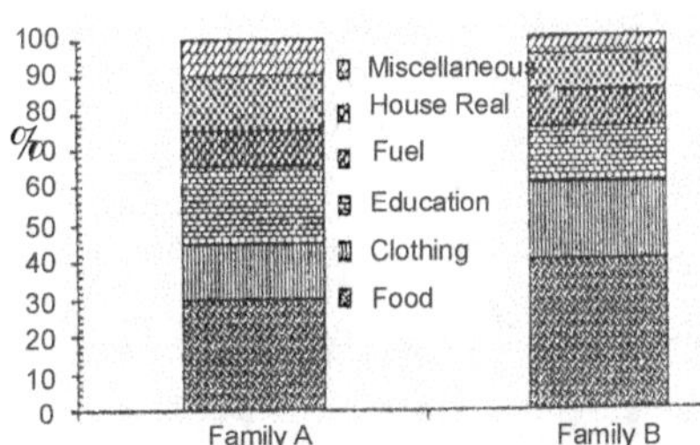

10. What fraction of the total expenditure is spent on education in family A?

A. 9/13

B. 2/3

C. 13/21

D. 1/5

11. If the total expenditure of family B is ₹ 10,000, then money spent on clothes by this family during the years is

A. ₹ 2,000   B. ₹ 600

C. ₹ 200   D. ₹ 6,000

12. If the total annual expenditure of family A is ₹ 30,000, the money spent on food, clothes and house rent is

A. ₹ 21,000   B. ₹ 18,000

C. ₹ 18,500   D. ₹ 15,000

13. What percentage is B's expenditure on food over A's expenditure on food, taking equal total expenditure?

A. 133.33%   B. 70%

C. 10%   D. 75%

EXPLANATORY ANSWERS

1. A: Average percentage increase $= \dfrac{200 - 100}{4} = 25\%$.

2. D: Price index of 1971-72 shows 133.3% increase which is maximum.

3. C:

Years	Per Capita Income Index	Price Index
71-72	48.20%	133.30%
81-82	67.88%	47.83%
91-92	19.87%	43.87%
01-02	Negative	47.52%

According to above table in 81-82. The Per capita income index increases at faster rate than the price index.

4. A:

5. C: In 2003, required percentage $= \dfrac{70}{50} \times 100 = 140\%$

In 2004, required percentage $= \dfrac{80}{70} \times 100 = 114.2\%$

In 2005, required percentage $= \dfrac{90}{70} \times 100 = 128.57\%$

Thus, in 2003 required percentage was maximum.

6. B: Required ratio = (50 + 100 + 80) : (70 + 80 + 100)
= 230 : 250 = 23 : 25

7. D: Required increase percentage
$$= \dfrac{100-50}{50} \times 100 \ = 100\%$$

8. A: Obviously that is R.

9. D: Obviously that year is 2007.

10. D: Required ratio $= \dfrac{20}{100} = \dfrac{1}{5}.$

11. A: Money spend on clothes by family B $= 1000 \times \dfrac{20}{100} = ₹\ 2000.$

12. B: Required expenditure $= 30000 \times \dfrac{(30+15+15)}{100} = ₹\ 18000.$

13. A: Required percentage $= \dfrac{40}{30} \times 100 \ = 133.33\%.$

———

23
FREQUENCY POLYGON

FREQUENCY POLYGON

Frequency Polygon are used to show how a quantity changes continuously. If the line goes up, the quantity is increasing; if the line goes down, the quantity is decreasing; if the line is horizontal, the quantity is not changing.

For Illustration:

Demand and Production of rubber (in thousand tons) in various years

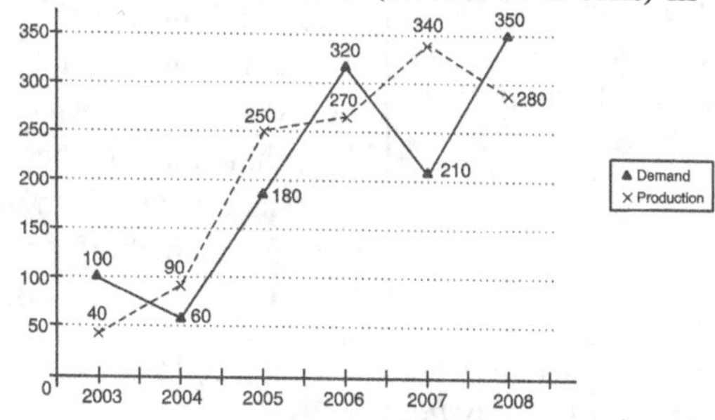

EXERCISE

Directions (Qs. 1 to 4) : *Study the given graph carefully to answer these questions.*

The following graph shows the ratio of imports to exports by two companies A and B over the years.

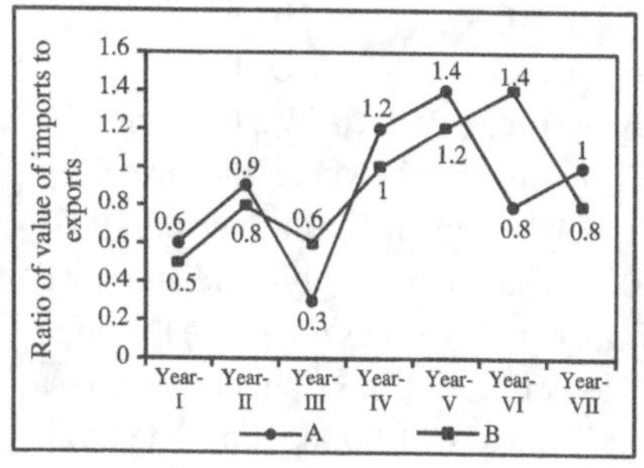

1. If the imports of company A in Year – VI were ₹ 10.40 crore, what were the exports of company A in the same year?
   A. 13 crore   B. 12.75 crore
   C. 12.50 crore D. 13.75 crore

2. It is supposed that Imports – Exports = 'x' for company A in Year-I and the imports of company A in Year-I were ₹ 3.6 crore, and it is also supposed that Imports – Exports = 'a' for company B in Year-V and the exports of company B in Year-V

were ₹ 5 crore. What is the relationship between 'a' and 'x'?

A. x > a

B. x = a

C. a > x

D. x ≠ a

3. If the exports of company B in Year-III were ₹ 2.19 crore, what were the imports of company B in the same year?

A. 3.65 crore

B. 1.314 crore

C. 1.214 crore

D. 1.414 crore

4. If the imports of company A in Year-V were ₹ 8.40 crore, what were the exports of company B in Year-VII?

A. 6 crore

B. 7.40 crore

C. 7.20 crore

D. Data inadequate

Directions (Qs. 5 to 8) : *The following graph shows the number of successful candidates from different schools (A to F) in different disciplines. Study the graph carefully to answer these questions.*

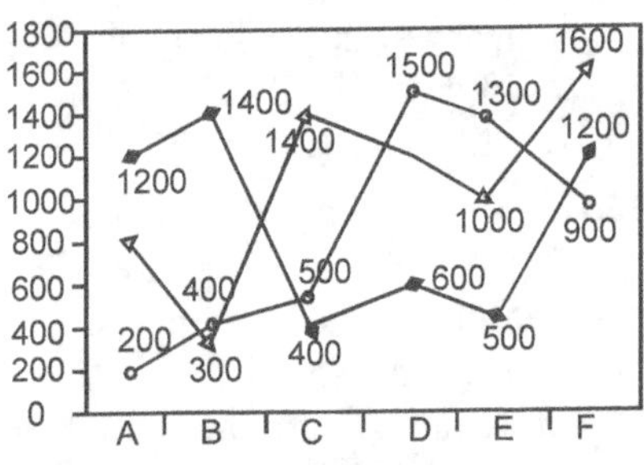

5. In which of the following institutes is the difference between the number of successful candidates in Engineering and that in Medical discipline the maximum?

A. F

B. C

C. B

D. D

6. The total number of successful candidates from Medical discipline is approximately what per cent more than that from Law?

A. 8%

B. 15%

C. 12%

D. 10%

7. The number of successful candidates from F in Engineering discipline is what per cent more than the number of successful candidates from A in Medical discipline?

A. 30%

B. 25%

C. $33\frac{1}{3}\%$

D. 20%

8. In which of the following institutes is the sum of the number of successful candidates in Engineering and Law disciplines 50% of the number of Medical students of the same institute?

A. C

B. E

C. D

D. B

Directions (Qs. 9 to 12) : Consider the following graph where the prices of timber are given for the period 1997-2003. The prices for plywood and sawn timber are given in ₹/m³ while the price of logs is given in ₹/tonne. Assume 1 ton is equal to 1,000 kg and one cu.m of log weigh 800 kg.

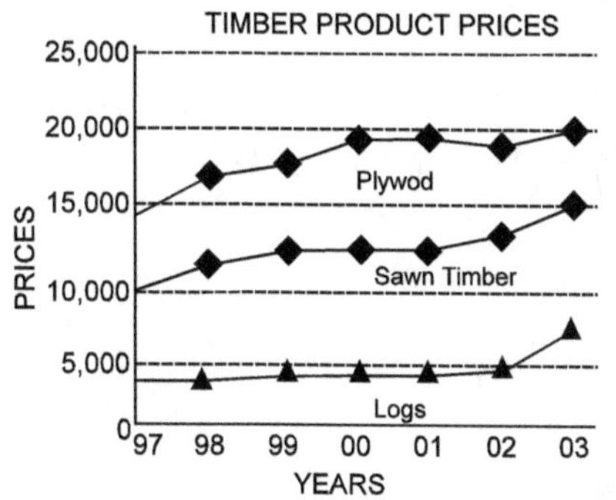

9. Which product had the largest percentage increase in price per cubic meter over the 7-year period ?
A. Sawn timber
B. Logs
C. Plywood
D. None of these

10. The maximum increase in price per cubic metre for any product over any two successive years was :
A. ₹ 2,500　　B. ₹ 3,125
C. ₹ 2,000　　D. ₹ 4,125

11. In 2003, the total sales of the company measured in cubic metres was made up of 40% plywood, 30% sawn timber and 30% logs. The average realisation per cubic metre in 2003 was closest to :
A. ₹ 16,500　　B. ₹ 13,500
C. ₹ 15,000　　D. ₹ 18,000

12. In 2004, the prices of plywood, sawn timber and logs went up by 5%, 1% and 10%, respectively, and the total sales were made up of 40% plywood, 30% sawn timber and 30% logs. The average realisation per cubic metre in 2004 was closest to :
A. ₹ 15,500　　B. ₹ 16,500
C. ₹ 14,500　　D. ₹ 18,500

EXPLANATORY ANSWERS

1. A:

2. C: $x = ₹\ 3.6$ crore $- ₹\ \dfrac{3.6}{0.6}$ crore $= -\ ₹\ 2.4$ crore

$a = ₹\ 5$ crore $\times 1.2 - ₹\ 5$ crore $= ₹\ 1$ crore

Thus, $a > x$.

3. B: Required exports = ₹ 2.19 crore × 0.6 = ₹ 1.314 crore.

4. D: There is no relation between imports of company A in year-V and exports of company B in year-VIII and the given data is not sufficient to answer the question.

5. B:

Institute	Required difference
A	1200 − 800 = 400
B	1400 − 300 = 1100
C	1400 − 400 = 1000
D	1200 − 600 = 600
E	1000 − 500 = 500
F	1600 − 1200 = 400.

6. D: Total number of successful candidates in
Medical = 5300, Law = 4800

$$\text{Required percentage} = \frac{5300 \times 4800}{4800} \times 100 = 10.4\% = 10\%.$$

7. C: Successful candidates from F in Engineering = 1600
Successful candidates from A in Medical = 1200

$$\text{Required percentage} = \frac{1600 - 1200}{1200} \times 100$$

$$= \frac{100}{3} = 33\frac{1}{3}\%.$$

8. D:

	A	B	C	D	E	F
Medical	1200	1400	400	600	500	1200
Engineering	800	300	1400	1200	1000	1600
Law	200	400	500	1500	1300	900

Hence, in B the total number of successful candidates of Engineering and Law is 50% of the number of candidates of Medical.

9. B: Increase in plywood = $\dfrac{(20,000 - 14000)}{14000} \times 100 = 42.86\%$

Increase in Sawn Timber = $\dfrac{15000 - 10000}{10000} \times 100 = 50\%$

Increase in Logs = $\dfrac{\dfrac{7500}{1.25} - \dfrac{4000}{1.25}}{\dfrac{4000}{1.25}} \times 100 = 87.5\%$

Hence, Logs had the largest increase in prices.

10. A: In plywood during 97 to 98 the price rise is about ₹ 2500 and it is maximum.

11. C: 40% of ₹ 20000 = $20000 \times \dfrac{40}{100}$ = ₹ 8000

30% of ₹ 15000 = $15000 \times \dfrac{30}{100}$ = ₹ 4500

30% of ₹ 7500 = $7500 \times \dfrac{30}{100}$ = ₹ 2250

Total = ₹ 8000 + ₹ 4500 + ₹ 2250 = ₹ 14750 ≈ ₹ 15000.
Hence, correct answer in C

12. A:

———————

24

PIE CHARTS

PIE CHARTS

These are used to show the share of various sectors in the total. They usually show the percentage share of each sector in the whole (taken as 100%). In such representation the total quantity in question is distributed over a total angle of 360°. The area of each sector is proportional to the relative frequency of the class represented by the sector.

$$\text{Sector angle} = \frac{\text{Class frequency}}{\text{Total frequency}} \times 360°$$

For Illustration:

Distribution of Expenditure of a family

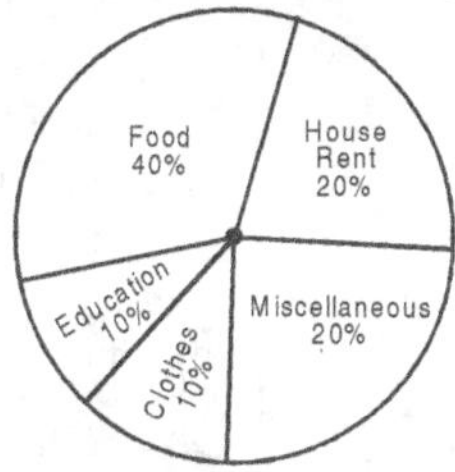

EXERCISE

Directions (Qs. 1 to 4) : *Study the pie-chart carefully to answer the questions that follow:*

Percentage-wise Break up of Students in terms of Specialization in MBA

TOTAL NUMBER OF STUDENTS = 8000

1. What is the total number of students having specialization in IR, Marketing and IT?
   A. 4640   B. 4080
   C. 4260   D. 4400

2. Students having IB as specialization forms **approximately** what per cent of students having Marketing as specialization?
   A. 116   B. 86
   C. 124   D. 74

3. What is the total number of students having IB as specilization?
   A. 1520   B. 1280
   C. 1360   D. 1120

4. What is the respective ratio of the students having Finance as specialization to that of students having HR as specialization?
   A. 11 : 19   B. 18 : 13
   C. 6 : 7   D. 12 : 21

Directions (Qs. 5 to 8) : *Study the graph below to answer these questions.*

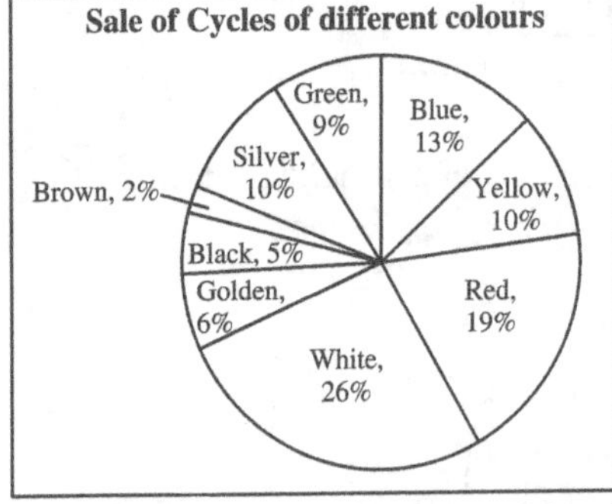

5. 50% of all the cycles consisted of which colours?
   A. Black, Golden, Blue, Red
   B. Blue, Black, Red, Silver
   C. White, Golden, Blue, Black
   D. Golden, Green, Black, White

6. Cycles of which colour when increased by two per cent and then combined with that of red cycles will make 30 per cent of the total?
   A. Golden
   B. Blue
   C. Black
   D. None of these

7. If in certain period the total production of all cycles was 95400 then how many more blue cycles were sold than green?
   A. 2580   B. 3618
   C. 2850   D. 3816

8. Cycles of which colour are 20% less popular than white coloured cycles?
   A. Black
   B. Golden
   C. Blue
   D. None of these

Directions (Qs. 9 to 12) : *Study the pir-chart below to answer these questions. The chart gives the composition of solar radiation.*

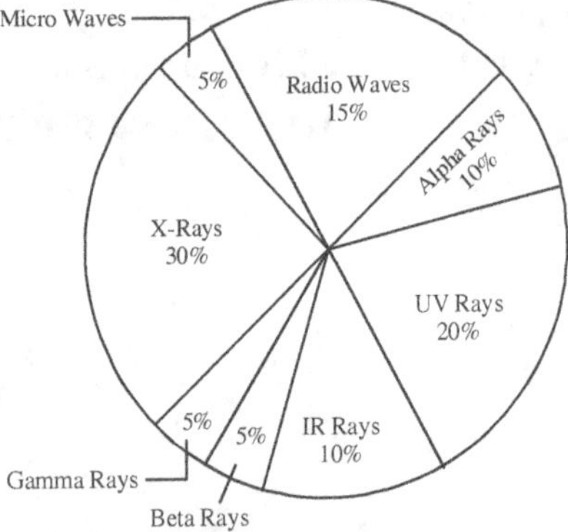

Total sun rays received in one minute = 3600 units

9. If the human body can withstand a maximum of 9720 units of IR rays when exposed to the sun continuously, then what is the maximum time in minutes that any person could stand in the sun without crossing the threshold limit of IR rays?

   A. 23   B. 19
   C. 27   D. 29

10. The amount of Beta rays in 10 minutes of the sun rays is how many times the amount of IR rays in 3 minutes of the sun rays?

   A. 1.44   B. 1.33
   C. 1.66   D. None of these

11. How many minutes of exposure to the sun in a day would be enough to ensure that the body receives enough amount of Vitamin D, given that the body requires 40 units of Vitamin D every day and that 30 units of Beta rays generate one unit of Vitamin D?

   A. $5\dfrac{1}{3}$ B. $5\dfrac{2}{3}$

   C. $6\dfrac{1}{3}$ D. $6\dfrac{2}{3}$

12. The amount of Alpha rays received in two minutes is how much more/less than the amount of Radio waves received in 4 minutes?

   A. 1320 units more
   B. 1200 units less
   C. 1440 units less
   D. 1600 units more

EXPLANATORY ANSWERS

1. D:

2. B: Required percentage $= \dfrac{19}{22} \times 100 = 86.36\% \approx 86\%$

3. A: Required number of Students $= \dfrac{19}{100} \times 8000 = 1520$

4. C: Required ratio $= 12 : 14 = 6 : 7$

5. C: Obviously, White, Golden, Blue and Black colours consists 50% of cycles.

6. D: Clearly, there is no such colours.

7. D: Required difference $= 95400 \times \dfrac{(13-9)}{100} = 954 \times 4 = 3816.$

8. D: There is no such coloured cycle which is exactly 20% less popular than White coloured cycles.

9. C: The maximum time $= \dfrac{9720}{\dfrac{3600 \times 10}{100}} = 27.$

10. D:

11. D: 40 units of vitamin D generate from

$$= 40 \times 30 = 1200 \text{ units of } \beta\text{-rays}$$

The amount of β-rays received in 1 min.

$$= \frac{5}{100} \times 3600 = 180 \text{ units}$$

Hence, required time $= \dfrac{1200}{180} = 6\dfrac{2}{3}$ min.

12. C: The amount of a-rays received in 2 min.

$$= \frac{10}{100} \times 3600 \times 2 = 720 \text{ units}$$

The amount of radio waves received in 4 min.

$$= \frac{15}{100} \times 3600 \times 4 = 2160 \text{ units}$$

Required difference $= 2160 - 720 = 1440$ units less.

25

MISCELLANEOUS QUESTIONS

1. When three right hand side digits of a number are 1,000 the number is divisible by:
   A. 4
   B. 5
   C. 9
   D. All the above

2. When the two right hand side digits of a number are 100, the number is divisible by:
   A. 2
   B. 4
   C. 5
   D. All the above

3. When the last digit of a number is 5, the number is divisible by:
   A. 3
   B. 5
   C. 25
   D. All the above

4. The H.C.F. of the product of first six odd numbers and the product of first six even numbers is:
   A. 45   B. 40
   C. 34   D. 30

5. $1\dfrac{1}{2}+\dfrac{1}{7}\times10\dfrac{1}{2}-2\dfrac{1}{3}\div1\dfrac{3}{4}$ of $1\dfrac{1}{3}$ is equal to:
   A. 1   B. 2
   C. 3   D. 4

6. $6\dfrac{1}{2}-\left[5\dfrac{1}{2}-\left\{4\dfrac{1}{2}-\left(3\dfrac{1}{2}-2\dfrac{1}{2}-\overline{\dfrac{1}{2}}\right)\right\}\right]$
   is equal to:
   A. 4   B. 3
   C. 2   D. 1

7. $\dfrac{1}{2}+\dfrac{2}{3}/\dfrac{3}{7}-\dfrac{1}{6}$ is equal to:
   A. $5\dfrac{4}{11}$ B. $3\dfrac{5}{11}$
   C. $4\dfrac{5}{11}$ D. $7\dfrac{6}{21}$

8. The sum of $\dfrac{1}{2},\dfrac{1}{4},\dfrac{1}{8}$ of a number is 28. The number is:
   A. 24   B. 28
   C. 32   D. 36

9. If 20 men can finish a piece of work in 10 days, how many persons can finish the same job in 4 days?
   A. 20   B. 30
   C. 40   D. 50

10. If 15 men can finish a job in 20 days, 25 men will finish the same job in:
    A. 8 days   B. 12 days
    C. 16 days   D. 12 days

144

EXPLANATORY ANSWERS

1. D: For example, consider the number 1000. The multiples of 1000 are 125 and 8, while the multiples of 125 and 8 are 5 and 4. Hence, the number is divisible by 4, 5 as well as 8.

2. D.

3. B.

4. A: First six odd numbers are 1, 3, 5, 7, 9, 11

Product of first six odd numbers $= 1 \times 3 \times 5 \times 7 \times 9 \times 11$
$$= 1 \times 3 \times 5 \times 7 \times 3 \times 3 \times 11$$

First six even numbers are 2, 4, 6, 8, 10, 12

Product of first six even numbers $= 2 \times 4 \times 6 \times 8 \times 10 \times 12$
$$= 2 \times 2 \times 2 \times 2 \times 3 \times 2 \times 2 \times 2 \times 2 \times 5 \times 2 \times 2 \times 3$$

The common factors are 3, 3, 5.

$\therefore$ H.C.F. $= 3 \times 3 \times 5 = 45.$

5. B:
$$1\frac{1}{2} + \frac{1}{7} \times 10\frac{1}{2} - 2\frac{1}{3} \div 1\frac{3}{4} \text{ of } 1\frac{1}{3} = \frac{3}{2} + \frac{1}{7} \times \frac{21}{2} - \frac{7}{3} \div \frac{7}{4} \text{ of } \frac{4}{3}$$
$$= \frac{3}{2} + \frac{3}{2} - \frac{7}{3} \div \frac{7}{3} = \frac{3}{2} + \frac{3}{2} - \frac{7}{3} \times \frac{3}{7} = \frac{3}{2} + \frac{3}{2} - 1 = \frac{3}{2} + \frac{1}{2} = 2.$$

6. A:
$$6\frac{1}{2} - \left[5\frac{1}{2} - \left\{4\frac{1}{2} - \left(3\frac{1}{2} - 2\overline{\frac{1}{2} - \frac{1}{2}}\right)\right\}\right]$$
$$= \frac{13}{2} - \left[\frac{11}{2} - \left\{\frac{9}{2} - \left(\frac{7}{2} - 2\right)\right\}\right] = \frac{13}{2} - \left[\frac{11}{2} - \left\{\frac{9}{2} - \frac{3}{2}\right\}\right]$$
$$= \frac{13}{2} - \left[\frac{11}{2} - 3\right] = \frac{13}{2} - \frac{5}{2} = 4.$$

7. C:
$$\frac{1}{2} + \frac{2}{3} / \frac{3}{7} - \frac{1}{6} = \frac{7}{6} / \frac{11}{42} = \frac{7}{6} \times \frac{42}{11} = \frac{49}{11} = 4\frac{5}{11}.$$

8. C: Let the number be x.

$$\therefore \frac{x}{2} + \frac{x}{4} + \frac{x}{8} = 28, \text{ or } \frac{7}{x} = 28 \qquad \therefore x = \frac{28 \times 8}{7} = 32.$$

9. D: Work can be finished in 10 days by 20 men

Work can be finished in 1 day by 20×10 men

Work can be finished in 4 days by $\dfrac{20 \times 10}{4} = 50$ men.

10. B: 15 men can finish the job in 20 days

25 men can finish the job in $\dfrac{20 \times 15}{25} = 12$ days.

1310

Reasoning and Analytical Ability

1

Analogies or Relationships

Wrong Analogy

In Analogy Tests the relationship between two given words is established and then applied to the other words. The type of relationship may vary, so while attempting such questions the first step is to identify the type of relationship.

EXERCISE

Directions : *In the questions given below establish the relationship between the two words. Then from the given options select one which has the same relationship as of the given two words.*

1. *Guilt* is to *Past* as *Hope* is to.....
   (a) Present (b) Future
   (c) Today (d) Despair

2. .... is to *Liquid* as *Mile* is to *Distance.*
   (a) Unit (b) Kilo
   (c) Scale (d) Litre

3. *Bench* is to *Judges* as *Chair* is to.......
   (a) Attorney (b) President
   (c) Lawyer (d) Ruler

4. *Psychology* is to *Emotions* as *Philosophy* is to.....

   (a) Knowledge (b) Scholar
   (c) Research (d) Wisdom

5. *Surgeon* is to *Scalpel* as *Sculptor* is to....
   (a) Pastle (b) Chisel
   (c) Pallet (d) Engraving

6. .... is to *Dumb* as *Light* is to *Blind.*
   (a) Voice (b) Language
   (c) Speech (d) Tongue

7. *Physicist is to Physics as* .... *is to Anatomy.*
   (a) Botany (b) Botanist
   (c) Body (d) Biologist

8. *Frequently* is to *Always* as *Seldom* is to......
   (a) Often
   (b) Rarely
   (c) Occasionally
   (d) Never

4

9. *Tailor* is related to *Cloth* in the same way as *Cobbler* is related to ....
   (a) Machine   (b) Leather
   (c) Stiching   (d) Mending

10. *Millionaire* is related to *Wealth* in the same way as *Genius* is related to ....
   (a) Capability   (b) Smartness
   (c) Intelligence(d) Awareness

EXPLANATORY ANSWERS

1. (b) : Feeling of guilt comes with mistakes in past and that of hope for a good future.

2. (d) : Liquid is measured in litres and distance in miles.

3. (b) : The seat of judges is bench and that of President a chair.

4. (d) : Psychology is the study of emotions as philosophy is of wisdom.

5. (b) : As scalpel is an instrument used by a surgeon so is chisel of a sculptor.

6. (c) : Blind cannot see the light and dumb cannot give speech.

7. (d) : Physicist deals with the subject Physics and biologist with subject anatomy.

8. (d) : The related words are near opposites.

9. (b) : Tailor makes clothes from cloth, cobbler makes shoes from leather.

10. (c) : A millionaire has lots of wealth, a genius has lots of intelligence.

Letter Analogy

In this type of analogy the relationship between two given set of letters is established and then applied to the other set to obtain the required set of letters as the answer. These letters can be moved some steps backward or forward; reversed in whole or in sections or have some common identity between each other.

EXERCISE

Directions : *In the questions given below one term is missing. Based on the relationship of the two given words find the missing term from the given options.*

1. GFC : CFG : : RPJ : ?
   (a) JRP   (b) JPR
   (c) PJR   (d) RJP

2. BCF : DEG : : MNQ : ?
   (a) OPR   (b) PQS
   (c) OPP   (d) QRT

3. UVW : SXU : : LMN : ?
   (a) JOL   (b) KNM
   (c) JKL   (d) MLO

4. BCDA : STUR : : KLMJ : ?
   (a) VWXU   (b) EFHG
   (c) SRTU   (d) QSRP

5. AEI : LPT : : CGK : ?
   (a) OSV   (b) RUY
   (c) TXC   (d) FJN

6. RUX : TRP : : BEH : ?
   (*a*) SQN   (*b*) QON
   (*c*) QOM   (*d*) QNL

7. RRS : XMW : : ITB : ?
   (*a*) PNE   (*b*) NOG
   (*c*) RSW   (*d*) OOF

8. LOM : NMK : : PKI : ?
   (*a*) RNK   (*b*) RSM
   (*c*) RMP   (*d*) RIG

9. ARQ : DTR : : JNG : ?
   (*a*) MPH   (*b*) PHJ
   (*c*) LPI   (*d*) GLE

10. BYDW : FVHT : : GQIO : ?
   (*a*) JLNP
   (*b*) QSTR
   (*c*) KMOL
   (*d*) KNML

ANSWERS

1	2	3	4	5	6	7	8	9	10
(*b*)	(*a*)	(*a*)	(*a*)	(*d*)	(*c*)	(*d*)	(*d*)	(*a*)	(*d*)

SOME SELECTED EXPLANATORY ANSWERS

1. The letters of the first group are reversed.

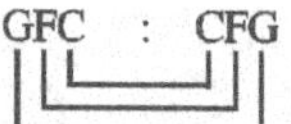

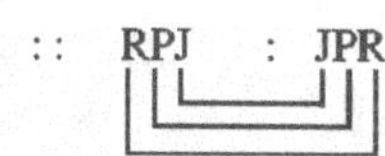

3. The three letters are moved –2, +2 and –2 steps respectively.

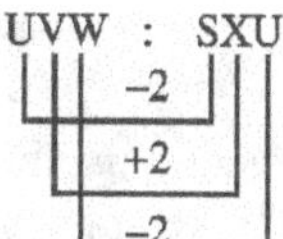

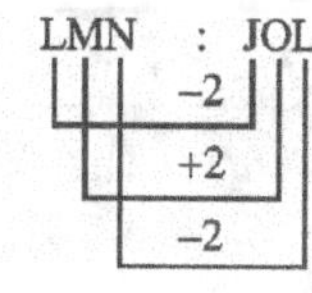

4. In each group the first three letters are consecutive and they follow the fourth letter.

5. In each group the letters jump three letters between them, *i.e.*, they are moving to the fourth letter.

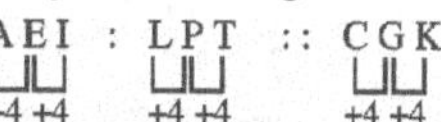

9. The three letters are moved 3, 2 and 1 step forward respectively.

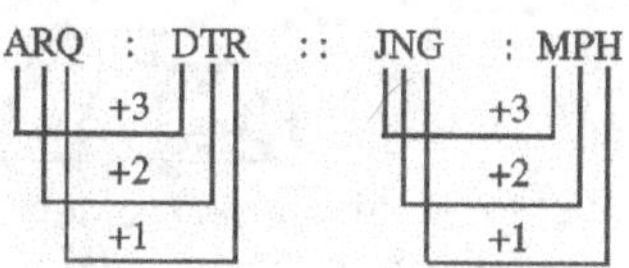

10. The letters are moved +4, –3, +4, –3 steps respectively

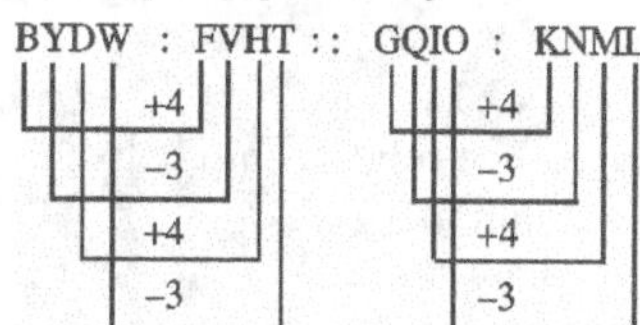

Number Analogy

In number analogy also, the relationship between the given numbers is detected and then applied to the second part to find the missing numbers.

Example

Directions : *Which number will come in the place of question mark?*

25 : 81 : : 36 : ?

   (*a*) 121   (*b*) 93   (*c*) 65   (*d*) 103

Ans. (*a*) **:** All the numbers are squares of different numbers.

$$\begin{array}{ccccccc} 25 & : & 81 & :: & 36 & : & 121 \\ \downarrow & & \downarrow & & \downarrow & & \downarrow \\ 5^2 & & 9^2 & & 6^2 & & 11^2 \end{array}$$

EXERCISE

Directions : *In the following questions, select the number from the given options which follows the same relationship as shared between the first two numbers.*

1. 18 : 27 : : 22 : ?

   (*a*) 42   (*b*) 39

   (*c*) 33   (*d*) 54

2. 14 : 20 : : 16 : ?

   (*a*) 23   (*b*) 10

   (*c*) 48   (*d*) 32

3. 8 : 27 : : 64 : ?

   (*a*) 277   (*b*) 125

   (*c*) 250   (*d*) 99

4. $\dfrac{1}{7} : \dfrac{1}{14} :: \dfrac{1}{9} : ?$

   (*a*) $\dfrac{1}{88}$ (*b*) $\dfrac{1}{80}$

   (*c*) $\dfrac{1}{81}$ (*d*) $\dfrac{1}{18}$

5. 0.16 : 0.0016 : : 1.02 : ?

   (*a*) 10.20   (*b*) 0.102

   (*c*) 0.0102   (*d*) 1.020

EXPLANATORY ANSWERS

1. (*c*) **:** In the given set, the numbers are multiples of 9 and in the second set, multiples of 11.

$$\begin{array}{ccccccc} 18 & : & 27 & :: & 22 & : & 33 \\ \downarrow & & \downarrow & & \downarrow & & \downarrow \\ 9\times2 & & 9\times3 & & 11\times2 & & 11\times3 \end{array}$$

2. (*a*) **:** The relationship between the numbers is :

$$\begin{array}{ccccccc} 14 & : & 20 & :: & 16 & : & 23 \\ \downarrow & & \downarrow & & \downarrow & & \downarrow \\ 7\times2 & & (7\times3)-1 & & 8\times2 & & (8\times3)-1 \end{array}$$

3. (*b*) **:** The numbers are cubes of different numbers.

$$\begin{array}{ccccccc} 8 & : & 27 & :: & 64 & : & 125 \\ \downarrow & & \downarrow & & \downarrow & & \downarrow \\ 2^3 & & 3^3 & & 4^3 & & 5^3 \end{array}$$

4. (*d*) **:** The first fraction is multiplied by half to obtain the second fraction.

$$\dfrac{1}{7} : \underset{\times\frac{1}{2}}{\underbrace{\dfrac{1}{14}}} :: \dfrac{1}{9} : \underset{\times\frac{1}{2}}{\underbrace{\dfrac{1}{18}}}$$

5. (*c*) **:** The decimals are divided by 100.

$$0.16 : \underset{\div 100}{\underbrace{0.0016}} :: 1.02 : \underset{\div 100}{\underbrace{0.0102}}$$

2
Series

Letter Series

In letter series the letters follow a definite order. The given series of letters can be in natural order or in reverse order or combination of both. The letters may be skipped or repeated or consecutive. The given series may be single or may even comprise of two different series merged at alternate positions. While attempting questions on letter series one should note the pattern of alphabet series.

Alphabets in natural series are :

A B C D E F G H I J K L M N O P Q R S T U V W X Y Z

1st   5th   10th   15th   20th   25th

Alphabets in reverse series are :

Z Y X W V U T S R Q P O N M L K J I H G F E D C B A

1st   5th   10th   15th   20th   25th

Note : On reaching Z, the series restarts from A and on reaching A, it restarts from Z.

Example

Directions : *Which of the given options will complete the given series?*

    B D F H J ?

   (*a*) L   (*b*) O   (*c*) M   (*d*) K

Ans. *(a)* : The series follows the pattern of moving the letters two steps forward.

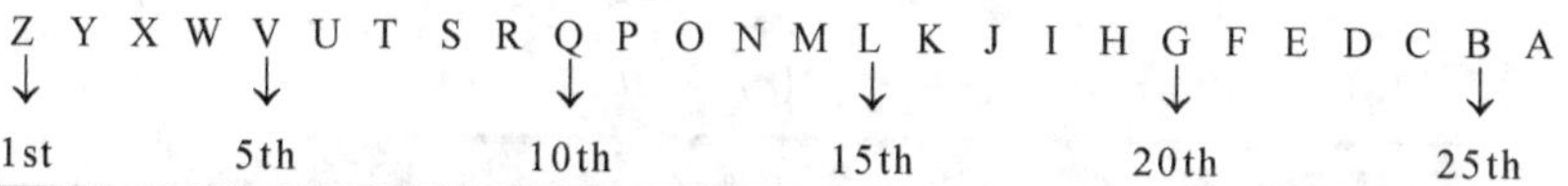

EXERCISE

Directions : *In each of the following series determine the order of the letters. Then from the given options select the one which will complete the given series.*

1. B Y C X D W E ?
- (a) S
- (b) T
- (c) U
- (d) V

2. A D C G E ?
- (a) G
- (b) J
- (c) I
- (d) L

3. X O I F ?
- (a) D
- (b) F
- (c) B
- (d) E

4. Z A A Y B B X C ?
- (a) W
- (b) C
- (c) V
- (d) D

5. A Z Y B X W C V U D T S E ?
- (a) R S
- (b) S T
- (c) R Q
- (d) Q R

6. R K F ? B
- (a) D
- (b) C
- (c) E
- (d) B

7. R Z J K S B C ?
- (a) W
- (b) K
- (c) L
- (d) X

8. A L W B M X C N ?
- (a) V
- (b) W
- (c) Y
- (d) X

9. LAZ, NEX, PIV, ?
- (a) SLS
- (b) QNS
- (c) RMT
- (d) RMS

10. EJOT, DHLP, CFIL, ?
- (a) BDFH
- (b) DGKL
- (c) DEIJ
- (d) BLHM

ANSWERS

1	2	3	4	5	6	7	8	9	10
(d)	(b)	(b)	(b)	(c)	(b)	(b)	(c)	(c)	(a)

SOME SELECTED EXPLANATORY ANSWERS

1. There are two alternate series.

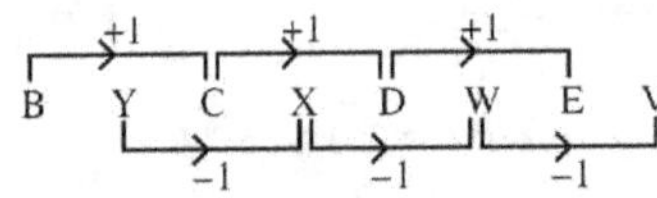

Series I : BCDE (natural order)
Series II : YXWV (reverse order)

3. The series follows the sequence of the difference decreasing by 3 *i.e.*

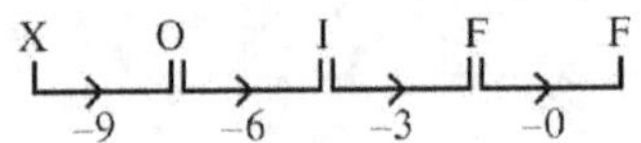

5. There are two alternate series.

Series I : ABCDE (in natural series)
Series II : ZY XW VU TS RQ
(double letter in reverse series)

6. The difference between the letters is reduced by two at each step.

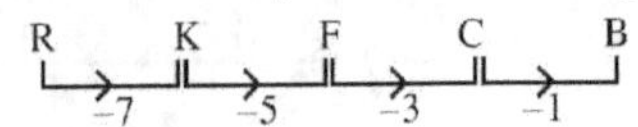

8. There are three alternate series.

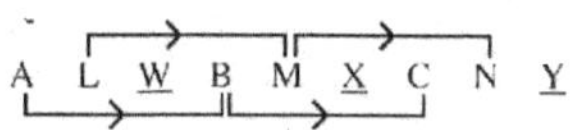

Series I : ABC
Series II : LMN
Series III : WXY

10. The letters in each group correspond to the letters in the next group in the manner –1, –2, –3, –4 respectively.

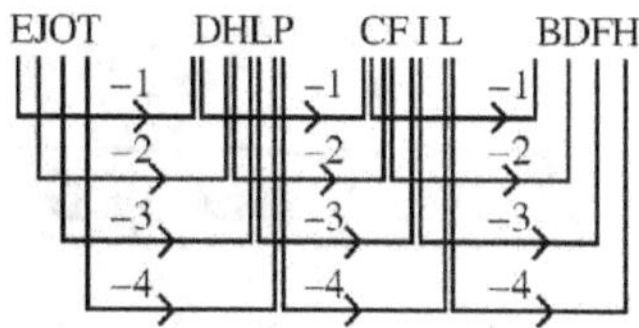

Wrong Letter Series

In this type of series the candidates are not required to find the letter or group of letters which will complete the given series but, they have to identify the letter or number which is wrong or misfit in the given series.

Example

Which of the following letters in the given series is wrong?

J M P T V Y

(*a*) J   (*b*) P   (*c*) T   (*d*) Y

Ans. (*c*) : The letters in this series are moved three steps forward, *i.e.,*

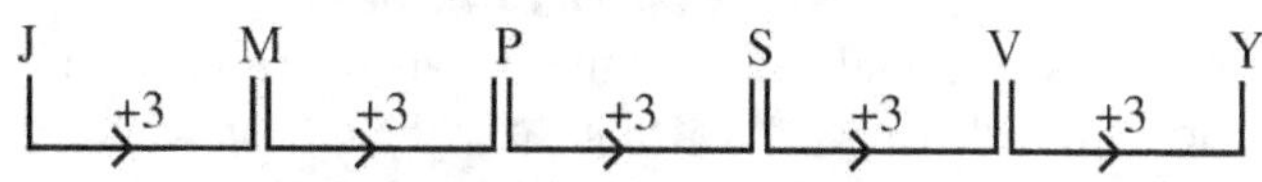

Letter 'T' should have been 'S'.

EXERCISE

Directions : *Which letter(s) in each of the following series is wrong or is misfit in the series?*

1. C H M S W B
(*a*) C
(*b*) S
(*c*) B
(*d*) W

2. Z A W B X C
(*a*) D   (*b*) C
(*c*) X   (*d*) W

3. D K R Y F L
(*a*) L
(*b*) D
(*c*) R
(*d*) Y

4. XW, DC, CB, NM, PQ
(*a*) NM   (*b*) CB
(*c*) PQ   (*d*) XW

5. Z T P K H F
(*a*) Z   (*b*) P
(*c*) T   (*d*) F

ANSWERS

1	**2**	**3**	**4**	**5**
(*b*)	(*d*)	(*a*)	(*c*)	(*b*)

SOME SELECTED EXPLANATORY ANSWERS

1. The letters in the series are moved five steps forward.

C H M R W B
+5 +5 +5 +5 +5

R should be in place of S.

3. The pattern in this series in moving the letters seven steps forward.

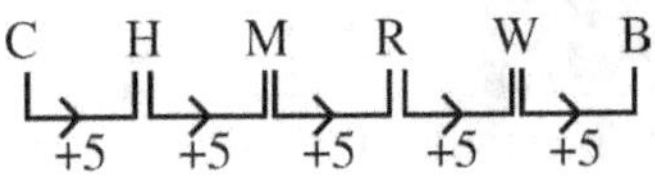

D K R Y F M
+7 +7 +7 +7 +7

M should be in place of L.

4. The series is made with any two consecutive letters written backwards.

XW DC CB NM QP
← ← ← ← ←

Q should come before P in the series.

Repeat Series

In this type of series small letters of the alphabet are used to make a set of letters which are repeated. The candidate has to find the set of letters which will fit the blanks left in the given series in such a manner that one section of the series is further repeated in the same manner.

Example

Which of the following groups of letters will complete the given series?

ba-b-aab-a-b

(*a*) baab (*b*) abba (*c*) abaa (*d*) babb

Ans. (*b*) : The series is baab, baab, baab. Here the section 'baab' is repeated in the series.

Solving steps : The candidate has to look for clues to solve such series pattern. 'aab' in the Series indicates that 'b' in this series is preceded by two 'a' so, the first blank and the last blank will be filled by 'a'. Now the first set is formed, *i.e.,* 'baab' in the beginning. This set is repeated, so the second and third blanks will have 'b' filling them. Now, solve the exercise given below to know the different ways in which these series are formed.

EXERCISE

Directions : *Which of the following groups of letters will complete the given series?*

1. b-abbc-bbca-bcabb-ab
   - (*a*) acba
   - (*b*) acaa
   - (*c*) cacc
   - (*d*) cabc

2. aca-ac--a-ac
   - (*a*) babc
   - (*b*) aaac
   - (*c*) cacc
   - (*d*) caca

3. ba-cb-b-bab-?
   - (*a*) acbb
   - (*b*) bcaa
   - (*c*) cabb
   - (*d*) bacc

4. ab-aa-caab-aab-a
   - (*a*) bcbc
   - (*b*) bbca
   - (*c*) cbcc
   - (*d*) caba

5. -bbcaa-bcaa-bc-a-bca
   - (*a*) bacab
   - (*b*) abbab
   - (*c*) abcba
   - (*d*) bcaab

EXPLANATORY ANSWERS

1. (*d*) : The series is bcab, bcab, bcab, bcab, bcab

2. (*c*) : The series is ac, ac, ac, ac, ac, ac

3. (*d*) : The series is babc, babc, babc

4. (*c*) : The series is abca, abca, abca, abca

5. (*b*) : The series is abbca, abbca, abbca, abbca

Number Series

In this type of series, the set of given numbers in a series are related to one another in a particular pattern or manner. The relationship between the numbers may be (i) consecutive odd/even numbers; (ii) consecutive prime numbers; (iii) squares/cubes of some numbers with/without variation of addition or subtraction of some number; (iv) sum/product/difference of preceding numbers; (v) addition/subtraction/multiplication/division by some number; and (vi) many more combinations of the relationships given above.

Example

Complete the given series.

2, 14, 98, 686, ?
- (*a*) 1976
- (*b*) 2548
- (*c*) 980
- (*d*) 4802

Ans. (*d*) : The numbers are multiplied by 7 to obtain the next numbers.

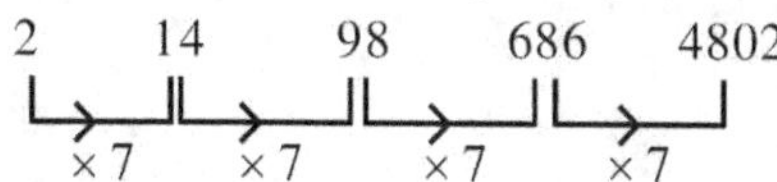

EXERCISE

Directions : *In the following questions, select the number(s) from the given options for completing the given series.*

1. 1, 8, 27, 64, 125, ?
   - (a) 172
   - (b) 176
   - (c) 216
   - (d) 189
2. 2, 3, 5, 7, 11, 13, ?
   - (a) 19
   - (b) 57
   - (c) 31
   - (d) 17
3. 80, 64, 48, 32, 16, ?
   - (a) 4
   - (b) 0
   - (c) 8
   - (d) 1
4. 3, 8, 13, 24, 41, ?
   - (a) 65
   - (b) 75
   - (c) 70
   - (d) 80
5. 9, 81, 90, 810, 819, ?
   - (a) 7371
   - (b) 900
   - (c) 8100
   - (d) 1638
6. 0, 8, 24, 48, 80, ?
   - (a) 110
   - (b) 96
   - (c) 120
   - (d) 140
7. 2, 4, 8, 3, 9, 27, 4, 16, ?
   - (a) 64
   - (b) 32
   - (c) 48
   - (d) 24
8. 27, 28, 25, 25, 23, 22, 21, ?
   - (a) 20
   - (b) 21
   - (c) 19
   - (d) 18
9. 80, 63, 72, 72, 64, 81, 56, ?
   - (a) 96
   - (b) 98
   - (c) 89
   - (d) 90
10. 0, 5, 22, 57, ?, 205
    - (a) 198
    - (b) 116
    - (c) 172
    - (d) 92

ANSWERS

1	2	3	4	5	6	7	8	9	10
(c)	(d)	(b)	(c)	(a)	(c)	(a)	(c)	(d)	(b)

SOME SELECTED EXPLANATORY ANSWERS

1. The sequence in the series is cube of numbers in their natural order.

2. The series consists of prime numbers in increasing order.

3. The numbers in the series are decreasing with the difference of 16 at each step.

5. The sequence in the series is × 9, + 9 which is repeated.

7. In this series 3 numbers form a set. The first number is in natural order. The second number is the square of above number. The third number is the cube of first number.

10. The series follows this sequence : cube of natural numbers starting from 1 minus odd numbers starting from 1.

$$0 \quad 5 \quad 22 \quad 57 \quad 116 \quad 205$$
$$\downarrow \quad \downarrow \quad \downarrow \quad \downarrow \quad \downarrow \quad \downarrow$$
$$1^3 - 1 \quad 2^3 - 3 \quad 3^3 - 5 \quad 4^3 - 7 \quad 5^3 - 9 \quad 6^3 - 11$$

Wrong Number Series

In this type of series the given series may be complete but what needs to be identified is the number in the given completed series which is disturbing the sequential pattern of that series and does not fit in with the relationship shared between the other numbers.

Example

Directions : *In each of the following series, one number is wrong. Select the answer from the given options.*

2, 4, 8, 16, 30, 64, 128

   (*a*) 8   (*b*) 128   (*c*) 30   (*d*) 4

Ans. (*c*) : The numbers in the series are multiplied by 2.

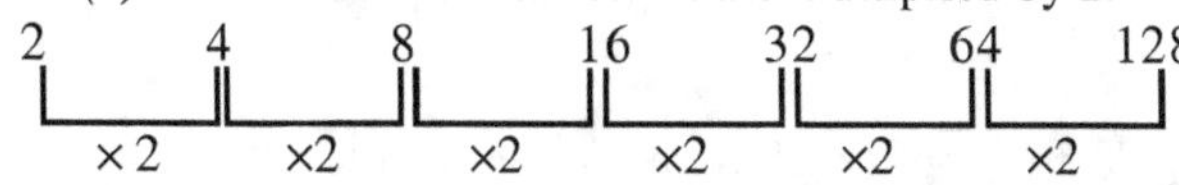

$$\therefore \ 32 \text{ should be in place of } 30.$$

EXERCISE

Directions : *In the given series find the number which is wrong.*

1. 5, 12, 16, 24, 27

   (*a*) 12   (*b*) 16

   (*c*) 24   (*d*) 27

2. 27, 36, 45, 60, 71, 99

   (*a*) 27   (*b*) 45

   (*c*) 60   (*d*) 71

3. 81, 64, 49, 35, 25, 16

   (*a*) 64   (*b*) 35

   (*c*) 25   (*d*) 16

4. 625, 125, 25, 5, 0

   (*a*) 0   (*b*) 125

   (*c*) 5   (*d*) 625

5. 25, 19, 17, 13, 11, 7

   (*a*) 25   (*b*) 17

   (*c*) 13   (*d*) 7

EXPLANATORY ANSWERS

1. (*c*) : The sequence in the series is +7, +4 which is repeated, *i.e.*,

5   12   16   23   27

   +7   +4   +7   +4

$\therefore$ 23 should be in place of 24.

2. (*d*) : All other numbers are divisible by 3.

3. (*b*) : The sequence is the square of the number in decreasing order starting from 9, *i.e.*,

$9^2 \ = 9 \times 9 \ = 81$

$8^2 \ = 8 \times 8 \ = 64$

$7^2 \ = 7 \times 7 \ = 49$

$6^2 \ = 6 \times 6 \ = 36$

$5^2 = 5 \times 5 = 25$

$4^2 = 4 \times 4 = 16$

$\therefore$ 36 should be in place of 35.

4. (a) : The number in the series are divided by 5 to get the next number

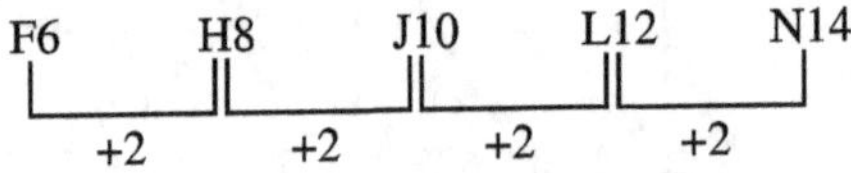

$\therefore$ 1 should be in place of 0 digit.

5. (a) : Other numbers are prime numbers.

Mixed Series

Mixed series comprises of the combination of letters and numbers. In this type of series the letters and numbers may have a common sequence pattern or may have separate sequence patterns.

Example

What should come in the place of question mark in the following letter-number combination?

F6, H8, J10, L12, ?

(a) N15   (b) O14   (c) N14   (d) O13

Ans. (c) : The letters are moved two steps forward and the number indicates the position of the letter in the alphabet series.

F6   H8   J10   L12   N14

+2   +2   +2   +2

EXERCISE

Directions : *In each series given below, what would come in place of the question-mark?*

1. 2B, 4C, 8E, 14H, ?
   (a) 20L
   (b) 22L
   (c) 21I
   (d) 16K

2. C(1)L, F(4)O, I(9)R, L(16)U, ?
   (a) P(27)W
   (b) N(24)Y
   (c) M(23)X
   (d) O(25)X

3. 3F, 6G, 11I, 18L, ?
   (a) 27P
   (b) 21O
   (c) 27Q
   (d) 25N

4. W(1)A, X(4)Z, Y(9)Y, ?, A(25)W
   (a) X(11)Z
   (b) Z(21)A
   (c) Z(16)X
   (d) Z(14)X

5. 81Y, 27S, 9N, 3J, ?
   (a) 0H   (b) 1G
   (c) 0F   (d) 1E

EXPLANATORY ANSWERS

1. (b) : The sequence of numbers is +2, +4, +6 +8 and sequence of letters is +1, +2, +3, +4.

2. (d) : The corresponding letters are moved 3 steps forward and the sequence of numbers is +3, +5, +7, +9.

3. (a) : The sequence of numbers is +3, +5, +7, +9 and the letters are moved 1, 2, 3, 4 steps forward.

4. (c) : The letters on the left are in reverse series, the letters on the right are in natural series, and the numbers are squares of numbers in natural order starting from 1.

5. (b) : The numbers are divided by 3 at each step and the letters are moved 6, 5, 4, 3 steps backward.

□□□

3
Classification

In this type of classification, five words are given out of which four are almost same in matter or meaning and only one word is different from the common four. One has to find out the word which is different from the rest.

Example

Directions : *In the following questions spot the odd one out.*

    (*a*) Father   (*b*) Mother   (*c*) Friend   (*d*) Brother

Ans. *(c)* : All other are blood relations.

EXERCISE

Directions : *In each of the following questions, four words are alike in some manner. Spot the odd one out.*

1. (*a*) Ornate   (*b*) Pleasant
   (*c*) Decorate   (*d*) Beautify
2. (*a*) Polo   (*b*) Chess
   (*c*) Ludo   (*d*) Squash
3. (*a*) Tutor   (*b*) Principal
   (*c*) Pupil   (*d*) Professor
4. (*a*) Pond   (*b*) River
   (*c*) Stream   (*d*) Brook
5. (*a*) Quotation (*b*) Duty
   (*c*) Tax   (*d*) Octroi

EXPLANATORY ANSWERS

1. *(b)* : All other words have the same meaning.

2. *(a)* : All others are indoor games.

3. *(c)* : All others are instructors. Pupil learns from the instructor.

4. *(a)* : All others are running forms of water.

5. *(a)* : All others are forms of taxes.

Odd One Out–Letters

In this classification of letters, four groups of letters or a series of letters is given as options. One has to select the option as answer which does not share the commonness of the others.

Example

Directions : *Find the odd one out in the following letters :*

    (*a*) NOP   (*b*) RTU   (*c*) JKL   (*d*) EFG

    Ans. (*b*) : In each group the letters are consecutive. In this option the first two letters jump one letter (S) inbetween.

EXERCISE

Directions : *Three of the following four in each question are alike in a certain way and so form a group. Select the group of letters that does not belong to that group.*

1. (*a*) ACE   (*b*) LOR
      (*c*) GIK   (*d*) VXZ

2. (*a*) TSR   (*b*) LKJ
      (*c*) PQO   (*d*) HGF

3. (*a*) EF LM   (*b*) KJ SR
      (*c*) XW HG   (*d*) ED YX

4. (*a*) JOPK   (*b*) BOPC
      (*c*) QOPR   (*d*) TOPS

5. (*a*) DfH   (*b*) MoQ
      (*c*) UwY   (*d*) lnO

EXPLANATORY ANSWERS

1. (*b*) : The sequence in each group is +2. Only option B has sequence in +3, *i.e.,*

$$A\,B\,C\,D\,E \quad\quad L\,M\,N\,O\,P\,Q\,R$$
$$+2\ \ +2 \quad\quad\quad +3 \quad\quad +3$$

$$G\,H\,I\,J\,K \quad\quad V\,W\,X\,Y\,Z$$
$$+2\ \ +2 \quad\quad\quad +2\ \ +2$$

2. (*c*) : The sequence of alphabet in each group is in reverse order. Only option C has sequence in disturbed order.

3. (*a*) : Two consecutive alphabet in each group are in reverse sequence (–1), *i.e.,*

$$K\,J\ \ S\,R;\ \ X\,W\ \ \ H\,G;$$
$$-1\ \ \ -1 \quad\ -1 \quad\ \ -1$$

$$E\,D\ \ \ Y\,X$$
$$-1\ \ \ \ -1$$

Only in option (a) the sequence is in natural order (+1), *i.e.,*

$$E\,F \quad\ L\,M$$
$$+1 \quad\quad +1$$

4. (d) : In each group, letters 'OP' are common. The two corner alphabet are in natural order (+1); *i.e.,*

JOPK ; BOPC ; QOPR
 +1   +1   +1

Only in option (d) they are in reverse order (–1); *i.e.,*

TOPS
–1

5. (d) : In other groups, only the alphabet in the centre is of lower case. In this option letter 'L' on the left is also in lower case.

Odd One Out–Numbers

In this type of classification, different numbers are given as options. These numbers have some commonness; except one which is the odd one. One has to identify the similarity and then strike the odd one out as answer option.

Example

Directions : *Find the odd number from the given options.*

  (a) 62   (b) 121   (c) 36   (d) 256

Ans. (a) : The other numbers are squares of :
11, (= 121), 6 (= 36) and 16 (= 256)

EXERCISE

Directions : *In each of the following questions, there are four options. Three numbers, in these options, are alike in certain manner. Only one number does not fit in. Choose the one which is different from the rest.*

1. (a) 1948   (b) 2401
   (c) 966   (d) 1449

2. (a) 129   (b) 130
   (c) 131   (d) 132

3. (a) 3215   (b) 9309
   (c) 4721   (d) 2850

4. (a) 64   (b) 84
   (c) 16   (d) 36

5. (a) 24   (b) 90
   (c) 54   (d) 36

EXPLANATORY ANSWERS

1. (a) : Other numbers are divisible by 7.

2. (c) : 131 is a prime number.

3. (b) : In other numbers, no digit is repeated.

4. (b) : All other numbers are perfect squares.

5. (a) : In other numbers, the sum of both the digits is 9.

4

Coding and Decoding

Coding is a secretive language which is used to change the representation of the actual term/word/value. This coded language can be framed by *(i)* moving the letters one or more steps forward or backward; *(ii)* substituting numbers for letters and vice–versa; *(iii)* writing the letters of the given word in reverse order in part or in whole; and *(iv)* replacing the letters in their natural series by the same positioned letters in their reverse series.

Alphabet in natural series are :

A B C D E F G H I J K L M N O P Q R S T U V W X Y Z

1st   5th   10th   15th   20th   25th

Alphabet in reverse series are :

Z Y X W V U T S R Q P O N M L K J I H G F E D C B A

1st   5th   10th   15th   20th   25th

Note : On reaching Z, the series restarts from A and on reaching A, it restarts from Z.

Example

If FACE is coded as GBDF, then BADE will be coded as :

(*a*) CBEF   (*b*) CEBF   (*c*) CFBE   (*d*) CBFE

Ans. *(a)* **:** The word is coded by moving the letters one step forward.

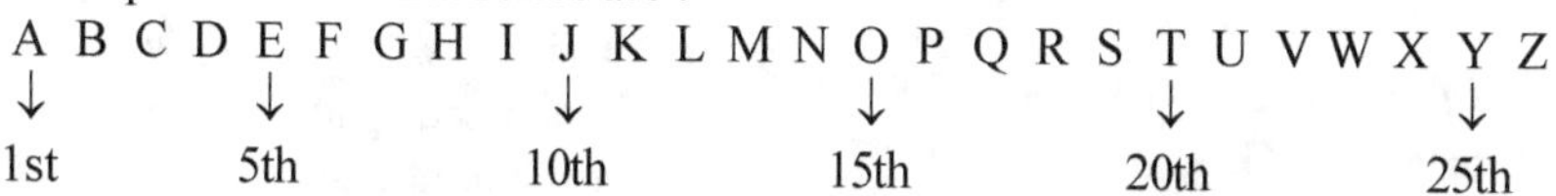

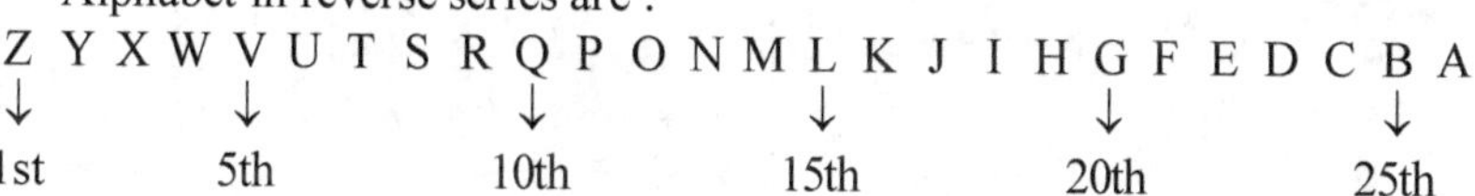

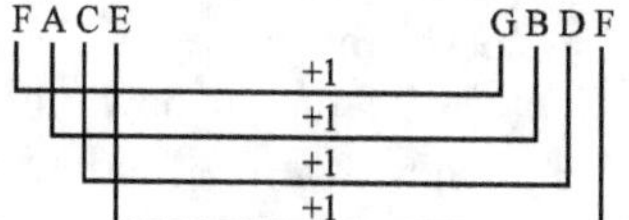

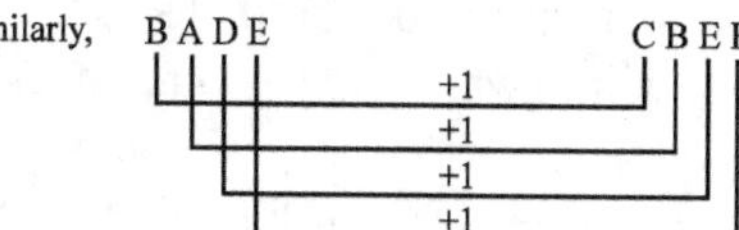

19

EXERCISE

Directions (Qs. 1 to 10): *In the following questions select the right option which indicates the correct code for the word or letter given in the question.*

1. If CHAIR is coded as FKDLU then RAID is coded as :
   (a) ULGD   (b) ULKG
   (c) ULDG   (d) UDLG

2. In a code language COME is written as XLNV and ABLE as ZYOV. How will MOLLY be written in that code?
   (a) NLOBO   (b) NLBOO
   (c) LNOOB   (d) NLOOB

3. If ACTION is coded as ZXGRLM, then HEALTH will be coded in the same way as :
   (a) SVZOGS   (b) TVZOGT
   (c) RUZPGR   (d) QVGOZQ

4. If 'w' is coded as 'a', 's' as 'r' and 'r' as 'w', how will 'answer' be written?
   (a) wnsaes   (b) anraew
   (c) anrwas   (d) wnraes

5. If MUSK is coded as 146816, then ZERO will be coded as :
   (a) 113811   (b) 122912
   (c) 15915   (d) 2651815

6. In a certain code LIBERATE is written as 56403170, TRIBAL will be written in the same code as :
   (a) 734615   (b) 736415
   (c) 136475   (d) 034615

7. If 341782 denotes MONKEY and 0596 denotes RAGS, then 75195044 will denote.
   (a) KANGAROO
   (b) PALMANTT
   (c) HANGAMEE
   (d) KARNAGOO

8. If ADD is coded as WOO, SUM as QJM and TOTAL as KPKWX, then TOADS will be coded as :
   (a) KPOWQ   (b) KPWQO
   (c) KPWOQ   (d) KPWOJ

9. If BOOK is coded as CNPJ, then MOON will be coded as :
   (a) MPNN   (b) NNPM
   (c) PNMN   (d) NMPN

10. DAZE is written as 41265 in a certain code. How will BOY be written in the same code?
    (a) 41425   (b) 5120
    (c) 21525   (d) 359

Directions (Qs. 11 to 15): *In the following questions study the coded patterns and then select the right option from the given alternatives.*

11. In a certain language, (a) 'go ju mi' stands for 'plenty of money'; (b) pao ju go nei vu' for 'money creates lots of problems'; (c) 'kol vu nei' for 'problems create tension'; and (d) 'sol tun ju haw' for 'still money is needed'. Which of the following words stand for 'money'?

21

(*a*) nei   (*b*) ju
(*c*) haw   (*d*) go

12. In a certain language, (a) 'FOR' stands for 'old is gold'; (b) 'ROT' stands for 'gold is pure'; (c) 'ROM' stands for 'gold is costly'. How will 'pure old gold is costly' be written?
 (*a*) TFROM   (*b*) FOTRM
 (*c*) FTORM   (*d*) TOMRF

13. In a certain code '415' means 'milk is hot'; '18' means 'hot soup'; and '895' means 'soup is tasty'. What number will indicate the word 'tasty'?
 (*a*) 9   (*b*) 8
 (*c*) 5   (*d*) 4

14. In a certain code '643' means 'she is beautiful', '593' means 'he is handsome', and '567' means 'handsome meets beautiful'. What number will indicate the word 'meets'?
 (*a*) 5   (*b*) 3
 (*c*) 7   (*d*) 6

15. In a certain code language, (a) 'dugo hui mul zo' stands for 'work is very hard'; (b) 'hui dugo ba ki' for 'Bingo is very smart'; (c) 'nano mul dugo' for 'cake is hard', and (d) 'mul ki qu' for 'smart and hard'. Which of the following words stand for 'Bingo'?
 (*a*) jalu   (*b*) dugo
 (*c*) ki   (*d*) ba

Directions (Qs. 16 to 20): *Read the given coded information and choose the correct answer from the given options.*

16. If 'water' is called 'blue', 'blue' is called 'red', 'red' is called 'white', 'white' is called 'sky', 'sky' is called 'rain', 'rain' is called 'green', 'green' is called 'air' and 'air' is called 'table', which of the following is the colour of milk?
 (*a*) white   (*b*) rain
 (*c*) sky   (*d*) green

17. If 'light' is called 'dark', 'dark' is called 'green', 'green' is called 'blue', 'blue' is called 'red', 'red' is called 'white' and 'white' is called 'yellow', what is the colour of blood?
 (*a*) red   (*b*) dark
 (*c*) white   (*d*) yellow

18. If 'sky' is called 'sea', 'sea' is called 'water', 'water' is called 'air', 'air' is called 'cloud' and 'cloud' is called 'river', then what do we drink when thirsty?
 (*a*) sky   (*b*) air
 (*c*) water   (*d*) sea

19. If 'yellow' means 'red', 'white' means 'green', 'red' means 'orange', 'blue' means 'white' and 'green' means 'blue', then the colour of sky is :
 (*a*) white   (*b*) green
 (*c*) blue   (*d*) yellow

20. If 'land' is called 'sky', 'sky' is called 'air', 'air' is called 'water', 'water' is called 'sand' and 'sand' is called 'solid', where do fishes swim?
 (*a*) air   (*b*) sky
 (*c*) water   (*d*) sand

ANSWERS

1	2	3	4	5	6	7	8	9	10
(d)	(d)	(a)	(b)	(b)	(b)	(a)	(c)	(b)	(c)
11	12	13	14	15	16	17	18	19	20
(b)	(a)	(a)	(c)	(d)	(c)	(c)	(b)	(a)	(d)

SOME SELECTED EXPLANATORY ANSWERS

4. Alphabet whose codes are given

w → a
s → r
r → w

All other alphabet will remain unchanged, so, 'answer' will be coded as :

5. The coded number signifies the position of the alphabet in its reverse order of the alphabetical series (ZYXW...)

M U S K → MUSK
↓ ↓ ↓ ↓
14th 6th 8th 16th → 146816
Similarly,
Z E R O → ZERO
↓ ↓ ↓ ↓
1st 22nd 9th 12th → 122912

6. The letters of the word TRIBAL are picked from LIBERATE. So will be the coded numbers.
L I B E R A T E →
given word
5 6 4 0 3 1 7 0 → codes
Similarly,
T R I B A L → word to be coded
7 3 6 4 1 5 → answer codes

7. The numbers represent letters and to find the answer, select the respective letters.
3 4 1 7 8 2 0 5 9 6 → codes
M O N K E Y R A G S → letters
So,
7 5 1 9 5 0 4 4 → codes
K A N G A R O O → answer letters

8. The letters of the words are coded by substituted letters. To find the answer codes, select the respective substituted letters.
A D D SUM TOTAL → letters
W O O QJM KPKWX → sub-stituted letters codes
So,
T O A D S → letters
K P W O Q → substituted answer letter codes

10. The letters of the word are coded by the numbers representing their position in the natural series.
D A Z E → letters
4 1 26 5 → position of letters in natural series

Similarly,

BOY → letters

2 15 25 → position of letters in natural series

11. *Code*   *Sentence*

1. go *ju* mi   plenty of *money*

2. pao *ju* go   *money* creates lots of

   nei vu   problems

3. kol vu nei   problems create tension

4. sol tun *ju* haw   still *money* is needed

In 1st, 2nd and 4th codes and their sentences the word 'ju' is repeated and so is 'money'.

13. *Code*   *Sentence*

1. 415   milk is hot

2. 18   hot soup

3. 8 95   soup is *tasty*

From 3rd code and its sentence neither number '9' is repeated nor the word 'tasty'.

15. *Code*   *Sentence*

1. *dugo hui* mul zo   work *is very hard*

2. *hui dugo* **ba** *ki*   **Bingo** *is very smart*

3. nano mul *dugo*   cake is *hard*

4. mul *ki* qu   *smart* and hard

From 2nd code and its sentence, neither 'ba' nor 'Bingo' is repeated. (Words repeated are in italics)

16. Colour of milk is 'white' and 'white' is called 'sky'.

17. Colour of blood is 'red' and 'red' is called 'white'.

18. We drink 'water' when we are thirsty and 'water' is called 'air'.

19. Colour of sky is 'blue' and 'blue' means 'white'.

20. Fishes swim in 'water' and 'water' is called 'sand'.

5

Direction Sense

In these type of tests, the directions in questions needs to be perceived. Such questions are based on the direction chart.

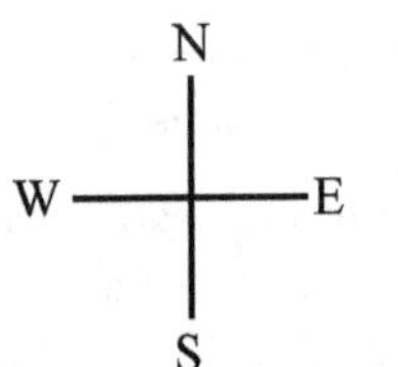

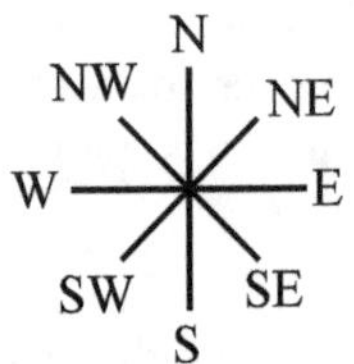

N = North S = South E = East W = West

The sense of the different directions are guided by the left and right turns or angular turns.

EXERCISE

Directions : *In the following questions, select the right answer from the given options to depict the correct direction/distance.*

1. A man travels 100 km towards South. From there he turns right and travels 100 km and again turns right to travel 50 km. Which direction is he in from his starting point?
   (*a*) North   (*b*) North-East
   (*c*) East   (*d*) South-West

2. A train runs 120 km in West direction, 30 km in South direction and then 80 km in east direction before reaching the station. In which direction is the station from the train's starting point?
   (*a*) South-West (*b*) North-West
   (*c*) South-East (*d*) South

3. Facing the West direction, Priya jogs for 20 m, turns left and goes further 40 m. She turns left again and jogs for 20 m. Then she turns right to go 20 m to reach the park. How far is the park from her starting point and in which direction?

(*a*) 20 m South   (*b*) 40 m West
(*c*) 60 m South   (*d*) 100 m East

4. If all the directions are rotated, *i.e.,* if North is changed to West and East to North and so on, then what will come in place of North-West?
   (*a*) South-West   (*b*) North-East
   (*c*) East-North   (*d*) East-West

5. A and B start together from one point. They walk 10 km towards North. A turns left and covers 5 km whereas B turns right and covers 3 km. A turns left again and covers 15 km whereas B turns right and covers his 15 km. How far is A from B?
   (*a*) 18 km   (*b*) 10 km
   (*c*) 5 km   (*d*) 8 km

6. Tarun is walking towards East. What direction he should not follow if he should walk towards North?
   (*a*) right, right, left, right, right
   (*b*) right, right, left, left, left
   (*c*) right, right, right
   (*d*) right, left, right, left

7. Sony and Moni start walking from a point. Sony walks in West direction and Moni in South direction. After covering 20 km, Soni turns left and walks 15 km. Moni walks 10 km, turns left and walks 5 km. Soni, then turns left again and walks 25 km, whereas Moni turns right and walks 5 km. How far are Sony and Moni from each other?

(*a*) 5 km
(*b*) They are back at the starting point
(*c*) They are at same place at the finishing point
(*d*) Data is insufficient

8. I was walking in South-East direction. After a while I turned 90° to the right and walked ahead. Later I turned 45° to the right. In which direction am I walking now?
   (*a*) North   (*b*) North-East
   (*c*) South-West   (*d*) East

9. Two friends Jack and Bunny start a race, and together they run for 50 mts. Jack turns right and runs 60 mts while Bunny turns left and runs 40 mts. Then Jack turns left and runs 50 mts while Bunny turns right and runs 50 mts. How far are the two friends now from each other?
   (*a*) 60 mts   (*b*) 100 mts
   (*c*) 20 mts   (*d*) 150 mts

10. A policeman left his police post and proceeded south 4 km, after hearing a loud sound from point A. On reaching the place he heard another sound and proceeded 4 km to his left to the point B, only to find that the sound was coming from left of B. From B he proceeded left to reach that place 4 km away. In which direction he has to go to reach his police post?
    (*a*) North   (*b*) South
    (*c*) East   (*d*) West

ANSWERS

1	2	3	4	5	6	7	8	9	10
(d)	(a)	(c)	(a)	(d)	(d)	(c)	(a)	(b)	(d)

SOME SELECTED EXPLANATORY ANSWERS

2.

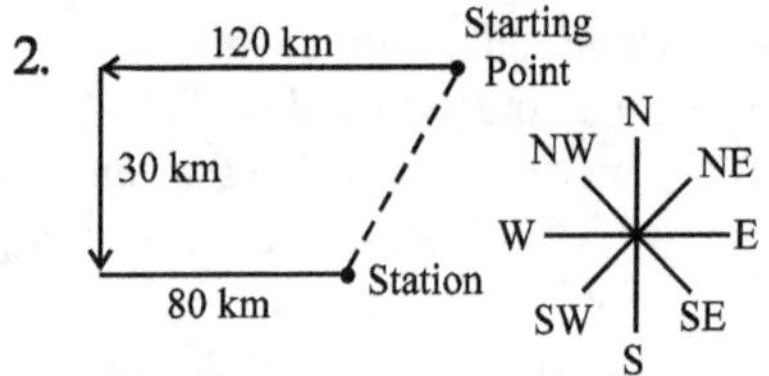

3. $(40 + 20) = 60$ metres South

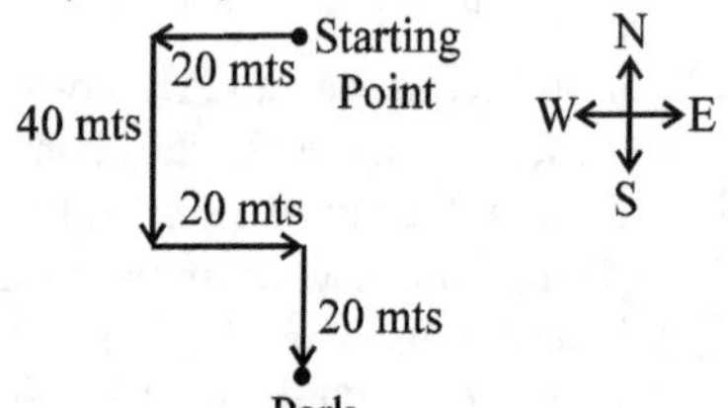

5.

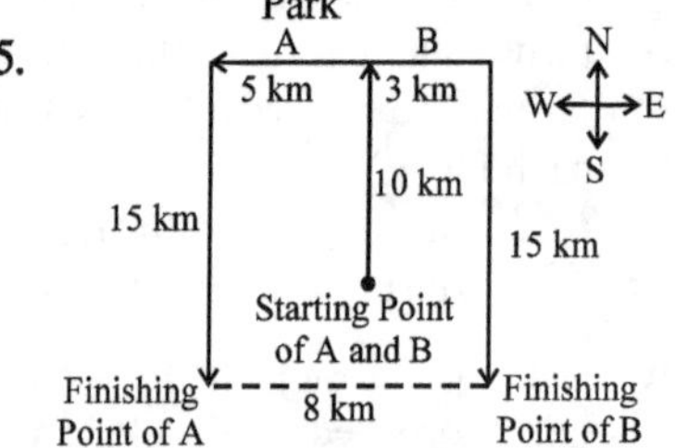

6.

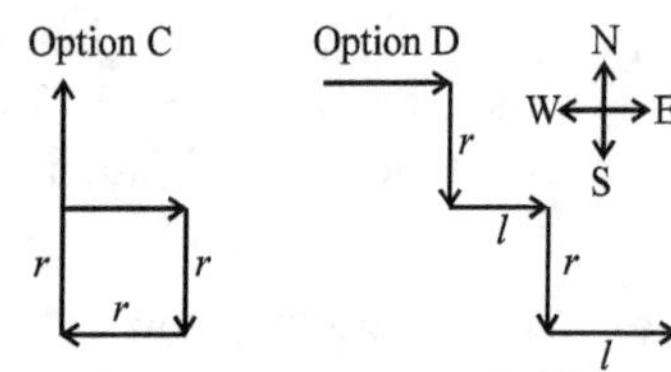

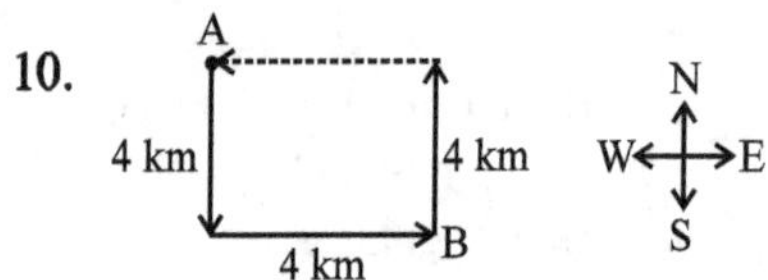

10.

6

Blood Relations

While attempting questions on blood relations, one should be clear of all the relation patterns that can exist between any two individuals. These type of questions are given mainly to test one's relationship ability.

EXERCISE

Directions : *In each of the following questions keenly study the relationship mentioned between the persons, and then from the given options select the right relationship as the answer.*

1. A lady said, "The person standing there is my grandfather's only son's daughter". How is the lady related to the standing person?
   (*a*) Sister   (*b*) Mother
   (*c*) Aunt   (*d*) Cousin

2. Ajay is the brother of Vijay. Mili is the sister of Ajay. Sanjay is the brother of Rahul and Mehul is the daughter of Vijay. Who is Sanjay's Uncle?
   (*a*) Rahul
   (*b*) Ajay
   (*c*) Mehul
   (*d*) Data inadequate

3. A man introduced the boy coming with him as "He is son of the father of my wife's daughter". What relation did the boy bear to the man?
   (*a*) Son-in-law   (*b*) Son
   (*c*) Brother   (*d*) Father

4. If Amit's father is Billoo's father's only son and Billoo has neither a brother nor a daughter, what is the relationship between Amit and Billoo?
   (*a*) Uncle — Nephew
   (*b*) Father — Daughter
   (*c*) Father — Son
   (*d*) Cousins

5. Pointing to a woman in the photograph a man said, "She is the daughter of my grandmother's only son. How is the woman related to the man?

27

(*a*) Mother
(*b*) Daughter
(*c*) Sister-in-law
(*d*) Sister

6. Pointing to a photograph, a woman said, "She is the only daughter of my mother's father." How is the woman related to the person in the photograph?
(*a*) Mother
(*b*) Grandmother
(*c*) Daughter
(*d*) Cannot be determined

7. Ram is the brother of Shyam and Mahesh is the father of Ram. Jagat is the brother of Priya and Priya is daughter of Shyam. Who is the uncle of Jagat ?
(*a*) Shyam
(*b*) Mahesh
(*c*) Ram
(*d*) Data insufficient

8. Introducing a man, a woman said, "His wife is the only daughter of my father". How is the man related to the woman?
(*a*) Husband
(*b*) Father
(*c*) Father-in-law
(*d*) Brother

9. If Maya is the only daughter of Richa's grandmother's brother, how is Maya's daughter related to Richa?
(*a*) Niece   (*b*) Cousin
(*c*) Aunt   (*d*) Mother

10. Pointing to a woman, a man said, "Her husband's mother is the wife of my father's only son". How is the man related to the woman?
(*a*) Son
(*b*) Brother-in-law
(*c*) Uncle
(*d*) Father-in-law

ANSWERS

1	2	3	4	5	6	7	8	9	10
(*a*)	(*d*)	(*b*)	(*c*)	(*d*)	(*c*)	(*c*)	(*a*)	(*b*)	(*d*)

SOME SELECTED EXPLANATORY ANSWERS

2. 1. Mili ——→ Ajay ——→ Vijay
     (sister)   (brother) ↓

                     Mehul
                 (daughter)

   2. Sanjay ——→ Rahul
           (brother)

There are two sets of relationship. Information given is incomplete and no relation can be established between the two sets.

3. The relationship chart based on problem is :

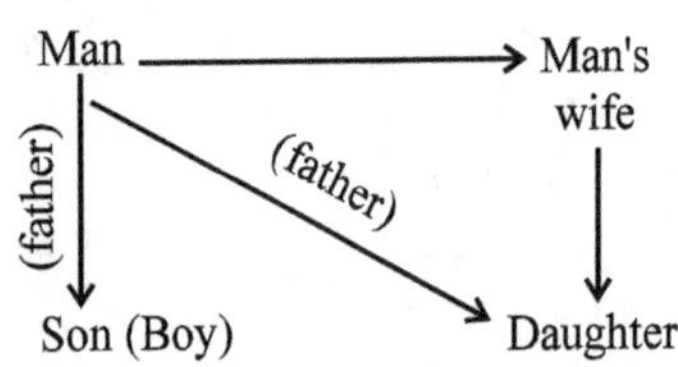

'Father of the man's wife's daughter' is the man himself and the boy in question is the man's son.

5.

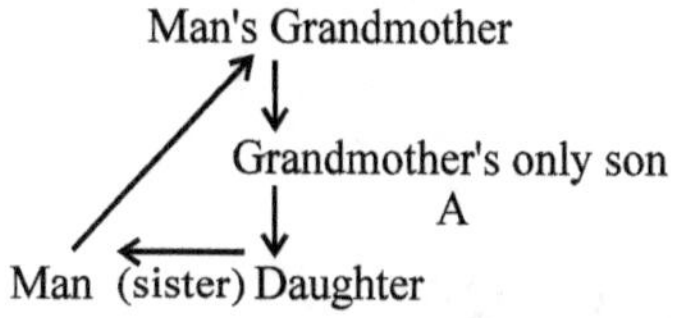

Man's Grandmother

Grandmother's only son
A

Man (sister) Daughter

'My grandmother's only son' is the father of the man, and 'daughter of my grandmother's only son' is the sister of the man.

6.   Woman's mother's father

↕

Person in photograph
(woman's mother/only daughter)
↑ (daughter)
Woman

'Only daughter of my mother's father' is the person in the photograph and she is also the mother of the woman. So, the woman is the daughter of the person in the photograph.

8.

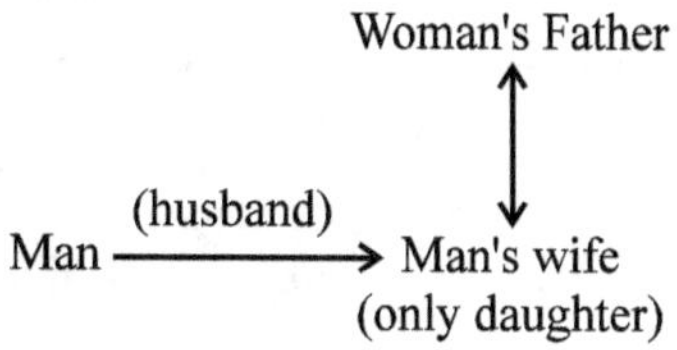

Woman's Father

(husband)
Man ⟶ Man's wife
(only daughter)

'Only daughter of my father' is the woman herself and the man is her husband.

7

Arranging in Order

In these type of questions arrangement of given options is done on the basis of dictionary, size, rank, weight, natural sequence etc in ascending or descending order.

EXERCISE

1. If the following words are arranged in natural order, what will come in the last place in ascending order?
   1. Captain
   2. Brigadier
   3. Major
   4. Lieutenant-General
   5. Lieutenant
   (*a*) Lientenant-General
   (*b*) Brigadier
   (*c*) Captain
   (*d*) Major

2. If these words are arranged according to dictionary then what word will come in the third place?
   1. Originality
   2. Originally
   3. Originator
   4. Original
   5. Originate

   (*a*) Originality   (*b*) Originator
   (*c*) Originate   (*d*) Originally

3. What will be the natural order of the following?
   1. Independence Day
   2. Christmas
   3. Diwali
   4. Holi
   5. Republic Day
   (*a*) 5 4 1 3 2   (*b*) 5 1 4 3 2
   (*c*) 4 1 5 3 2   (*d*) 2 3 4 1 5

4. If the following words are arranged in ascending order what word will be in the fourth place?
   1. Air commodore
   2. Wing Commander
   3. Pilot Officer
   4. Squadron Leader
   5. Air Marshal
   (*a*) Air Marshal
   (*b*) Air Commodore

30

(*c*) Wing Commander
(*d*) Pilot Officer

5. What will be the natural order of the following words according to size?

1. Dog   2. Horse
3. Ant   4. Giraffe
5. Mouse

(*a*) 3 5 1 2 4   (*b*) 3 1 5 2 4
(*c*) 3 5 1 4 2   (*d*) 3 5 2 1 4

ANSWERS

1	2	3	4	5
(*a*)	(*d*)	(*a*)	(*b*)	(*a*)

SOME SELECTED EXPLANATORY ANSWERS

1. The arrangement of ranks in ascending order is—Lieutenant, Captain, Major, Brigadier, **Lieutenant-General.**

2. The dictionary order of words is–Original, Originality, **Originally,** Originate, Originator.

3. The natural order of National Holidays in Calendar is—Republic Day (January), Holi (March), Independence Day (August), Diwali (October/November), Christmas (December).

4. The arrangement of ranks in ascending order is—Pilot Officer, Squadron Leader, Wing Commander, **Air Commodore,** Air Marshal.

5. The natural order of living beings according to increasing size is—Ant, Mouse, Dog, Horse, Giraffe.

8

Calendar, Clock & Time

These are mathematical problem based on calculations of time by a clock or calendar and computations of speed or distances.

EXERCISE

1. If the day before yesterday was Thursday, when will Sunday be?
   (*a*) Tomorrow
   (*b*) Day after tomorrow
   (*c*) Today
   (*d*) Two days after today

2. Radha remembers that her father's birthday is after 16th but before 21st of March, while her brother Mangesh remembers that his father's birthday is before 22nd but after 19th of March. On which date is the birthday of their father?
   (*a*) 19th
   (*b*) 20th
   (*c*) 21st
   (*d*) Cannot be determined

3. A clock is so placed that at 12 noon its minute hand points towards north-east. In which direction does its hour hand point at 1.30 P.M.?
   (*a*) East   (*b*) West
   (*c*) North   (*d*) South

4. A couple married in 1980 had two children, one in 1982 and the other in 1984. Their combined ages will equal the years of the marriage in?
   (*a*) 1986   (*b*) 1985
   (*c*) 1987   (*d*) 1988

5. Manoj left home for the bus stop 15 minutes earlier than the usual time. It takes 10 minutes to reach the stop. He reached the stop at 8.40 a.m. What time does he usually leave home for the bus stop?
   (*a*) 8.30 a.m.
   (*b*) 8.55 a.m.
   (*c*) 8.45 p.m.
   (*d*) None of these

6. If the third day of a month is Monday, which of the following

will be the fifth day from 21st of that month?

(*a*) Tuesday   (*b*) Monday

(*c*) Wednesday (*d*) Thursday

7. Keshav runs a factory in three shifts of eight hours each with 210 employees. In each shift minimum of 80 employees are required to run the factory effectively. No employee can be allowed to work for more than 16 hours a day. At least how many employees will be required to work for 16 hours every day?

(*a*) 30

(*b*) 60

(*c*) Data inadequate

(*d*) None of these

8. A clock shows the time as 3 : 30 p.m. If the minute hand gains 2 minutes every hour, how many minutes will the clock gain by 4 a.m.?

(*a*) 23 Minutes   (*b*) 24 Minutes

(*c*) 25 Minutes   (*d*) 26 Minutes

9. A train started from station 'A' and proceeded towards station 'B' at a speed of 48 km/hr. Forty-five minutes later another train started from station 'B' and proceeded towards station 'A' at 50 km/hr. If the distance between the two stations is 232 km, at what distance from station 'A' will the trains meet?

(*a*) 132 km   (*b*) 144 km

(*c*) 108 km   (*d*) 160 km

10. My uncle shall visit me after 64 days of my father's birthday. If my father's birthday falls on Tuesday, what shall be the day on my Uncle's visit?

(*a*) Wednesday (*b*) Sunday

(*c*) Tuesday   (*d*) Monday

ANSWERS

1	2	3	4	5	6	7	8	9	10
(*a*)	(*b*)	(*a*)	(*a*)	(*d*)	(*c*)	(*d*)	(*c*)	(*a*)	(*a*)

SOME SELECTED EXPLANATORY ANSWERS

1.
Thursday – Day-before-yesterday
Friday   – Yesterday
Saturday – Today
Sunday   – Tomorrow

4. 1982 – 2 years later – 1st child
1984 – 4 years later – 2nd child
Total age of children — 2 years.
1985 — 5 years later — Total age of children : 4 years.

1986 — 6 years later — Total age of children : 6 years.

5. Manoj reached the bus stop at 8.40 a.m. He left his home at 8:40 – 10 minutes = 8:30 a.m. He left 15 minutes earlier than usual, so his actual time of leaving home is 8:30 am + 15 minutes = 8:45 a.m.

6. 3rd day of the month is Monday
5th day from 21st is 26th
$26 - 3 = 23$ days
23 days later, 23/7 leaves 2 days.
So, two days ahead of Monday will be Wednesday.

8. Hours between 3:30 p.m. and 4 a.m. are — 12½ hours. Number of minutes gained will be $12½ \times 2 = 25$ minutes.

9.

$$\frac{d}{48} = \frac{232 - d}{50} + \frac{3}{4}$$

i.e.,

$$\frac{d}{48} = \frac{464 - 2d + 75}{100}$$

$100\,d = (539 - 2d)\,48$

$100\,d = 25872 - 96\,d$

$196\,d = 25872$

$d = 25872 \div 196 = 132$ km.

10. My father's birthday is on Tuesday.
$64 \div 7$ gives 1 as remainder
So, 63rd day will be Tuesday and one day ahead is the day when uncle shall visit i.e., on Wednesday.

9

Rows and Ranks

These type of problems need easy calculations to find out the number of objects in a row, lane or queue or to find a person's rank in a class of certain number of students; or to find the total number of students.

EXERCISE

1. Mahesh and Suresh are ranked 11th and 12th respectively from the top in a class of 41 students. What will be their respective ranks from the bottom?
   (a) 32nd and 33rd
   (b) 29th and 30th
   (c) 30th and 31st
   (d) 31st and 30th

2. Uma ranked 8th from the top and 37th from bottom in a class. How many students are there in the class?
   (a) 47   (b) 46
   (c) 45   (d) None of these

3. In a queue, Sadiq is 14th from the front and Joseph is 17th from the end, while Jane is in between Sadiq and Joseph. If Sadiq be ahead of Joseph and there be 48 persons in the queue, how many persons are there between Sadiq and Jane?

   (a) 5   (b) 6
   (c) 7   (d) 8

4. Rohan ranked eleventh from the top and twenty-seventh from the bottom among the students who passed the annual examination in a class. If the number of students who failed in the examination was 12, how many students appeared for the examination?
   (a) 48
   (b) 49
   (c) 50
   (d) Cannot be determined

5. Some boys are sitting in a row. P is sitting fourteenth from the left and Q is seventh from the right. If there are four boys between P and Q, how many boys are there in the row?
   (a) 19   (b) 21
   (c) 25   (d) 23

ANSWERS

1	2	3	4	5
(d)	(d)	(c)	(b)	(c)

SOME SELECTED EXPLANATORY ANSWERS

2.
$$\text{Uma}$$
8th — 37th

Total number of students in the class are :

$(8 + 37) - 1 = 44.$

4.
Rohan
11th — 27th

Number of students who passed the examination $(11 + 27) - 1 = 37$

Those who failed $= 12$

Total number of students who appeared in the examination

$= 37 + 12 = 49.$

5.
P   Q
14th   4   7th

The number of boys in the row are :

$(14 + 4 + 7) = 25.$

❏❏❏

10

Symbol Substitution

Questions in these category are easy to attempt. Candidates must be quick in substituting symbols and calculations. The common pattern of questions asked are given below.

EXERCISE

1. If '✱' denotes '×', 'Δ' denotes '÷', '□' denotes '−', '●' denotes '+', 'α' denotes '=' and 'β' denotes ≠, then which of the following euations is correct?
   (a) $2 \square 10 ✱ 4 \Delta 5 \alpha 5 ● 12 \Delta 6$
   (b) $27 \Delta 9 ● 6 \beta 3 ✱ 6 \square 9$
   (c) $4 \Delta 2 ✱ 0 \alpha 7 \Delta 1 ✱ 0$
   (d) $5 ● 6 \Delta 3 \square 2 \alpha 8 \Delta 4 ✱ 3$

2. If ↓ stands for '÷', ↑ stands for '×', → stands for '+' and ← stands for '−', then

   $25 ↓ 5 → 3 ↑ 6 ← 8 = ?$
   (a) 9   (b) 12
   (c) 16   (d) 15

3. If the + and × signs of the following equations are interchanged, which will be the correct equation?
   (a) $7 \times 5 + 3 = 20$
   (b) $4 + 9 \times 1 = 42$
   (c) $6 \times 5 + 8 = 46$
   (d) $2 + 11 \times 4 = 28$

4. If '+' stands for multiplication, '×' stands for addition, '÷' stands for subtraction and '−' stands for division, then what will be the result of the following equation?
   $7 \times 4 ÷ 10 \times 2 + 5 = ?$
   (a) 7   (b) 0
   (c) 11   (d) 15

5. If 'A' means '÷', 'B' means '+', 'C' means '×' and 'D' means '−', then
   $12 \, C \, 4 \, A \, 24 \, D \, 10 \, B \, 1 = ?$
   (a) $11\dfrac{1}{3}$ (b) 23
   (c) -7 (d) $16\dfrac{4}{5}$

Directions (Qs. 6 to 8): *Find out the one word among the options which* *cannot be formed by using the letters of the word as given in each question.*

6. ROTATION
   (a) TORN   *(b)* NOTE
   (c) TART   *(d)* RAIN

7. PHILOSOPHY
   (a) SOIL   *(b)* SHIP
   (c) SOLO   *(d)* SPIN

8. SLAVATION
   (a) SNORT   *(b)* LATVIA
   (c) SALIVA   *(d)* AVAIL

Directions (Qs. 9 and 10): *Find out the one word among the options which can be formed by using the letters of the word as given in each question.*

9. INVESTIGATE
   (a) INVERT   *(b)* GLIDE
   (c) STING   *(d)* ACTED

10. MAJORITY
   (a) MORE   *(b)* JURY
   (c) READ   *(d)* TRAY

ANSWERS

1	2	3	4	5	6	7	8	9	10
(c)	*(d)*	*(c)*	*(c)*	*(c)*	*(b)*	*(d)*	*(a)*	*(c)*	*(d)*

SOME SELECTED EXPLANATORY ANSWERS

2. $25 \div 5 + 3 \times 6 - 8$
$5 + 18 - 8 = 15$

3. After interchanging the signs the equations are :
   (a) $7 + 5 \times 3 = 22$ which is wrong
   (b) $4 \times 9 + 1 = 37$ which is wrong
   (c) $6 + 5 \times 8 = 46$ which is correct
   (d) $2 \times 11 + 4 = 26$ which is wrong

4. $7 + 4 - 10 + 2 \times 5$
$7 + 4 - 10 + 10 = 11$

5. $12 \times 4 \div 24 - 10 + 1$
$2 - 10 + 1 = -7$

11

Statement Analysis

In these type of questions, a few statements are given. Certain facts are broken up and mentioned in these statements. What is required is to analyse the statements, arrange and sort out the given facts and then answer the questions related to the given statements.

EXERCISE

1. Among five friends, A is heavier than B; C is lighter than D; B is lighter than D but heavier than E. Who among them is the heaviest?
   - (*a*) B
   - (*b*) C
   - (*c*) A
   - (*d*) Can't say

2. Pune is bigger than Jhansi, Sitapur is bigger than Chittor. Raigarh is not as big as Jhansi, but is bigger than Sitapur. Chittor is not as big as Sitapur. Which is the smallest?
   - (*a*) Jhansi
   - (*b*) Pune
   - (*c*) Chittor
   - (*d*) Sitapur

3. Ajay works more than Ram. Alok works as much as Raju. Pankaj works less than Alok. Ram works more than Alok. Who works the most of all?
   - (*a*) Ajay
   - (*b*) Ram
   - (*c*) Alok
   - (*d*) Raju

4. Among five friends P, Q, R, S and T, who is the youngest? To arrive at the answer which of the following information given in the statements (A) and (B) is sufficient?
   (A) R is younger than P and T.
   (B) S is younger than Q.
   - (*a*) Only A alone is sufficient
   - (*b*) Either A or B is sufficient
   - (*c*) Both A and B together are needed
   - (*d*) Both A and B together are not sufficient

5. A is elder to B while C and D are elder to E who lies between A and B. If C be elder to B, which one of the following statements is necessarily true?
   - (*a*) E is elder to B
   - (*b*) A is elder to C
   - (*c*) C is elder to D
   - (*d*) D is elder to C

Directions (Qs. 6 and 7) : *Read the following directions and answer the questions given below :*
There are five persons in a group. Out of these two are men. Only three persons know swimming, of which one is a man. There is a couple, of which the husband knows swimming. A is the younger sister of D and B is the husband of E. C is a swimming champion.

6. The two women who know how to swim are:
   (*a*) A and C   (*b*) C and D
   (*c*) D and E   (*d*) A and E

7. The two persons who do not know how to swim are :
   (*a*) B and D   (*b*) D and E
   (*c*) A and E   (*d*) A and D

Directions (Qs. 8 to 10) : *Read the following statements and answer the questions given below :*

Rajat, Sushil and Nagesh play football, hockey and cricket. Rajat, Ramu and Nagesh play hockey, cricket and basketball. Rajat, Sushil, Mayank and Nagesh play football and cricket.

8. Which game is played by all the boys?
   (*a*) Hockey   (*b*) Basketball
   (*c*) Football   (*d*) Cricket

9. Who does not play football?
   (*a*) Rajat   (*b*) Nagesh
   (*c*) Sushil   (*d*) Ramu

10. Which of the following two boys play all the games?

    (*a*) Nagesh, Rajat
    (*b*) Mayank, Ramu
    (*c*) Ramu, Nagesh
    (*d*) Sushil, Mayank

Directions (Qs. 11 to 15) : *Read the following information and answer the questions given below:*
   (*i*)   P, Q, R, S, T and U are six members in a family in which there are two married couples.
   (*ii*) T a teacher is married to the doctor who is mother of R and U.
   (*iii*) Q the lawyer is married to P.
   (*iv*) P has one son and one grandson.
   (*v*)   Of the two married ladies one is a housewife.
   (*vi*) There is also one student and one male engineer in the family.

11. Who among the following is the housewife?
    (*a*) Q   (*b*) P
    (*c*) S   (*d*) T

12. Which of the following represents the group of females in the family?
    (*a*) QTR
    (*b*) PSR
    (*c*) PSU
    (*d*) Data inadequate

13. Which of the following is true about the granddaughter in the family?
    (*a*) She is a student
    (*b*) She is an engineer
    (*c*) She is a lawyer
    (*d*) Data Inadequate

14. How R is related to U?
  (*a*) Brother
  (*b*) Sister
  (*c*) Brother and Sister
  (*d*) Data inadequate

15. How is P related to R?
  (*a*) Grandfather
  (*b*) Mother
  (*c*) Sister
  (*d*) Grandmother

ANSWERS

1	2	3	4	5	6	7	8	9	10
(*d*)	(*c*)	(*a*)	(*d*)	(*a*)	(*a*)	(*b*)	(*d*)	(*d*)	(*a*)

11	12	13	14	15
(*b*)	(*d*)	(*a*)	(*c*)	(*d*)

SOME SELECTED EXPLANATORY ANSWERS

1. The five friends in descending order of weight are : A/D, B/C, E or A/D, B, C/E. Either A or D is the heaviest.

2. The order of cities in descending order of size is : Pune, Jhansi, Raigarh, Sitapur, Chittor.

3. On the basis of doing work, the descending order will be : Ajay, Ram, Alok/Raju, Pankaj.

4. Statements are not inter-related.

5. The order in descending seniority will be : A/C/D, E, B.

Chart for Answers 8 to 10

Boy	Games Played
Rajat	Football, Hockey, Cricket, Basketball
Sushil	Football, Hockey, Cricket, Basketball
Nagesh	Football, Hockey, Cricket, Basketball
Ramu	Hockey, Cricket, Basketball
Mayank	Football, Cricket

Chart for Answers 11 to 15

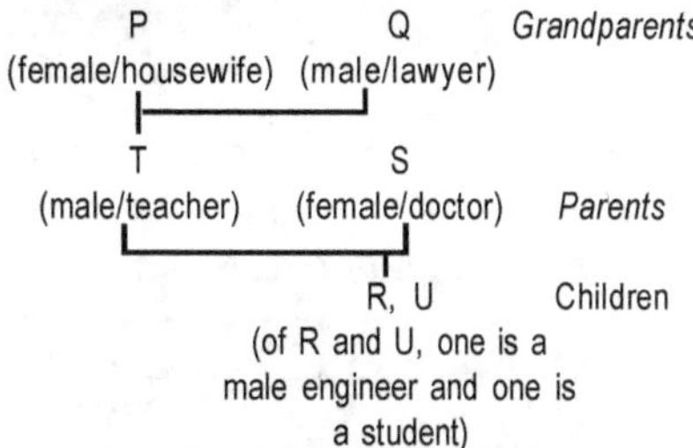

11. One married lady S who is mother of R and U is a doctor. Q the lawyer is married to P. Of the two married ladies one is a house-wife. As Q is a lawyer the other married lady who is a housewife should be P.

12. Sex of R and U is not given.

13. P has one son T and one grandson either R or U one of whom is an engineer. So, the granddaughter is a student.

14. Sex of R and U is not given, but as both are children of S and one is a male engineer, the relationship between the two is of brother and sister.

12

Missing Numbers

Playing with numbers and mathematical skills are needed to attempt these type of tests. The candidates have to work out the right combination of arithmetical symbols to arrive at the answer options which will take the place of the interrogation sign in the given questions.

EXERCISE

Directions : *In each question given below which one number can be placed at the sign of interrogation?*

1. 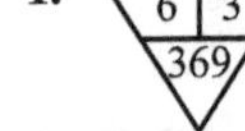

(a) 693   (b) 939
(c) 981   (d) 993

2. 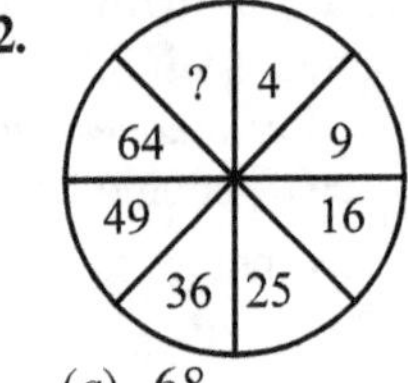

(a) 68   (b) 100
(c) 72   (d) 81

3. 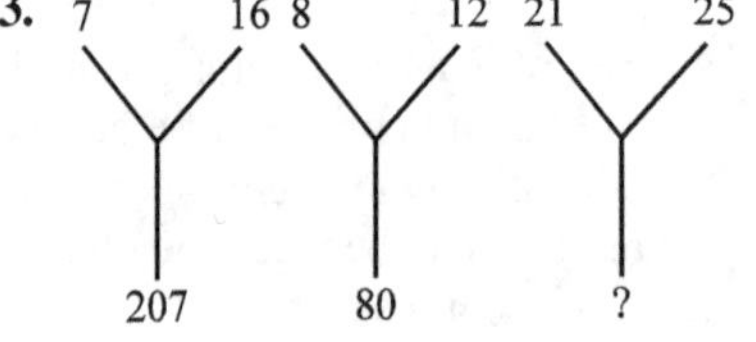

(a) 425   (b) 184
(c) 241   (d) 210

4.

14	9	4
12	7	2
10	5	0
16	11	?

(a) 9   (b) 6
(c) 3   (d) 7

5. 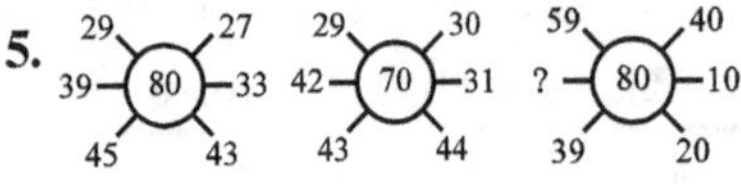

(a) 69   (b) 49
(c) 50   (d) 60

6. 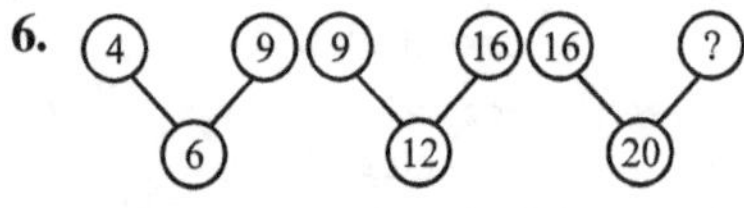

(a) 21   (b) 25
(c) 50   (d) 60

7. 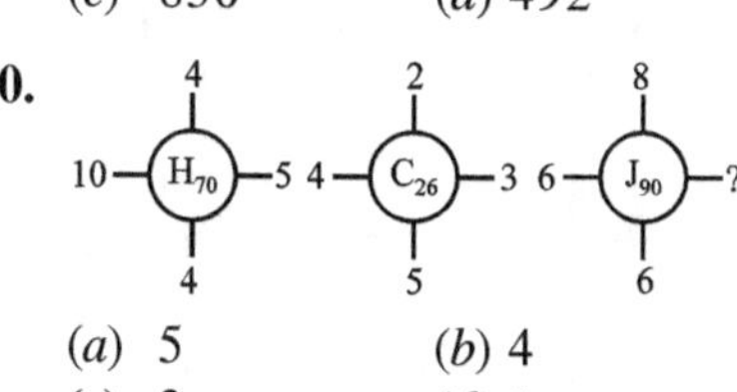

(a) 8   (b) 14
(c) 10   (d) 6

8.

42	(21)	22
78	(?)	84
162	(18)	99

(a) 12   (b) 13
(c) 60   (d) 72

9.

(a) 960   (b) 628
(c) 830   (d) 492

10.

(a) 5   (b) 4
(c) 2   (d) 1

ANSWERS

1	2	3	4	5	6	7	8	9	10
(c)	(d)	(b)	(b)	(a)	(b)	(c)	(b)	(c)	(b)

SOME SELECTED EXPLANATORY ANSWERS

1. The squares of two numbers on the top placed side by side gives the number inside the bottom triangle, *i.e.*,
6^2 and $3^2 = 369$
2^2 and $5^2 = 425$, similarly
3^2 and $9^2 = 981$.

2. Starting from number 4 the numbers are the squares of numbers in natural order *i.e.*, $2^2 = 4$, $3^2 = 9$, $4^2 = 16 \ldots\ldots 9^2 = 81$.

3. The number at the bottom is the difference of the squares of two numbers at the top, *i.e.*,
$16^2 - 7^2 = 256 - 49 = 207$
$12^2 - 8^2 = 144 - 64 = 80$,
Similarly
$25^2 - 21^2 = 625 - 441 = 184$.

6. Square of number at the bottom is equal to the product of two numbers at the top, *i.e.*,
$6^2 = 4 \times 9$, *i.e.*, 36
$12^2 = 9 \times 16$, *i.e.*, 144, similarly
$20^2 = 16 \times ?$, *i.e.*, 400. The missing number is $400 \div 16 = 25$.

7. The number inside each triangle is the difference of the numbers at its base *i.e.*
$10 - 4 = 6$, $18 - 4 = 14$ and
$18 - 10 = 8$
$14 - 8 = 6$, $22 - 8 = 14$ and
$22 - 14 = 8$,
Similarly
$11 - 5 = 6$, $15 - 5 = 10$ and
$15 - 11 = 4$.

8. The number inside the brackets is obtained by multiplying the number on the left by 2 and then dividing the product by the sum of digits of number on the right, *i.e.,*

$(42 \times 2) \div (2 + 2) = 21$

$(162 \times 2) \div (9 + 9) = 18$, similarly

$(78 \times 2) \div (8 + 4) = 13$.

9. The number in the centre is the product of all the 4 numbers minus 10, *i.e.,*

$(3 \times 5 \times 2 \times 6) - 10 = 170$

$(8 \times 1 \times 4 \times 9) - 10 = 278$,

Similarly,

$(10 \times 6 \times 7 \times 2) - 10 = 830$.

10. Letter H is 8th in order of alphabetical series. Taking the sum of numbers placed vertically outside the circle + 8; multiplying it by the number on the right; then subtracting from the product the number on the left, gives the number inside the circle, *i.e.,*

Step I $\rightarrow$ $4 + 8 + 4 = 16$

Step II $\rightarrow$ $16 \times 5 = 80$

Step III $\rightarrow$ $80 - 10 = 70$

Letter C is 3rd in order, so

Step I $\rightarrow$ $2 + 3 + 5 = 10$

Step II $\rightarrow$ $10 \times 3 = 30$

Step III $\rightarrow$ $30 - 4 = 26$

Similarly, J is 10th in order, so

Step I $\rightarrow$ $8 + 10 + 6 = 24$

Step II $\rightarrow$ $24 \times ?$

Step III $\rightarrow (24 \times ?) - 6 = 90$

Simplifying the above equation :

$$24 \times ? = 90 + 6, \text{ i.e., } 96$$

$$? = 96 \div 24 = 4.$$

□□□

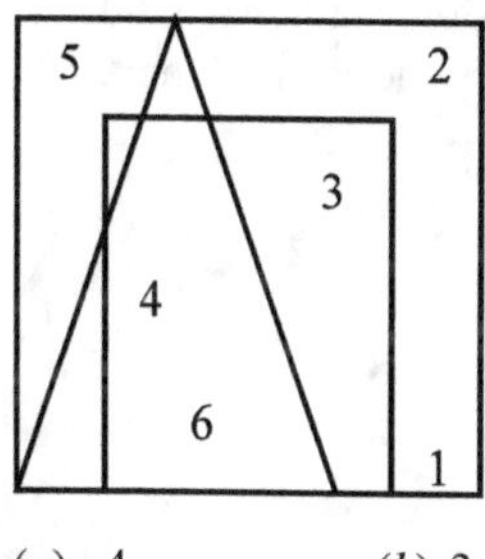

13

Venn Diagrams & Logical Diagram

In these type of questions, diagrammatic representation presents a logical illustration of particular class or statements based on which the questions are asked. A clear view of the diagram makes the concepts clear for attempting such questions.

EXERCISE

1. What is the number which is common to only two geometrical figures?

(a) 4   (b) 3
(c) 5   (d) 2

Directions (Qs. 2 & 3) : *In the following diagram, rectangle represents Hindi Announcers, circle represents English Announcers, square represents French Announcers, and triangle represents German Announcers.*

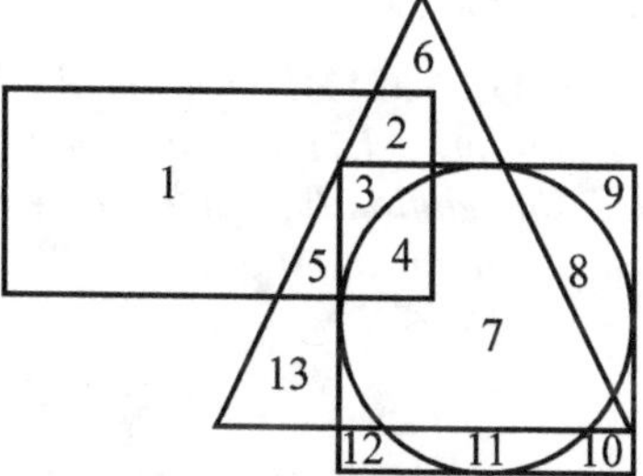

2. Which area represents those announcers who can present programmes in Hindi, French and German only?
(a) 1   (b) 2
(c) 3   (d) 4

3 Which area represents those announcers who can present programmes in French and English only?
(a) 7   (b) 9
(c) 11   (d) 13

Directions (Qs. 4 & 5): *Study the diagram to answer these questions.*

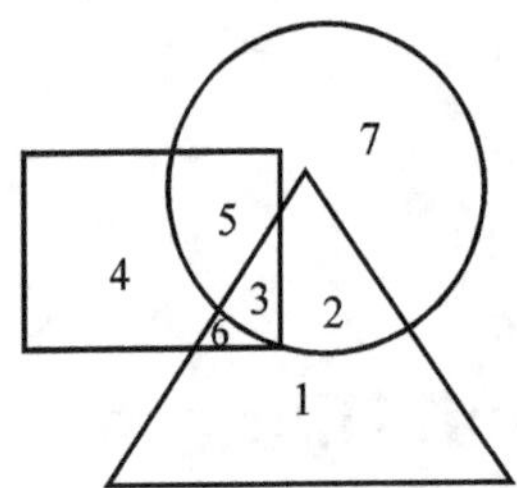

4. Which number is in all the geometrical figures?
   (*a*) 5   (*b*) 6
   (*c*) 2   (*d*) 3

5. Number 6 is in :
   (*a*) Rectangle and triangle
   (*b*) Circle and traingle
   (*c*) Rectangle and circle
   (*d*) Rectangle only

Directions (Qs. 6 to 15): *From the five logical Diagrams, select one which best illustrates the relationship among three given classes in the questions 1 to 10.*

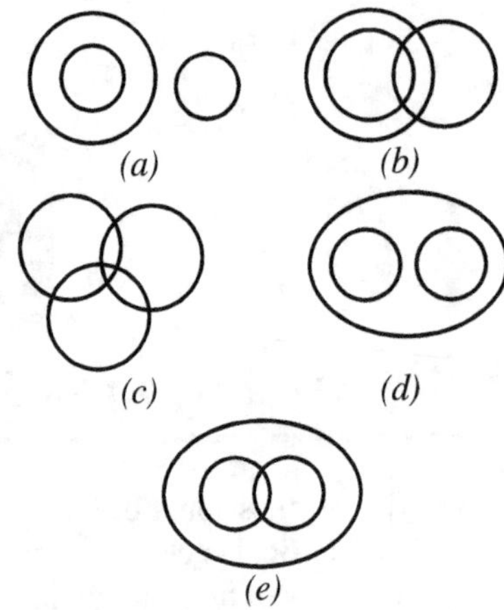

6. Birds, fruits, mangoes
7. Criminals, lawyers, bandits
8. Swimmers, bachelors, men
9. Smart, engineers, women
10. Vegetables, potatoes, brinjals
11. Grapes, sweet, fruit
12. Doctors, architects, humans
13. Scholars, people, Indians
14. Children, naughty, studious
15. Pens, pencils, stationery

ANSWERS

1	2	3	4	5	6	7	8	9	10
(*b*)	(*c*)	(*c*)	(*d*)	(*a*)	(*a*)	(*a*)	(*b*)	(*c*)	(*d*)

11	12	13	14	15
(*b*)	(*d*)	(*e*)	(*c*)	(*d*)

SOME SELECTED EXPLANATORY ANSWERS

1.

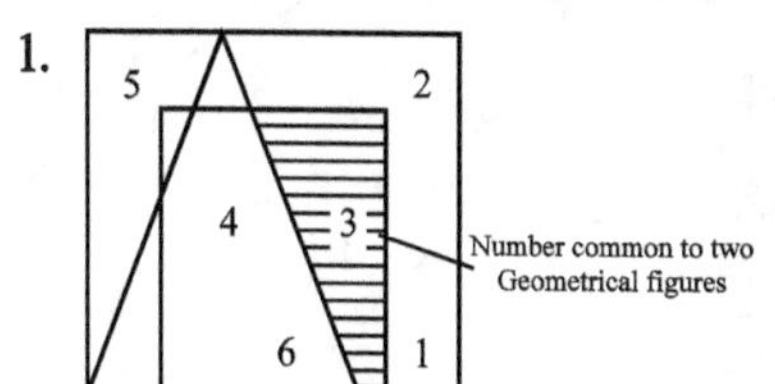

Note : Numbers 4 and 6 are common to all three geometrical figures.

2–3.

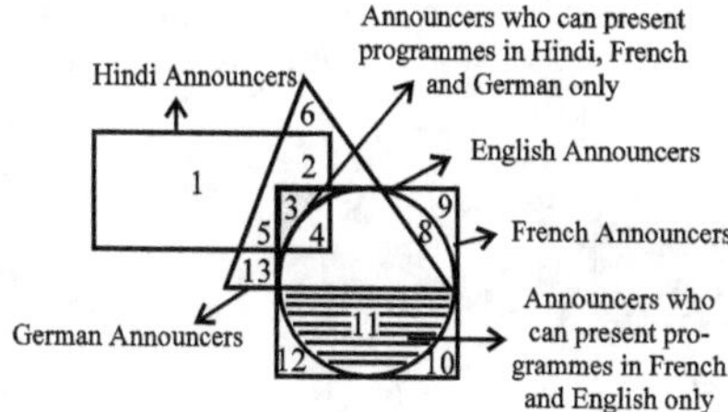

4–5.

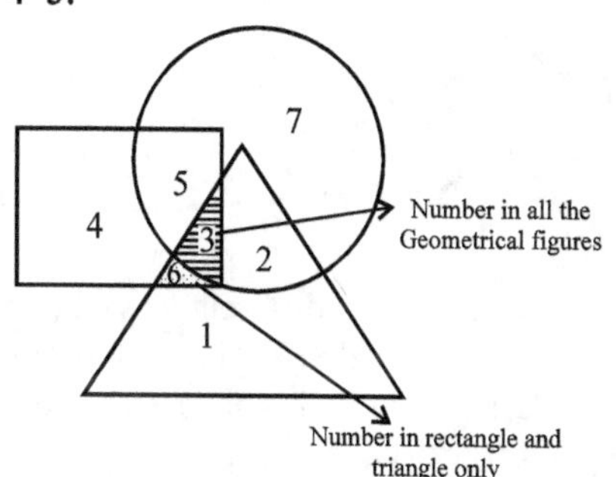

6.

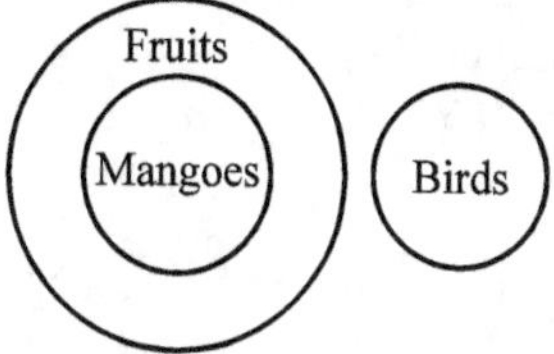

All mangoes are fruits, but neither fruits, nor mangoes can be birds.

8.

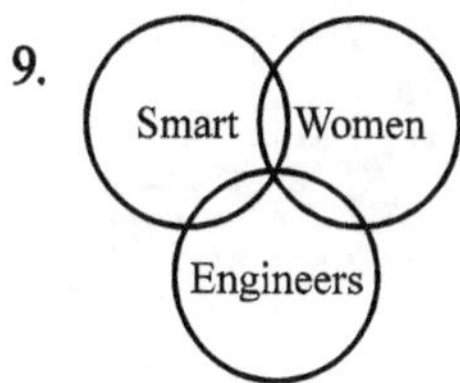

All bachelors are men and some men and bachelors can be swimmers.

9.

Some women can be smart and some women can be engineers and vice–versa. Some engineers can be women and some engineers can be smart and vice–versa.

13.

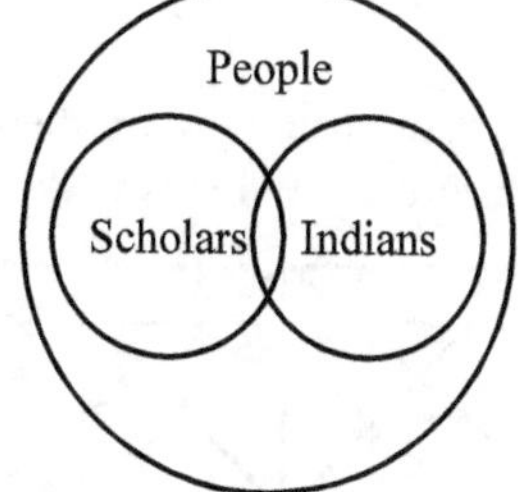

Some Indians can be scholars and some scholars can be Indians. All scholars and Indians are people.

14

Diagrammatic Puzzle

This test aims to judge your space visualisation, keen observation and analytical aptitude. In this test diagrams are given which may look puzzling. Questions are asked on the diagrams.

EXERCISE

1. How many squares are there in the figure given below?

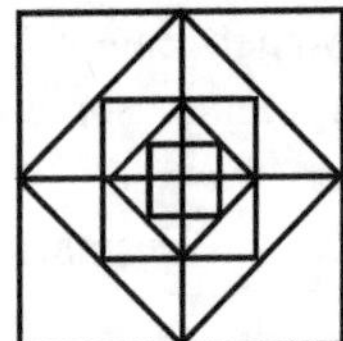

   (a) 12   (b) 13
   (c) 16   (d) 17

2. How many triangles are there in the figure given below?

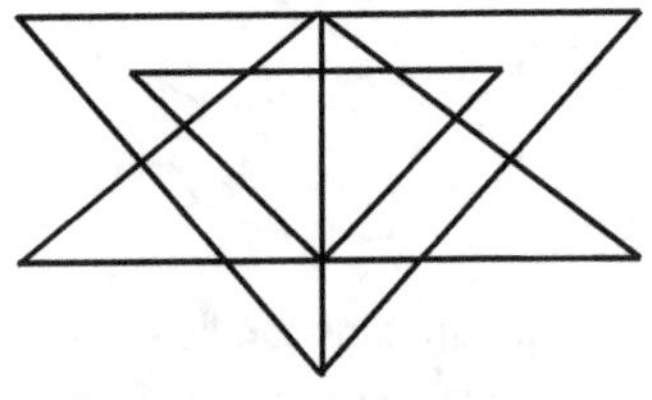

   (a) 25   (b) 23
   (c) 21   (d) 27

3.

In how many different ways can the word **THINKER** be read from left to right in this diagram, each letter connecting to its neighbour along one of the marked lines.

   (a) 16   (b) 12
   (c) 8   (d) 20

4. Two positions of a dice are shown below.

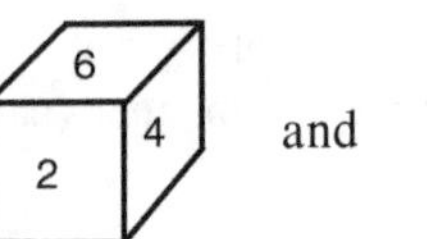

When 2 is at the bottom, what number will be at the top?

(a) 1   (b) 3
(c) 4   (d) 5

5. Six sides of a block are coloured Green, Blue, Red, Yellow, Orange and White in the following manner:

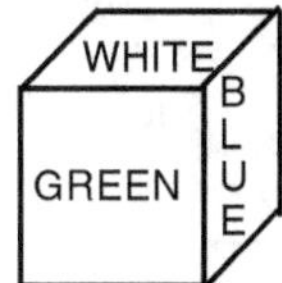

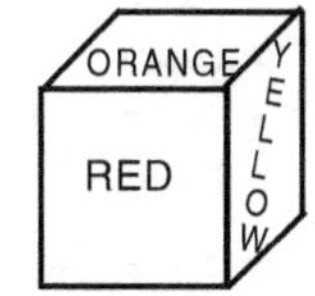

When Blue is on the top, which colour will be at the bottom?

(a) Orange   (b) Red
(c) White   (d) Yellow

Directions (Qs. 6 to 8): *The figures given below show three positions of the same dice having 1, 2, 3, ...6 circles on its six faces. Answer these questions based on this dice.*

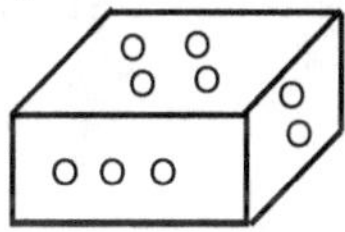
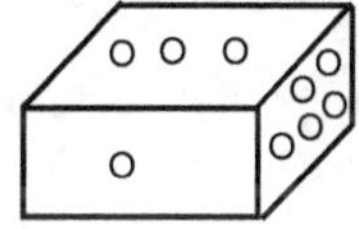
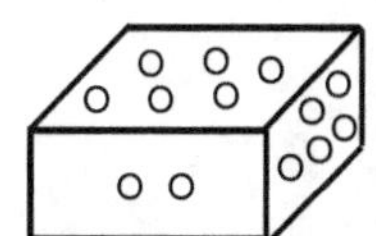

6. The number of circles on the face opposite to the one having three circles is:

(a) 6   (b) 5
(c) 7
(d) None of these

7. What is the number of circles on the face at the bottom of the first cube?

(a) 6
(b) 1
(c) 5
(d) None of these

8. How many circles will be there on the top face in the figure shown?

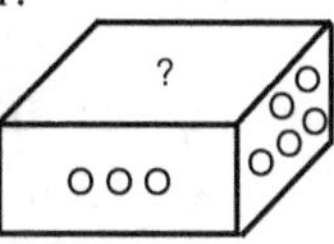

(a) 2   (b) 1
(c) 6   (d) 4

Directions (Qs. 9 & 10): *A toy cube has pictures of different fruits on its six faces. The top face has the picture of orange. Banana is adjacent to melon and orange. Apple is not at the bottom of the cube and melon is opposite the peach.*

9. A cube is coloured with different colours on each side. Red is at the base and white at the top. The colours green, yellow, blue and purple respectively are painted on the four sides of the cube, in the clockwise direction. When the yellow side is changed as the base of the cube, which colour will be on the top?

(a) BLUE   (b) GREEN
(c) PURPLE   (d) RED

10. A four centimetre cube has been painted blue on all its sides. It is then cut into one cm cubes. How many cubes will be there with only one side painted?

(a) 24   (b) 16
(c) 8   (d) 32

ANSWERS

1	2	3	4	5	6	7	8	9	10
(d)	(d)	(d)	(b)	(b)	(a)	(c)	(a)	(c)	(a)

SOME SELECTED EXPLANATORY ANSWERS

6. 2, 4, 1 and 5 circles are neighbouring faces of 3.

7. 5 circles' face has neighbouring faces with 1, 3, 2 and 6 circles. Hence 4 and 5 circles faces form opposite pairs.

9. The sides are painted green, yellow, blue and purple respectively. So the colour opposite each will be the alternate one, *i.e.*, when yellow colour is at the base purple colour will be at the top.

10. One side of the cube has four such cubes, therefore six sides of the cube will have 24 such cubes with only one side painted.

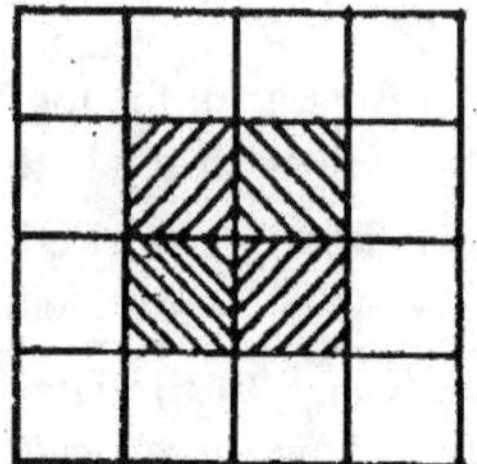

□□□

═══ NON-VERBAL ═══

1

Series

In this form of non-verbal series, which are the most common, four or five consecutive problem figures form a definite sequence and one is required to select the one figure from the given set of Answer Figures that will continue the same sequence.

One has to try different set of moves, changes, replacements, rotations, repetitions and a lot more variations to arrive at the logical pattern making the series. Practising alone will sharpen one's skill of solving such sequences.

Example

Directions : *Which of the given options will complete the given series?*

Problem Figures

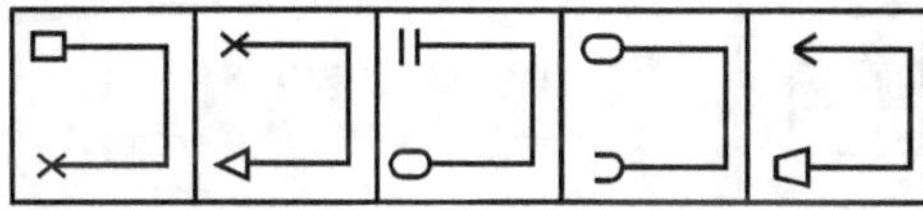

Answer Figures

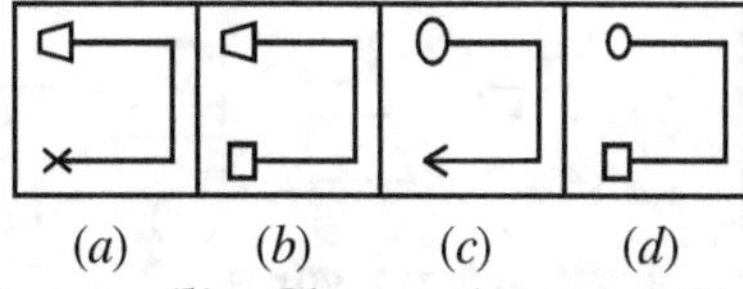

(a)   (b)   (c)   (d)

Answer (b) : Observe the series. Figure one corelates to figure two in the manner that the places of both the elements on the left are inter changed and then the element at the bottom is replaced by a new element. Similarly, Figure three corelates to figure four and answer figure 'B' corelates to figure five.

EXERCISE

Direction : *Each of the following questions consist of problem figures followed by answer figures. Select a figure from amongst the answer figures which will continue the same series or pattern as established by the problem figures.*

1. Problem Figures

Answer Figures

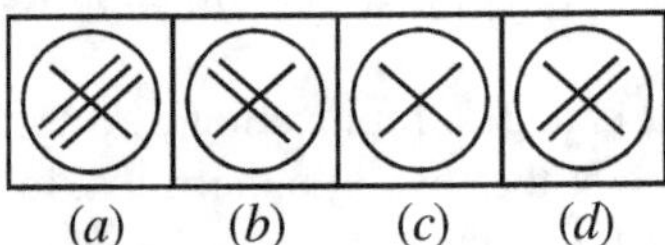

(a)　　(b)　　(c)　　(d)

2. Problem Figures

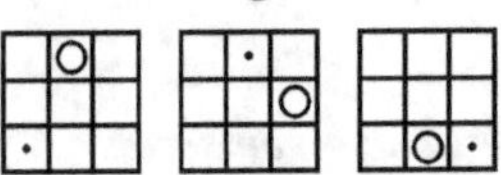

Answer Figures

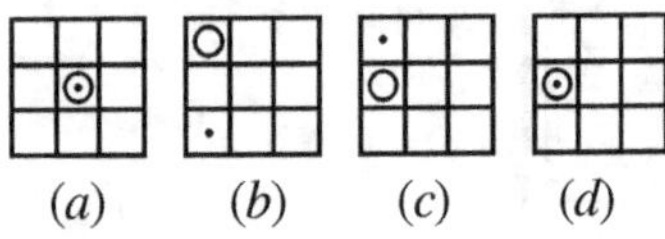

(a)　　(b)　　(c)　　(d)

3. Problem Figures

Answer Figures

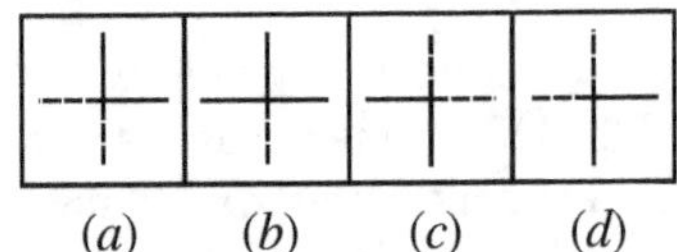

(a)　　(b)　　(c)　　(d)

4. Problem Figures

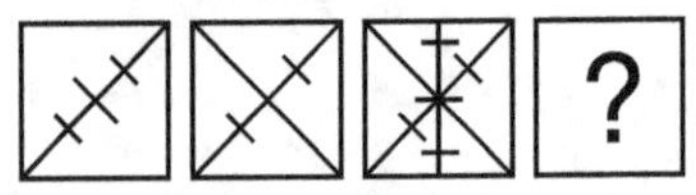

Answer Figures

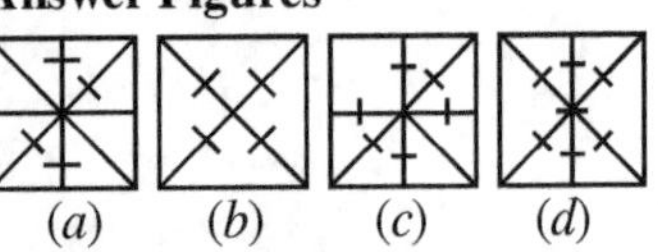

(a)　　(b)　　(c)　　(d)

5. Problem Figures

Answer Figures

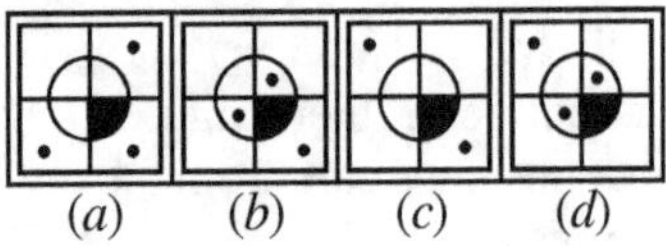

(a)　　(b)　　(c)　　(d)

6. Problem Figures

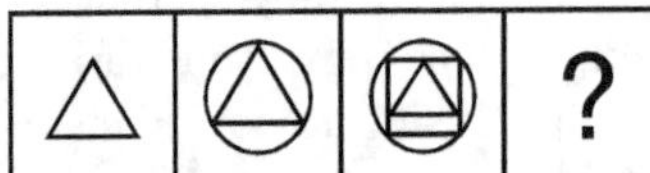

Answer Figures

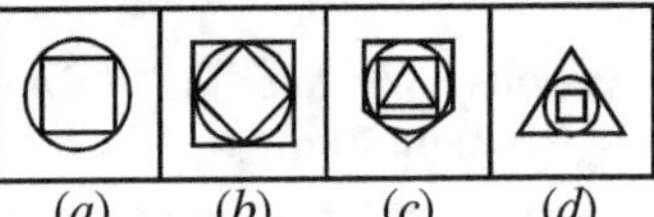

(a)　　(b)　　(c)　　(d)

7. Problem Figures

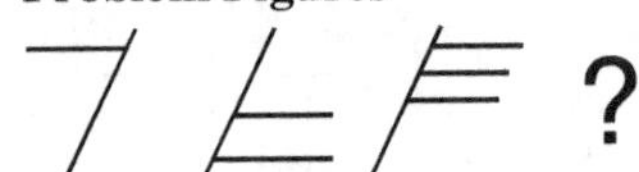

Answer Figures

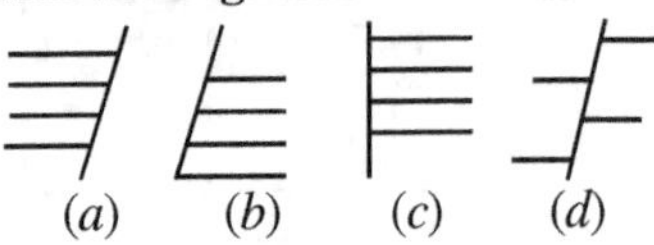

(a)　　(b)　　(c)　　(d)

8. Problem Figures

Answer Figures

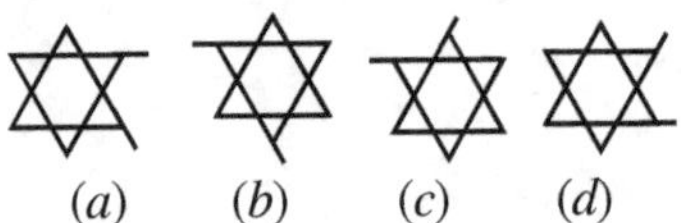

(a)　　(b)　　(c)　　(d)

9. Problem Figures

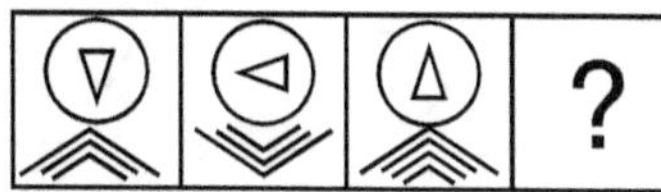

Answer Figures

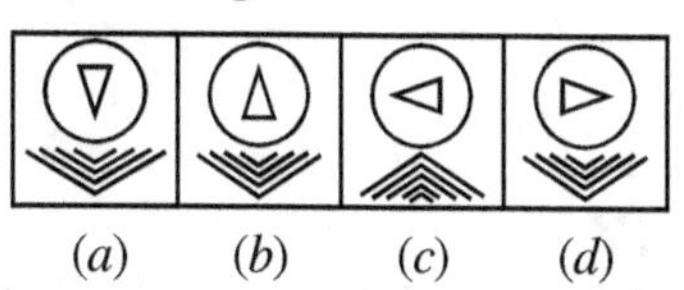

    (*a*)   (*b*)   (*c*)   (*d*)

10. Problem Figures

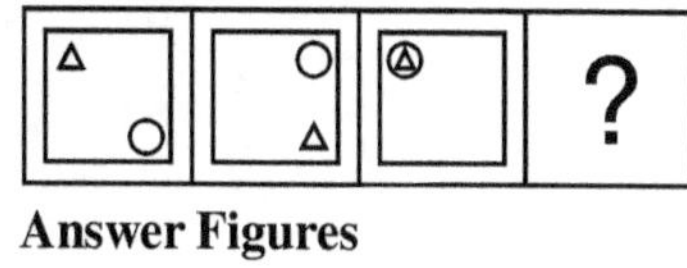

Answer Figures

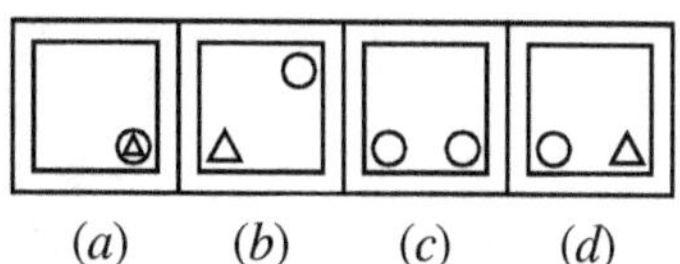

    (*a*)   (*b*)   (*c*)   (*d*)

ANSWERS

1	2	3	4	5	6	7	8	9	10
(*d*)	(*d*)	(*a*)	(*a*)	(*d*)	(*c*)	(*a*)	(*d*)	(*d*)	(*d*)

SOME SELECTED EXPLANATORY ANSWERS

2. The circle and the dot are moved two and three sections clockwise respectively.

3. The cross is turned 90° clockwise at each step.

5. The complete figure is turned 90° clockwise at each step.

6. A new figure is added to the previous set of figures at each step.

8. The star shape is rotated 90° anticlockwise at each step.

10. The triangle is moved diagonally to and fro and the circle one step anticlockwise to get the next figure.

2

Analogy

Analogy is a process of reasoning between two parallel cases. It relates to agreement or correspondence in certain respects between two things. It is a process whereby the underlying relationship that exists between two figures, designs or patterns is determined. Under the process, one has to discover the features common to the two figures or designs. This common feature is a model or base. The question seeks solution on the basis of this model or base.

Example

Directions : *Which of the given options will complete the given series?*

Problem Figures

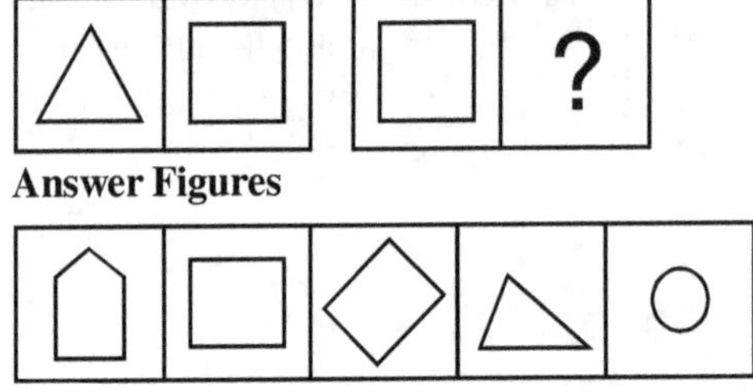

Answer Figures

Answer A : Study the two figures in the first part of the Problem Figures. They are a triangle and a square. The first figure (a triangle) has three angles and three sides, while the second figure (a square) has four angles and four sides. The relationship between them is—the second figure has one angle and one side more than what the first figure has.

On this analogy the figure to suit in the space marked by ? should be one with 5 angles and 5 sides (one angle and one side more than what the first figure of the second part of the Problem Figures has).

54

EXERCISE

Directions : *The second figure in the first unit of the Problem Figures bears a certain relationship to the first figure. Similarly, one of the figures in the Answer Figures bears the same relationship to the first figure in the second unit of the Problem Figures. Locate the figure which would fit the question mark.*

1. Problem Figures

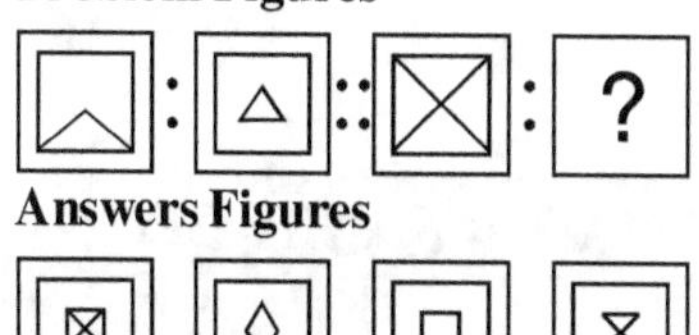

Answers Figures

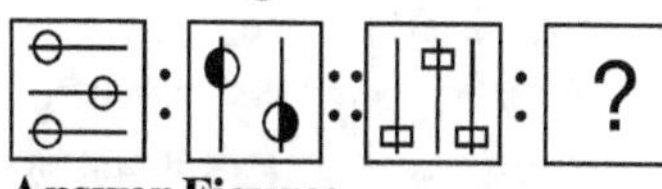

(a)　　(b)　　(c)　　(d)

2. Problem Figures

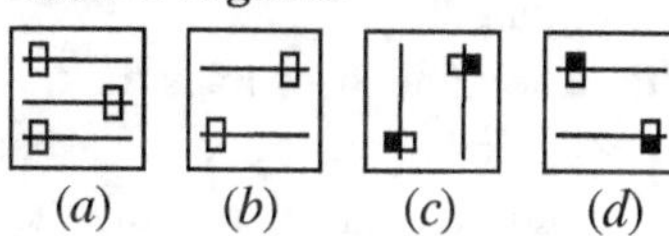

Answer Figures

(a)　　(b)　　(c)　　(d)

3. Problem Figures

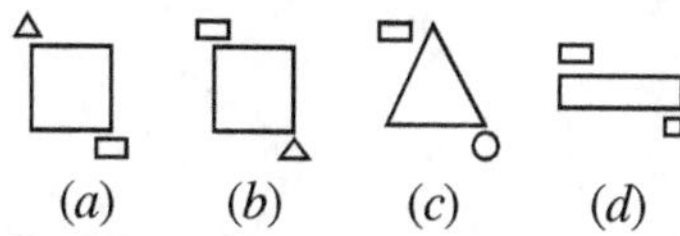

Answer Figures

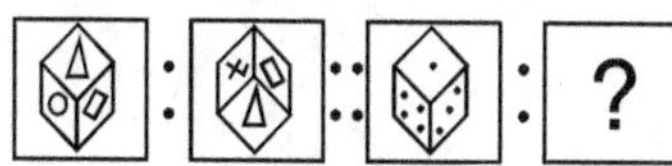

(a)　　(b)　　(c)　　(d)

4. Problem Figures

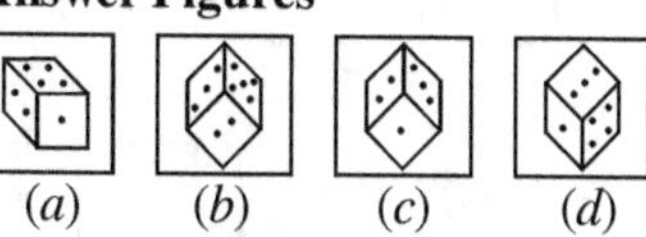

Answer Figures

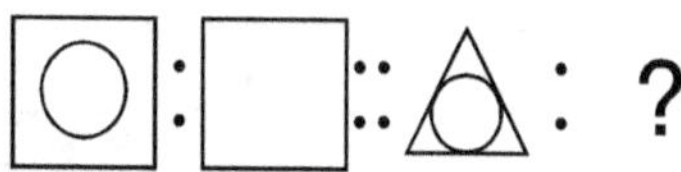

(a)　　(b)　　(c)　　(d)

5. Problem Figures

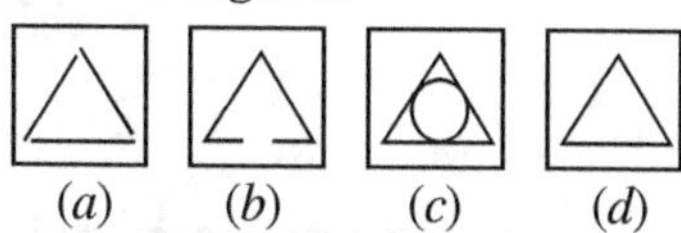

Answer Figures

(a)　　(b)　　(c)　　(d)

6. Problem Figures

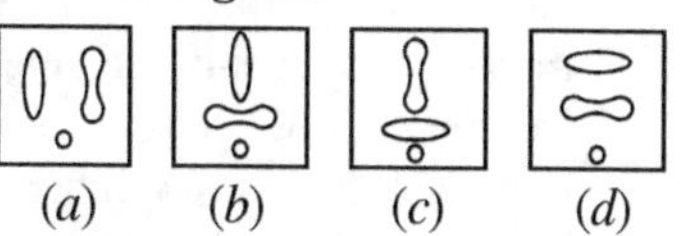

Answer Figures

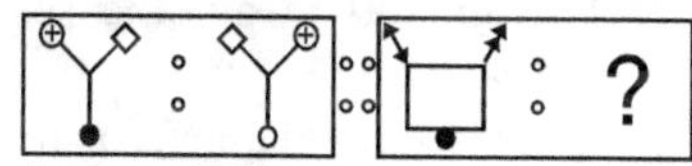

(a)　　(b)　　(c)　　(d)

7. Problem Figures

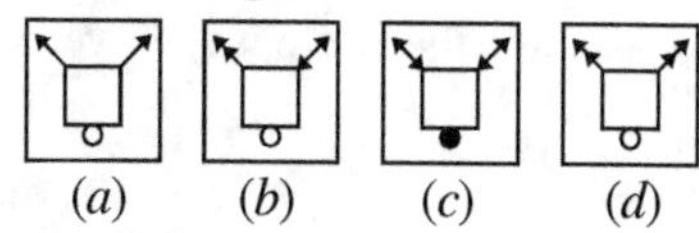

Answer Figures

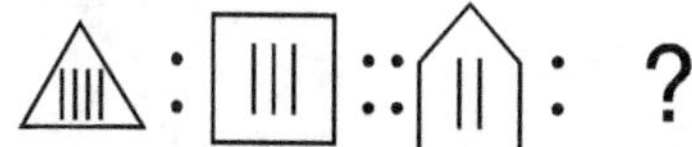

(a)　　(b)　　(c)　　(d)

8. Problem Figures

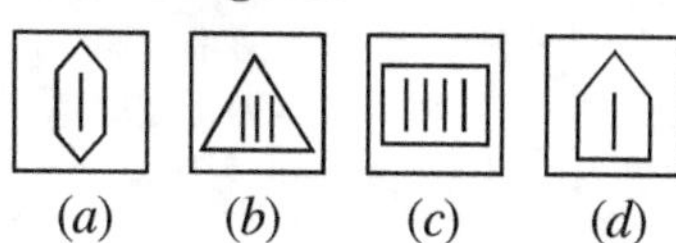

Answer Figures

(a)　　(b)　　(c)　　(d)

9. Problem Figures

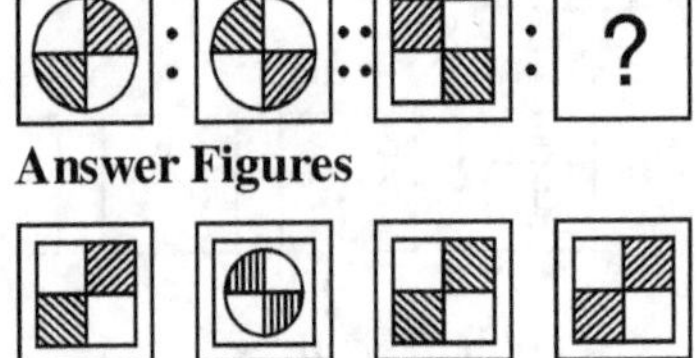

Answer Figures

(a)   (b)   (c)   (d)

10. Problem Figures

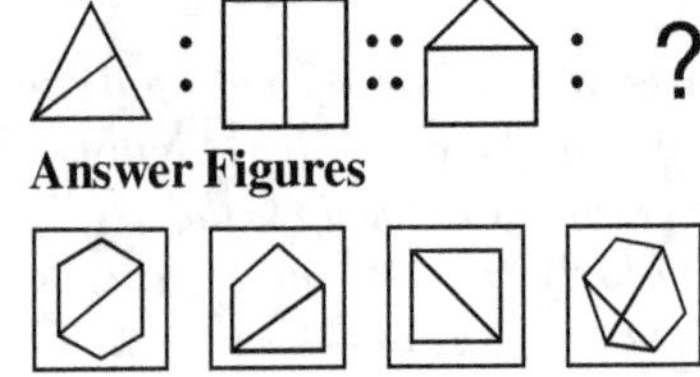

Answer Figures

(a)   (b)   (c)   (d)

ANSWERS

1	2	3	4	5	6	7	8	9	10
(d)	(d)	(a)	(c)	(d)	(b)	(b)	(a)	(a)	(a)

SOME SELECTED EXPLANATORY ANSWERS

3. The element at the bottom is moved to the diagonal corner, the element in the top is enlarged and moved to the centre and element in the middle is reduced and moved to the bottom right corner.

5. The inner shape in the first figure is removed to get the second figure.

7. The places of elements on the top are interchanged and the shade inside the circle is removed.

8. One of the vertical lines is removed and the number of lines making the second figure is increased by one.

9. First figure is rotated 90° anticlockwise to get the second figure.

10. The number of lines making the second figure is one more than the number of lines making the first figure.

3

Classification

Classification means arranging the given content in groups or classes having qualities of same kind. In classification type questions, the figures or items are sorted out in groups on the basis of their similarities in qualities in shapes, size, pattern, structure, genus, order, species, grade, style, constituents and other specifications, and thus the answer is found out.

Example

Directions : *Find the figure which is different from all given figure?*

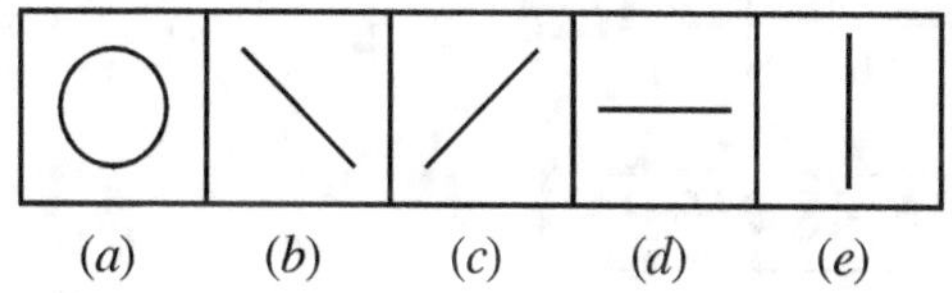

$$(a) \qquad (b) \qquad (c) \qquad (d) \qquad (e)$$

Answer (a) : A is a circle, whereas B, C, D and E are straight lines pointing to different directions. Note that the common characteristic in each of the four figures B, C, D and E is that they are straight lines. Thus, they belong to a class. As against these figures, A is a circle and does not belong to that class.

Therefore, the figure that does not belong to the class is A.

EXERCISE

Directions : *In each of the following questions one of the figures is different from the rest. Spot the figure.*

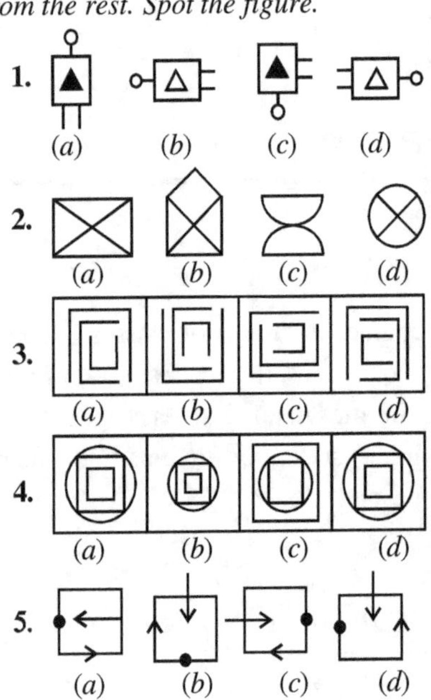

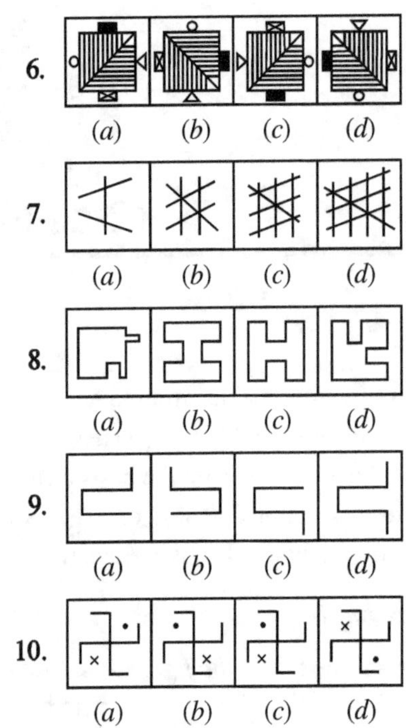

ANSWERS

1	2	3	4	5	6	7	8	9	10
(c)	(c)	(d)	(c)	(a)	(c)	(d)	(a)	(d)	(c)

SOME SELECTED EXPLANATORY ANSWERS

2. All other figures are divided into four parts.

3. Only in this figure the middle and the centre shapes are opposite to each other.

4. In all other figures the middle and the centre designs are identical.

6. All other figures can be rotated into each other.

8. In all other figures the cuts are identical along the two sides of the square.

9. Only in this figure both ends of the design are drawn further.

10. In all other figures the dot and the cross are in diagonally opposite sections of the shape.

4

Mirror Image

These type of problems are based on the mirror images or reflections of number, letters and figures. While attempting such questions one must be able to visualise clearly the questioned reflections, be they on vertical plane or on horizontal plane.

EXERCISE

Directions (Qs. 1 to 4): *In each question below which is the exact mirror image if the mirror is held vertically?*

1. CHIDE

   A. EDIHƆ   B. EDIHƆ
   C. CHIDE   D. ƆHIDE

2. 4320

   A. ४३५0   B. ४३20
   C. ०३५४   D. ०३२४

3. MJ7KL

   A. WۺLKꓶ   B. WۺꓶKꓶ
   C. WۺꓶꓘL   D. WۺꓶꓘL

4. ↓OF2xq

   A. ↑OꟻƧxd   B. ↑OꟻƧxd
   C. ↑OꟻƧxp   D. ↑OƧꟻxd

Directions (Qs. 5 to 10) : *In each question given below which one would be the mirror image of the given figure when the mirror is placed along the line shown in each figure.*

5. Problem Figure

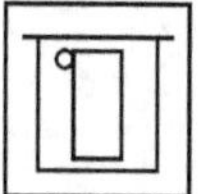

Answer Figures

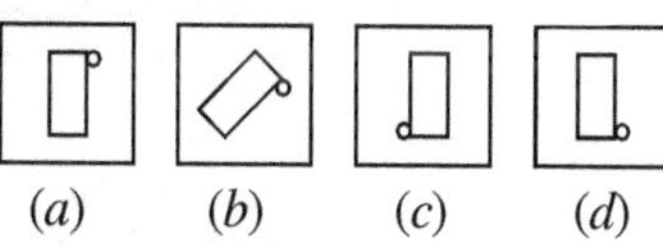

  (a)   (b)   (c)   (d)

6. Problem Figure

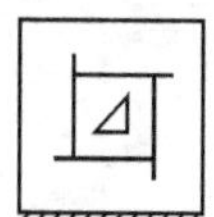

Answer Figures

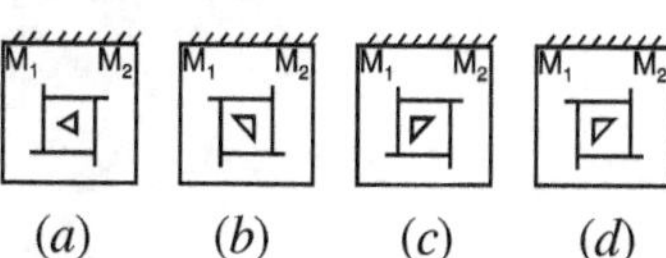

  (a)   (b)   (c)   (d)

7. Problem Figure

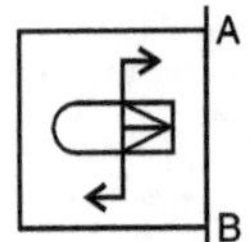

Answer Figures

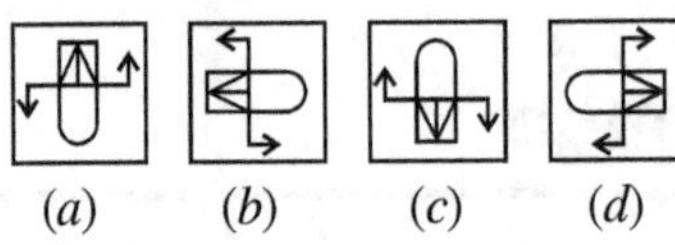

(a)   (b)   (c)   (d)

8. Problem Figure

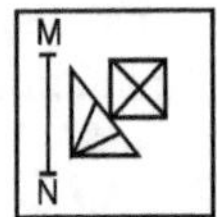

Answer Figures

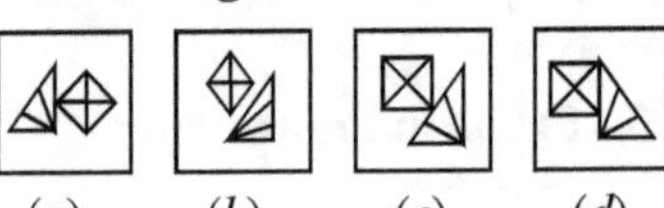

(a)   (b)   (c)   (d)

9. Problem Figure

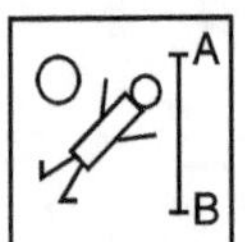

Answer Figures

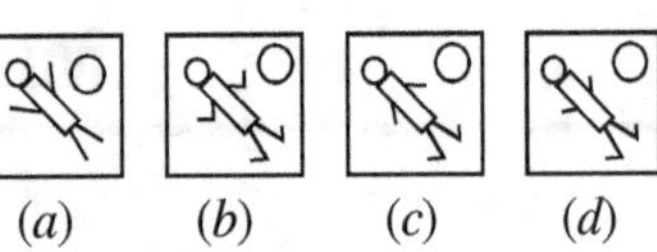

(a)   (b)   (c)   (d)

10. Problem Figure

Answer Figures

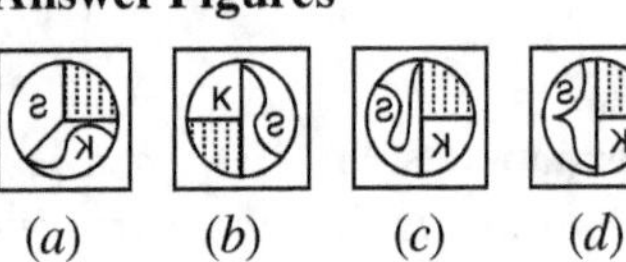

(a)   (b)   (c)   (d)

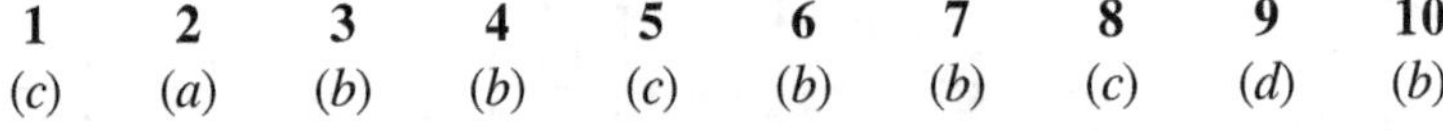

ANSWERS

1	2	3	4	5	6	7	8	9	10
(c)	(a)	(b)	(b)	(c)	(b)	(b)	(c)	(d)	(b)

□□□

5

Syllogism

In this reasoning pattern the two premises are followed by two conclusions drawn from them. Four options (*a*), (*b*), (*c*) and (*d*) are given as answers. Based on the two statements the candidate has to select the right option as answer.

Example

Directions : *In the questions below the answer is given as :*
   (*a*) if only conclusion I follows.
   (*b*) if only conclusion II follows.
   (*c*) if neither I nor II follows, and
   (*d*) if both I and II follows.

   Q. *Statements*   *I :* All officers are lazy.
                    II : Some men are officers.
          Conclusions I : All lazy are men.
                    II : Some men are lazy.

Ans. (b): When all officers are lazy and some men are officers then some men must be lazy. Therefore, conclusion II is correct.

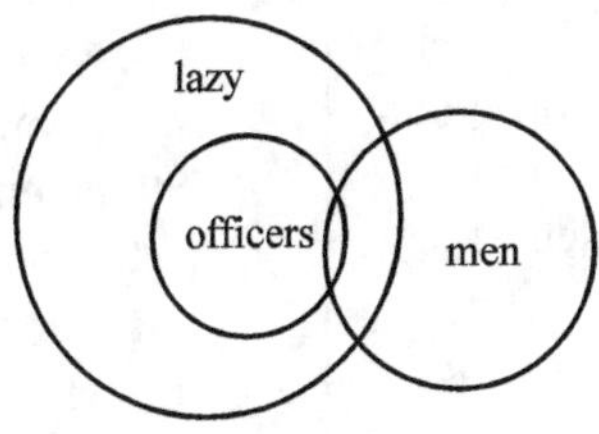

EXERCISE

Directions : *In each question below are given two statements followed by two conclusions numbered I and II. You have to take the two given statements to be true even if they seem to be at variance from commonly known facts and then decide which of the given conclusions logically follows from the two given statements, disregarding commonly known facts. Read both the statements and—*

Give answer (a) if only conclusion I follows; give answer (b) if only conclusion II follows; give answer (c) if neither I nor II follows and give answer (d) if both I and II follows.

1. **Statements**
   I. All tomatoes are red.
   II. All grapes are tomatoes.
   Conclusions
   I. All grapes are red.
   II. Some tomatoes are grapes.

2. **Statements**
   I. All painters are smilling.
   II. Some authors are painters.
   Conclusions
   I. All smiling authors are painters.
   II. Some authors are smiling.

3. **Statements**
   I. All peons in this office are efficient.
   II. Ramu is not efficient.
   Conclusions
   I. Ramu is not peon in this office.
   II. Ramu should be more efficient.

4. **Statements**
   I. All weavers are hard working.
   II. No hard working men are foolish.
   Conclusions
   I. No weavers are foolish.
   II. Some foolish are weavers.

5. **Statements**
   I. All fishes are cars.
   II. All cars are vegetables.
   Conclusions
   I. Some vegetables are cars.
   II. Some vegetables are fishes.

6. **Statements**
   I. Some dogs are pups.
   II. All horses are pups.
   Conclusions
   I. Some dogs are horses.
   II. Some horses are dogs.

7. **Statements**
   I. All beautiful women are mothers.
   II. All mothers are understanding.
   Conclusions
   I. All beautiful women are understanding.
   II. All mothers are beautiful women.

8. **Statements**
   I. Some toys are tables.
   II. No table is black.
   Conclusions
   I. Some toys are black.
   II. Some toys are not black.

9. Statements
   I. All rivers are mountains.
   II. Some rivers are deserts.
Conclusions
   I. Some mountains are deserts.
   II. Some deserts are not mountains.

10. Statements
   I. All men are horses.
   II. All horses are elephants.
Conclusions
   I. All men are elephants.
   II. All elephants are men.

ANSWERS

1	2	3	4	5	6	7	8	9	10
(d)	(b)	(a)	(a)	(d)	(c)	(a)	(c)	(d)	(a)

SOME SELECTED EXPLANATORY ANSWERS

1. When all tomatoes are red and all grapes are tomatoes, then all grapes are also red. When all grapes are tomatoes, then some tomatoes must be grapes. Therefore, both conclusions I and II are correct.

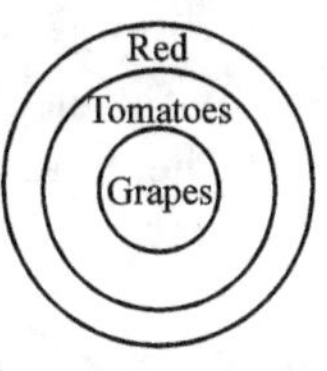

2. When all painters are smiling and some authors are painters, then some authors are smiling. Therefore, only conclusion II is correct.

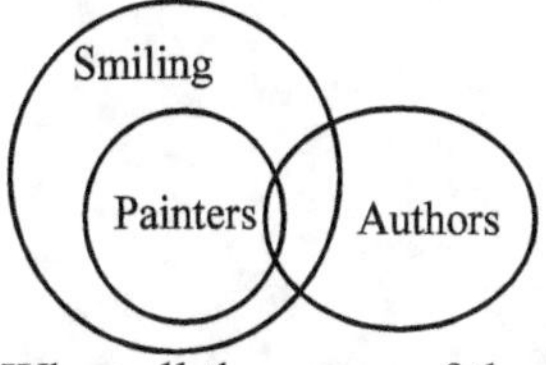

3. When all the peons of the office are efficient, then Ramu cannot be a peon in this office. Therefore, only conclusion I is correct.

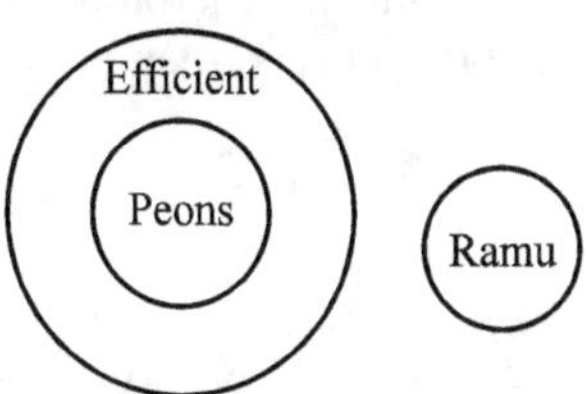

4. When all weavers are hardworking and no hardworking men are foolish, then no weavers are foolish. Therefore, only conclusion I is correct.

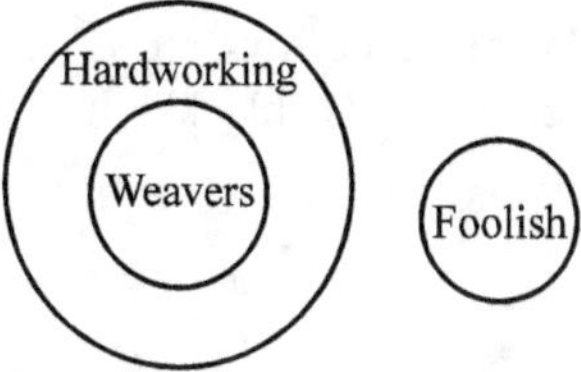

5. When all fishes are cars and all cars are vegetables, then all fishes will naturally be vegetables. This means that some vegetables are fishes. And when all cars are vegetables, then some vegetables

will be cars naturally. Therefore, both the conclusions I and II are correct.

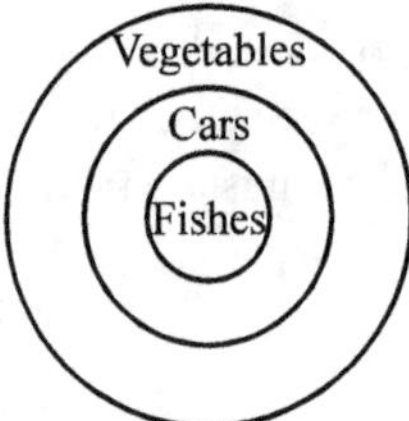

7. When all beautiful women are mothers and all mothers are understanding, then naturally all beautiful women are understanding. All mothers need not be beautiful women. Therefore, only conclusion I is correct.

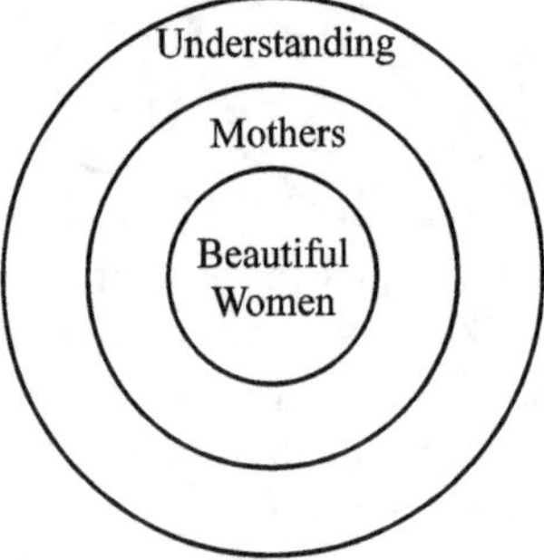

8. When some toys are tables and no table is black, then it is

indicated that some toys can be black, as all toys are not tables. On the other hand, some toys may not be black. Therefore, there is a possibility that some toys may or may not be black. As such, either conclusion I or conclusion II can be correct.

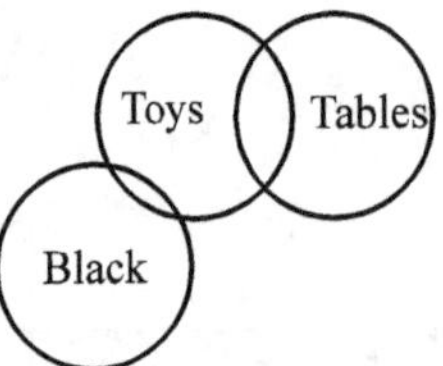

10. When all men are horses and all horses are elephants then, naturally all men are elephants, but all elephants need not be men. Therefore, only conclusion I is correct.

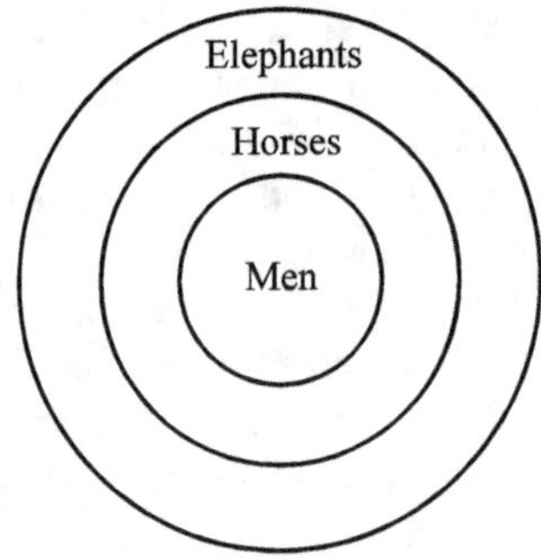

Objective General Knowledge

History

1. 'Abhinav Bharat' was organized by
   A. Bhai Parmanand
   B. Khudiram Bose
   C. Vir Savarkar
   D. None of these
2. The ancient name of Bengal was
   A. Kamrupa B. Vasta
   C. Gauda   D. Vallabhi
3. Ashoka belonged to:
   A. Maurya dynasty
   B. Gupta dynasty
   C. Kushan dynasty
   D. Saka dynasty
4. Morish traveller, Ibn Batutah, came to India during the time of
   A. Ala-ud-din Khilji
   B. Firoz Shah Tughluq
   C. Balban
   D. Muhammad-bin-Tughluq
5. The relics of Indus Valley Civilisation indicates that the main occupation of the people was
   A. Agriculture
   B. Cattle rearing
   C. Commerce
   D. Hunting
6. The Mahabalipuram temples were built by the king of .... dynasty
   A. Gupta
   B. Chola
   C. Pallava
   D. Kushana
7. The first telegraph line between Calcutta (Kolkata) and Agra was opened in
   A. 1852   B. 1853
   C. 1854   D. 1855
8. The first discourse of Buddha in Sarnath is called
   A. Mahabhiniskraman
   B. Mahaparinirvana
   C. Mahamastakabhisheka
   D. Dharmachakrapravartan
9. The political and cultural centre of the Pandyas was
   A. Vengi
   B. Madurai
   C. Kanchipuram
   D. Mahabalipuram
10. What is the correct chronological order of the dynasties in which they invaded India?
    1. Huns   2. Kushanas
    3. Aryans   4. Greeks
    A. 4, 3, 2, 1 B. 3, 4, 2, 1
    C. 4, 2, 3, 1 D. 3, 4, 1, 2
11. Who wrote Mitakshara, a book of Hindu law?
    A. Nayachandra
    B. Amoghvarsa
    C. Vijnaneswara
    D. Kumban
12. Gupta empire declined in the fifth century A.D. as a consequence of
    A. Chalukya raids
    B. Greek invasion
    C. Hun invasion
    D. Pallava raids

13. Who founded the Hindu Shahi dynasty of Punjab?
A. Vasumitra
B. Kallar
C. Jayapala
D. Mahipala

14. The main external threat to the Sultanate of Delhi was posed by the
A. Mughals
B. Afghans
C. Iranians
D. None of these

15. Who among the following was a leading exponent of Gandhian thoughts?
A. J.L. Nehru
B. M.N. Roy
C. Vinoba Bhave
D. Jayaprakash Narayan

16. Who were the immediate successors of the Imperial Mauryas in Magadha?
A. Kushanas
B. Pandyas
C. Satvahanas
D. Sungas

17. Both Mahavira and Buddha preached during the reign of
A. Ajatashatru
B. Bimbisara
C. Nandivardhan
D. Uday

18. Jahangiri Mahal is located in
A. Delhi
B. Fatehpur Sikri
C. Agra Fort
D. Sikandara

19. The main contribution of the Chola dynasty is in the field of
A. Systematic provincial administration
B. A well planned revenue system
C. A well organised central government
D. An organised local self government

20. Who founded the philosophy of Pustimarga?
A. Chaitanya
B. Nanak
C. Surdas
D. Ballabhacharya

21. Which of the following battles changed the destiny of a Mughal ruler of India?
A. Haldighati
B. Panipat II
C. Khanwah
D. Chausa

22. "The Vedas contain all the truth" was interpreted by
A. Swami Vivekanand
B. Swami Dayanand
C. Swami Shraddhanand
D. S. Radhakrishnan

23. Match the colums

Column I	Column II
(a) Second Battle of Panipat	1. Decline of Vijayanagar empire
(b) Second Battle of Tarain	2. British rule in India
(c) Battle of Talikota	3. Turkish rule in India
(d) Battle of Plassey	4. Mughal rule in India
	5. Slave dynasty in India

Codes:

	(a)	(b)	(c)	(d)
A.	2	3	4	1
B.	3	1	2	4
C.	5	3	2	1
D.	4	3	1	2

24. Babur entered India for the first time from the west through
    A. Kashmir B. Sind
    C. Punjab D. Rajasthan
25. Which was the first among the following?
    A. Doctrine of Lapse
    B. Subsidiary Alliance
    C. Permanent Settlement
    D. Double Government
26. The name of Lord Cornwallis is associated with the
    A. Dual government
    B. Maratha wars
    C. System of subsidiary
    D. Permanent settlement
27. Sir Charles Wood's Despatch of 1854 dealt with
    A. Administrative reforms
    B. Social reforms
    C. Economic reforms
    D. Educational reforms
28. Which of the following pairs is correct?
    A. Ashvaghosa — Vikramaditya
    B. Banabhatta — Harshvardhan
    C. Harisena — Kanishka
    D. Kalidasa — Samudragupta
29. 4th July, 1776 is important in world history because
    A. battle fo Plassey started
    B. Sea route to India was discovered
    C. English King Charles II was executed
    D. American Congress adopted the Declaration of Independence
30. Rawlatt Act was passed in the year
    A. 1917   B. 1919
    C. 1921   D. 1923
31. The court language of Delhi Sultanate was
    A. Urdu   B. Persian
    C. Hindi   D. Arabic
32. Where did Buddha attain Mahaparinirvana?
    A. Kushinagar
    B. Kapilvastu
    C. Pava
    D. Kundagramma
33. In Afghanistan, two towering Buddha statues were destroyed at
    A. Kandahar B. Yakaolong
    C. Bamiyan D. Mazar-i-Sharif
34. Kalibangan, the Indus Valley site is in
    A. Rajasthan
    B. Gujarat
    C. Madhya Pradesh
    D. Uttar Pradesh
35. Which of the following materials was mainly used in the manufacture of harappan seals?
    A. Terracota B. Bronze
    C. Copper   D. Iron
36. The Grand Trunk Road in India was got constructed by
    A. Ashoka   B. Shershah Suri
    C. Akbar   D. Humayun
37. 'Tripitaka' is the religious book of the
    A. Jains   B. Buddhists
    C. Sikhs   D. Hindus

38. Which among the following states was forced to merge itself with the Union of India after 1947?
    A. Hyderabad
    B. Kashmir
    C. Patiala
    D. Mysore
39. Alexander the Great died in 323 B.C. in
    A. Persia
    B. Babylon
    C. Macedonia
    D. Taxila
40. Who gave the slogan—"Jai Hind"?
    A. Subhash Chandra Bose
    B. Jawaharlal Nehru
    C. Moti Lal Nehru
    D. Mahatma Gandhi
41. The most glorious king of the Chola dynasty who conquered Ceylon was
    A. Rajaraja I
    B. Rajaraja II
    C. Rajendra Chola
    D. Gangai Konda Chola
42. Name the Chera King known as the "Red Chera", who built a temple for Kannagi?
    A. Elara
    B. Karikala
    C. Senguttuvan
    D. Nedenjerai Alan
43. The first Indian ruler to accept Subsidiary Alliance offered by Lord Wellesley in 1798 was
    A. Nawab of Oudh
    B. Nizam of Hyderabad
    C. Nawab of Carnatic
    D. King of Mysore

44. The first Viceroy of India was
    A. Lord Hastings
    B. Lord Canning
    C. Lord Minto
    D. Lord Curzon
45. The Satavahanas formerly worked as local officials under the
    A. Nandas   B. Mauryas
    C. Cholas   D. Cheras
46. Who was the first woman President of the Indian National Congress?
    A. Sarojini Naidu
    B. Bhikaji Cama
    C. Annie Besant
    D. Vijaya Lakshmi Pandit
47. During the Indian Freedom Struggle, who of the following founded the Parathana Samaj?
    A. Atmaram Pandurang
    B. Gopal Hari Deshmukh
    C. Ishwar Chandra Vidyasagar
    D. Keshav Chandra Sen
48. Which one of the following periodicals was published by Mahatma Gandhi during his stay in South Africa?
    A. Afrikanes
    B. Indian Opinion
    C. India Gazette
    D. Navjivan
49. During the Civil Disobedience Movement, who led the 'Red Shirts' of North-Western India?
    A. Abul Kalam Azad
    B. Khan Abdul Ghaffar Khan
    C. Mohammad Ali Jinnah
    D. Shaukat Ali

50. Match List-I with List-II and select the correct answer using the codes given below the lists—
    List-I
    (Name of the Author)
    (a) Abul Fazal
    (b) Nizamuddin Ahmed
    (c) Krishnadeva Raya
    (d) Kalhana
    List-II
    (Name of the Book)
    1. Tabqat-i-Akbari
    2. Akbarnama
    3. Rajatarangini
    4. Amuktamalyada
    Codes:

	(a)	(b)	(c)	(d)
A.	2	4	1	3
B.	3	1	4	2
C.	2	1	4	3
D.	3	4	1	2

51. Which one of the following pairs is not correctly matched?
    A. Sheikh Shihab-ud-din Suharawardi — Sufi Saint
    B. Chaitanya Maha Prabhu — Bhakti Saint
    C. Minhaj-us Siraj — Founder of Sufi order
    D. Lalleshwari — Bhakti Saint

52. Who of the following kings was an ardent follower of Jainism?
    A. Bimbisara
    B. Mahapadma Nanda
    C. Kharavela
    D. Pulakesin II

53. To which dynasty did Ashoka belong?
    A. Vardhana B. Maurya
    C. Kushan D. Gupta

54. Which one of the following battles was fought between Babar and the Rajputs in 1527?
    A. The First Battle of Panipat
    B. The Battle of Khanwah
    C. The Battle of Ghagra
    D. The Battle of Chanderi

55. Aryabhat,ta and Varahamihira belong to which age?
    A. Guptas B. Cholas
    C. Mauryas D. Mughals

56. Consider the· following statements about Amir Khusro:
    1. He was a disciple of Nizamuddin Auliya.
    2. He was the founder of both Hindustani classical music and Qawwali.
    Which of the statements given above is/are correct?
    A. 1 only
    B. 2 only
    C. Both 1 and 2
    D. Neither 1 nor 2

57. Panini, the first Grammarian of Sanskrit language in India, lived during the
    A. 2nd Century B.C.
    B. 6th-5th Century B.C.
    C. 2nd Century A.D.
    D. 5th-6th Century A.D.

58. Who among the following was associated with the foundation of Ghadar party?
    A. Lala Lajpat Rai
    B. Lala Hardayal
    C. C.R. Das
    D. Bipin Chandra Pal

59. The Treaty of Bassein (1802) was signed between
    A. Madhav Rao and the British
    B. Baji Rao II and the British
    C. Mahadji Scindia and the British
    D. Holkar and the British

60. The words 'Satyameva Jayate' in the State Emblem of India, have been adopted from which one of the following?
    A. Brahma Upanishad
    B. Mudgala Upanishad
    C. Maitreyi Upanishad
    D. Mundaka Upanishad

61. Match List-I with List-II and select the correct answer using the codes given below the lists—

    List-I
    (Symbol)
    (*a*) Elephant
    (*b*) Tree
    (*c*) Empty Throne
    (*d*) Horse

    List-II
    (Important event of life of Buddha)
    1. Renouncement of worldly pleasures
    2. Birth of Buddha
    3. Enlightenment
    4. Representation of royalty

    Codes:

	(*a*)	(*b*)	(*c*)	(*d*)
A.	2	4	3	1
B.	3	1	4	2
C.	3	4	1	2
D.	2	3	4	1

62. When was Mahatma Gandhi, the father of the nation, born?
    A. 1889   B. 1859
    C. 1869   D. 1879

63. Chinese pilgrim Hiuen-Tsang came to and lived in India under whose rule?
    A. Harshavardhan
    B. Chandragupta Maurya
    C. Ashok
    D. Samudragupta

64. Who had founded the Slave dynasty in India?
    A. Qutb-ud-din Aibak
    B. Iltutmish
    C. Mohammed Gauri
    D. Balban

65. Which British Governor-General had started the *Doctrine of Lapse* policy in India?
    A. Lord William Bentinck
    B. Lord Dalhousie
    C. Lord Canning
    D. Lord Hardinge

66. "Liberty is our birth right, we shall seize it." Who said it?
    A. Bhagat Singh
    B. Ramprasad Bismil
    C. Bal Gangadhar Tilak
    D. Mahatma Gandhi

67. The most important Sufi shrine in India is located at
    A. Pandua
    B. Bidar
    C. Ajmer
    D. Shahjahanabad

68. The 'Ajivikas' were a
    A. Sect contemporary to the Buddha
    B. Breakaway branch of the Buddhists
    C. Sect founded by Charvaka
    D. Sect founded by Shankara-charya

69. The Indian Universities were first founded during the time of
A. Macaulay
B. Warren Hastings
C. Lord Canning
D. Lord William Bentinck

70. One of the following was **not** involved in the Chittagong Armoury Raid, 1934. Who was he?
A. Kalpana Dutt
B. Surya Sen
C. Pritilata Woddedar
D. Dinesh Gupta

71. Which of the following is associated with Sufi saints?
A. Tripitaka B. Dakhma
C. Khanqah D. Synagogue

72. Which Indian statesman used these, magic words, "Long years ago we made a tryst with destiny, and now the time comes when we shall redeem our pledge ... "?
A. Mohandas Karamchand Gandhi
B. Sardar Vallabhbhai Patel
C. Netaji Subhas Chandra Bose
D. Jawaharlal Nehru

73. In which century did French Revolution begin?
A. 16th century
B. 17th century
C. 18th century
D. 19th century

74. Under whose patronage was the Khandariya Mahadeo Temple at Khajuraho built?
A. Solankis
B. Rashtrakutas
C. Tomaras
D. Chandellas

75. During the period of which of the following was 'Panchtantra' written?
A. Nandas B. Mauryas
C. Guptas D. Sungas

76. Who wrote the book called Kitab-i-Nauras?
A. Amir Khusro
B. Badauni
C. Ibrahim Adil Shah II
D. Ala-ud-din Bahmani

77. Who among the following, Mughal rulers granted the English Company *Dewani* over Bengal, Bihar and Orissa, by Treaty of Allahabad?
A. Ahmad Shah
B. Alamgir II
C. Shah Alam II
D. Akbar Shah II

78. During the Indian freedom struggle, what accusation was made against Master Amir Chand, Awadh Bihari, Bal Mukund and Basant Kumar Biswas?
A. Assassination of the Commissioner of Poona
B. Throwing a bomb on Viceroy's procession in Delhi
C. Attempt to shoot the Governor of Punjab
D. Looting an armoury in Bengal

79. Which of the following pairs is/are correctly matched?
1. Regulating Act : Hastings
2 Widow Remarriage Act : Bentinck
3. Vernacular Press Act : Lytton

Select the correct answer using the codes given below:
A. 1 only   B. 2 and 3
C. 1 and 3   D. 1, 2 and 3

80. Which among the following is referred to as the Montague-Chelmsford Reforms?
A. Indian Council Act, 1909
B. Government of India Act, 1919
C. Rowlatt Act
D. Government of India Act, 1935

81. Consider the following statements:
1. Lord Cornwallis introduced the Permanent Land Settlement in Bengal.
2. Lord Wellesley introduced the Subsidiary Alliance system.
Which of the statements given above is/are correct?
A. 1 only
B. 2 only
C. Both 1 and 2
D. Neither 1 nor 2

82. Who was the Governor-General when the Revolt of 1857 started?
A. Lord Canning
B. Lord Cornwallis
C. Lord Dalhousie
D. Lord Ellenborough

83. Which of the following pairs is correctly matched?
A. Mahatma   : Home Rule
   Gandhi
B. Annie   : Non-Coopera-
   Besant   tion Movement
C. Jawaharlal : Khilafat
   Nehru   Movement
D. Lala   : Hindustan
   Hardayal   Ghadar Party

84. For which of the following movements did Mahatma Gandhi give the slogan "Do or Die"?
A. Kheda Satyagraha
B. Non-Cooperation Movement
C. Civil Disobedience Movement
D. Quit India Movement

85. Who among the following was the founder of the Servants of India Society?
A. Bal Gangadhar Tilak
B. Dadabhai Naoroji
C. Gopal Krishna Gokhale
D. Lala Lajpat Rai

86. Which of the following pairs is *not* correctly mathced?
A. Lord Wellesley : Subsidiary
                    Alliance
B. Lord Dalhousie : Doctrine of
                    Lapse
C. Lord Ripon   : Vernacular
                    Press Act
D. Lord Curzon   : Partition of
                    Bengal

87. Which of the following territories was outside the boundaries of the Mughal Empire during the reign of Akbar?
A. Khandesh B. Kabul
C. Bijapur   D. Kashmir

88. Which Sultan of Delhi enforced a strict market control system during his time?
A. Ala-ud-din Khilji
B. Mohammad-bin-Tughlaq
C. Firoz Shah Tughlaq
D. Bahlol Lodi

89. Which of the following pairs is *not* correctly matched?
   A. Kautilya : Arthashastra
   B. Hala : Gathasaptasati
   C. Banabhatta : Buddha Charita
   D. Kalidasa : Abhijnana Shakuntalam

90. With which of the following countries is the famous 'October Revolution' associated?
   A. China   B. Cuba
   C. France   D. Russia

91. Who is the author of "Das Kapital"?
   A. Karl Marx
   B. Friedrich Engels
   C. Joseph Stalin
   D. Vladimir Lenin

92. Who was the Commander of the American forces during the American War of Independence?
   A. Alexander Hamilton
   B. Thomas Jefferson
   C. George Washington
   D. Major Samuel Shaw

93. Who fought the Battle of Buxar?
   A. Humayun and Sher Shah Suri
   B. Ahmad Shah Abdali and Marathas
   C. English and Mir Kasim
   D. English and Marathas

94. Who of the following started the newspaper 'Samvad Kaumudi' in the early 19th century?
   A. Ishwar Chandra Vidyasagar
   B. Keshav Chandra Sen
   C. Raja Rammohan Roy
   D. Satyendranath Tagore

95. Match List-I (Movements) with List-II (Leaders) and select the correct answer using the codes given below the lists:

List-I (Movements)	List-II (Leaders)
A. Home Rule movement	1. Maulana Abul Kalam Azad
B. Bhudan movement	2. Bal Gangadhar Tilak
C. Aligarh movement	3. Sayyid Ahmad Khan
D. Khilafat movement	4. Vinoba Bhave

Codes:

	(a)	(b)	(c)	(d)
A.	1	4	3	2
B.	2	4	3	1
C.	2	3	4	1
D.	1	3	4	2

96. When the Moroccan traveller Ibn Batutah visited India, who was the Delhi Sultan?
   A. Jalaluddin Khilji
   B. Ala-ud-din Khilji
   C. Giasuddin Tughlaq
   D. Muhammad-bin Tughlaq

97. The Lingaraja Temple built during the medieval period is at
   A. Bhubaneswar
   B. Khajuraho
   C. Madurai
   D. Mount Abu

98. Which of the following is Considered as an encyclopaedia of Indian medicine?
   A. Charakasamhita
   B. Lokayata

C. Brihatsamhita

D. Suryasiddhanta

99. Which of the following is not included in the 'eight-fold path' of Buddhism?

A. Right Speech

B. Right Contemplation

C. Right Desire

D. Right Conduct

100. During India's freedom struggle, the 'Sepoy Mutiny' started from which of the following places?

A. Agra   B. Gwalior

C. Jhansi   D. Meerut

Geography

101. Match List-I (Historical Site) with List-II (State) and select the correct answer using the codes given below the lists:

List-I (Historical Site)	List-II (State)
(a) Shore temple	1. Karnataka
(b) Bhimbetka	2. Tamil Nadu
(c) Kesava temple (Hoysala (Monuments)	3. Kerala
(d) Hampi	4. Madhya Pradesh
	5. Rajasthan

Codes :

	(a)	(b)	(c)	(d)
A.	3	5	2	1
B.	2	4	1	1
C.	3	4	2	2
D.	2	5	1	4

102. Where are the maximum numbers of major ports located in India?

A. Maharashtra

B. Kerala

C. Goa

D. Tamil Nadu

103. Match List-I (Beach Resort) with List-II (State) and select the correct answer using the codes given below the lists:

List-I (Beach Resort)	List-II (State)
(a) Digha	1. Kerala
(b) Covelong	2. West Bengal
(c) Cherai	3. Maharashtra
(d) Murud-Janjira	4. Tamil Nadu

Codes :

	(a)	(b)	(c)	(d)
A.	2	4	1	3
B.	3	1	4	2
C.	2	1	4	3
D.	3	4	1	2

104. Match List-I (Produce) with List-II (Major Producer State) and select the correct answer using the codes given below the lists:

List-I (Produce)	List-II (Major Producer State)
(a) Rubber	1. Andhra Pradesh
(b) Soyabean	2. Tamil Nadu
(c) Groundnut	3. Madhya Pradesh
(d) Wheat	4. Kerala
	5. Uttar Pradesh

Codes :

	(a)	(b)	(c)	(d)
A.	4	1	2	5
B.	5	3	1	4
C.	4	3	1	5
D.	5	1	2	4

105. Match List-I (Railway Zone) with List-II (Headquarters) and select the correct answer using the codes given below the lists:

List-I	List-II
(Railway Zone)	**(Headquarters)**
(a) East-Central Railway	1. Hubli
(b) North-Western Railway	2. Allahabad
(c) North-Central Railway	3. Hajipur
(d) South-Western Railway	4. Jabalpur
	5. Jaipur

Codes :

	(a)	(b)	(c)	(d)
A.	3	5	2	1
B.	2	1	4	5
C.	3	1	2	5
D.	2	5	4	1

106. Match List-I (Wildlife Sanctuary) with List-II (State) and select the correct answer using the codes given below the lists:

List-I	List-II
(Wildlife Sanctuary)	**(State)**
(a) Bhitar Kanika	1. Andhra Pradesh
(b) Pachmarhi	2. Karnataka
(c) Pocharam	3. Madhya Pradesh
(d) Sharavathi	4. Orissa
	5. Uttar Pradesh

Codes :

	(a)	(b)	(c)	(d)
A.	4	2	1	3
B.	1	3	5	2
C.	4	3	1	2
D.	1	2	5	3

107. Which one of the following is *not* a tributary of the river Godavari?

A. Koyna B. Manjra

C. Pranhita D. Wardha

108. Which one of the following is the correct statement?

A. Spring tides occur on the full moon day only

B. Neap tides occur on the new moon day only

C. The West coast of India experiences tides four times a day

D. Tides do not occur in the gulfs

109. Which one of the following pairs is *not* correctly matched?

City	River
A. Ahmedabad:	Sabarmati
B. Hyderabad :	Musi
C. Lucknow :	Gomti
D. Surat :	Narmada

110. Match List-I (Famous Place) with List-II (Country) and select the correct answer using the codes given below the lists:

	List-I (Famous Place)	List-II (Country)

(*a*) Alexandria   1. Turkey
(*b*) Blackpool   2. Great
     Pleasure Beach   Britain
(*c*) Constantinople 3. Italy
(*d*) Florence   4. Greece
             5. Egypt

Codes :

	(*a*)	(*b*)	(*c*)	(*d*)
A.	1	3	4	2
B.	5	2	1	3
C.	1	2	4	3
D.	5	3	1	2

111. Match List-I (Institute) with List-II (City) and select the correct answer using the codes given below the lists:

	List-I (Institute)	List-II (City)

(*a*) Rashtriya   1. Hyderabad
     Sanskrit
     Vidyapeeth
(*b*) Maharishi   2. Varanasi
     Sandipani
     Rashtriya
     Veda Vidhya
     Pratishthan
(*c*) Central   3. Mysore
     Institute
     of Indian
     Languages
(*d*) Central   4. Tirupati
     Institute of
     English and
     Foreign
     Languages
             5. Ujjain

Codes :

	(*a*)	(*b*)	(*c*)	(*d*)
A.	2	3	1	5
B.	4	5	3	1

112. Consider the following statements:
1. Kaziranga National park is a World Heritage Site recognised by the UNESCO
2. Kaziranga National Park is a home to sloth bear and hoolock gibbon.

Which of the statements given above is/are correct?
A. 1 only
B. 2 only
C. Both 1 and 2
D. Neither 1 nor 2

113. Which country among the following is the biggest producer of cotton?
A. China
B. India
C. Indonesia
D. USA

114. Where is the Holy Shrine of Imam Ali in Najaf located?
A. Saudi Arabia
B. Iraq
C. Iran
D. Kuwait

115. Match List-I (Institute) with List-II (Location) and select the correct answer using the codes given below the lists:

	List-I (Institute)	List-II (Location)

(*a*) Indian   1. Faridabad
     Institute of
     Public
     Administration

(*b*) V.V. Giri National Labour Institute   2. Bangalore

(*c*) National Institute of Financial Management   3. NOIDA

(*d*) National Law School of India University   4. Mumbai

    5. Delhi

Codes :

	(*a*)	(*b*)	(*c*)	(*d*)
A.	1	2	4	3
B.	5	3	1	2
C.	1	3	4	2
D.	5	2	1	3

116. Which river feeds "Tehri dam"?
   A. Alaknanda
   B. Bhagirathi
   C. Gandak
   D. Ghaghara

117. Which of the following winds are known as "Anti-trade winds"?
   A. Chinook
   B. Cyclones
   C. Typhoons
   D. Westerlies

118. Geostationary orbit is at a height of
   A. 6 km
   B. 1000 km
   C. 3600 km
   D. 36000 km

119. The orbits of planets around the Sun can be
   A. Elliptic and parabolic
   B. Parabolic and hyperbolic
   C. Circular and hyperbolic
   D. Circular and elliptic

120. What is Super Nova?
   A. A black hole
   B. A dying star
   C. An asteroid
   D. A comet

121. Which State is irrigated by the Gang Canal?
   A. Uttar Pradesh
   B. Bihar
   C. West Bengal
   D. Rajasthan

122. Among the following Indian cities, which one is located most southward?
   A. Hyderabad
   B. Visakhapatnam
   C. Panaji
   D. Belgaum

123. Match List I (National Highway) with List II (Connected Cities) and select the correct answer using the codes given below the Lists:

List-I (National Highway)	List-II (Connected Cities)
A. NH 3	1. Delhi-Lucknow
B. NH 4	2. Agra-Bikaner
C. NH 11	3. Agra-Mumbai
D. NH 24	4. Chennai-Thane (Mumbai)

Codes :

	(*a*)	(*b*)	(*c*)	(*d*)
A.	3	1	2	4
B.	2	4	3	1
C.	3	4	2	1
D.	2	1	3	4

124. Match List-I (Defence Institute) with List-II (City) and select the correct answer using the codes given below the Lists:

List-I	**List-II**
(Defence Institute)	**(City)**
(*a*) College of Defence Management	1. Panchmarhi
(*b*) Army Air Defence College	2. Bengaluru
(*c*) Army Supply Corps (ASC) Centre and College	3. Secunderabad
(*d*) Army Education Corps (AEC) Training College and Centre	4. Gopalpur

Codes :

	(*a*)	(*b*)	(*c*)	(*d*)
A.	3	4	2	1
B.	1	2	4	3
C.	3	2	4	1
D.	1	4	2	3

125. Which of the following are Defence Public Sector Undertakings?

1. Goa Shipyard Limited
2. The Bharat Dynamics Limited
3. Mishra Dhatu Nigam Limited

Select the correct answer using the codes given below:

A. 1 and 2   B. 2 and 3
C. 1 and 3   D. 1, 2 and 3

126. Which one of the following pairs is *not* correctly matched?

A. Gol Gumbaz : Hyderabad
B. Tomb of Itmad-ud-daula : Agra
C. Tomb of Sher Shah : Sasaram
D. Tomb of Rani Rupmati : Ahmedabad

127. Where is the Baglihar Hydro-electric Project located?

A. Firozepur District of Punjab
B. Doda District of Jammu and Kashmir
C. Faridkot District of Punjab
D. Baramulla District of Jammu and Kashmir

128. Match List-I (Temple/Cathedral) with List-II (Place) and select the correct answer using the code given below the Lists:

List-I (Temple/Cathedral)

(*a*) Brihadeswara Temple
(*b*) Vishwanatha Temple
(*c*) Kamakhya Temple
(*d*) Santhom Cathedral

List-II (Place)

1. Guwahati
2. Chennai
3. Thanjavur
4. Khajuraho

Codes :

	(*a*)	(*b*)	(*c*)	(*d*)
A.	3	2	1	4
B.	1	4	3	2
C.	3	4	1	2
D.	1	2	3	4

129. Match List-I (World Heritage Site) with List-II (State) and select the correct answer using the code given below the Lists:

List-I (World Heritage Site)
(*a*) Manas Wildlife Sanctuary
(*b*) Mahabodhi Temple Complex
(*c*) Group of Monuments, Pattadakal
(*d*) Nandadevi National Park

List-II (State)
1. Bihar
2. Uttarakhand
3. Asom
4. Karnataka

Codes :

	(*a*)	(*b*)	(*c*)	(*d*)
A.	2	4	1	3
B.	3	1	4	2
C.	2	1	4	3
D.	3	4	1	2

130. Consider the following statements:
1. Black soils occur mainly in Maharashtra, Western Madhya Pradesh and Gujarat.
2. Alluvial soils are confined mainly to the northern plains.

Which of the statements given above is/are correct?
A. 1 only
B. 2 only
C. Both 1 and 2
D. Neither 1 nor 2

131. What is the new name of the old colony of Northern Rhodesia?
A. Zambia   B. Zimbabwe
C. Uganda   D. Tanzania

132. Which is the smallest (in area) of the following Union Territories?
A. Chandigarh
B. Dadra and Nagar Haveli
C. Daman and Diu
D. Lakshadweep

133. The Sundarbans or the 'Mangrove' forests are found in
A. Kutch Peninsula
B. Western Ghats
C. Konkan Coast
D. Deltaic West Bengal

134. On which river has the Hirakud dam been built?
A. Mahanadi
B. Godavari
C. Cauvery
D. Periyar

135. Where is "Ground Zero"?
A. Greenwich
B. New York
C. Indira Point
D. Sriharikota

136. The maximum concentration of scheduled caste population is in the
A. Indo-Gangetic Plains
B. North-East India
C. Western Coast
D. Eastern Coast

137. When was the first passenger train run in India?
A. January 1848
B. April 1853
C. May 1857
D. April 1852

138. Which is the major area where 'Garba' dance form is common?
A. Maharashtra   B. Gujarat
C. Rajasthan   D. Punjab

139. Where is India's most prized tea grown?
A. Jorhat   B. Darjeeling
C. Nilgiris   D. Mannar

140. Which is the largest cotton growing State in India?
A. Maharashtra
B. Madhya Pradesh
C. Andhra Pradesh
D. Gujarat

141. Which one of the following is the first shipyard of India?
A. Cochin
B. Visakhapatnam
C. Mazagaon
D. Paradeep

142. Which of the following Indian States is the largest producer of Cardamom?
A. Kerala
B. Tamil Nadu
C. Karnataka
D. Jammu & Kashmir

143. Vikram Sarabhai Space Centre is located in
A. Peenya
B. Ahmedabad
C. Thiruvananthapuram
D. Dehradun

144. The Sardar Sarovar Dam is associated with
A. Tapti river valley project
B. Mahanadi river valley project
C. Narmada project
D. Bhakra-Nangal project

145. In which of the following states in India is the bird, Great Indian Bustard found?
A. Rajasthan
B. Bihar

C. Karnataka
D. Andhra Pradesh

146. The Indian state with smallest population is
A. Sikkim
B. Arunachal Pradesh
C. Goa
D. Mizoram

147. On which of the following rivers Nasik is situated?
A. Ganges
B. Krishna
C. Godavari
D. Cauvery

148. Atacama Desert is in
A. South America
B. North America
C. South Africa
D. Russia

149. Which place in India is a reference for determining Indian Standard Time?
A. Delhi   B. Allahabad
C. Kolkata D. Mumbai

150. Which of the following does not share a boarder with India?
A. Pakistan
B. Bangladesh
C. Burma
D. Afghanistan

151. The Dachigam Wildlife Sanctuary is in
A. Himachal Pradesh
B. Asom
C. Jammu & Kashmir
D. Karnataka

152. How many days does the moon take to complete 1 revolution around the earth?

A. $26\frac{1}{3}$ days

B. $27\frac{1}{3}$ days

C. $24\frac{1}{3}$ days

D. $28\frac{1}{2}$ days

153. A high growth rate of population is characterised by
A. High birth and high death rates
B. High birth and low death rates
C. Low birth and low death rates
D. Low birth and high death rates

154. The Indian Sub-continent was originally a part of
A. Jurassic-land
B. Angara-land
C. Aryavarta
D. Gondwana-land

155. The tropical grassland is called
A. Pampas   B. Llanas
C. Savanah D. Veld

156. The atmosphere is heated mainly by
A. Insolation
B. Conduction
C. Radiation
D. Convection

157. Which one of the following countries is the largest producer of uranium in the world?

A. Canada   B. South Africa
C. Namibia D. USA

158. Which of the following methods does not help in conserving soil fertility and moisture?
A. Contour ploughing
B. Dry farming
C. Strip cropping
D. Shifting agriculture

159. Mudumalai Wildlife Sanctuary is located in the State of
A. Kerala
B. Karnataka
C. Tamil Nadu
D. Andhra Pradesh

160. The narrow stretch of water connecting two seas is called
A. Bay   B. Peninsula
C. Isthmus   D. Strait

161. The topography of plateau is ideal for
A. Cultivation
B. Forestry
C. Mining
D. Generation of hydel power

162. Naga Khasi and Garo hills are located in
A. Purvanchal Ranges
B. Karakoram Ranges
C. Zaskar Ranges
D. Himalayas Ranges

163. In which of the following States, Jawahar Tunnel is located?
A. Himachal Pradesh
B. Jammu & Kashmir
C. Uttarakhand
D. Goa

164. Where was India's first submarine museum established?
A. Kochi
B. Panjim
C. Visakhapatnam
D. Mumbai

165. Which two countries are connected by an under-water tunnel?
A. England and Spain
B. Malaysia and Singapore
C. England and Belgium
D. France and England

166. Which of the following is correctly matched with regard to thermal power projects?
A. Korba — Uttar Pradesh
B. Ramagundam — Tamil Nadu
C. Talcher — Andhra Pradesh
D. Kawas — Gujarat

167. Sundarbans of Eastern India is an example of
A. Forest Ecosystem
B. Mangrove Ecosystem
C. Grassland Ecosystem
D. Marine Ecosystem

168. The deepest trench of the world—'The Mariana Trench' is located in the
A. Indian Ocean
B. Atlantic Ocean
C. Arctic Ocean
D. Pacific Ocean

169. Which of the following is a landlocked sea?
A. Timor Sea
B. Arafura Sea
C. Greenland Sea
D. Aral Sea

170. Match the dams and the states in which they are situated:

	Dam	State
(a)	Hirakud	1. Chhattisgarh
(b)	Mettur	2. Orissa
(c)	Mahanadi	3. Karnataka
(d)	Almatti	4. Tamil Nadu

Codes :

	(a)	(b)	(c)	(d)
A.	3	2	4	1
B.	2	4	1	3
C.	1	3	2	4
D.	4	1	3	2

171. Which of the following territories does not have a border with Arunachal Pradesh?
A. Asom
B. Nagaland
C. Bhutan
D. Manipur

172. Which of the following 'rivers does *not* originate in the Indian territory?
A. Mahanadi
B. Brahamaputra
C. Ravi
D. Chenab

173. Land and sea-breezes occur due to
A. Conduction
B. Convection
C. Radiation
D. Tides

174. Which of the following is *not* correctly matched with regard to Project Tiger Reserves?
A. Sariska — Alwar
B. Valmiki — Hazaribagh
C. Pench — Garhwal
D. Nagarjunasagar — Sri Sailam

175. Trade winds blow from the
   A. Equatorial low pressure
   B. Polar high pressure
   C. Subtropical high pressure
   D. Subpolar low pressure

176. Most of the Indians belong to which of the following racial stocks?
   A. Caucasoid
   B. Negroid
   C. Australoid
   D. Mongoloid

177. Which of the following signifies the American Indians living in the US?
   A. Bushmen
   B. Alpine
   C. Amerindus
   D. Mestizoes

178. Which region is most famous for citrus fruits?
   A. Deserts
   B. Monsoon regions
   C. Temperate grasslands
   D. Mediterranean regions

179. The leading sulphur producing country in the world is
   A. USA   B. Russia
   C. Japan   D. Mexico

180. The largest producer of mercury is
   A. USA   B. Canada
   C. China   D. Spain

181. The largest amount of saffron comes from
   A. Uttar Pradesh
   B. Tamil Nadu
   C. Jammu and Kashmir
   D. Kerala

182. The boundary between Germany and Poland is called the
   A. Hindenberg Line
   B. Maginot Line
   C. Durand Line
   D. 17th Parallel

183. The boundary between North and South Korea is marked by the
   A. Radcliffe Line
   B. 38th Parallel
   C. 49th Parallel
   D. 17th Parallel

184. Which countries are separated by the 49th Parallel?
   A. France and Germany
   B. USA and Mexico
   C. USA and Canada
   D. Russia and China

185. Echo-sounding is the technique applied to
   A. Measure the depth of the sea
   B. Measure the amplitude of sound waves
   C. Record earthquake waves
   D. Record the density of air in the atmosphere

186. On which of the rivers is the famous Kariba Dam situated?
   A. Nile   B. Niger
   C. Zambezi   D. Amazon

187. The northernmost limit of India is
   A. 36°4' N latitude
   B. 37°8' N latitude
   C. 37°6' N latitude
   D. 36°12' N latitude

188. The length of India's coastline is about
    A. 4,500 km
    B. 5,900 km
    C. 7,000 km
    D. 7,516 km

189. The total area of India is about
    A. 31 lakh sq km
    B. 33 lakh sq km
    C. 320 lakh sq km
    D. 35 lakh sq km

190. Where is the Gulf of Mannar located?
    A. West of Gujarat
    B. East of Tamil Nadu
    C. West of Kerala
    D. South of Kanyakumari

191. The Sivaliks stretch between
    A. Indus and Sutlej
    B. Potwar Basin and Teesta
    C. Sutlej and Kali
    D. Sutlej and Teesta

192. The territorial waters of India extend up to
    A. 12 nautical miles
    B. 6 nautical miles
    C. 15 nautical miles
    D. 10 nautical miles

193. The deepest lake in the world is
    A. Pushkar Lake
    B. Lake Superior
    C. Victoria Lake
    D. Baikal Lake

194. Simlipal Tiger Reserve is located at
    A. Assam
    B. Gujarat
    C. Orissa
    D. Bihar

195. Which of the following rivers flow through a rift valley?
    A. Ganga
    B. Narmada
    C. Brahmaputra
    D. Krishna

196. What is the most important characteristic of the islands (Indian) located in the Arabian Sea?
    A. They are all very small in size
    B. They are all of coral origin
    C. They have a very dry climate
    D. They are extended parts of the mainland

197. The Thar Desert is believed to be expanding. The most suitable way to check it would be by
    A. Afforestation
    B. Artificial rain
    C. Canal irrigation
    D. Using the area for cattle rearing

198. Which one is a land-locked State?
    A. Gujarat
    B. Andhra Pradesh
    C. West Bengal
    D. Bihar

199. Which area in India gets the summer monsoon?
    A. The Himalayas
    B. The Eastern Ghats
    C. The Western Ghats
    D. The Indo-Gangetic plains

200. In which of the following areas is maximum precipitation received from the summer monsoon?
    A. The Coromandel coast

B. The North-Eastern hilly region
C. The Central Indian hills
D. The Western Himalayas

Indian Polity and Constitution

201. Which Schedule of the Constitution lists the languages recognised by it?
A. Eighth Schedule
B. Sixth Schedule
C. Seventh Schedule
D. Ninth Schedule

202. Which of the following Union Territories has a Chief Minister?
A. Andaman and Nicobar Islands
B. Puducherry
C. Chandigarh
D. Dadra and Nagar Haveli

203. Who among the following administers the Oath of Office to the President of India?
A. The Vice-President of India
B. The Chief Justice of India
C. The Chairman of Rajya Sabha
D. The Prime Minister

204. Parliament of India consists of
A. Directly elected members only
B. Directly elected and nominated members
C. Directly elected and indirectly elected members
D. Directly elected, indirectly elected and nominated members

205. In a Unitary Government
A. All powers are vested in the Centre
B. Powers are divided between the Centre and the States under a Constitution
C. Powers are divided by mutual consent of the Centre and the States through Parliamentary statute
D. The Judiciary must be independent

206. Article 360 of the Constitution of India relates to
A. National Emergency
B. Emergency in a State
C. To conduct Parliament Elections
D. Financial Emergency

207. Panchayati Raj was recommended by
A. Sarkaria Commission
B. Fazlali Commission
C. Balwantrai Mehta Committee
D. Rajamannar Committee

208. Name the first woman Governor of an Indian State
A. Padmaja Naidu
B. Lakshmi N. Menon
C. Sarojini Naidu
D. Sucheta Kriplani

209. Gangtok is the capital of
A. Nagaland
B. Meghalaya
C. Sikkim
D. Arunachal Pradesh

210. Who appoints the Chief Justice of a High Court in India?

A. The President of India
B. The Governor of the State concerned
C. The Chief Justice of the Supreme Court
D. An Appointment Committee in the Union Ministry of Law

211. In India, how did the Planning Commission come into existence?
    A. By an Act of Parliament
    B. By an executive order
    C. Under the provisions of the Constitution
    D. As an attached office of the Union Ministry of Finance

212. Which is the first executive tier of the Panchayati Raj system from below?
    A. Gram Sabha
    B. Gram Panchayat
    C. Mandal Parishad
    D. Panchayat Samiti

213. After the Constitution of India, came into force, when did the Parliament enact the Untouchability (Offences) Act?
    A. 1953   B. 1954
    C. 1955   D. 1956

214. Which of the following pairs is *not* correctly matched?

State/U.T.	High Court
A. Goa	— Bombay
B. Andaman and Nicobar Islands	— Calcutta
C. Sikkim	— Guwahati
D. Puducherry	— Madras

215. The procedure for the Amendment of the Constitution of India is given under
    A. Article 315
    B. Article 358
    C. Article 360
    D. Article 368

216. Which of the following Articles of the Constitution of India has provision for the President to proclaim emergency?
    A. Article 352
    B. Article 355
    C. Article 356
    D. Article 360

217. Which of the following offices is held during the pleasure of the President of India?
    A. Vice-President
    B. Chief Justice of India
    C. Governor of a State
    D. Chairman of the Union Public Service Commission

218. Article 370 of the constitution is applicable to the state of
    A. Nagaland
    B. Mizoram
    C. Manipur
    D. Jammu & Kashmir

219. In the parliamentary practices when did the "Zero-hour" interventions emerge in India?
    A. 1952   B. 1962
    C. 1972   D. 1982

220. "Vote on Account" means legislative vote
    A. On the Appropriation Bill
    B. On the Finance Bill

C. On the accounts and audit report submitted by the CAG

D. Authorising expenditure in respect of the demands for grants pending the passing of the Appropriation Bill

221. Which of these words is not in the preamble of the constitution of India?
A. Socialist
B. Sovereign
C. Secular
D. Public Welfare

222. Which of the following has **not** been mentioned in the Indian Constitution as a Right?
A. Political and Social Rights
B. Educational Rights
C. Economic Rights
D. Religious Rights

223. Which one of the following is **not** stated in the Preamble of the Indian Constitution?
A. Justice
B. Fraternity
C. Adult franchise
D. Equality of status

224. In framing the Constitution of India, from which country did we borrow the scheme of the federal set up?
A. U.S.A.   B. U.K.
C. Canada   D. Switzerland

225. Who among the following was **not** a member of the Constituent Assembly set up in July 1946?
A. Dr. Rajendra Prasad
B. K.M. Munshi

C. Mahatma Gandhi
D. Abul Kalam Azad

226. Which article of the Indian Constitution provides for the institution of Panchayati Raj?
A. Art. 36   B. Art. 39
C. Art. 40   D. Art. 48

227. Which of the following is a bulwark of personal freedom?
A. Mandamus
B. Habeas Corpus
C. Quo Warranto
D. Certiorari

228. Who is the highest civil servant of the Union Government?
A. Attorney-General
B. Cabinet Secretary
C. Home Secretary
D. Principal Secretary to the Prime Minister

229. Article 1 of the Constitution declares India as
A. Federal State
B. Quasi-Federal State
C. Unitary State
D. Union of States

230. Which functionary can be invited to give his opinion in the Parliament?
A. Attorney-General of India
B. Chief Justice of India
C. Chief Election Commissioner of India
D. Comptroller and Auditor-General of India

231. Which of the following countries has an Unwritten Constitution?
A. USA   B. UK
C. Pakistan D. India

232. The Drafting Committee of the Constitution, including the chairman, comprised of
    A. Seven members
    B. Five members
    C. Nine members
    D. Three members

233. Which one of the following exercised the most profound influence on the Indian Constitution?
    A. The Government of India Act 1935
    B. The US Constitution
    C. British Constitution
    D. The UN Charter

234. Which one of the following features was borrowed by the Indian Constitution from the British Constiution?
    A. Parliamentary system of government
    B. Rule of Law
    C. Law-making procedure
    D. All the above

235. India borrowed the idea of a federal system with a strong centre from
    A. USA   B. Canada
    C. Australia D. New Zealand

236. The emergency provisions of the constitution of India were greatly influenced by
    A. The Government of India Act 1935
    B. The Weimar Constitution of Germany
    C. The Constitution of United States

    D. The Constitution of Canada

237. India borrowed the idea of Directive Principles of State Policy from the Constitutions of
    A. The Weimar Republic of Germany
    B. The Republic of Ireland
    C. The South Africa
    D. None of the above

238. If the President wishes to tender his resignation before the expiry of his normal term, he has to address the same to
    A. The Vice-President of India
    B. The Speaker of Lok Sabha
    C. The Chief Justice of India
    D. The Election Commission

239. Who among the following got the Bharat Ratna Award before becoming the President of India?
    A. Dr. Zakir Hussain
    B. Dr. Rajendra Prasad
    C. V.V. Giri
    D. Dr. S. Radhakrishnan

240. The Council of Ministers is collectively responsible to
    A. The President of India
    B. The Parliament
    C. The Prime Minister
    D. The Rajya Sabha

241. The office of the Prime Minister of India
    A. Has been created by the Constitution
    B. Is extra-constitutional growth
    C. Has been created by a Parliamentary Statute
    D. Is the combination of all the above

242. The minimum age at which a person can be appointed Prime Minister of India?
    A. 21 years B. 25 years
    C. 30 years D. 35 years
243. The first Amendment of the constitution was made in the year:
    A. 1950   B. 1949
    C. 1954   D. 1958
244. Which of the following is the maximum time limit of 'Zero Hour' during the Parliament session in India?
    A. 30 minutes
    B. One hour
    C. Two hours
    D. None of the above
245. Who among the following summons the joint session of Lok Sabha and Rajya Sabha?
    A. Speaker
    B. Chairman of Rajya Sabha
    C. President
    D. Minister of Parliamentary Affairs
246. Which of the following is India's Contribution to parliamentary system of democracy?
    A. Zero Hour
    B. Cut Motion Resolution
    C. Adjournment Motion
    D. Guillotine
247. The total number of members in the Legislative Council of a State cannot exceed
    A. one-fourth of the total number of members in the Legislative Assembly
    B. one-third of the total number of members of the legislative Assembly
    C. one-sixth of the total number of members of the Legislative Assembly
    D. No such limit has been fixed
248. Sikkim was made an integral part of India under the
    A. 42nd Amendment
    B. 40th Amendment
    C. 39th Amendment
    D. 36th Amendment
249. The number of Anglo-Indians who can be nominated by the President to the Lok Sabha is
    A. 2   B. 3
    C. 4   D. 5
250. Money Bills can be introduced in the State Legislature with the prior consent of
    A. the Speaker
    B. the Chief Minister
    C. the Governor
    D. the President

Economy

251. The apex bank for industrial credit in India is
    A. RBI   B. NABARD
    C. ICICI   D. IDBI
252. The prominent function of the Central Statistical Organisation is
    A. To determine the money supply
    B. To collect national income estimates
    C. To collect employment details
    D. To determine prices

253. Planning and control are related in such a way that
A. Planning precedes control
B. Control precedes planning
C. Both are concurrent
D. Both go hand in hand with each other in a cyclical manner

254. 'Gresham's Law' states that
A. Good money drives away bad money out of circulation
B. Bad money drives away good money out of circulation
C. Good money promotes bad money in the system
D. Bad money promotes good money in the system

255. National income refers to
A. Money value of goods and services produced in a country during a year
B. Money value of stocks and shares of a country during a year
C. Money value of capital goods produced by a country during a year
D. Money value of consumer goods produced by a country during a year

256. Which of the following taxes is/are lived by the Union and collected and appropriated by the States?
A. Service tax
B. Stamp duties
C. Estate duty
D. Passenger and goods tax

257. Which of the following is *not* shared by the Centre and the States?
A. Income tax
B. Excise duty
C. Corporation duty
D. Sales tax

258. Expenditure on which of the following is *not* considered as an investment in the theory of income determination?
A. Factory construction
B. A computer
C. Increase in stocks of unsold goods
D. Stocks or shares in a joint stock company

259. With what aspect of commerce are "Bull" and "Bear" associated?
A. Banking
B. E-Commerce
C. International trade
D. Stock market

260. FDI means—
A. Foreign Direct Investment
B. Full Dog Cost
C. Full Direct Cost
D. Finance Institute

261. If the tax rate increases with the higher level of income, it shall be called
A. Proportional tax
B. Progressive tax
C. Lump sum tax
D. Regressive tax

262. In India, one-rupee coins and notes and subsidiary coins are issued by
A. The Reserve Bank of India
B. The Central Government
C. The State Bank of India
D. The Unit Trust of India

263. Which is the highest body that approves Five-Year Plans in the country?
A. NITI Aayog
B. Union Cabinet
C. National Development Council
D. Parliament

264. Prime cost is equal to
A. Variable cost plus administrative cost
B. Variable cost plus fixed cost
C. Variable cost only
D. Fixed cost only

265. New capital issue is placed in
A. Secondary market
B. Grey market
C. Primary market
D. Black market

266. Bank deposits that can be withdrawn without notice are called
A. Account payee deposits
B. Fixed deposits
C. Variable deposits
D. Demand deposits

267. An expenditure that has been made and cannot be recovered is called
A. Variable cost
B. Opportunity cost
C. Sink cost
D. Operational cost

268. The practice of selling goods in a foreign country at a price below their domestic selling price is called
A. 'Diplomacy'
B. 'Discrimination'
C. 'Dumping'
D. 'Double pricing'

269. Who propounded the 'market law'?
A. Adam Smith
B. J.B. Say
C. T.R. Malthus
D. Dravid Ricardo

270. National income is based on the
A. total revenue of the state
B. production of goods and services
C. net profit earned and expenditure made by the state
D. the sum of all factors of incomes

271. 'Utility' in economics means the capacity to
A. provide comforts
B. earn an income
C. satisfy human wants
D. satisfy human motives

272. Labour welfare does not include
A. education facilities
B. health facilities
C. housing facilities
D. quick promotion in job

273. 'Sellersmarket' denotes a situation where
A. Commodities are available at competitive rates
B. Demand exceeds supply

C. Supply exceeds demand

D. Supply and demand are evenly balanced

274. "Legal Tender Money" refers to

A. Cheques

B. Drafts

C. Bills of exchange

D. Currency notes

275. The sum total of incomes received for the services of labour, land or capital in a country is called

A. Gross domestic product

B. National income

C. Gross domestic income

D. Gross national income

276. The measurement of poverty line is based on the criteria of

A. Their dwelling houses

B. The nature of employment

C. Coloric consumption

D. Level of education

277. Capital is that wealth

A. Which is used for the production of wealth

B. Which is kept in boxes and lockers

C. Which is buried in the land

D. Which is stored for consumption

278. The poverty line has been defined in the

A. Seventh Five–Year Plan

B. Sixth Five–Year Plan

C. Eight Five–Year Plan

D. Fifth Five–Year Plan

279. Perfect market means there are

A. Many sellers and many buyers

B. A few sellers and a few buyers

C. A few sellers and many buyers

D. A few buyers and many sellers

280. A hard currency is the one

A. Whose external value is increasing

B. Which can be acquired only with official permission

C. Which can be obtained only against sale of gold

D. Which is really accepted in international transactions

281. Which of the following is not a Central Government Tax?

A. Income Tax

B. Customs

C. Land Revenue

D. Corporation Tax

282. Who is called the father of White Revolution?

A. Dr. Kurien Verghese

B. Nanjunda Swamy

C. M.S. Swaminathan

D. U.R. Rao

283. The major source of revenue in India is through

A. Direct Taxes

B. Indirect Taxes

C. Internal Borrowings

D. External Borrowings

284. The Reserve Bank of India was established in

A. 1927   B. 1935

C. 1947   D. 1949

285. Finance Commission is appo-
inted by
A. Prime Minister
B. President of India
C. Ministry of Finance
D. None of these

286. Which of the following groups
suffer the most from inflation?
A. Debtors
B. Creditors
C. Business class
D. Holders of real assets

287. Which one of the following is
not an example of indirect tax?
A. Sales tax
B. Excise duty
C. Customs duty
D. Expenditure tax

288. The major aim of devaluation
is to
A. Encourage imports
B. Encourage exports
C. Encourage both exports and
imports
D. Discourage both exports and
imports

289. Which of the following is a cash
crop?
A. Wheat
B. Rice
C. Sugarcane
D. Maize

290. NAFED is connected with
A. Animal husbandry
B. Conservation of fuels
C. Agricultural marketing
D. Agricultural implements

291. Which Commission replaced
Planning Commission in 2015?
A. NIYAM Aayog
B. NAGRIK Aayog
C. NITI Aayog
D. None of these

292. The one-rupee notes bear the
signatures of the
A. Governor, Reserve Bank of
India
B. Secretary, Ministry of
Finance
C. Deputy Governor, Reserve
Bank of India
D. Joint Secretary, Ministry of
Finance

293. Whose approval is necessary
before the Five-Year Plan can
start?
A. The Finance Minister
B. National Development Cou-
ncil
C. The Prime Minister
D. Parliament

294. NABARD stands for
A. National Bank of
Agriculture and Regional
Development
B. National Bank for Agricul-
ture and Rural Development
C. National Bureau of Aeronau-
tical Research and Develop-
ment
D. None of these

295. 'Bottle neck inflation' means
A. No rise in prices despite increase in aggregate demand
B. Rise in prices without increase in the aggregate demand

C. Decline in prices due to increase in aggregate demand

D. None of these

296. The main cause of International Trade is
A. Equal cost difference
B. Absolute cost difference
C. Comparative cost difference
D. Equal and comparative cost difference

297. Which one of the following taxes is not shared by the Central Government with the States?
A. Union excise duties
B. Customs duty
C. Income tax
D. Estate duty

298. A dualistic economy is one in which
A. both rich and poor people co-exist side by side
B. it has both foreign trade and internal trade
C. industry and agriculture exist side by side
D. modern sector and traditional sector exist side by side

299. Whose signatures are found on the 10 rupee note in India?
A. Prime Minister of India
B. President of India
C. Finance Minister of India
D. Governor, Reserve Bank of India

300. "Green Revolution" began in India during the year
A. 1967-68 B. 1966-67
C. 1968-69 D. 1969-70

General Science

301. Deep blue colour is imparted to glass by the presence of
A. Cobalt Oxide
B. Cupric Oxide
C. Ferrous Oxide
D. Nickel Oxide

302. Which of the following fibres is least prone to fire?
A. Nylon   B. Cotton
C. Rayon   D. Terry Cott

303. Which of the following is used as a filler in rubber tyres?
A. Carbon black
B. Coal
C. Coke
D. Graphite

304. Which of the following alloys is used for making magnets?
A. Duralumin
B. Stainless Steel
C. Alnico
D. Magnalium

305. Which of the following elements is obtained from sea weeds?
A. Argon
B. Sulphur
C. Vanadium
D. Iodine

306. Where are Mesons found?
A. Cosmic rays
B. X-rays
C. γ-rays
D. Laser beams

307. Milk tastes sour when kept in the open for sometime due to the formation of
A. Lactic acid
B. Citric acid
C. Acetic acid
D. Carbonic acid

308. Polythene is industrially prepared by the polymerisation of
A. Methane
B. Styrene
C. Acetylene
D. Ethylene

309. Which of the following chemicals responsible for the depletion of ozone layer in the atmosphere?
A. Nitrous oxide
B. Carbon dioxide
C. Chlorofluorocarbons
D. Sulphur dioxide

310. Plants die in winter by frost because
A. There is no transpiration
B. No photosynthesis takes place at such low temperatures
C. Respiration ceases at such low temperatures
D. Of desiccation and mechanical damage to tissues

311. Which of the following is *not* a constituent of chlorophyll?
A. Hydrogen
B. Magnesium
C. Carbon
D. Calcium

312. Which is the chief nitrogenous waste in humans?
A. Ammonia
B. Urea
C. Uric acid
D. Ammonium nitrate

313. Which is the largest living bird?
A. Peacock   B. Ostrich
C. Dodo   D. Turkey

314. Hormones are normally absent in
A. Rat   B. Monkey
C. Bacteria D. Cat

315. Dengue fever is caused by
A. Fungi   B. Bacteria
C. Protozoa D. Virus

316. Which of the following is considered to be good cholesterol?
A. VLDL   B. LDL
C. HDL   D. Triglycerides

317. "Thalassaemia" is a hereditary disease affecting
A. Blood   B. Kidney
C. Lungs   D. Heart

318. Which of the following is a proper food chain showing a producer, a herbivore and the carnivore?
A. Grass-Insect-Elephant
B. Plants-Rabbit-Tiger
C. Fish-Insect-Whale
D. Tiger-Rabbit-Owl

319. Aspirin is
A. Methoxy Benzoic acid
B. Methyl Salicylate
C. Acetyl Salicylic acid
D. Phenyl Salicylate

320. The medical instrument sphygmomanometer is used to examine
A. hormonal activity
B. brain tumor
C. the functions of intestine
D. blood pressure

321. Onion is a modified form of
A. stem   B. root
C. leaves   D. fruit

322. Weight of the body
    A. remains the same everywhere on the earth's surface
    B. is maximum at the poles
    C. is maximum at the equator
    D. is more on mountains than plains

323. Most of the nutrients are absorbed into blood through
    A. large intestine
    B. mouth
    C. small intestine
    D. abdomen

324. The path of Halley's comet in its orbit around the Sun is
    A. circular
    B. elliptical
    C. parabolic
    D. hyperbolic

325. Atoms of the same element having the same atomic number but different atomic weights are called
    A. Isotopes   B. Polymers
    C. Isomers   D. Isobars

326. The chief constituent of gobar gas is
    A. Nitrogen
    B. Ethane
    C. Hydrogen
    D. Methane

327. Law of heredity was put forward by
    A. Mendel   B. Mendeleev
    C. Pavlov   D. Koch

328. A device used for converting a.c. into d.c. is called
    A. Transformer
    B. Rectifier
    C. Induction oil
    D. Dynamo

329. An antibiotic is
    A. A chemical synthesised by a human cell against a micro-organism
    B. A chemical synthesised by a micro-organism against another micro-organism
    C. A substance produced by blood cells against bacteria
    D. A substance produced by blood cells against infection

330. Which one of the following can be synthesized by Liver?
    A. Vitamin-A
    B. Vitamin-E
    C. Vitamin-D
    D. Vitamin-K

331. Fluid part of blood devoid of corpuscles is called
    A. Tissue fluid
    B. Plasma
    C. Serum
    D. Lymph

332. Heart murmur indicates a
    A. Defective valve
    B. Poor oxygenation
    C. Dislocation of the heart
    D. Improper development of muscles

333. The language used in writing the scientific name of animals is
    A. French   B. Latin
    C. German   D. Dutch

334. Energy of Ultra-violet rays is greater than
    A. Infra-red rays

    B. Gamma rays
    C. X-rays
    D. Cosmic rays

335. By-product obtained by soap-industry is
    A. Caustic soda
    B. Glycerol
    C. Naphthalene
    D. Caustic potash

336. Ripe grapes contain
    A. Fructose
    B. Sucrose
    C. Galactose
    D. Glucose

337. Polythene is polymer of
    A. Ethylene
    B. Propylene
    C. Acetylene
    D. Aniline

338. Which one of the following is pure water?
    A. Rain water
    B. Filter water
    C. Tubewell water
    D. Distilled water

339. Which silver salt is used for making film for photography?
    A. Silver bromide
    B. Silver chloride
    C. Silver sulphate
    D. Silver nitrate

340. To an astronaut sky appears
    A. White
    B. Rich blue
    C. Light blue
    D. Dark

341. The instrument used to measure the speed of the wind is
    A. Altimeter
    B. Anemometer
    C. Chronometer
    D. Dosimeter

342. Who defined the law of gravitation?
    A. Newton   B. Archimedes
    C. Galileo   D. Faraday

343. The metal used to make lightning conductors is
    A. Iron   B. Aluminium
    C. Copper   D. Zinc

344. 'IC' in computers stands for
    A. Integrated Charge
    B. Integrated Current
    C. Integrated Circuits
    D. Internal Circuits

345. A hydrogen balloon floats up because of
    A. Air pressure decreases with decrease in height
    B. Air pressure decreases with decrease in weight
    C. Weight of the balloon is less than the weight of air displaced by it
    D. The pressure inside the balloon is more than the pressure outside it

346. In a rechargeable cell what kind of energy is stored within the cell?
    A. Electrical energy
    B. Potential energy
    C. Chemical energy
    D. Kinetic energy

347. M.R.I. stands for
    A. Metered Resonance imaging
    B. Magnetic Resonance Imaging

C. Magnetic Reaction Imaging
D. Metered Reaction Imaging

348. The American space shuttle which exploded in space killing astronaut Kalpana Chawla, was known as
A. Challenger
B. Columbia
C. Discovery
D. Columbus

349. For determination of the age of which among the following is carbon dating method used?
A. Fossils
B. Rocks
C. Trees
D. A and B

350. Which is the hottest planet in the Solar System?
A. Jupiter   B. Saturn
C. Venus   D. Uranus

State

351. Telangana became India's 29th State in
A. 2014   B. 2013
C. 2012   D. 2011

352. In which State would you find Jim Corbett National Park?
A. Assam
B. Uttar Pradesh
C. Maharashtra
D. Uttarakhand

353. Jharia mines are situated in which of the following States?
A. Jharkhand
B. West Bengal
C. Bihar
D. Odisha

354. 'Sardar Sarovar' project is in which of the following States?
A. Rajasthan
B. Madhya Pradesh
C. Uttar Pradesh
D. Gujarat

355. The new name of Rajasthan canal is
A. Gandhi canal
B. Indira Gandhi canal
C. Jawahar canal
D. Subhash canal

356. Which of the following lakes in Rajasthan is saline?
A. Ana Sagar
B. Pichola
C. Sambhar
D. Jaisamand

357. In which state is the district of Udham Singh Nagar situated?
A. Punjab
B. Uttarakhand
C. Uttar Pradesh
D. Rajasthan

358. Which amongst the following States has the highest population density as per census 2011?
A. Kerala
B. Madhya Pradesh
C. Uttar Pradesh
D. Bihar

359. Which one among the following states is smallest in area?
A. Andhra Pradesh
B. Gujarat
C. Karnataka
D. Tamil Nadu

360. In which State is Nalsarovar Bird Sanctuary located?

A. Maharashtra
B. Odisha
C. Gujarat
D. Rajasthan

361. Which of the following is the 28th State of India?
A. Jharkhand
B. Uttarakhand
C. Chhattisgarh
D. Gorkhaland

362. In which State is Ghana Bird Sanctuary located?
A. U.P.
B. M.P.
C. Assam
D. Rajasthan

363. Which of the following States does not have border with China?
A. Uttarakhand
B. U.P.
C. H.P.
D. Sikkim

364. What is the capital of the State of Chhattisgarh?
A. Raipur
B. Patna
C. Jamshedpur
D. Bokaro

365. With which State would you associate the festival of Dev Devali?
A. Bihar
B. West Bengal
C. Uttar Pradesh
D. Maharashtra

366. Areawise, which is the smallest State in India?
A. Goa   B. Sikkm
C. Manipur D. Tripura

367. The capital of Lakshadweep is
A. Aizwal   B. Port Blair
C. Kavaratti D. Agartala

368. The famous Kanha Wildlife Sanctuary is located in the State of:
A. Assam
B. Bihar
C. Madhya Pradesh
D. Karnataka

369. Which one of the following State is most populous?
A. Odisha
B. Uttar pradesh
C. Maharashtra
D. Bihar

370. Bhangra is a folk dance of
A. Punjab
B. Madhya Pradesh
C. Odisha
D. Assam

371. Kaziranga Animals Sanctuary is situated in the State of
A. Assam
B. Uttar Pradesh
C. Madhya Pradesh
D. Rajasthan

372. Konark temple is situated in the State of
A. Odisha
B. Kerala
C. Madhya Pradesh
D. Andhra Pradesh

373. The State which produces maximum Uranium in India is
A. Rajasthan
B. Kerala
C. Jharkhand
D. West Bengal

374. Lumbini, the birth place of Gautam Buddha is in
A. Bihar   B. Sikkim
C. Nepal   D. Uttar Pradesh

375. Which of the following is the least densely populated State?
A. Sikkim
B. Meghalaya
C. Mizoram
D. Arunachal Pradesh

376. "Dudhawa National Park" is situated in
A. Madhya Pradesh
B. Bihar
C. Uttar Pradesh
D. Karnataka

377. Sandal wood is found in
A. Tamil Nadu
B. Himachal Pradesh
C. Karnataka
D. Maharashtra

378. The chief producer of 'Jute' in India is
A. West Bengal
B. Karnataka
C. Tamil Nadu
D. Asom

379. The Ghat and Bhor Ghat are the important passes in
A. Kerala
B. Maharashtra
C. Gujarat
D. Rajasthan

380. The famous monolithic statue of Jain Saint Bahubali is situated in the state of
A. Andhra Pradesh
B. Bihar
C. Karnataka
D. Tamil Nadu

381. Which state of India is the largest exporter of marine products?
A. Andhra Pradesh
B. Gujarat
C. Kerala
D. Maharashtra

382. After Uttar Pradesh, which State leads in the production of sugarcane?
A. Bihar
B. Andhra Pradesh
C. Maharashtra
D. Tamil Nadu

383. Goa was liberated from the Portuguese in
A. 1964   B. 1961
C. 1963   D. 1962

384. The State which accounts for more than 90 per cent of total rubber production in India is
A. Karnataka
B. Kerala
C. Tamil Nadu
D. Andhra Pradesh

385. Which one of the following States has no common border with UP?
A. Punjab
B. Haryana
C. Madhya Pradesh
D. Uttarakhand

386. Name the State in which the Hirakud Dam is located?
A. Orissa   B. Karnataka
C. U.P.   D. Gujarat

387. Panna in Madhya Pradesh is associated with
A. Manganese
B. Mica
C. Copper
D. Diamond

388. The holy city Hardwar is in which of the State?
- A. Uttar Pradesh
- B. Haryana
- C. Bihar
- D. Uttarakhand

389. According to the census of 2011 the only State in India that shows excess of females over males is
- A. Uttar Pradesh
- B. Kerala
- C. Maharashtra
- D. Jammu and Kashmir

390. Which States share the Tungabhadra multipurpose project?
- A. Karnataka and Madhya Pradesh
- B. Orissa and Madhya Pradesh
- C. Andhra Pradesh and Karnataka
- D. Tamil Nadu and Andhra Pradesh

Organisations

391. The headquarter of World Trade Organisation (WTO) is located at
- A. Rome
- B. New York
- C. Geneva
- D. Washington DC

392. Which of the following countries is not a member of SAARC?
- A. Nepal
- B. China
- C. Pakistan
- D. India

393. Where is SAARC secretariat situated?
- A. Islamabad
- B. Colombo
- C. New Delhi
- D. Kathmandu

394. What is the activity of the INTERPOL?
- A. Central record keeping agency of the international crimes
- B. Investigative agency of the UN
- C. An organisation to coordinate the police activities of the participating nations
- D. A terrorist outfit

395. The six official languages of the UN are Russian, Chinese, English, French, Spanish and
- A. Hindi
- B. Urdu
- C. Arabic
- D. Japanese

396. What does SAPTA stands for?
- A. South Asian Preferential Trade Agreement
- B. South Asian Post Trade Agreement
- C. SAARC Preferential Trade Agreement
- D. SAARC Prevention Trade Agreement

397. The Association of South East Asian Nations (ASEAN) has its headquarters at
- A. Manila
- B. Jakarta
- C. Kuala Lumpur
- D. Bangkok

398. The normal term of office of UN Secretary General is
A. 3 years
B. 4 years
C. 5 years
D. 6 years

399. Which of the following countries is not a member of the G-7 Group?
A. France
B. Italy
C. Spain
D. Germany

400. Which of the following is NOT a permanent member of the UN Security Council?
A. Germany
B. France
C. Great Britain
D. China

401. The first Secretary General of the United Nations was:
A. Mrs. Vijay Lakshmi Pandit
B. Trygve Lie
C. Dag Hammarskjoeld
D. U. Thant

402. Who was the first Indian to be the President of U.N. General Assembly?
A. Natwar Singh
B. V.K. Krishna Menon
C. Smt. Vijay Lakshmi Pandit
D. Romesh Bhandari

403. Where is the headquarters of the International Court of Justice?
A. The Hague (Netherlands)
B. Paris (France)
C. Rome (Italy)
D. Washington (U.S.A)

404. How many Judges are there in the International Court of Justice?
A. 9   B. 10
C. 11   D. 15

405. When was the United Nations Organisation founded?
A. 20th October, 1945
B. 11th, November, 1944
C. 24th October, 1945
D. 26th June, 1945

406. The headquarters of the Organisation of Petroleum Exporting Countries is at
A. Teheran
B. Vienna
C. Abu Dhabi
D. Doha

407. How many members does the Security Council of UN have?
A. Ten   B. Fifteen
C. Sixteen   D. Twenty

408. Which country is not a member of ASEAN?
A. Indonesia
B. Cambodia
C. Singapore
D. Philippines

409. Where is the Head Quarter of Asian Development Bank?
A. Washington
B. Manila
C. Paris
D. Canberra

410. The headquarters of the U.N.O. is located in
A. Washington
B. New York
C. Philadelphia
D. Chicago

Awards

411. 'Pulitzer' prizes are awarded to Americans for excellence in
A. Films
B. Social work
C. Journalism
D. Medicine

412. When was the Nobel Prize started?
A. 1901   B. 1905
C. 1934   D. 1900

413. 'Bharat Ratna' Award was given for the first time in
A. 1956   B. 1957
C. 1952   D. 1954

414. Saraswati Samman is awarded by
A. K.K. Birla Foundation
B. Government of India
C. Bharatiya Jnanpith
D. Sahitya Academy

415. Who was the first Asian to win a Nobel Prize?
A. Hideki Yuka
B. Har Gobind Khurana
C. C.V. Raman
D. Rabindranath Tagore

416. The highest Gallantry Award given in India is
A. Ashok Chakra
B. Mahavir Chakra
C. Param Vir Chakra
D. None of these

417. On which day every year National Awards for Teachers are announced?
A. September 5
B. November 14
C. November 19
D. August 15

418. Dronacharya Awards are given
A. to outstanding athletes
B. to outstanding coaches
C. for best performance in archery
D. for invention in science

419. Dr. C.V. Raman was awarded Nobel Prize in
A. Chemistry
B. Literature
C. Physics
D. Medicine

420. The first recipient of Rajiv Gandhi Khel Ratna Award is
A. Leander Paes
B. Viswanathan Anand
C. Kapil Dev
D. Limba Ram

421. The highest civilian award of India is
A. Bharat Ratna
B. Padam Vibhushan
C. Padam Bhushan
D. Padma Shri

422. Which of the following Indians awarded 'Legion D Award', the highest civilian award of France?
A. Satyajit Ray
B. Pandit Ravi Shankar
C. Lok Nayak Jayaprakash
D. J.L. Nehru

423. Dhanvantari Awards are given for the best performance in the field of
A. Medical Sciences
B. Nuclear Sciences
C. Economics
D. Space Research

424. Nobel Prizes are not given for which of the following fields?
A. Music   B. Chemistry
C. Peace   D. Physics

425. Dadasaheb Phalke Award is given for:
A. drama   B. social welfare
C. films   D. literature

426. In which year Nehru Award for International Understanding was instituted?
A. 1969   B. 1984
C. 1964   D. 1966

427. Who among the following has not been awarded the Bharat Ratna?
A. Indira Gandhi
B. Mahatma Gandhi
C. Sardar Patel
D. Radhakrishnan

428. Which one of the following is the second highest Civilian award in India?
A. Padma Shri
B. Bharat Ratna
C. Padma Bhushan
D. Padma Vibhushan

429. 'Victory Medal' is awarded in:
A. the USA
B. the UK
C. Russia
D. France

430. National film Awards were instituted in the year
A. 1954   B. 1950
C. 1961   D. 1969

431. In which year was the Nobel Prize for Economics announced for the first time?
A. 1969   B. 1901
C. 1919   D. 1970

432. Borlaug Award was instituted for recognising outstanding contribution in the field of
A. agriculture
B. ecology
C. journalism
D. medicine

433. Jesse Owens Global Award is given in the field of
A. Literature
B. Journalism
C. Science
D. Sports

434. Noble Alfred Bernhard after whom Nobel Prizes are given was
A. Engineer
B. Chemist
C. Both (A) and (B)
D. Doctor

435. Who was the first winner of Nehru Award for International Understanding?
A. Martin Luther King
B. Mother Teresa
C. U. Thant
D. Dr. Jonas Salk

Sports

436. In which International Championship, 'Thomas Cup' is given
A. Football
B. Cricket
C. Badminton
D. Tennis

437. 'Gambit' is related to which among the followings sports?
A. Carrom B. Bridge
C. Chess D. Billiards

438. The term 'Grandmaster' is used in which of these games?
A. Chess B. Judo
C. Bridge D. Karate

439. In the game of Volleyball, the number of players on each side is
A. Eight B. Five
C. Seven D. Six

440. The term ''Cue'' is associated with which game?
A. Hockey B. Football
C. Billiards D. Cricket

441. With which game is Geet Sethi Associated?
A. Basketball
B. Snooker
C. Chess
D. Tennis

442. How many players are there in each side in the game of Netball?
A. 7 B. 6
C. 9 D. 11

443. 'Uber Cup' is associated with which of the following?
A. Tennis B. Badminton
C. Chess D. Cricket

444. Where is the annual Australian Open Tennis tournament held?
A. Sydney B. Melbourne
C. Canberra D. Brisbane

445. The Olympic Motto is
A. Health is wealth
B. Promote Universal brother-hood
C. Faster, higher, stronger
D. Excellence is the goal

446. The term 'Tee' is associated with which of the following sports?
A. Polo B. Table Tennis
C. Golf D. Judo

447. Which Indian sportsman is known as Hockey Wizard throughout the world?
A. A.B. Subbiah
B. Jude Felix
C. Dhyan Chand
D. Ajitpal Singh

448. When did India become World Cricket champion?
A. 1980 B. 1982
C. 1983 D. 1986

449. ''Googly'' is associated with:
A. Cricket B. Table-Tennis
C. Hockey D. Billiards

450. With which game are the terms bull's eye, muzzle and plug associated?
A. Shooting B. Solitaire
C. Billiards D. Rowing

451. Who is the first Indian to take a hat trick in an international test?
A. Kapil Dev
B. Jasu Patel
C. Harbhajan Singh
D. B.S. Chandrashekhar

452. Who was declared by wisden as '' The Best Indian Bowler of the Century'' (20th Century)?
A. Kapil Dev
B. B.S. Chandrashekhar

C. B.S. Bedi
D. Subhash V. Gupte

453. " Jab" and "Parry" are terms used in which sport?
A. Wrestling
B. Boxing
C. Billiards
D. Weightlifting

454. India's national game is
A. Football B. Cricket
C. Tennis   D. Hockey

455. Davis Cup is associated with the sport of
A. Tennis   B. Football
C. Cricket   D. Hockey

456. The term 'breast stroke' is associated with:
A. Skating
B. Croquet
C. Swimming
D. Rifle Shooting

457. What is the National Game of the USA?
A. Cricket   B. Baseball
C. Soccer   D. Billiards

458. Roger Federer is associated with
A. Hockey   B. Lawn Tennis
C. Golf   D. Badminton

459. 'Merdeka Cup' is associated with
A. Golf   B. Football
C. Squash   D. Hockey

460. Who among the following has become the first woman in the world to swim across seven seas?
A. Shikha Tandon
B. Bula Chowdhury
C. Amanda Beard
D. Arti Saha

Books

461. The famous book 'Geet Govind' is written by
A. Banabhatt
B. Jaydev
C. Mirabai
D. Kalidas

462. 'Ain-e-Akbari' was written by
A. Farista   B. Ibn Batuta
C. Abul Fazal   D. Birbal

463. Who wrote " Vande Mataram"?
A. Rabindra Nath Tagore
B. Sumitra Nandan Pant
C. Bankim Chandra Chatterji
D. Vivekanand

464. Who among the following is the author of 'Das Kapital'?
A. Lenin
B. J.M. Keynes
C. Robert Owen
D. Karl Marx

465. 'Panchatantra' was written by
A. Jai Dev
B. Ved Vyas
C. Bhavbhuti
D. Vishnu Sharma

466. Patanjali is well known for the compilation of
A. Yoga Sutra
B. Panchatantra
C. Brahma Sutra
D. Ayurveda

467. Who among the following has written the book, 'The Wings of Fire: An Autobiography'?
A. K.R. Narayan
B. Sobha De

C. A.B. Vajpayee
D. A.P.J. Abdul Kalam

468. Who compiled the 'Adi Granth'?
A. Guru Nanak
B. Guru Ramdas
C. Guru Arjun
D. Guru Gobind Singh

469. The famous book 'Anandmath' was authored by
A. Rabindranath Tagore
B. Bankim Chandra Chattopadhyaya
C. Sarojini Naidu
D. Sri Aurobindo

470. Which one of the following pairs is *not* correctly matched?
A. Mudrarakshasa : Visakhadatta
B. Rajtarangini : Kalhana
C. Kadambari : Bana Bhatta
D. Ratnavali : Bilhana

471. 'Harry Potter and the Deathly Hallows' is written by
A. Robert Ludlum
B. J.K. Rowling
C. Sidney Sheldon
D. Spencer Johnson

472. 'Arthashastra' was written by
A. Kalidas
B. Kautilya
C. R.K. Narayan
D. Bana Bhatta

473. Name the author of book "The Post Office (Dak Ghar)"?
A. R.K. Narayan
B. Rabindra Nath Tagore
C. Prem Chand
D. Krishan Chandra

474. Who wrote the nursery rhyme, "Twinkle, twinkle, little star"?
A. Lovelace
B. Ann Taylor
C. William Ross Wallace
D. William Shakespeare

475. Ashtadhyayi is a book written by
A. Panini
B. Patanjali
C. Vishnu Sharma
D. None of these

476. 'Prithviraj Raso' was written by:
A. Kalhan
B. Chand Bardai
C. Bhavbhuti
D. Bhule Shah

477. The book 'Prison Diary' was written by
A. Mahatma Gandhi
B. V.D. Savarkar
C. Jai Prakash Narayan
D. Morarji Desai

478. "Runs and Ruins" is written by
A. Nawab Pataudi
B. Vivian Richards
C. Clive Lloyd
D. Sunil Gavaskar

479. Who is the author of the book, 'The God of small Things'?
A. Ali Sardar Jafri
B. Vikram Chandra
C. Padma Seth
D. Arundhati Roy

480. India-2020 is a book written by
A. Montek Singh Ahluwalia
B. A.P.J. Abdul Kalam
C. G. Ganeshan
D. Indra Kumar Gujral

Computer

481. Which one of the following has earned the title "Father of Modern Computer"?
A. Blaise Pascal
B. Charles Babbage
C. Herman Hollerith
D. Jack Kilby

482. Which one of the following is the first generation computer?
A. UNIVAC-1
B. EDVAG
C. IBM 1201
D. IBM 1104

483. Which one of the following is a hardware?
A. Integrated circuit
B. Compiler
C. DOS
D. FORTRAN

484. What is the measuring unit of memory?
A. Watt
B. Words
C. Bit
D. None of these

485. How many bits are there in one byte?
A. 1
B. 2
C. 8
D. 1024

486. Digital computers deal with
A. discrete quantities
B. physical quantities
C. both discrete and physical quantities
D. neither discrete nor physical quantities

487. What is nibble?
A. A group of 2 bits
B. A group of 4 bits
C. A group of 8 bits
D. A group of 12 bits

488. Which one of the following is not a package?
A. BASIC
B. dBase
C. Pagemaker
D. Wordstar

489. Who invented the punched card?
A. Jack Kilby
B. John Napier
C. Gottfried Leibnitz
D. None of these

490. Which of the following does not represent an I/O device?
A. Speaker which beeps
B. Plotter
C. Joystick
D. ALU

491. A set of instructions is called a
A. compiler
B. program
C. assembler
D. information

492. Data is a collection of
A. raw material
B. number of alphabets
C. facts and entities relevant to user
D. input material for a computer

493. Which one of the following is part of the CPU?
A. Memory
B. Compiler
C. Control unit
D. Joystick

494. Which one of the following is not a system software?
A. Operating system
B. Compiler

C. Assembler
D. Software for railway reservation

495. What are the main limitations of computers?
A. Lack of decision-making power
B. Zero IQ
C. Lack in innovations
D. All the above

496. What do you understand by IPO cycle?
A. Information and Programming Operations cycle
B. Innovating and Programming Operations cycle
C. Input-Program-Output cycle
D. None of these

497. Calculations are made in computer with the help of its
A. Memory
B. ALU
C. CU
D. Input device

498. Results are obtained from computer through its
A. input unit
B. output unit
C. CPU
D. memory

499. Who, among the following invented the method of logarithm?
A. John Napier
B. Blaise Pascal
C. Joseph Jacquard
D. Charles Babbage

500. The modern age of data processing began with the completion of the computer

A. Analytical Engine
B. Napier's 'Logs' and 'Bones'
C. ENIAC
D. Leibnitz's Calculator

Miscellaneous

501. Who is called the First Citizen of India?
A. President of India
B. Prime Minister of India
C. Mahatma Gandhi
D. Dr. B.R. Ambedkar

502. Panini was a famous scholar of
A. Language and grammar
B. Ayurveda
C. Astronomy
D. Biology

503. Which of the following is not a mineral?
A. Slate
B. Limestone
C. Coal
D. Calcite

504. The state of rising prices due to an enhancement in the quantity of money in circulation, is termed as
A. Inflation
B. Deflation
C. Demonetisation
D. Devaluation

505. Name the minerals that are essential for bone and teeth formation in human
A. Calcium and Phosphorus
B. Magnesium and Potassium
C. Sodium and Iron
D. Iodine and Sulphur

506. Ripe mangoes contain
  A. Vitamin A
  B. Vitamin B
  C. Vitamin C
  D. Vitamin E

507. In which one of the following places, the boiling point of water is the highest?
  A. Dead Sea
  B. Mt. Everest
  C. Nile Delta
  D. Sunderbans Delta

508. The primary colours used in a colour TV are
  A. Green, Yellow, Violet
  B. Violet, Red, Orange
  C. Blue, Green, Red
  D. Blue, Geen, Violet

509. Which one of the following is not a Fundamental Right guaranteed by the Indian Constitution?
  A. Freedom to manage religious affairs
  B. Free and compulsory education up to primary stage
  C. Prohibition of employment of children in factories
  D. Freedom to propagate religion

510. The chief merit of a federal government is that it
  A. Ensures a strong government at the centre
  B. Integrates national unity with regional autonomy
  C. Keeps a check on the multiparty system
  D. Is very less expensive

511. The first Assamese to become the President of India was
  A. Saiyeda Anowara Taimur
  B. Gopinath Bordoloi
  C. Fakhruddin Ali Ahmed
  D. Syed Abdul Malik

512. Match List I with List II and select the correct answer using the codes given below the lists:

List-I	**List-II**
(a) Amjad Ali Khan	1. Flute
(b) Bismillah Khan	2. Sarod
(c) Hari Prasad Chaurasia	3. Tabla
(d) Alla Rakha	4. Shehnai

Codes:

	(a)	(b)	(c)	(d)
A.	2	1	3	4
B.	4	2	1	3
C.	2	4	1	3
D.	1	2	3	4

513. A dentist's mirror is a
  A. Cylindrical mirror
  B. Plane mirror
  C. Convex mirror
  D. Concave mirror

514. Which of the following is the largest producer of raw silk?
  A. Asom
  B. Karnataka
  C. Andhra Pradesh
  D. Jammu and Kashmir

515. The Gandhara School of Sculpture was a blend of
  A. Indian and Greek styles
  B. Indian and Persian styles
  C. Purely Indian in origin
  D. Indian and South East Asian style

516. Which one of the following languages is used in Tripura?
A. Hindi   B. Mizo
C. Khasi   D. Bengali

517. How many schedules are there in the Constitution of India?
A. Eight   B. Ten
C. Twelve   D. Fourteen

518. The term 'cloning' is related with
A. Environment
B. Genetics
C. Space technology
D. Trade

519. The planet nearest to the Earth is
A. Jupiter   B. Venus
C. Mercury   D. Mars

520. Hard water can be used in
A. Boilers
B. Textile industry
C. Paper industry
D. Drinking

521. Ras Leela, Yaosang, Lai Haraoba are the festivals of
A. Assemese people
B. Karbi people
C. Manipuri people
D. Bodo people

522. The Tigris river flows mainly through
A. Turkey   B. Syria
C. Iraq   D. Iran

523. "India is a secular State". It means that the Indian State
A. Favours irreligious citizens
B. Favours the religions of the majority community

C. Favours the religions of the minority community
D. Favours no particular religion

524. The second largest linguistic unit in India is
A. Tamil   B. Hindi
C. English D. Telugu

525. The oldest inhabitants of India are considered to be
A. Mongoloids
B. Negritos
C. Indo-Aryan
D. Mediterranean

526. The International Date Line passes through
A. Malacca Strait
B. Gibraltar Strait
C. Bering Strait
D. Florida Strait

527. The last three digits of a PIN code represent
A. Zone
B. Subzone
C. Sorting District
D. Mailing route

528. Which state has the largest number of sugar mills?
A. Punjab
B. Haryana
C. Tamil Nadu
D. Uttar Pradesh

529. The first oil well in India was dug at
A. Bombay High
B. Moran
C. Digboi
D. Naharkatiya

530. Which of the following is *not* a rabi crop?
A. Wheat   B. Maize
C. Mustard   D. Gram

531. The state with the largest area under waste land is
A. Gujarat
B. Madhya Pradesh
C. Jammu and Kashmir
D. Rajasthan

532. Mixed farming involves
A. Growing more than one crop on a farm
B. Growing specialised crops
C. Growing crops and keeping livestock
D. Intensive and extensive agriculture

533. The country with the highest population density is
A. China   B. Bangladesh
C. India   D. France

534. When the first metal came into being, it was used for
A. Pot making
B. House-building
C. Clearing jungles
D. Making wheels

535. To whom does Vasudeva-Krishna address all his teachings in the Bhagvad Gita?
A. Arjuna
B. Duryodhana
C. Yudhishthira
D. The common people

536. Who raised the simple slogan 'Do or Die' for the Quit India Movement?
A. Mahatma Gandhi
B. Subhash Chandra Bose
C. Jawahar Lal Nehru
D. J.B. Kripalani

537. The salary and perquisities of the Prime Minister of India are decided by the
A. Constitution
B. Cabinet
C. Parliament
D. President

538. At what age can one exercise the right to vote in the general elections?
A. 18 years B. 21 years
C. 25 years D. 19 years

539. The Supreme Court was set up
A. By an act of Parliament
B. By the Constitution
C. Under the Government of India Act, 1935
D. By the Presidential order

540. A party to be recognised as a National Party must be in at least_____states.
A. Three   B. Four
C. Five   D. Six

541. Which of the following places is well known for the embroidery form of ''Chikankari''?
A. Hyderabad
B. Jaipur
C. Bhopal
D. Lucknow

542. Match the following

Folk form	**States where popular**
(*a*) Heer song	1. Bengal
(*b*) Bhatiali song	2. Punjab

(*c*) Garba dance　　3. U.P.
(*d*) Raas dance　　4. Gujarat

	(*a*)	(*b*)	(*c*)	(*d*)
A.	1	2	3	4
B.	1	3	2	4
C.	2	1	4	3
D.	2	3	4	1

543. Which is the most ancient musical instrument of India?
A. Flute　　B. Tabla
C. Veena　　D. Sitar

544. Who was the pioneer of the Bengal School of Art?
A. Nandlal Bose
B. B.C. Sanyal
C. Jamini Roy
D. Abanindranath Tagore

545. The proposed sea-route ''Sethu Samudram'' is a canal through which of the following sea-lanes?
A. Gulf of Mannar
B. Malacca Strait
C. Gulf of Kutch
D. Andaman and Nicobar Islands

546. The English established their first factory in India at
A. Bombay (Mumbai)
B. Surat
C. Sutanati
D. Madras (Chennai)

547. Which one of the following is a political right?
A. Right to freedom
B. Right to contest elections
C. Right to equality before law
D. Right to life

548. The main function of the judiciary is
A. Law formulation
B. Law execution
C. Law adjudication
D. Law application

549. 'Sakshat' is
A. A missile
B. An artificial satellite
C. A railway project
D. A website

550. Who started the first English newspaper in India?
A. Bal Gangadhar Tilak
B. Raja Rammohan Roy
C. J.A. Hickey
D. Lord William Bentinck

551. Mahatma Gandhi's autobiography—'My Experiments with Truth' was originally written in—
A. English　　B. Hindi
C. Marathi　　D. Gujarati

552. Who commanded the army of Bahadur Shah Zafar in 1857 revolt in Delhi ?
A. Azimulla
B. General Bakht Khan
C. Haqim Ahsanulla
D. Khan Bahadur

553. People greet one another in French language with—
A. GutenTag
B. Bonjour
C. Ahlan Wasahlan
D) None of these

554. Which among the following is *not* a correct match—
A. Thomas Cup—Badminton
B. Rovers Cup—Hockey
C. Deodhar Trophy—Cricket
D. Durand Cup—Football

555. What is Gene ?
   A. A segment of RNA, DNA and Histone
   B. A segment of DNA and RNA
   C. A segment of DNA
   D. A segment of DNA and Histone

556. Water pollution is mainly caused by-
   A. Pesticides
   B. NH_3
   C. Industrial waste
   D. Detergent

557. In the constitution of India, India has been described as—
   A. A federation
   B. A secular of federation
   C. A quasi-federal organization
   D. A union of states

558. Damodar Valley Project is sponsored by West Bengal and—
   A. Orissa
   B. Jharkhand
   C. U.P.
   D. All the above

559. Which among the following is a riverine port ?
   A. Cochin   B. Kolkata
   C. Kanca   D. Mormugao

560. Budapest is the capital of—
   A. Haiti
   B. Honduras
   C. Hungary
   D. Czech Republic

561. Among the following, which state capital is not situated near the bank of a river ?
   A. Lucknow   B. Patna
   C. Bombay   D. Kolkata

562. Which is the storehouse of salt in human body ?
   A. Liver   B. Skin
   C. Kidneys   D. Neck

563. Pyorrhoea affects which part of the body ?
   A. The gums
   B. The teeth
   C. Salivary glands
   D. Lips

564. Who was the author of 'Geet Govind' ?
   A. Vidyapati   B. Jayadeva
   C. Magha   D. Sriharsha

565. Thermocole is made from—
   A. Polystyrene
   B. Perspex
   C. Polythene
   D. Teflon

566. Printing for the blind was invented by—
   A. Berliner
   B. N.R.Finsen
   C. Louis Braile
   D. J. L. Baird

567. Which is the heaviest flying bird?
   A. Bustard
   B. Penguin
   C. Ostrich
   D. Vulture

568. Economic development of a country is directly based on—
   A. Natural resources
   B. Capital formation
   C. Availability of market
   D. None of these

569. The term Ikebana is associated with which country ?
   A. Thailand   B. Japan
   C. England   D. Australia

570. The largest irrigation canal in India is called the—
A. Yamuna canal
B. Sirhind canal
C. Lower Baridoab canal
D. Indira Gandhi canal

571. Horns of most mammals are made of—
A. Bones
B. Cartilage
C. Keratin
D. Chitin

572. Rigveda is divided into how many Mandals ?
A. 10 mandals
B. 7 mandals
C. 15 mandals
D. 20 mandals

573. The constitution of UNO is known as—
A. Peace agreement
B. Magna Carta
C. Declaration
D. Charter

574. December 10 is observed as—
A. World Mental Health Day
B. World Sight Day
C. World Red Cross Day
D. Human Rights Day

575. The Durand Line is the international border between—
A. Afghanistan and Pakistan
B. Iran and Syria
C. India and Bangladesh
D. India and Nepal

576. Washington is situated at the bank of—
A. Vistula
B. Moskava
C. Potomac
D. Tagus

577. The term 'Rook' is linked with—
A. Golf
B. Archery
C. Chess
D. Badminton

578. 'Fan', a widely spoken language of the world belongs to—
A. Laos
B. Kenya
C. Tibet
D. Myanmar

579. Which among the following is matched incorrectly ?
A. Mahatma Gandhi — Bapu
B. Lajpat Rai — Punjab Kesari
C. C.F. Andrews— Deshabandhu
D. Subhash Chandra Bose — Netaji

580. Supreme Court in India was established in Calcutta in :
A. 1771
B. 1774
C. 1775
D. 1776

581. The first radio-programme in India was broadcast by Radio Club of Bombay in:
A. 1924
B. 1923
C. 1926
D. 1927

582. In India, the first state to institute a Human Rights Commission is :
A. A.P.
B. Kerala
C. W. Bengal
D. Rajasthan

583. The 'Vikram Sarabhai Space Centre is located at :
A. Bangalore
B. Hyderabad
C. Chennai
D. Thiruvananthapuram

584. The first film actor to be nominated to Rajya Sabha was :
A. Ashok Kumar
B. Dilip Kumar
C. Jeevan
D. Prithviraj Kapoor

585. The first Indian Institute of Technology was set up in India in 1950 at :
A. Kolhapur   B. Kanpur
C. Kharagpur   D. Bangalore

586. Which state has the maximum forest cover amongst all Indian States and Union Territories?
A. T.N.   B. A.P.
C. M.P.   D. U.P.

587. Manas Wildlife Sanctuary housing tigers is in:
A. Sikkim
B. Asom
C. Karnataka
D. Arunachal Pradesh

588. Who wrote 'Long Walk To Freedom' ?
A. Nelson Mandela
B. Aung San Su Kyi
C. Abraham Lincoln
D. Moti Lal Nehru

589. The currency of Bhutan is :
A. Lote   B. Rupiah
C. Ngultrum   D. Shekel

590. Who discovered X-rays in 1895 ?
A. Mackintos
B. B. Certois
C. Belard
D. Prof. Roentgen

591. The melting point of iron is :
A. 1600°C   B. 1535°C
C. 1765°C   D. 1650°C

592. The headquarters of European Union is :
A. Rome   B. Paris
C. Brussels   D. Dublin

593. Commonwealth Day is observed by Member Countries on :
A. 26 August
B. 24 May
C. 27 December
D. 29 January

594. IMF (International Monetary Fund) was established in :
A. 1950   B. 1965
C. 1945   D. 1980

595. The distance covered by wheeled vehicle is measured by :
A. Sextant
B. Odometer
C. Speedometer
D. Stroboscope

596. Diphtheria, a disease, attacks :
A. Lungs   B. Eyes
C. Gums   D. Throat

597. Phrenology is the study of :
A. Language
B. Teeth
C. Skull and brain
D. Nerves

598. If the President of India wants to submit his resignation, to whom, would he submit his resignation?
A. Speaker of the Lok Sabha
B. Chief Justice of Supreme Court
C. Vice President
D. Prime Minister

599. Rose is the national emblem of :
A. Italy   B. Iran
C. Israel   D. Iraq

600. 'Akash' is India's—
A. Air to air missile
B. Anti-tank guided missile
C. Surface to surface missile
D. Surface to air missile

601. Tapti river originates from :
  A. Amarkantak
  B. Panchmarhi
  C. Trimbakeshwar
  D. Satpura range

602. The first municipal corporation in India was established in Madras in :
  A. 1687   B. 1699
  C. 1685   D. 1690

603. RAW (Research and Analysis Wing) works under:
  A. Ministry of Home
  B. Ministry of Personnel
  C. PMO
  D. Cabinet Secretariat

604. The first spacecraft sent by Europe to the moon is :
  A. Atlantis   B. Discovery
  C. Odyssey   D. SMART-I

605. Siyam is the old name of :
  A. Vietnam   B. Thailand
  C. Myanmar   D. Laos

606. The number of states which do not touch international boundary and are completely landlocked is :
  A. 3   B. 7
  C. 5   D. 6

607. Which state of India touches the boundary of most other states?
  A. A.P.   B. M.P.
  C. Asom   D. U.P.

608. Which of the Mughal rulers promoted painting most?
  A. Babar   B. Akbar
  C. Jahangir   D. Shahjahan

609. The subject matter of the fourth schedule of the Constitution of India is :
  A. Administration of tribal areas
  B. Forms of oath or Affirmation
  C. Languages
  D. Allocation of seats of the Rajya Sabha to states

610. Vice-President is the part of :
  A. Legislature
  B. Executive
  C. Rajya Sabha
  D. None of these

ANSWERS

1	2	3	4	5	6	7	8	9	10
C	C	A	D	C	C	B	D	B	B

11	12	13	14	15	16	17	18	19	20
C	C	C	D	C	D	B	C	D	D

21	22	23	24	25	26	27	28	29	30
B	B	D	B	D	D	D	B	D	B

31	32	33	34	35	36	37	38	39	40
B	A	C	A	A	B	B	B	A	A

41	42	43	44	45	46	47	48	49	50
C	C	B	B	B	C	A	B	B	C

51	52	53	54	55	56	57	58	59	60
C	C	B	B	A	C	B	B	B	D

61	62	63	64	65	66	67	68	69	70
D	C	A	A	B	C	C	A	C	D
71	72	73	74	75	76	77	78	79	80
C	D	C	D	C	C	C	B	C	B
81	82	83	84	85	86	87	88	89	90
C	A	D	D	D	C	C	A	C	D
91	92	93	94	95	96	97	98	99	100
A	C	C	C	B	D	A	A	C	D
101	102	103	104	105	106	107	108	109	110
B	D	A	C	A	C	A	A	D	B
111	112	113	114	115	116	117	118	119	120
B	C	A	B	B	B	D	D	D	B
121	122	123	124	125	126	127	128	129	130
D	C	C	A	D	A	D	C	B	C
131	132	133	134	135	136	137	138	139	140
B	D	D	A	B	A	B	B	B	D
141	142	143	144	145	146	147	148	149	150
B	A	C	C	A	A	C	A	B	D
151	152	153	154	155	156	157	158	159	160
C	B	B	C	C	D	A	D	C	D
161	162	163	164	165	166	167	168	169	170
B	D	B	C	D	D	B	D	D	B
171	172	173	174	175	176	177	178	179	180
D	B	B	C	C	C	A	D	A	C
181	182	183	184	185	186	187	188	189	190
C	A	B	C	B	C	C	D	B	D
191	192	193	194	195	196	197	198	199	200
D	A	D	C	B	B	A	D	D	C
201	202	203	204	205	206	207	208	209	210
A	B	B	D	A	D	C	C	C	A
211	212	213	214	215	216	217	218	219	220
B	B	C	C	D	A	C	D	B	D
221	222	223	224	225	226	227	228	229	230
D	C	C	A	C	C	B	A	D	A
231	232	233	234	235	236	237	238	239	240
B	A	A	A	A	B	B	A	D	B
241	242	243	244	245	246	247	248	249	250
D	B	A	B	C	C	B	D	A	C
251	252	253	254	255	256	257	258	259	260
D	B	D	B	A	B	C	D	D	A

261	262	263	264	265	266	267	268	269	270
B	A	C	C	C	D	C	C	B	B

271	272	273	274	275	276	277	278	279	280
C	D	B	D	D	C	A	D	A	D

281	282	283	284	285	286	287	288	289	290
C	A	B	B	B	B	D	B	C	C

291	292	293	294	295	296	297	298	299	300
C	B	D	B	B	C	B	D	D	A

301	302	303	304	305	306	307	308	309	310
A	B	A	C	D	A	A	D	C	A

311	312	313	314	315	316	317	318	319	320
D	C	B	C	D	C	A	B	C	D

321	322	323	324	325	326	327	328	329	330
A	B	C	B	A	D	A	B	B	D

331	332	333	334	335	336	337	338	339	340
B	A	B	A	C	C	A	A	D	D

341	342	343	344	345	346	347	348	349	350
B	A	B, C	C	C	C	B	B	A	C

351	352	353	354	355	356	357	358	359	360
A	D	A	D	B	C	B	D	D	C

361	362	363	364	365	366	367	368	369	370
A	D	B	A	D	A	C	C	B	A

371	372	373	374	375	376	377	378	379	380
A	A	C	C	D	C	C	A	B	C

381	382	383	384	385	386	387	388	389	390
D	C	B	B	A	A	D	D	B	C

391	392	393	394	395	396	397	398	399	400
C	B	D	C	C	A	B	C	C	A

401	402	403	404	405	406	407	408	409	410
B	C	A	D	C	B	B	B	B	B

411	412	413	414	415	416	417	418	419	420
C	A	D	A	D	C	A	B	C	B

421	422	423	424	425	426	427	428	429	430
A	A	A	A	C	C	B	D	A	A

431	432	433	434	435	436	437	438	439	440
A	A	D	B	C	C	C	A	D	C

441	442	443	444	445	446	447	448	449	450
B	A	B	B	C	C	C	C	A	A

451	452	453	454	455	456	457	458	459	460
C	B	B	D	A	C	B	B	B	B

461	462	463	464	465	466	467	468	469	470
B	C	C	D	D	A	D	C	B	D
471	472	473	474	475	476	477	478	479	480
B	B	B	B	B	B	C	D	D	B
481	482	483	484	485	486	487	488	489	490
B	A	A	D	C	A	B	A	D	D
491	492	493	494	495	496	497	498	499	500
B	C	C	D	D	D	B	B	A	A
501	502	503	504	505	506	507	508	509	510
A	A	C	A	A	A	A	C	C	B
511	512	513	514	515	516	517	518	519	520
C	C	D	A	A	D	C	B	B	A
521	522	523	524	525	526	527	528	529	530
C	C	D	D	B	C	C	D	C	C
531	532	533	534	535	536	537	538	539	540
D	C	B	A	A	A	C	A	B	B
541	542	543	544	545	546	547	548	549	550
D	C	A	D	A	B	B	C	D	C
551	552	553	554	555	556	557	558	559	560
D	B	B	B	C	C	D	B	B	C
561	562	563	564	565	566	567	568	569	570
C	B	A	B	A	C	A	B	B	D
571	572	573	574	575	576	577	578	579	580
C	A	D	D	A	C	C	D	C	B
581	582	583	584	585	586	587	588	589	590
B	C	D	D	C	C	B	A	C	D
591	592	593	594	595	596	597	598	599	600
B	C	B	C	B	D	C	C	B	D
601	602	603	604	605	606	607	608	609	610
B	A	D	D	B	C	D	C	D	B

1904

ESSAY & LETTER WRITING

Essays

The Independence Day

India became independent on 15th August, 1947 after a long struggle. Jawaharlal Nehru who had spent the prime of his life in British jails while fighting against the mighty British empire, became the first Prime Minister of India and hoisted the Indian flag, tricolor, on the ramparts of the Red Fort in Delhi at 12:00 pm as the zero hour for 15th August started on this date in 1947. He called the moment India's "tryst with destiny".

Since then 15th August is celebrated every year as Independence Day. The main festival is held in Delhi. The Prime Minister of India hoists the tricolor early in the morning on the ramparts of the Red Fort before a mammoth gathering of Indian and foreign dignitaries, VIPs and common people. He makes a speech from behind a bullet proof glass cabin. In his speech, he explains the achievements and policies of the government and highlights the projects in hand and what the country wants to be and to what side her efforts are directed. He lists the major problems of the country and how the government wants to address and harness them.

Small functions are held in all towns and cities and even in some big villages. In state capitals, the Chief Ministers and at other places Governors and other dignitaries such as Deputy Commissioners senior police officers, Mayors of Municipal Corporation, Chairmen of Municipal Committees, etc. hoist the national flag. In schools and colleges the Presidents of Managing Committees or Principals of the institutions concerned do the ceremony. In all cases, the function always ends with the recitation of the National Anthem with due respect and regard.

Diwali

Diwali is perhaps the most famous festival of India. It comes off twenty days after Dussehra. It occurs mostly towards the end of October or in November.

On the day of Diwali, Lord Rama returned home after killing the cruel demon king Ravana. Then the people of Ayodhya illuminated their houses. It is since then that Diwali is celebrated all over India with great pomp and show.

Many days before Diwali, people get their houses whitewashed. On the day of Diwali, they wear new clothes. Particularly, the children are fond of new clothes.

People distribute and exchange sweets. The markets and bazaars are tastefully decorated. At night, the houses are illuminated with electric and earthen ware lamps and candles.

On this day, the businessmen start new account books. Some people indulge in drinking and gambling. That is very bad.

Diwali is an important day for people of all communities in India for one reason or the other. On this day people of all communities greet each other and exchange sweets with each other. People worship goddess Lakshmi at night. Many people fire crackers. That should be avoided as crackers pollute the atmosphere. If children insist on firing crackers, their parents must stand close to them to avoid any accident.

Diwali can be very helpful in bringing about national integration. People of all communities should join hands to change Diwali into a national festival, as in fact, it is not the festival of just one community.

Holi

Holi is one of the most famous festivals of India. It usually comes off in the month of March, mostly in the first or second week of this month.

Holi is called the festivals of colours, just as Diwali is called the festivals of lights. Holi denotes the victory of truth over falsehood and good over evil.

There is a story behind this festival. It is said that once there was a king. His name was Hiranyakashyap. He had declared himself to be God and asked people to worship him. But his own son Prahlad, refused to obey him. He refused to accept him as God or incarnation of God.

Hiranyakashyap was very angry with Prahlad. He wanted to punish him for disobeying him. He had a sister, Holika. She had got a boon that fire could not burn her. She took the little child, Prahlad, in her lap and sat on a heap of burning wood.

It so happened that Holika herself was burnt in fire but fire could cause no harm to Prahlad. God had saved him. Holika's boon could not work because she was trying to use it for an evil purpose. Fire could do no harm to Prahlad because of his firm faith in God and his unflinching determination to follow the path of truth.

It is said that since then Holi is being celebrated in India. It is celebrated mostly in north India. On this day people smear each other's face with dry colour or they sprinkle liquid colour on each other out of love and enhance fun and happiness.

It is sad that some people start quarrelling with each other over the question of sprinkling colour on one another. The people also exchange sweets on this day. The day can be used as one for enhancing the spirit of national integration, as the people of all communities participate in it.

My Country

The name of my country is India. It is a very big country. In the matter of population it is next only to China. Its population is more than 121 crore of people.

India is divided into several States. Some of the big States are Uttar Pradesh, Madhya Pradesh, Bihar, Maharashtra, Rajasthan, etc. Among the Union Territories there are Chandigarh, Pondicherry (Puducherry), etc.

Jammu and Kashmir lies in the north of India. The southernmost Indian State is Tamil Nadu. India is spread from Kashmir to Kanya Kumari and from Assam to Gujarat.

The Indian people believe in different religions. They eat different kinds of food and wear different kinds of clothes. They speak different languages. But they are all Indians.

India is an ancient country. It remained under foreign rule for many centuries. In 1947, it became independent. It adopted a democratic set up. It became a republic in 1950.

India is a sovereign, secular country. All the citizens of India have equal rights. They have some fundamental rights and duties.

Among India's neighbours are China, Myanmar, Bangladesh, Nepal, Bhutan, Pakistan and Afghanistan.

India is a peaceloving country. It wants friendship with all the countries of the world, particularly with its neighbours.

India is making a rapid progress in all fields, particularly in telecommunications. It is paying attention to industrialization on war footing. It is already self-sufficient in food. For having become a big military and economic power, India is now known as "The Asian Tiger".

India is trying to tackle the problems of unemployment, illiteracy, disease, corruption, poverty, etc. Let us hope for the best.

Child Labour

Great poets like Wordworth and Tagore were great lovers of children. Among the Indian leaders, Jawaharlal Nehru was known for his great affection for children. President A.P.J. Abdul Kalam will also go in history as a true lover of children.

All parents love their children even more than their own life but it is a pity many of them are forced by the circumstances to send their children for doing some labour instead of going to school. Now, education for children in the age group of 6 to 14 has been made a fundamental right. Primary education is compulsory. Mid-day meals have been started in government schools to check the number of drop outs.

In spite of this, many poor parents do not send their children to school. Even those who are sent there, give up studies after the completion of primary education and in many cases even before its completion and that even ignoring the incentive of the mid-day meals.

The reason for this scenario is that many parents while feeling the pangs of poverty, want their children to be self-supporting even in that tender age. They themselves cannot earn much and want the children to work and augment the income of the family. Many children in poor families have to leave their hearths and homes to fend for themselves.

These poor children work in brick kilns, in restaurants and hotels, at shops and in houses of well-to-do people. Some of them who can't do much progress turn into the thieves, pickpockets, chain-snatchers, etc. and join the ranks of antisocial elements. Some of them even start taking drugs.

In order to prevent the practice of child labour some concrete, drastic steps should be taken by all concerned. Every child's attendance at school must be ensured. An awakening should be brought about among the poor families in this regard. Until, the income of these marginal families is increased no incentives or inducements may be able to deliver the goods.

Unemployment

Our country is said to be progressing by leaps and bounds in the matter of economy. But this progress is so lopsided that the net result has been the sharp increase in the number of the unemployed people.

At present we have hordes of unemployed young men and women of every kind and in all fields. We have both educated and uneducated unemployed people. We have skilled and unskilled unemployed youth. We have un-employed people both in urban and rural areas. Even degree holders such as engineers and MBAs are unemployed, not to speak of simple graduates in humanities, sciences and commerce.

Our universities are producing so many graduates all of whom the industry and other institutions cannot absorb. Many young people who can afford are trying to find jobs overseas. That also results in brain drain on a colossal scale.

There should be some planning in the matter of producing skilled and highly qualified graduates and post-graduates in various disciplines. It should be correlated to the necessity or possibility of job creation.

It is now almost certain that agriculture in our country is not able to absorb many more workers, skilled or others. The main remedy lies in rapid industrialisation. It is heartening to note that many new courses are being started by our universities and other institutions like IITs, ITIs, etc. Another positive factor is the large number of scientifically skilled people in our country who have the capacity and capability to absorb and grasp all the new research that is being made in various fields in the world. However, the unemployed people want concrete results and not mere policies.

The policy of reservation is also responsible to a great extent in the matter of unemployment. Similarly, corruption and nepotism have also accentuated the problem. Let the government and all others concerned with this topic do their best to overcome this problem.

Price Rise

Price rise is one of the most ticklish current problems. Whenever we go to make some purchases in the market, we learn to our great disappointment that the prices of most of the commodities have risen and sometimes quite exorbitantly.

There are several reasons for this steep rise in prices. One reason is the shortfall in production. This happens particularly when the country or a part of it is witnessed by floods or famine. Strikes result in fall in industrial production.

Sometimes, one feels baffled when one learns that there has been a bumper crop and still there is scarcity of essential commodities in the market. This usually happens due a number of reasons. One reason is the defective distribution system. Sometimes, there is over-production of some agricultural product in one State but it does not reach other States for lack of wagons, boxes, etc. It is generally seen there is surplus production of wheat in States like Punjab and Haryana but this surplus produce is not swiftly transferred to other States. Similarly, the bumper product of apples in Himachal Pradesh does not reach other States.

Another reason for the scarcity of commodities in the market even during times of profusion is the tendency of wholesalers and capitalists to hoard the products and create a scarcity in the market.

There are several other reasons for price rise. Some of such reasons are black market, corruption, faulty taxation system, wastage, expenditure on luxuries, bloated bureaucracy drawing heavy salaries, excessive profit charged by manufacturers on their products, etc.

In order to check price rise, effective steps should be taken and at the same time excessive circulation of money should also be checked. It should be ensured that imports are decreased and at the same time exports are increased.

Population Control

In the matter of population, India is the second largest country in the world. In this respect, she is next only to China, but she has a much smaller land mass as compared to China.

India's population crossed the mark of 1.21 billion in March 2011. At the time of Independence, it was only about 35 crore. It means in just about 63 years, it has increased four-fold, and that after all the various efforts put in at Central, State and local levels through various means.

India has one of the most liberal laws on abortion in the world. But this has resulted in another malady and that is the menace of female foeticide which is the result of easy availability of scanning machines in all cities and towns and which has brought the female ratio in certain States like Punjab and Haryana to an alarmingly low level.

In spite of all the efforts to give a fillip to literacy, a great mass of people is still illiterate, particularly in rural and slum areas. These people are traditionally-minded. They think that every child is the gift of God. Moreover, they are not much aware of the methods and devices of family planning. Some people, especially those belonging to the lower strata of society think that if they have more hands in the family, their income can increase. But they do not care or know that every new comer also comes with a mouth which is to be fed.

The population explosion has to a great extent nullified the tremendous progress India has made after Independence. The result is that a vast majority of the Indians is still steeped in stark poverty.

The multiplying numbers require more food, clothing, housing, healthcare, education, employment, etc. Certainly, in the long run neither food nor jobs and other provisions, supplies and facilities can keep pace with the numbers. So, the best way and the only way is to check population for which drastic measures should be adopted. Those with large families should be made to pay heavy taxes and those having small families of one or two children only should be rewarded.

The Postman

The postman is a very useful member of society. He brings us dak from our friends and relatives who live at long distances from us. He brings us messages of joy and sorrow. He does his duty in sun and shower.

The postman is perhaps at the lowest level in the posts and telegraphs set up. He is the least literate and accordingly gets the lowest pay per month. He is only a step higher than sweepers and khalasis.

A postman is not a totally illiterate person. Otherwise, he would not be able to read even the address on letters. He is perhaps at least a matriculate. If a postman is hardworking and continues his studies during his spare time and passes graduation, he can rise at least to the post of a clerk in a post office.

The postman has to do his duty whether he is appointed in an urban or a rural area. His duty starts in the morning and ends late in the afternoon or in the evening.

The postman often goes to far off places on his bicycle. He should be provided at least less with a moped. He gets a uniform annually, but his pay is very low whereas his duty is hard and strenuous.

In rural areas, the postman has sometimes to read letters to illiterate recipients. Rarely, he may even have to write a letter for them.

He brings letters, inland letters, postcards, money orders, parcels and telegrams. People wait for him eagerly. Though he is fobidden to accept any gift from anybody, some people force him to accept a gift on certain occasions such as Diwali, New Year's Day or some marriage or birth in the family.

In any case, he is a lovable person who deserves better treatment from the authorities in the matter of pay-fixation, allowances, etc.

Mahatma Gandhi

Mahatma Gandhi's full name was Mohan Das Karamchand Gandhi. He was born on 2nd October, 1869 at Porbandar in Gujarat.

As a student, he was not quite brilliant. But, under the influence of his mother, he had a highly religious, upright mind. It is well-known to all that he refused to copy a word probably "kettle" even when he was asked by his class teacher to do so. It was clear that he was a child of truth, character, honesty and integrity and no temptation could bow him down. He was a spiritual anarchist. He reversed the dictum — 'God is truth' with 'truth is God'.

He was married when he was only thirteen years old. He went to England for higher studies when he was nineteen. He took some vows before his mother before leaving for England. These included not taking wine or meat and not casting a lustful eye on any woman.

He became a Barrister and returned to India in 1891 and started practice at Rajkot and Mumbai (then Bombay). He could not succeed as a lawyer.

He went to Africa in 1893. He fought for justice for Indians there during his twelve year stay there. After his return to India in 1914, he chose Gopal Krishna Gokhale to be his mentor.

He toured the countryside and acquainted himself with the views and aspirations of the Indian people. At first he started the Non-Cooperation Movement. He wanted to attain Swaraj by peaceful means. After the Chauri-Chaura incident, he took back the movement.

Then he started the Civil Disobedience Movement on 6th April, 1930 which led to the famous Dandi March. There was picketing of foreign goods during this movement.

He started the Quit India Movement on August 8, 1942. Now, there was mass movement against the British Rule. During this period most of the Indian leaders were put behind the bars.

India attained Independence on August 15, 1947 but the great Mahatma was assassinated by Nathu Ram Godse on 30th January, 1948.

He will always be remembered as an apostle of peace, love, truth and non-violence and one of the greatest Indians and world leaders.

Co-education

There was a time when it was believed that boys and girls should be taught in separate institutions. In ancient gurukuls, there were only boys who were given education then. In spite of this, women generally had good education in ancient India.

After Independence, several education commissions and committees were set up. They generally advocated co-education in schools upto 10+2 level and separate education for boys and girls at the university level till graduation.

This policy is now by and large being followed in our country. There is, however, co-education again at post-graduation level.

Some people believe that co-education should not be there. In their opinion this can lead to attraction between boys and girls which is neither good for their health, nor character, nor studies.

Some other people are of the view that co-education can bring about a healthy competition between boys and girls and thus it can be of mutual benefit to both sexes. It can mean better desicipline since in the presence of girls the boys will not talk irrelevantly or obscenely in the class.

The most potent argument advanced by co-education lovers is that it can help both boys and girls in the development of their personality. They can come out of their enclosed shell-like personality and get rid of their unwarranted hesitation and shyness.

This can make boys and girls more expressive, progressive and forward in outlook and attitude to life which can be of great advantage to both sexes.

It must, however, be noted that some reservations are also there and even in a country like England, exclusive schools for girls are now being set up.

A Railway Journey

Children generally love to go out. As such, they are very fond of making journeys frequently. They love all kinds of journeys. I have frequently travelled by bus with my parents to different places. However, last Sunday I had a memorable journey by rail.

We reached the station at about 10.00 a.m. The train was to start at 10.15 a.m. My father bought tickets for mother and me as also for himself.

Immediately, we moved to platform No.1 where the train was to arrive shortly. We had not been there on the platform for more than a minute or two when the train arrived. We at once boarded it. We had first class tickets with us. So, we found no difficulty in boarding the train.

I got a seat near the window. Soon, the train started. I felt thrilled. I saw the platform moving backwards. At first the train was slow but soon it gathered speed. Within a few minutes, it gained the speed of the wind.

All the houses, poles, fields and trees seemed to be running backwards. I saw farmers working in the fields. Animals were also grazing there. Some women were picking up weeds from the fields.

It was an express train. So, it did not halt at small stations. Even at big stations and junctions, it halted only for a few minutes. As the train halted some people bought eatables and drinks from the vendors at the platforms. Some vendors also came within the compartments. A travelling ticket Examiner came and checked our tickets.

It was late in the afternoon that the train reached Kolkata. We alighted from it and through the exit gate came out. Again our tickets were checked, now at the gate. We left for our uncle's house where we had to go.

A Visit to the Taj

The Taj Mahal is a world famous mausoleum. It is situated on the bank of the river Yamuna near Agra. It was built by the Mughal Emperor Shah Jahan in the middle of the seventeenth century.

Shah Jahan built this monument in memory of his beloved wife, Mumtaz Mahal. It is said that more than twenty thousand masons and workers took more than twenty years in building this monument.

The Taj is made of pure white marble. It is one of the wonders of the world. Tagore called it " a tear frozen on the face of eternity."

Even after about four centuries when it was built, it has not lost its beauty. When the Mathura Oil Refinery was set up, there was a wide spread fear about the safety of the glory of the Taj. However, at the instance of the Supreme Court, timely remedial measures were taken.

Before we reach the main building of the Taj, we walk on a path which has tall attractive cypress trees on either side. Behind the cypress trees there are vast luxurious grassy lawns.

There is a large central dome over the main building, having four spiralling minarets on each of the four sides of the building. The graves of Shah Jahan and Mumtaz Mahal lie in a dark chamber beneath the central dome.

Thousands of visitors and tourists visit the Taj annually. It is a sight to see in the moonlight, especially on the full moon night.

I visited the Taj last Monday and I would like to visit it more than once again.

A Visit to the Zoo

Last Sunday, my elder brother took me to the zoo. He bought tickets at the gate and we went straight inside the Zoo.

The first thing that I saw was a vast lake. A large number of ducks and swans of different varieties were swimming in the lake. There were also a large number of migratory birds in the lake. These birds were seasonal visitors and had migrated temporarily from different countries, particularly very cold countries like Russia.

As we moved foward, we saw lions, tigers, bears and wolves in cages. Some of the wolves were roaring. Others were eating meat. In this section of the zoo, we also saw several other animals which are generally found in a wild state only. Among such animals were hyenas, jackals, foxes, panthers, leopards, etc.

I felt most amused when I saw a hippopotamus. I had never seen such an ugly creature before. Then we saw zebras and other animals.

In one of the sections of the zoo, we saw birds of different kinds such as sparrows and parrots of many colours and kinds. I was amused to see an ostrich. I also saw some penguins and kiwis in the zoo.

The creatures which most amused me were the monkeys and apes which were jumping from one branch of the tree to the other. The sight of the deer running on grass was also quite impressive. The kangaroo also offered an interesting figure.

It was in the afternoon that I had an elephant ride which turned out to be the grand finale to the visit. As I returned home, I was full of joy and enthusiasm.

A Railway Accident

Railway accidents are very comman these days. However, it can be guessed that when thousands of trains run over the rail track every day and some mishap sometimes cannot be ruled out. Accidents may occur due to some mechanical failure, but often they occur due to human error.

Day before yesterday, a horrible accident took place between two trains near the local railway station. It so happened that the Rajdhani Express was coming at full speed. It was a through train and was thus not to stop at this station.

The station master gave the wrong signal and the Rajdhani Express rammed into the passenger train which was approaching the station from the opposite direction.

The two mightly engines struck each other like two fearful demons. Both of them were smashed and the drivers and cleaners of both of them were killed on the spot.

Two bogies of the Rajdhani Express were destroyed, while four front bogies of the passenger train also met the same fate.

It was early in the morning. As we heard the cries of passengers, we rushed to the spot. It was a horrible sight. About two hundred passengers had been killed. Thousands of the passengers were injured. Volunteers from the adjoining areas had come to look after the injured passengers.

The railway safety system should be brushed up to make travel risk-free.

T.V.

Television is one of the greatest inventions of the modern age. Its brief name is TV. It is also sometimes called the Idiot Box and the Small or Silver Screen. The word 'small' naturally brings into mind the cinema in comparison to which it has a small screen and hence presents images on a small scale whereas the cinema screen offers them life size.

Before the advent of television, radio ruled the roost in the houses of the common people. Now, we have TV sets in most of the houses of people in our country. The installation of satellites of varying degrees and purposes in space by some countries and now our own country, has given a fillip to TV as to products in other fields such as Infor-mation Technology, Telecommunication, etc.

At first, black and white T.V was introduced in our country. Colour TV came only later. Surprisingly, colour TV was introduced in Bangladesh earlier than in India.

The advantages of TV are many and varied. Now, there are several TV channels. We also have several private TV companies besides Doordarshan, now under Prasar Bharti, such as Zee TV, Star TV, Jain TV, Sony TV, etc. There is the Cable System and Direct to Home (DTH) has also now been started.

We see over TV films, matches, discoveries, advertisement, happenings, speeches, etc. Most of these we see live. There are so many TV serials which are instructive and humorous and some of them are especially meant for a section of society such as children, women, sportspersons, farmers, students, youth etc. Some serials are quite interesting while others are just boring.

We should not sit too close to the TV set. Some children who sit too close to it get their eyesight weakened. We should also not become addicts to TV. TV should not be watched at the cost of studies.

Merits and Demerits of Science

Science is a mixed bag. It has in it merits as well as demerits. Science has made life for the common man very comfortable in the modern age. Now even an average man can afford to enjoy the comfort of such things as electricity and electrical devices such as the fan, the bulb desert cooler, the refrigerator, TV etc. Well-to-do people have other devices in their homes such as telephone, electric oven, computer, AC, etc. Those who can afford have cars. Medical science has prologed man's existence on earth for a number of years. There are food and clothing for all. Many people live in good houses. All this has been possible only because of science.

Science has some demerits also. It has given so much power to man which probably he cannot keep under his control. Science has also given to man some destructive articles such as guns, pistols, the rifles, cannon, bombs, warplanes, warships, torpedoes, missiles, etc.

Man is today sitting on a huge stockpile of explosive material which can destroy his very existence on earth in the twinkling of an eye even as a result of slight error or misunderstanding on his part.

Unless man destroys weapons of mass destruction, he cannot have real happiness on this earth. So, preparation for war negates all efforts of man towards progress. Progress may seem to be impressive and even tremendous but at present it is not free from corresponding dangers which are disastrous and fatal in nature.

Global Warming

The most prominent among the green-houses gases is the carbon dioxide. The maximum amount of this gas is produced in America and Europe.

The greenhouse gases raise the atmospheric temperature. It is told by the Intergovernmental Panel on climatic change that the Global Mean Tempera-ture of the atmosphere has risen by about one degree Fahrenheit (0.55 degree Celsius) in the 20th century. About half of it has risen in just 20 years. It is estimated by the scientists that the temperature may rise by another half a degree in the next 20 years. By the end of 21st century the world may get warmer by about 3.5 degrees.

The effect of this global rise in temperature is stupendous. It is likely to bring about severe climatic changes. It can lead to greater evaporation of water from oceans and water reservoirs. This means that world will become rainier and more moist. This can make the northern latitudes greener. But it can also cause devastating floods, as the rainfall pattern changes the world over.

One greatly devastating affect of the greenhouses gas can be visualised from the almost certain possibility that the global warming will make the snow on mountains melt more quickly. This will mean more water in oceans and accordingly, some islands and sea-coasts in certain parts of the world may get submerged. Such affects are already being witnessed in certain parts of the world.

It is of utmost importance that the production of greenhouse gases at such an alarming scale should be checked. This will also reduce pollution all over the world, particularly in urban areas. The burning of coal, oil, wood, fossil fuel and emissions from factories, motor vehicles, etc., leakage of gases from refrigerators, etc. all add to the quantity of greenhouse gases in atmosphere and the global warming. Some gases used in refrigerators and perfumes are greatly responsible for thinning of the ozone layer over the earth's atmosphere. This also leads to global warming.

The remedy lies in checking those practices and in making the increasing use of renewable energy.

Electricity

Electricity is one of the most important discoveries of science in the modern age. Electricity is there in the charged clouds and that is why they thunder so loudly. Probably, man took an idea from the clouds and this helped him in discovering electricity.

Electricity is a blind energy and is thus ruthless in its power, working and effect. Man has, however, found out the means to harness it with the help of insulators which he has discovered through experiments for the purpose.

Today, electricity is produced in several ways, that is, through hydraulic means, through wind power, through the use of coal, through nuclear power and so on. Now, even house waste is being used to generate electricity and energy. Solar energy is a common word these days. Energy comes to us mostly in the form of electricity, though some other shapes and forms may also be there.

In the modern age, we cannot think of life without electricity. Day in and day out, we are always surrounded by objects and machines which work with electricity. Some of these common household objects and devices are the electric bulb, the fluorescent tube, the electric fan, the desert cooler, the air conditioner, the room heater, the electric microwave oven, the mixer, the juicer, the toaster, the refrigerator, the geyser, etc.

Almost all the factories run with electricity. Computer which has changed the face of life on earth is also run with electricity. Even objects such as the mobile phone, etc. which work with the help of satellite use computer for certain purposes such as recording, bill charging, etc.

Thus, it is basically electricity which has revolutionized life on earth and other revolutionary things get sustenance from electricity.

An Earthquake

So far, no foolproof method has been devised to predict an approaching earthquake. Some people, especially in China, believe that just before an earthquake occurs, birds and animals start behaving in strange manner.

Scientist have created artificial earthquakes in the laboratories to apprise the people of their various aspects. But, it is not essential that the earthquakes should always occur in the same manner. Some earthquakes are said to start from 30 to 100 kilometres below the surface of the earth and others from 100 to 650 kilometres below it. The earthquake that started, as recorded in history, at the deepest level under the earth so far, occurred in Bolivia in 1994.

A violent earthquake shook the city of Bam, 1285 km southeast of Teheran in Iran at 5.28 a.m. (07.28 IST) on 26 December 2003. The earthquake was of the magnitude of 6.3 on the Richter scale. Its epicenter was outside Bam, about 1000 km southeast of Tehran. The quake hit the city when most of the people were in bed.

The city had a population of 80,000 and death toll was high. It was estimated that more than 40,000 people had died. The citadel of Bam was destroyed. The oldest part of the fortress dates to about 2000 years ago, but most of it was built in the 15th to 18th centuries and attracted thousands of tourists every year.

Telephone links with Bam were severed and the authorities were in contact with the city area through radio and satellite phone links. More than 90 percent buildings in the city were demolished. Thousands of people were injured. Power and water supplies were also snapped. This hampered relief efforts.

The international community came to the rescue of the Iranian people and tents, blankets, canned food, bread, clothing and medicines were donated liberally by some countries and sent to affected area.

Another quake rock South Asia. Jammu & Kashmir and Pakistan are badly hit by the killer quake raising the death toll to 80000 in Pakistan and more than 1500 in Batalik village of Jammu & Kashmir. India extended her hands for help of earthquake victims in Pakistan also.

Water

Water is one of the most precious things on earth. Its real value is realized only by one who needs water sorely and is unable to get it. When a soldier is seriously wounded in a battle, he needs water urgently and if he is unable to get it ask him the value of water when he is on the verge of death.

It is a pity that the real value of water is not realized. So much water is wasted. Indeed, we have no civic sense and so much water goes down the drain when we keep the taps running even when we are not using water.

God is so kind to us. He has given us so much water whether when we deserve it or not. When it rains, tons of water flows down to the seas and oceans through the water channels as we fail to harness it. It is of paramount importance that we should build dams, tanks and reservoirs to store water for the lean summer season when water is scarce even in rivers and canals.

We need water for drinking, bathing, washing and irrigational purposes. Thus, we need a lot of water daily. We must utilize it properly without wasting it.

It is something deplorable that even more that 55 years after Independence still people in several villages and slum areas do not get pure and enough drinking water.

We'll have to take some urgent measures in regard to management of water as the underground table-table in many States, particularly northern States, is falling sharply. If we fail to adopt a viable policy regarding water, we may have to fight disputes and battles for water as we used to fight for petrol and other resources of energy.

Place of Women in Society

Women form about one half of the total population of the world. Thus, they have every right to enjoy equal rights and duties with men.

It is, however, unfortunate that women have been neglected during the ages, particularly since the middle ages when they were pushed behind the four walls of the house and were forbidden to undertake any work which required calibre, enterprise and responsibility. They were considered weak, frail and inferior.

In ancient times women enjoyed high status in society. No yajna was considered complete unless a woman was present there. It is said that some women sages also wrote certain hymns of the Rig Veda.

In the present age, there has been a lot of awakening among women in many countries, particularly the countries which are partially or completely westernized.

Women have now got the right to vote. They have equal fundamental rights and duties with men. They are considered fit to be selected to most of the jobs. Now, we have women officers, judges, magistrates, advocates, teachers, doctors, pilots, engine drivers, architects, engineers, entrepreneurs, managers, etc. In fact, they are there in every field including sports, religion, dance, music, film industry, manufacturing industry, publishing industry, etc.

Modern women, especially in high society, are generally highly educated. But the condition of women in lower society, particularly in rural and slum areas, is still far from satisfactory. These women are still steeped in ignorance, illiteracy and superstition.

Crimes against women such as rapes, murders, exploitation, etc. are increasing these days in spite of the National Commission for Women and so many other bodies to look after the welfare of women. Day in and day out, we have so many dowry deaths. It is the need of the hour that more attention should be paid to women's welfare and uplift.

Pleasures of Reading

It is a well-recognized fact that most of the people in India, particularly in north India are not much interested in reading. Most of the people read only if they must. Students are encouraged by teacher to read just the books of their courses and nothing more and in many cases, and that quite pitiably, people shirk even buying books of courses. This is not true of paupers and poor people only. Even millionaires and those quite philanthropic and fond of donating money for good social purposes, fight shy of buying books for they are least interested in reading books and brushing or updating their knowledge.

Superstitions play a vital role in the people's mental make-up in our country. Even educated people think that the ever-changing pattern of news of different kinds will shake their faith. In other words, they are not ready to accept reason as a guiding force in their life. They feel contented while remaining steeped in the dark alleys of blind faith and superstition.

Reading books, however, is recommended not just for augmenting one's knowledge Reading provides a sort of pleasure which is not attainable anywhere else. When a person starts reading a good novel such as one by Dickens or a fictional story such as by Ruskin Bond, one cannot desire to lay down the book till the story is finished.

Pleasure provided by good books is exhilarating and elevating. We should, however,beware of writings which are degenerative in nature. A judicious selection of books or the guidance of an experienced person is necessary before we decide about the books that we should read.

Freedom of the Press

If one thing of which even the crookedest politicians and bureaucrats may be afraid is the press. It is rightly called the fourth estate. In any government, especially that having a democrative set-up, the three important organs are the legislature, the judiciary and the executive. The press may be regarded as the fourth organ.

The press brings to surface all the machinations of the clever politicians through simple informative statements and comments. The word Newspapers is almost synonymous with the word press. These newspapers are widely read even by the commonest people. Thus, if a politician falls in the eyes of the newspapers, he also loses favour with the common people whom he has to go for votes sooner or later.

The newspapers carry news, advertisements, readers' views, editorials, book reviews, cartoons, pictures, quizzes, etc. The word news is sometimes written in capital letters NEWS to convey the sense of North, East, West and South respectively which implies that they bring news from all directions or from all over the world. But we know that the newspapers carry information even from the skies. For instance, they tell us when an eclipse is to take place, when a storm is likely to approach a particular sea-coast, when the sun is going to flare up, when a comet will touch the atmosphere of the earth, etc. They also tell us about the weather.

In the newspapers we read editorials which carry comments on different policies of the government and other matters. Sometimes, these editorials are biased in favour of or against a particular political party or other organisation. So, we must read them most objectively. If we want to express our views, we can write a simple letter to the editor. Thus, newspapers are something useful, unavoidable and even indispensable in the modern age.

Tourism

Over the years, tourism has grown as a flourishing industry. Some countries, even small ones, like Singapore, the Carribeans, Japan, Hong-Kong (now under China), Thailand and even Malaysia have made great progress with the earnings obtained from tourists.

In India, earnings to the government and people from tourism as compared to such countries are only fractional. There may be several reasons for this.

Tourism in India can become a viable industry if effective and concerted steps are taken. First of all, red-tapism should be ended. All bottlenecks and harassments to tourists that scare them should be removed. People at the helms of tourist affairs such as officials of ministry of tourism, hoteliers emporium-owners, etc. should be taught etiquette and given lessons in ideal behaviour that should be meted out to tourists.

India has innumerable attractions for tourists. Throughout the country there are numerous beauty and scenic spots. There are very good hotels in big cities and tourist complexes on highways. There are several places where the tourists can enjoy adventure games. There are so many ancient temples, mosques, forts and other historical places in India which the tourists from various countries would like to visit.

Our embassies should supply to the people and governments of other countries all the important information regarding objects and places which can attract the tourists. The coming of the tourists to India and their stay here should be made easier, smoother and more comfortable as far as possible.

Advertising

We live in a world where advertising is everything. When we are watching any TV serial, we are disturbed again and again by advertisements of various products and brands such that sometimes we feel bored and even chagrined.

Open the page of any newspaper or magazine. You will find advertisements galore on almost every page as if we had purchased the said newspaper or magazine only for these advertisements.

In the newspapers we get advertisements of varied type. There we have matrimonial advertisements demanding bridegrooms and brides having particular features and qualities.

In the educational advertisements we learn about various courses and the names of institutions and universities where we can get them. There are several government advertisements in which a particular policy or project of the government is highlighted.

In commercial advertisements mostly inserted by different companies on the TV or in newspapers and magazines, we learn about the qualities of different brands of articles in interesting ways. Some advertisements are just visual. Others combine something visual with some catchy slogan. Many a time, some famous actor or actress or singer or sports personality is roped in to cash on his or her popularity. Thus, we have well-known advertisements for various brands by Sachin, Amir Khan, Salman Khan, Kapil Dev, Shah Rukh Khan, Daler Mehandi, etc.

Some advertisements are quite interesting. Others are disgusting and at times even atrocious. The most hatable advertisements are those where gender bias is displayed

or where scantily clad women are brought to focus. Advertisements must be healthy, meaningful and intelligent. They should be prepared with due care and censored by the authorities.

In fact, advertising is a sophisticated and intelligent art and it must be recognized as such.

CRPF

Before Independence, the CRPF was known as the Crown, Representative Police. It was created at Neemuch on 27th July, 1939.

Ten CRPF jawans sacrificed their lives at Hot Springs on 21st October 1959 during the Chinese aggression. Since then 21st October is observed as Police Commemoration Day throughout the country.

The Force proved its mettle during the Indo-Pak wars of 1965 and 1971. Earlier, on 9th April 1965, it repulsed a Pakistani attack on the Gujarat border, killing 34 Pakistani soldiers. Since then, 9th April is observed as 'Day of Valour' in the Force.

The Force has done its duty excellently on several occasions such as a part of the Indian Peace Keeping Force (IPKF) in Sri Lanka during Rajiv Gandhi's Prime Ministership, in Haiti, Cambodia, Bosnia, Herzegovina, Kosovo, etc as a part of UN Peace Keeping Mission.

Its one particular moment of valour, adherence to duty and national pride came when the Force valiantly fought and foiled the terrorist attack on Indian Parliament on December 13, 2001. In this operation, one Mahila Constable of the Force sacrificed her life while doing her duty.

The Force has commendable job in fighting the terrorists more than four thousand of whom have been killed and about 45,000 captured in about seven thousand encounters in which over one thousand jawans of the Force have also sacrificed their lives at the call of duty.

The Force has got several Awards including 1 George Cross, 1 Ashok Chakra, 1 Vir Chakra, 4 Shaurya Chakra, etc. and several Police Medals as well as President's Police Medal.

The Force has done commendable job in establishing peace in riot-hit areas as in Punjab during the 1980's and is now busy in confidence building measures (CBM) in J & K and North-Eastern States.

The Force has also shown spectacular achievements in National and International Games and won thousands of Gold, Silver and Bronze Medals and even 8 Arjuna and Rajiv Gandhi Khel Ratna Awards.

Now the Force is undergoing a major expansion programme to perform its duty towards the nation even more perfectly in view of the rising demands on it because of the contemporary necessities.

Healthcare

According to the Nobel Laureate Prof. Amartya Sen, a nation can progress only if it takes education and health on priority basis.

Some people have natal or prenatal deformative features and maladies. That is pitiable and we should hope that some of these can be cured partially or completely. Such cases are, however, rare. Most of the people are born normal and can maintain good physical and mental health through conscious efforts.

Though exact parameters for maintaining good health can be pronounced only by the experts in the line, we can think a few things which a layman knows or can know and tell easily and which are easily intelligible and practicable.

First of all, one must take a balanced diet. It is not only the intake or non-intake of a particular type of diet which is important, but also the total caloric intake per day is also a very significant factor. We shall take all the food ingredients – fat, carbohydrates, proteins, mineral, vitamins and fibrous foods in the required quantity, preferably under the guidance and supervision of a dietician.

Similarly, daily and regular exercise of the kind as specified by a medical expert for each individual should be taken. There is also a question of regular rest and hours of sleep. A period of rest and leisure should not be considered waste of time. There is also a necessity for the proper dose of amusement and entertainment. Regular walks in the morning and evening can be of great value.

We should try to avoid tension, stress, strain and a unnecessary worry in life. Laughter is a great tonic. We should remember that cheerfulness and contentment have a great role to play in maintaining good health in life.

Causes of Heart Attack

Previously, it was believed that heart attack occurred to men only after 50 and to women only after menopause. Now, this belief has been shattered. Now, we hear men and women getting heart attack in forties and even in thirties.

Another belief that was there was that men were more prone to heart attack than women. Biologically, this may be true. But, now, because of several reasons, we find even several women having heart attack.

In the modern age, a saying which is getting to be poverbial runs thus: "At forty you can have it all---a lucrative job, a car, a house and a heart attack !"

Quite clearly, in most respects, heart attack is related to life-style. A sedentary life-style where you have good and rich diet, luxuries and all the comforts of life but no physical activity or exercise, is the sure way to heart attack.

Many people in India, particularly people in north India, in spite all of diffusion of medical knowledge, believe in taking heavy amounts of fat which is rich in cholesterol that deposits in arteries and finally leads to heart attack and stroke.

Added to this taking of rich, high caloric fat are the due menaces of drinking and smoking. They raise the blood pressure and damage the heart muscle.

Therefore, on the one hand stress, strain and tension in life should be reduced. On the other hand, only simple, low caloric diet should be taken. Vegetarian diet is preferable to non-vegetarian diet. Consumption of alcohol and cigarettes should be reduced if not altogether cut. One should also learn the art of yoga, meditation and positive thinking to eliminate worry and tension in life.

The Secret of Success

In the modern age, every man wants to make a quick buck. It is because we live in a materialistic world where money thinks, talks, acts and rules. A man without money has no status in life. This is the reason that those who cannot make money through honest means, resort to several corrupt practices to become rich overnight.

As we generally see in life, a corrupt man, however, clever he may be, is caught in the long run and he has to spend his life behind the bars. Such a man can hardly be called a successful man.

It is thus that a person who wants to be really successful in life, must adopt some fair means for the purpose. It is rightly said that nothing can be received without giving. One receives only in proportion to what one gives. So, sacrifice is the first and foremost requirement for achieving success.

A shopkeeper who adulterates food and other items or one who gives short measures loses his customers and ultimately goes bankrupt. On the other hand, a shopkeeper who is fair in his dealings attracts customers and grows rich in the long run.

A student who does not work hard and wants to get through various examinations by copying from books and other classmates, loses grip over all subjects and ends as a dullard and a failure in life. So, the real secret of success lies in hard work. There is no other miracle which can bring about success.

Patriotism

When we think of the importance of patriotism, four kinds of people haunt our mind. People of the first kind are those who are chauvinists. They are obsessed with the idea of patriotism. They are practically fascists like Hitler and Mussolini. Such people may be imperialistic like Churchill.

The second kind of people are traitors like Quisling. But unlike Quisling, such people generally remain hidden under the surface. Many of them may pose to be great patriots but actually they may be outright traitors.

The third kind of people may be just indifferent to the idea of patriotism and they may maintain this indifferent attitude at all times even in the times of calamities and natural disasters.

The fourth kind of people who may be the commonest, may be of the type who remain indifferent to the idea generally but rise to occasion in time of war, floods, earthquakes, cyclones, famines or other disasters and national calamities.

To these kinds may be added a fifth kind. Such people may be more dangerous and treacherous than ordinary traitors. These are the people who engage themselves in anti-national activities such as terrorism, communalism, fake currency making, scams, smuggling, selling sensitive military and other information to the enemies of the country, etc.

We must bear in mind that the nation whose people do not have the spirit of patriotism in them, will just disintegrate sooner or later. We must bow to our country which is our motherland where we are born and which supplies us everything we need.

The man who does not love his country is just a dead soul as Sir Walter Scott has said :

'Breathes there the man with soul so dead,

Who never to himself hath said,

"This is my own, my native land !"

Leisure

Human body is a machine. Like any other machine, it requires rest after working for some time. W.H. Davies has expressed his views about the modern life which is full of stress and strain in the following words:

"What is this life if full of care?

We have no time to stand and stare."

Excessive worry about time is the bane of modern man. The doctrine that not a minute should be wasted is fraught with danger. It simply exhorts continuous work day and night and negates the idea of leisure.

Leisure is essential for our physical and mental health. A person who has done strenuous physical work for a few hours, needs rest after that. Similar is the case with one who has engaged himself in some mental work or intellectual activity for some time. This is the reason in all schools, colleges and other institutions, in offices and factories there is recess or lunch period. Even shops in posh markets close for an hour or so for lunch which also includes period for recess and refreshment.

One who has done hard physical work for some time, may study some interesting story book or have a look at the pages of an illustrated magazine during the leisure time. He may watch T.V if he doesn't have a book or is not inclined to read.

A person who has done some hard mental or intellectual work for sometime, may indulge in some physical activity such as a game of badminton, gardening, etc. for the purpose of replenishing the mental stamina.

The period of leisure should not be considered waste of time, even if one just spends this time in gossiping instead of indulging in any useful physical or mental activity. It should be regarded as worthwhile. However, the leisure time should be limited and should not be prolonged inordinately so as to encroach upon the working hours.

The Animal World

Scientific and archaelogical discoveries tell us that man has probably emerged from animals through the process of evolution. 'The Origin of Species', the world famous work by Darwin, specifically highlights this point, may be more theoretically and philosophically than scientifically. If we look at the human body carefully, we learn that even at present man is not much different from animals in various aspects. At best, he is an evolved animal.

The animals are like human beings in many respects. They have feelings like us. They feel heat and cold and pain like us. They love, hate and fear like human beings. They do not have a developed brain. Hence, probably they cannot think. The toughest thing against them is that if they cannot speak and express their views. If they could speak, they would at least say :-

"O dear human being you are known as homo sapien. You call yourself the crown of creation. You claim to take upon yourself the responsibility of the protection of all creatures, big and small. Please don't be cruel to me. I do feel pain like you and my heart too beats loudly and fearfully as cruelty is inflicted on me."

Indeed, it is a pity that man should be so cruel to animals when animals are so useful to him. Animals provide man with so many of his necessities of life. Ans overwhelming number of people in the world are non-vegetarians who eat meat of animals. Fishes are rich in Omega-3 which is so useful for human heart and for controlling cholesterol.

We get hides from animals which are used for making shoes, bags, purses, etc. We get wool from sheep. Seal oil is used by people in snowy regions. We get milk from cows, buffaloes, goats, etc. Some animals are used as beasts of burden, for instance, the camel, the donkey, the mule, the ox, etc. Horse is used for riding. Oxen are used for drawing carts. Snake poison is used as a medicine.

Similarly, numerous animals are used for numerous purposes. Man does thousands of medical and scientific experiments on animals for various purposes. If still man is not thankful to animals, shouldn't we term him as an ungrateful, if not a detestable, cruel, cunning brat?

Letters

INFORMAL LETTERS

1. Letters to Father

1. Letter to father requesting him to allow you to join an educational tour.

Boys Hostel-II
39, New Convent School
Gwalior
July 21,........

My dear Father

The tour of our school students is leaving next week for some prominent historical cities such as Agra, Mathura, Delhi, Panipat, Kurukshetra, Amritsar, etc.

It will be a twenty student tour for about ten days and will be led by Shri Prem Prakash, our teacher of history who is a renowned scholar. He will explain to us every significant thing which has some historical and educational value.

The tour will cost only ₹ 500/- per student including boarding, lodging, transport and other expenses.

Dear father, it is a rare chance. Kindly allow me to join this tour and send me ₹ 500/- at the earliest.

Convey my regards to mamma.

Yours affectionately
(Krishna Gulati)

2. Letter to father requesting him to increase your monthly allowance.

16 Girls Hostel
Government High School
Sector 29, Faridabad
November 12, 2.......

My dear Father

You will be glad to learn that I'm doing very well in my studies. During the last examination, the result of which is out today, I have secured the first position in the aggregate marks.

There are, however, certain problems which I'm facing now. The school authorities have substantially increased the school fees and that quite arbitrary. The washerman has increased the charges. Then I need a number of books and items of stationery for which I have no money.

I shall, therefore, be grateful if you increase my monthly allowance from the present ₹ 1500 to 2000

Convey my love to Sunny and Kanu.

Your loving daughter
(Reena)

2. Letters to Mother

1. Letter to mother describing how you saved a drowning child.

15 Boys Hostel-I
New Pahari School
Hamirpur
July 15,...............

My dear Mother

Yesterday was Sunday. I went to the canal that flows near our hostel early in the morning. I have a hearty bath and a short swimming bout there every Sunday.

Hardly had I jumped into the canal when I heard loud cries from a distance. I came out of the canal and rushed to the side from where the cries were coming.

I saw an old woman crying loudly on the bank of the canal. Her only grand son was drowning in the canal. I at once jumped into the canal and brought out the child. The woman was highly thankful to me and wanted to give me a reward, but I refused to accept it.

Convey my love and regards to Papa.

Yours loving son
(Inder Prakash)

2. Letter to mother describing the Annual Prize Distribution Function in your school.

10 Girls' Hostel-I
New Anglican School
Dehra Dun.
January 12 ....

My dear Mother

The Annual Prize Distribution Function was held in my school yesterday. Mrs. Gautama Garg, the Deputy Commissioner was the chief guest.

The function was held in the school hall which was tastefully decorated with ribbons, balloons and bunting.

The chief guest arrived in time. She along with the Principal and the President, School Managing Committee sat on the dais.

The President of Managing Committee welcomed the chief guest. Then there was a hilarious cultural programme. After that the Principal highlighted the attainments of the school during the year. The chief guest gave away the prizes. In her speech, she praised the school for its achievements. The function ended with the National Anthem.

Love to papa.

Your loving daughter
(Preeti)

3. Letters to Sister

1. Letter to sister recommending some books to her.

53, Hanuman Enclave
Lahori Gate, Delhi.
May 5,...............

My dear Sister

I learn from your letter which I received yesterday that you have got holidays for two months on account of summer vacation. You say that you are likely to feel bored during this long vacation and your coming here for several reasons is not possible.

My dear sister, you should know that books can prove your best friends in such moments and you'll never feel bored if you read them. I recommend the following books.
1. Harry Potter by JK Rowling.
2. Rupa Book of Stories by Ruskin Bond.
3. Gulliver's Travels by Jonathan Swift.
4. Treasure Island by R.L. Stevenson

Love from papa and mamma.

Your loving brother
(Krishna Kumar)

2. To sister exhorting her to learn some hobbies during the vacation.

15 Boys Hostel-III
Sacred Heart Convent School, Nagpur
May 2 ....

My dear Sister

I learn from your letter which I received yesterday that your school has closed for summer vacation.

I shall remain occupied here due to the summer camp which is being held in our school during the vacation. So, I may not give you company for play this summer. However, you can keep occupied by joining some hobby classes during the vocation. I recommend the following hobbies for you :

1. Knitting
2. Sewing
3. Toy-making
4. Painting
5. Music classes
6. Computer classes
7. Cookery
8. English speaking course.

You may make your own selection.

Yours affectionately
(Dalip Rahi)

4. Letters to Uncle

1. Letter to uncle for his birthday gift.

72 Kareem Baksh Road
Ilahi Street,
Qadian (Punjab)
15 August ....

My dear Uncle

Yesterday my birthday was celebrated with usual fervour. All my friends and relatives were present. I felt your absence greatly.

However, quite in the midst of the celebrations, the postman delivered the parcel from you. I opened it with bated breath and was overjoyed when I found the beautiful glittering gold wrist watch in it.

I at once wore the watch on my wrist and I am glad to say that it keeps correct time to the fraction of a second. I was in dire need of a watch. Now I'll never be late for school.

Uncle, I do not find the words enough to thank you. Simply accept my humble thanks and do attend my next birthday in person.

Convey my compliments to aunt.

Yours affectionately
(Sunil Dhingra)

5. Letters to Friend _______________________________

1. To friend inviting him to a hill station.

18 Ridge
Shimla
May 6..........

My dear Govind/Friend

I reached Shimla yesterday. I was tired of the scorching heat of the plains.

I'm glad to state that Shimla is just like a paradise. It is rightly called like Mussourie, the Quean of Hills. It is all pleasant here. A cool breeze is always blowing. The rain is frequent but it is not inundating as in the plains.

All around Shimla there are lush green forests of pine and other trees. There are sparkling springs everywhere.

I, therefore, invite you to come here and stay with me during the summer vacation. Then we'll visit Jakhu, Kufri and other places and have frequent walking trips in forests and over the hills. I live here with my uncle who is a very generous, jolly person.

Convey my regards to your revered parents.

Yours sincerely
(Puneet Papneja)

2. To friend congratulating him on his success in a examination.

17 Suleman Avenue
Bareilly
April 22............

My dear Birbal/Friend

I'm glad to learn from today's newspaper that you have passed the 10+2 examination getting very high marks. Your name appears in the merit list.

Your grand success is not a surprise to me. I expected it. Moreover, you are a brilliant student and last year in particular you worked very hard.

Please accept my heartiest congratulations and convey the same to your revered parents also.

I hope you'll arrange a grand party for your friends like me as I've no patience on such occasions

Yours sincerely
(Sohan Saxena)

3. *To your friend clearing a misunderstanding.*

92 Bahadurgarh Road,
Hanumanpura, Ajmer.
20 February ....

My dear Wilaiti

In your recent letter you have expressed a great deal of anger for my unbecoming behaviour to you at the function, as you allege.

Reality, dear friend, is quite contrary to what you have said. Actually, when you were delivering your speech at the function, it was not I who was hooting and whistling. It was, in fact, Piloo Micky, who is already known for such pranks. He was mimicking my voice and I heavily reprimanded him for this. He has expressed his regrets and is ready to reiterate them to your face.

I hope you'll now give up your dislike for me and be my bosom friend as usual.

Convey my best wishes to all at home

Yours ever
(Daulat Deshi)

FORMAL LETTERS & APPLICATIONS

1. Applications to Principal

1. *To Principal for fee concession.*

To,

    The Principal
    ATK school, Paharganj
    New Delhi.

Sir

I am a brilliant student of your school. I always stand first in my class. I'm also good at sports and extra-curricular activities.

However, my father is a very poor man He is a peon in a private firm. His salary is very low. He is unable to pay my school fees.

I'll, therefore, be grateful if you grant me full fee concession.

Thanking you.

Yours obediently
(Simple Satija)
Roll No.21
Class 10th
12 November....

*2. **To Principal for remission of a fine.***

To,

> The Principal
> DKL School
> Lahori gate
> Delhi.

Sir

Yesterday I reached the school late by five minutes and I was fined ₹ 10 by my class teacher.

Actually, I had reached the school on time. I was detained at the gate for about ten minutes. It was because frisking of students of 10+2 who had to appear in the Annual Board Examination was going on and I had to wait. I was not told by the security guard that the back gate of the school had been opened for students of other classes.

I'll therefore, be grateful if you remit the fine imposed on me for no fault of mine.

Thank you.

> Yours obediently
> (Santripta Saini)
> Roll No. 11
> Class 9th Red
> 16 July............

2. Application For A Post

*2. **Application for the post of a receptionist.***

69, Deepawali Area
Near Durga Temple
Patna.

> 16, August ....
> M/S Dilawar Software works
> 52 Mukherjee Marg
> Kolkata

Sirs

Sub : Posts of Receptionists.

In reference to your advertisement for the posts of receptionists in your various branches in Bengal and Bihar, I hereby apply for one of the posts.

I'm a Bachelor in Computer Applications (BCA) from Patna University. My date of birth is .... I have worked for one year as a computer operator at Simmy Graphics, Gaya.

I have a charming personality and I can speak English, Hindi, Odiya and Bengali fluently. At school and college I won several awards and prizes in studies, sports and histrionics.

I'm enclosing copies of all the necessary testimonials. If I'm selected. I'll work most diligently.

Thank you.

Yours faithfully
(Smriti Chatterjee)

3. Letters to the Editor

1. Letter to the Editor of a newspaper expressing your views on environmental pollution.

To Dalapura
Jagatari
July 15 ....
To,
 The Editor
 The Hindustan Times
 Delhi
Sir

Environmental pollution has reached its peak level in our country. In particular our cities are no longer livable.

Air pollution is being caused by ruthless cutting down of trees, chimneys of factories, emissions from motor vehicles, burning of coal, wood and other fossil fuel, etc.

Soil and water pollution is being caused by factory effluents, excessive use of pesticides and insecticides, etc.

Noise pollution is being caused by loudspeakers, high volumes of radio and TV sets, horns and buzzers, loud voices in markets, etc.

Pollution of all these kinds is dangerous for mankind. Effective steps should be taken to check it in every possible way.

Thank you.

Yours truly
(Somnath Singla)

OFFICIAL & BUSINESS LETTERS

1. Letter to postmaster against a postman.

....

....

To

    The Postmaster

    ....

    ....

Sir

The postman of our locality does not deserve to be allowed to remain in service. At least, he must be transferred from our locality.

He is not regular in delivering the post. Then he throws the letters, including registered letters, in the open or hands them over to children.

During the last one month, I have lost a number of important letters. Even money order for ₹ 500 sent to me by my brother from Chennai two months ago hasn't reached me. It seems the postman, Mr Ashok Sehgal, is a pastmaster in the matter of embezzlement.

I hope you'll take an early action on my complaint.

Thank you.

Yours faithfully

(______________)

3. Write a letter to a book seller placing an order for books.

....

....

To

    M/S Kapoor Book Trading Co.

    Rose Books Market, Jaipur

Sir

Please send the following books one copy each through VPP as early as possible. I'm enclosing a bank draft for Rs. 50/ as advance money for the books. All the books are published by Ramesh Publishing House, New Delhi.

1. Improvement in English Course.
2. How to Write Correct English
3. Advance General English
4. English Hindi Grammar.
5. Exploring English

Thank you.

Yours faithfully

(____________)

1604

PRECIS WRITING

(1)

(Solved)

The two great epics of ancient India—The Ramayana and the Mahabharata—probably took shape in the course of several hundred years, and even subsequently additions were made to them. They deal with the early days of the Indo-Aryans, their conquests and civil wars, when they were expanding and consolidating themselves, but they were composed and compiled later. I do not know of any books anywhere which have exercised such a continuous and pervasive influence on the mass mind as these two Dating back to a remote antiquity, they are still a living force in the life of the Indian people, not in the original Sanskrit, except for a few intellectuals, but in translations and adaptations, and in those innumerable ways in which tradition and legend spread and become a part of the texture of a people's life. They represent the typical Indian method of catering all together for various degrees of cultural development, from the highest intellectual to the simple unread and untaught villager. They make us understand somewhat the secret of the old Indians in many ways and graded in castes, in harmonizing their discords, and giving them a common background of heroic tradition and ethical living. Deliberately they tried to build up a unity of outlook among the people which was to survive and overshadow all diversity

----- J.L. Nehru
(words: 224)

Precis

The two great epics of ancient India are the Ramayana and the Mahabharata. Their subject matter is the Indo-Aryan exploits for conquest, expansion and consolidation, though the books were compiled later. They are the unique books written in Sanskrit which has had such a forceful influence on the Indian mass mind since antiquity. They are available in several translations and adaptations. They express the unity in diversity of the Indian culture in all its graded forms.

Heading: **The Two Great Epics of Ancient India.**
　or
The Ramayana and the Mahabharata

(2)

We often blame the government for all ills and consciously or unconsciously try to turn a belind eye on government's positive steps in any field. As, for instance, in the case of small scale industry, the central government had taken several definitive steps. There is a appreciative statement from a state minister hailing the Centre for formulating schemes like special economic zones, assistance to states for infrastrucutre development for export, apparel parks and industrial cluster development schemes, etc.

Now, it is for the concerned industry to take advantage of the scheme. It is true that the condition of the industrial units, particularly the small scale industrial units is in a bad state. To add fuel to fire, the stand off between Indian and Pakistani troops worsened the position in Jammu and Kashmir and in Punjab. In J and K the central government. has given some sort of special package to the small scale units. It is for this reason that the Punjab state minister for Industries and Commerce appealed to the central government in the following words.

"Because of being a border state, SSI units in Punjab are precariously placed vis-a-vis their counterparts in other parts of the country. Recent tension on the borders has further put the SSI units on their toes, therefore, a special package is needed to compensate the entrepreneurs on the pattern of Jammu and Kashmir where the benefits of transport subsidy and income tax concession have been granted to the industrial units."

That was in 2002. Now, with the change of guard at the centre, Small Scale Industry, not only in one state but throughout the country expects a lot from the new government. (words: 297)

Precis

The Central government has taken several positive steps in regard to small scale industry. Some of these steps are creation of special economic zones, assistance to states for infrastructure development, apparel parks and industrial cluster development schemes, etc.

In border states like J and K and Punjab the stand-off between Indian and Pakistani troops added to the woes of small scale industry. J and K was given a special package comprising subsidies, tax concession, etc. Later, Punjab also demanded it.

Now, its the change of government at the centre and states expect much from the union government.

(words: 96)

Title: Small Scale Industry or

States and Small Scale Industry.

2

(3)

The profitable avenues offered by agricultural pursuits to young Indians of education are never dwelt upon in political discourses. Yet with the so-called learned professions over crowded with anxious aspirants, there are opportunities here full of attraction for men who are willing to devote themselves to strenuous work. The trouble hitherto experienced in agricultural schools has been that the students attending them have been animated mainly by a desire to obtain employment with the government. Yet men of experience in agriculture maintain that farming would be a profitable pursuit for educated young men properly trained for their task and that the diversion of a proportion of the rising generation of this class to the soil would help materially in the agricultural regeneration of India. It would be well, indeed, if instead of bewailing the congestion which exists in Medicine and Law, more of our Indian public men were to direct the attention of the educated youth of the country to this field. The Swarajists for their part seem desirous of creating discontent among the rural population not for discontent that impels men to strive to attain higher things but the discontent which is capable of being guided into evil channels, to the injury of the individual and the prejudice of the commonwealth. The thoughtful man realises that the prosperity of the people is no bar to national development, the converse, indeed, is the case. The dictates of true patriotism then call for enthusiastic support for the policy foreshadowed by His Excellency the Viceroy and the Secretary of State for India, which is contemptuously dismissed by the Swarajist leader as "some agricultural scheme".

Precis : Agriculture and Employment
Agriculture, undoubtedly, offers vast opportunities to educated Indians when the so-called learned professions are overcrowded. But the pity is that even the agricultural graduates are after government service. Our public men should strive to divert a certain proportion of these persons from Law and Medicine to Agriculture. The Swarajists, instead of creating discontent among the rural population, should follow the policy chalked out by His Excellency the Viceroy and the Secretary of State for India.

(4)

The government at the centre, the state governments and the PSUs are now trying their best to get rid of their surplus staff. It is not possible to dismiss them en mass or to retire them compulsorily.

The banks and many government departments have started attractive voluntary retirement schemes (VRSs), sometimes termed as "Golden Handshake." Here is a report regarding such a scheme for government doctors in one of the states:

According to the notification issued by the state government in May, 2002, the doctors in regular service with an experience of minimum 8 years can avail themselves of the leave. In the meantime, if the doctor's private practice picks up, he/she can opt for the Voluntary Retirement Scheme (VRS) and all retirement benefits will be provided to him under the Premature Retirement Rules, 1975.

As per the notification, the doctor can take up to five years leave. A three-year leave can be sanctioned first, which can further be extended to another two years. During this period, doctors will not be entitled to the Non-Practice Allowance or any other allowance. Even if the doctor fails to do well in private practice during the period of leave, he will be able to get his government salary. This leave will be deducted from the doctor's "leave account", according to the directions.

Meanwhile, no fresh recruitment can take place in the absence of the doctor applying for long leave. The doctors applying for long leave cannot rejoin their government duties before three years. The "special leave" will be given to the applicant once in his entire service.

This facility for a long leave (say, of 3 to 5 years) should be provided to government employees in all departments in all states so that they can start their own business or join service elsewhere in some private concern. If they get success in their new venture, they can select for voluntary retirement. Otherwise, they can rejoin their old post after the expiry of the long leave (without pay and allowances).

This way, there is possibility of a large amount of expenditure on salaries being saved as a long term measureble At present, a large amount of the government exchequer is spent on paying salaries to its staff. In some states, the government expenditure on salaries, allowances and pensions and other benefits is about 80/ per cent or more of the government revenue. So, very little money for development purposes is left with the government.

Precis : Russia's Importance in the War

The operations in the East and Russia's activity must be watched for their importance. In spite of Germany's efforts to divide the Entente Powers, these are pledged not to make peace separately and it needs to be recognised that the cause of the West is bound up with Russia, without whose cooperation, France and Belgium could not have been saved.

(5)

The first and most obvious reflections which arise in a man, who changes the city for the country, are upon the different manners of the people whom he meets within those two different scenes of life. By manners, I do not mean morals but behaviour and good-breeding as they show themselves in the town and in the country.

And here, in the first place, I must observe a very great revolution that has happened in this article of good, breeding. Several obliging deferences, condescensions and submissions, with many outward forms and ceremonies that accompany them, were first of all, brought up among the politer part of mankind, who lived in courts and cities and distinguished themselves from the rustic part of the species (who on all occasions acted bluntly and naturally) by such a mutual complaisance and intercourse of civilities. These forms of conversation by degrees multiplied and grew troublesome; the modish world found too great a constraint in them, and have therefore thrown most of them aside. At present, therefore, an unconstrained carriage and a certain openness of behaviour, are the height of good-breeding. The fashionable world is grown free and easy; our manners sit more loose upon us. In a word, good-breeding shows itself most where to an ordinary eye it appears the least.

If after this we look on the people of mode in the country, we find in them the manner of the last age. They have no sooner fetched themselves up to the fashion of the polite world, but the town has dropped them, and are nearer to the first state of nature than to those refinements which formerly reigned in the court, and still prevail in the country. A polite country squire shall make you as many bows in half an hour as would serve a courtier for a week. There is infinitely more to do about place and precedency in a meeting of justices' wives than in an assembly of duchesses.

Precis : Town and Country Life
The most important thing that a person, while travelling from a town to the country, marks is the difference in manners between the people. No doubt, several civilities and ceremonies were first cultivated by the citizens and the courtiers who distinguished themselves in that respect from the unpolished village-dwellers. Gradually these formalities multiplied and some of them had to be shunned off by citizens to free themselves from troublesome ones. At present a certain candour and freedom from formalities constitute marks of refinement in the city. In the country, however, the modes of last age, extra-courteousness, etc. predominate.

5

On a green knoll above the plain of the Arve, between Cluse and Bonneville, there was, in the year 1860, a cottage inhabited by a well-doing family — man and wife, three children and the grandmother. I call it a cottage but in truth, it was a large chimney on the ground, wide at the bottom, so that the family might live round the fire lighted by one small broken window and entered by an unclosing door. The family, I say was "well doing"; at least, it was hopeful and cheerful; the wife healthy, the children, for Savoyards, pretty and active, but the husband threatened with decline from exposure under the cliffs of the mont Vergi by day and to draughts between every plank of his chimney in the frosty nights.

"Why could he not plaster the chinks?" asks the practical reader. For the same reason that your child cannot wash its face and hands till you have washed them many a day for it and will not wash them when it can till you force it.

I passed this cottage often in my walks, had its window and door mended; sometimes mended also a little the meal of sour bread and broth and generally got kind greeting and smile from the face of young or old; which greeting this year, narrowed itself into the half-recognising stare of the elder child and the old woman's tears for the father and mother were both dead, one of sickness, the other of sorrow. It happened that I passed not alone but with a companion, a practised English joiner who, while these people were dying of cold, had been employed from six in the morning to six in the evening, for two months in fitting without nails, the panels of single door in a large house in London. Three days of his work taken, at the right time, from fastening the oak panels with useless precision and applied to fasten the larch timbers with decent strength, would have saved these Savoyards lives.

Precis : Useful and Useless Work

In 1860, a dilapidated cottage in Savoy was inhabited by a family all of whom, except the father were healthy. The father was ill owing to exposure at work and in the draughty cottage which he had neither the ability nor the initiative to repair. The writer having had the cottage partly repaired and their meals improved, was cheerfully welcomed, until one year, passing with a skilled joiner, he learned that father and mother died of illness and grief respectively. His friend had been for two months elaborately fitting the penels of one door in London; but had he occupied, at an opportune time, three days of that period on the cottage, the parents would not have died.

There have been other men of our own generation, though very few, who, without equalling, have approached Macaulay in power of memory and who have certainly exceeded him in the unfailing accuracy of their recollections. and yet not in accuracy as to dates or names or quotations, or other matters of hard fact, when the question was one simply between aye and no. In these he may have been without a rival. In a list of Kings Popes or Senior Wranglers, Prime Ministers, battles palaces as to the houses in Pall Mall or about Leicester Square, he might be followed with implicit confidence. But a large and an important class of human recollections are not of this order; recollections for example of characters, of feelings, of opinions, of the intrinsic nature, details, and bearings, of occurrences. And here it was that Macaulay's wealth "was unto him an occasion of falling." And that in two ways. First, the possessor of such a vehicle as his memory could not but have something of an overweening confidence in what it told him; and quite apart from any tendency to be vain or overbearing, he could hardly enjoy the benefits of that caution which arises from self-interest and the sad experience of so powerful a fancy could not but illuminate with the colours it supplied the matters which he gathered into his great magazine wherever the definiteness of their outline was not so rigid as to defy or disarm the action of the intruding and falsifying faculty. Imagination could not alter the date of the Battle of Marathon, the Council of Nice or the crowning of Pepin. But it might seriously or even fundamentally disturb of the balance of light and dark in his account of the opinions of Milton or of Laud or his estimate of the effects of the protectorate or the Restoration, of the character and even the adulteries of William III. He could detect justly this want of dry light in others; he probably suspected it in himself: but was hardly possible for him to be enough upon his guard against the distracting action of a faculty at once so vigorous, so crafty and so pleasurable in its intense activity.

Hence arose, it seems reasonable to believe that charge of partisanship against Macaulay as an historian, on which much has been and probably much more will be, said. He may not have possessed that nice tact of exact justice, which is among the very rarest, as well as the most precious, of human virtues. But there never was a writer less capable of international unfairness. This, during his lifetime, was the belief of his friends but was hardly admitted by opponents. His biographer has really lifted the question out of the range of controversy. He wrote for truth; but, of course, for truth such as he saw it; and his sight was coloured from within. This colour, once attached, was what in manufacture is called a mordant; it was a fast colour; he could not distinguish between what his mind had received and what his mind had imparted. Hence, when he was wrong, he could not see that he was wrong and of those calamities which are due to the intellect only and not the heart, there can hardly be greater.

Precis: Lord Macaulay

Macaulay's power of memory has rarely been surpassed though his accuracy has been exceeded. His dates, names, figures or hard matters of fact could implicity be accepted, but in regard to matters involving the exercise of jugement the wealth of his memory made him overconfident and his imaginative tendency disturbed the balance of light and dark in his estimates of characters and opinions. He perceived in others their want of dry light but he lacked it himself and in consequence, he has as a historian incurred the charge of partisanship. Not scrupulously just, he was nevertheless, never intentionally unfair. He really wrote for truth but truth as he saw it was coloured by his own fancy and he was unable to distinguish between what his mind received and what it imparted. Thus when he was wrong, he could not see that he was wrong. His intellect, not his heart, was at fault.

(8)

A young stag, as he bent over a spring to quench his thirst, saw himself reflected in the blue water below, and stood still to admire the picture. "Ah," he said, "what a splendid pair of horns I have. If the rest of my body was as beautiful, I should be the handsomest animal alive. But, I cannot bear to look at my ugly, thin legs. I am really ashamed of them."

Just then he heard the angry roar of a huge lion and was off like wind. The legs he had despised carried him so swiftly that very soon the lion was left far behind. But, as he was going through a wood, the splendid horns—that he loved so well—were caught in the branches of a thick bush and he was held a prisoner until the hungry lion came up and made and end of him.

So that, after all, the beautiful horns-which he had admired so much-were the cause of his death.

Precis:

On seeing his own reflection in water, a stag praised his beautiful horns but despised his thin legs. Just then he heard the roar of a lion and ran off. The legs that he had despised, carried him to a safe place but his horns caught in a bush till the lion came and devoured him.

8

COMPREHENSION

(1)

(Solved)

In a significant judgement, the Punjab and Haryana High Court ruled on 29 May 2002.

A hire purchase agreement may in substance be a loan transaction and the label of such an agreement is not conclusive. It is open to the court to determine whether a particular agreement is loan transaction or a hire-purchase agreement. In a loan agreement for financing goods on hypothecated basis, the creditor cannot forcibly repossess the hpothecated item, though he can enforce the security through the court."

The judge delivering the verdict further held: "If a specific clause is inserted in an agreement authorising the repossession of a vehicle or any other goods by the hypothecatee, such a clause may be unconscionable, unless otherwise shown by the hypothecatee".

Questions

1. What ruling did the court give regarding a loan transaction?
2. Who is to determine a transaction?
3. What can a creditor do and what can't he do in a loan agreement for financing goods on hypothecated basis?
4. About what clause did the court say that it may be unconscionable"?
5. Which court gave the said judgement and when?

Answers

1. The court ruled that the hire purchase agreement may in substance be a loan transaction and the value of such a transaction is not conclusive.
2. It is the court who is to determine such a transaction.
3. When there is a loan agreement for financing goods on hypothecated basis, the creditor cannot forcibly repossess the item that is hypothecated, but he can enforce the security through the court.
4. If in the agreement a specific clause is inserted which authorises the repossession of the hypothecated item by the hypothecatee, such a clause

may be unconscionable except when it is shown otherwise by the hypothecatee.

5. The said judgement was given by the Punjab and Haryana High Court on 29 May 2002.

(2)

India has signed the International Treaty on Plant Genetic Resources for Food and Agriculture.

The treaty will facilitate conservation and sustainable use of plant genetic resources of food and agriculture and fair and equitable sharing of the benefits arising out of their use for sustainable development of agriculture and food security.

Access to plant genetic resources for creating new plant varieties is to be ensured all over the world through this treaty. Developing nations which are gene rich but economically poor will get adequate compensation through fair and equitable share of benefits arising out of the use of plant genetic resources which have been conserved by the farmers over centuries. The "Farmers' Right" concept will help in global recognition of the important role played by farmers in crop improvement activities."

Questions

1. What is the name of the treaty which India has signed?
2. What will the treaty facilitate?
3. What kind of sharing will it ensure?
4. Over what part of the world will it have its effect?
5. How will the developing nations be benefited by it?
6. In what context are the "Farmers' Rights" mentioned in the passage?

Answers

1. The name of the treaty which India has signed is International Treaty on Plant Genetic Resources for Food and Agriculture."
2. The treaty will facilitate conservation and sustainable use of plant genetic resources of food and agriculture.
3. It will ensure the fair and equitable sharing of the benefits derived from the use of plant genetic resources.
4. It will have its effect all over the world.
5. The developing nations will be greatly benefitted by it. Many of these nations are rich in genetic resources though they are economically poor. They will be greatly benefited by getting adequate compensation.
6. "Farmers' Rights" are mentioned in the passge in connection with the important role played by them in crop improvement activities.

10

(3)

They had not been long together before. Darcy told her that Bingley was also coming to wait on her; and she had barely time to express her satisfaction and prepare for such a visitor, when Bingley's quick step was heard on the stairs, and in a moment he entered the room. All Elizabeth's anger against him had been long done away; but had she still felt any, it could hardly have stood its ground against the unaffected cordiality with which he expressed himself. On seeing her again, he inquired in a friendly, though general way, after her family, and looked and spoke with the same good-humoured ease that he had ever done.

Question

1. For whom do you think has the word 'they' been used in the first line of the given passage?
2. For whom do you think has the word 'her' been used in the same line?
3. Why had the lady mentioned in the passage barely time to express her satisfaction?
4. In what tone did the gentleman talk to the lady?
5. What was the effect of this talk on the lady?

Answers

1. The word "They" has been used in the first line of the passage for Darcy and Elizabeth.
2. The word "her" has been used in the same line for Elizabeth.
3. She had barely time to express her satisfaction because Bingley's step was suddenly heard on the stairs.
4. The gentleman talked to the lady in a genuinely cordial tone.
5. The effect of this talk was positive in the sense that the lady's anger, if any, was over.

(4)

In this way Indian mythology and old tradition crept into my mind and got mixed up with all manner of other creatures of the imagination. I do not think I ever attached very much importance to these stories as factually true, and I even criticized the magical and supernatural element in them. But they were just as imaginatively true for me as were the stories from the Arabian Nights or the Panchatantra, that storehouse of animal tales from which Western Asia and Europe have drawn so much. As I grew up other pictures crowded into my mind: fairy stories, both Indian and European, tales from Greek mythology, the story of Joan of Arc, Alice in Wonderland, and many stories of Akbar and Birbal, Sherlock Holmes, King Arthur and his Knights, the Rani of Jhansi-the young heroine of the Indian Mutiny-and tales of Rajput chivalry and heroism. These and many others

11

filled my mind in strange confusion, but always there was the background of Indian mythology which I had imbibed in my earliest years.

--- J. L. Nehru

Questions
1. What crept into author's mind during the earliest years of his life?
2. Did he ever consider these things to be factually true?
3. What did he criticize?
4. What crowded into his mind as he grew up?
5. In what context does the author mention the Arabian Nights and the Panchtantra?
6. What was always there as background in the author's mind?

Answers
1. Indian mythology and old tradition crept into author's mind during the earliest years of his life.
2. Perhaps he never considered these things to be factually true.
3. He criticized the magical and supernatural element in the old Indian mythology and traditon.
4. As he grew up, several other pictures crowded into his mind, much as Indian as well as Greek fairy tales, tales from Greek mythology, the story of Joan of Arc, Alice in Wonderland, stories of Akbar and Birbal, Sherlock Holmes, King Arthur and his knights, the Rani of Jhansi, Rajput chivalry and heroism, etc.
5. The author makes a mention of the Arabian Nights and the Pachtantra to inform the readers that he considered the Indian mythology and tradition in the same vien.
6. It was the Indian mythology which was always there as the background in the author's mind.

(5)

The new food policy, to be announced shortly, will provide special incentives for edible oil producers, especially rice bran oil producers in the country. Since the country is importing more than 40 lakh tonnes of edible oil annually the government plans to encourage farmers to plant cash crops on a large scale especially oilseeds instead of following the traditional wheat-paddy rotation.

This was stated today by Union Minister for Consumer Affairs, Food and Public Distribution Supply on June 30, 2002.

Responding to the demand to cut down duties on edible oils, he said: "The Centre is aware of the fact that high level of state and central duties is affecting the interests of producers, traders and consumers. That is one of the reasons the Central

12

government in the last budget had tried to rectify the import duty structure. It has given positive results."

Question

1. When will the new food policy be announced?
2. What will it provide?
3. What does the government plan to encourage and why?
4. What is the designation of the governmental authority mentioned in the passage?
5. Whose interests are mentioned in the passage and what is affecting them?
6. What had the central government tried in the last budget and what has been the effect?

Answers

1. The new food policy will be announced shortly.
2. It will provide special incentives for edible oil producers, especially rice bran producers in the country.
3. The government plans to encourage the planting of cash crops on a large scale, especially oil seeds.
4. The designation of the governmental authority mentioned in the passage is the Union Minister for Consumer Affairs, Food and Public Distribution Supply.
5. The interests of producers, traders and consumers are mentioned in the passage. The high level of state and central duties is affecting them.
6. The government had tried to rectify the import duty structure in the last budget. It has given positive results.

(6)

Has she come a full circle from her "liberated spirit" day? It would seem so. Once making strident call for freedom for women, she predicts today that there will be no great change in women's status in the next century. "They have to work out problems with men not without them," she says. "My good times today are eating and shopping to get rid of negative thoughts. But I want a marriage to go home to. I need a good man to take care of me. I need a solid base to my life. Work is one side of life. Emotional security is the other and both are necessary for every woman!"

Questions

1. From where has "A Particular Woman" come a full circle?
2. What was once her call?
3. What is her present prediction?
4. How does she think about men?

5. What does she think to be her good times at present?
6. Why does she want to marry?
7. What two things does she consider important for every woman?

Answers

1. "A Particular Woman" has come a full circle from her "liberated spirit" day.
2. Once her call was for freedom for women.
3. Her present prediction is that there will be "no great change" in women's status in the next century.
4. She thinks that women need men to take care of them. She believes that women can't get emotional security without men.
5. She thinks eating and shopping to get rid of negative thoughts are her good times at present.
6. She wants to marry to go home to and to get emotional security.
7. She thinks that work and emotional security are the two things which are important for every woman.

(7)

As the unbelievable news ragarding Hansie Cronje's involvement in "match-fixing" spread, the most affected were those nearest to him.

"A lot of us were shocked. It is a blow for us and we just have to refocus. I am going to go out there and try and do the best job I can," Pollock told Reuters at the ground.

"He [Cronje] is an integral part of the team and an always-reliable all-rounder. He is a top-class player and he is going to be a hard person to replace".

"There won't be a shortage of motivation when you play against Australia. We will be missing Hansie but I'm sure the guys will be able to motivate themselves," he said.

Australia's team manager Steve Bernard told AAP news agency in Durban that the match-fixing scandal had reduced the three-match series to a sideshow.

"People aren't talking about the cricket. They are talking about this controversy. It is a shadow over the series. This takes some glass away" Bernard said.

Questions

1. What unbelievable news is mentioned in the passage?
2. Briefly describe Pollock's reaction to the news.
3. Who was Steve Bernard?
4. What were his views in this connection.
5. Assign a suitable heading to the passage.

Answers

1. The unbelievable news mentioned in the passage is Hansie Cronje's involvement in "match-fixing."

2. Pollock got shocked on hearing the news. He had a high opinion of Cronje as
being a good player who was an all-rounder. During the ensuing match with
Australia, although Cronje's absence will be greatly felt by the South African
team, Pollock thinks that the guys will come over it through self-motivation.
3. Steve Bernard was Australia's team manager.
4. According to him the match-faxing scandal has reduced the three match
series to a sideshow.
5. Hansie Cronje and Match-fixing.

(8)

And rising as she thus spoke, she would have quitted the room, had not Mr. Collins thus addressed her:

"When I do myself the honour of speaking to you next on the subject. I shall hope to recieve a more favourable answer than you have now given me; though I am far from accusing you of cruelty at present, because I know it to be the established custom of your sex to reject a man on the first application, and perhaps you have even now said as much to encourage my suit as would be consistent with the true delicacy of the female character."

"Really, Mr. Collins," cried Elizabeth with some warmth, "you puzzle me exceedingly. If what I have hitherto said, can appear to you in the form of encouragement, I know not how to express my refusal in such a way as may convince you of its being one."

"You must give me leave to flatter myself, my dear cousin, that your refusal of my addresses is merely words of course. My reasons for believing it are briefly these: It does not appear to me that my hand is unworthy of your acceptance, or that the establishment I can offer would be any other than highly desirable. My situation in life, my connections with the family of de Bourgh, and my relationship to your own, are circumstances highly in my favour; and you should take it into further consideration, that in spite of your manifold attractions, it is by no means certain that another offer of marriage may ever be made to you. Your portion is unhappily so small that it will in all likelihood undo the effects of your loveliness and amiable qualifications. As I must therefore conclude that you are not serious in your rejection of me, I shall choose to attribute it to your wish of increasing my love by suspense, according to the usual practice of elegant females."

"I do assure you, sir, that I have no pretensions whatever to that kind of elegance which consists in tormenting a respectable man. I would rather be paid the compliment of being believed sincerely. I thank you again and again for the honour you have done me in your proposals, but to accept them is absolutely impossible. My feelings in every respect forbid it. Can I speak plainer? Do not

15

consider me now as an elegant female, intending to plague you, but as a rational creature, speaking the truth from her heart."

Questions

1. Between which two characters does the dialogue as given in the passage take place?
2. Why did the lady not quit the room?
3. How does the man mentioned in the passage take the rejection?
4. Mention briefly his reasons for delivering that his suit had not actually been rejected by the lady.
5. Explain briefly how the lady tried to convince the man that her rejection of him was genuine and not fake or pretended.

Answers

1. The dialogue as given in the passage takes place between Mr. Collins and Elizabeth.
2. The lady did not quit the room as Mr. Collins started addressing her in the manner as given in the passage.
3. The man mentioned in the passage took the rejection as a positive sign of the lady's finally accepting him after the first reaction was over.
4. He believed that his rejection of him by Elizabeth was only a manifestation of the true delicacy of the female character. He believed that there were sever factors encouraging his belief as such, such as his situation in life, his connections with the family of de Bourgh, his relationship to Elizabeth's family, etc.
5. The lady tried to convince Mr. Collins that her rejection of him was real and not feigned. She thanked him repeatedly for his proposal, but she told him that she was a rational creature and was not interested in torment him by making a pretended rejection of him. So, she should be taken seriously.

———————————

1809